Logoi and Muthoi

SUNY series in Ancient Greek Philosophy

Anthony Preus, editor

Logoi and Muthoi

Further Essays in
Greek Philosophy and Literature

Edited by
William Wians

Cover photograph [detail] © 2018 Museum of Fine Arts, Boston. *Two-handled jar (amphora) with Achilles and Ajax.* About 525–520 B.C. Place of Manufacture: Athens, Attica, Greece. By: the Andokides Painter; by: the Lysippides Painter. Ceramic, Black Figure and Red Figure (Bilingual). Henry Lillie Pierce Fund 01.8037.

Published by State University of New York Press, Albany

© 2019 State University of New York

All rights reserved

No part of this book may be used or reproduced in any manner whatsoever without written permission. No part of this book may be stored in a retrieval system or transmitted in any form or by any means including electronic, electrostatic, magnetic tape, mechanical, photocopying, recording, or otherwise without the prior permission in writing of the publisher.

For information, contact State University of New York Press, Albany, NY
www.sunypress.edu

Library of Congress Cataloging-in-Publication Data

Names: Wians, William Robert, editor.
Title: Logoi and muthoi : further essays in Greek philosophy and literature / edited by William Wians.
Description: Albany : State University of New York, 2019. | Series: SUNY series in ancient Greek philosophy | Includes bibliographical references and index.
Identifiers: LCCN 2018035998 | ISBN 9781438474892 (hardcover : alk. paper) | ISBN 9781438474908 (ebook)
Subjects: LCSH: Philosophy, Ancient. | Literature—Philosophy. | Greek literature—History and criticism. | Mythology, Greek.
Classification: LCC B178 .L639 2019 | DDC 180—dc23
LC record available at https://lccn.loc.gov/2018035998

10 9 8 7 6 5 4 3 2 1

Contents

List of Illustrations	vii
Acknowledgments	ix
From *Logos* and *Muthos* to . . . *William Wians*	1
1. *Xenia*, *Hiketeia*, and the Homeric Language of Morals: The Origins of Western Ethics *Kevin Robb*	17
2. The Muses' Faithful Servant: Moral Knowledge in Homer, Hesiod, and Xenophanes *William Wians*	55
3. How Philosophy is Rooted in Tradition: Stories Describing the Appearance of Man and Woman in Ancient Greece *Luc Brisson*	79
4. *Muthos* and *Logos* on New Year's Day: Trial and Error in Anaximander's Seasonal Sundial *Robert Hahn*	95
5. Tragic Values in Homer and Sophocles *Lawrence J. Hatab*	135
6. Sketches of Oedipus in Sophocles's Play about Tyranny *Marina Marren*	165

7. Helen and the Divine Defense: Homer, Gorgias, Euripides 197
   Ruby Blondell

8. The Hero and the Saint: Sophocles's Antigone and
   Plato's Socrates 223
   Roslyn Weiss

9. Myth and Argument in Glaucon's account of Gyges's Ring
   and Adeimantus's Use of Poetry 263
   Marina McCoy

10. Myth Inside the Walls: Er and the Argument of the *Republic* 279
    Pierre Destrée

11. Priam's Despair and Courage: An Aristotelian Reading of
    Fear, Hope, and Suffering in Homer's *Iliad* 297
    Marjolein Oele

12. Poets as Philosophers and Philosophers as Poets:
    Parmenides, Plato, Lucretius, and Wordsworth 319
    A. A. Long

Bibliography 335

About the Contributors 355

Index 359

Illustrations

Figure 4.1 A possible reconstruction of Anaximander's sundial with the gnomon set horizontally pointing southward and casting shadows on the north wall of a well in Chios.   102

Figure 4.2 Drum fragment from the Archaic Didymaion exhibiting *anathyrôsis* and a round *empolion* (*l*), and next to it (*r*) a drum exhibiting *anathyrôsis* found in Samos from Dipteros II.   104

Figure 4.3 Column-drum installation—*anathyrôsis* and *empolion* are exhibited as well as drum bosses and use of rope with lifting device, after Orlandos. The *anathyrôsis* and *empolion* technique allowed for each drum to be lined up perfectly, the circumference equidistant from the center, controlled by inner circular rings.   105

Figure 4.4 Circle/column-drum face bisected East-West with many local noon points running North-South.   106

Figure 4.5 Circle/column-drum face with only three shadow points: Summer Solstice, Equinox, and Winter Solstice.   107

Figure 4.6 Anaximander's Earth with Sun risings and settings on Solstices and Equinox.   108

Figure 4.7 Artifact, possibly a sundial, found at Qumran, first century BCE.   109

viii   Illustrations

Figure 4.8   Anaximander's sundial with two concentric circles, Summer and Winter Solstices (*l*); Anaximander's sundial with three concentric circles, Summer, Winter Solstices, Equinox (*r*).   110

Figure 4.9   Anaximander's sundial comparative: Miletos and Sparta.   112

Figure 4.10 Anaximander's sundial with diameter measurements for 1.000-foot and 1.500-foot gnomons in Miletos.   113

Figure 4.11 Anaximander's sundial comparative: Miletos and Naucratis (emphasizing smaller solstice circle diameters in Naucratis).   115

Figure 4.12 Anaximander's sundial comparative: Miletos and Naucratis (emphasizing the observer's location on the Earth's surface).   116

Figure 4.13 Scale model of Anaximander's Sundial with Summer and Winter Solstice "Sun Wheels."   117

Figure 4.14 The Celestial Sphere and the Obliquity of the Ecliptic: Identifying the exact moments of the Equinoxes.   119

Figure 4.15 Anaximander discovered the Equinox by bisecting the angle between the Summer and Winter Solstice risings, and the Summer and Winter Solstice settings.   120

Figure 4.16 Anaximander's sundial with two concentric circles, Summer and Winter Solstices, and hour-markers (*l*); Anaximander's sundial with three concentric circles, Summer, Winter Solstices, Equinox, and hour-markers (*r*).   121

Acknowledgments

As with the first volume *Logos and Muthos*, published by SUNY Press in 2009, completing *Logoi and Muthoi* has required the combined work of many parties. My first thanks go to my contributors, who have been unfailingly cooperative and patient. I am happy to thank Merrimack College for its support in the form of summer research grants that helped to advance the project, and Boston College, where I was able to teach a seminar on the themes of this volume. Finally, I want to thank Tony Preus, the series editor, and Andrew Kenyon, my editor at SUNY Press (with an able assist from Michael Rinella, my former editor). Once again, it has been a pleasure to work with the entire SUNY Press staff.

About the Cover

The cover image for this volume shows the second side of the vase from which the first volume also took its image (Museum of Fine Arts, Boston 01.8037). The vase is a type that is called 'bilingual,' meaning it uses black figure technique on one side and red figure on the other. The black figure side was used in 2009. As I wrote then, "The image of the warriors Ajax and Achilles seemingly at their ease playing dice was a popular subject for vase painters. But as Emily Vermuele suggests in her classic study, *Aspects of Death in Early Greek Art and Poetry* (Berkeley and Los Angeles: University of California Press, 1979, 80–82), the simple game of chance is a metaphor for the risks of mortal life. In fact, neither warrior would return from the war at Troy. Nevertheless, a measure of immortality is won for the heroes through the *kleos* preserved by the work of the artist. The vase is a powerful reminder to the modern viewer of both the persistence of *muthoi* in Greek culture and the subtlety with which they can convey their lesson."

From *Logos and Muthos* to . . .

William Wians

Logoi and Muthoi: Further Philosophical Essays in Greek Literature is a second volume of essays devoted to exploring philosophical themes in Greek literature. The first volume, *Logos and Muthos: Philosophical Essays in Greek Literature*, accomplished more (I hope) than to make the present title more or less inevitable. Its aim was to build on the now well-established recognition that the term pair *logos/muthos* is not equivalent to once common oppositions such as reason vs. myth or rational vs. irrational, while providing compelling alternatives to what once was called the Greek Miracle and the old opposition's narrative of progress from benighted credulity to at least the dawning of some form of critical enlightenment.

Given that *Logoi and Muthoi* has the same goal as the first volume, it is worth repeating the more expansive statement of purpose from the first volume's introduction:

> The title conveys the collection's two main intentions. First, not from *muthos* to *logos*, but *logos* **and** *muthos*, implying a whole range interactions, reactions, tensions and ambiguities arising between different forms of discourse. Scholarship in recent years has moved decisively beyond old assumptions of a simple progression from myth to reason, and the collection takes full advantage of that work. But the full emphasis of *Logos and Muthos* becomes apparent in the subtitle. All of the volume's chapters explore philosophical dimensions of

> literary authors—Homer, Hesiod and the Archaic poets, the tragic playwrights . . . figures and works not usually central to histories of ancient philosophy.
>
> The purpose of the collection is not, then, to mount another challenge to the old opposition, or to search for the 'beginnings of philosophy,' or to seek anything like a comprehensive definition of myth. . . . Rather, it intends to consider philosophical issues and ideas as they arise from or can be applied to literary, usually poetic, texts, to *muthoi* in one sense of the Protean term.[1]

The present volume has the same aim: to consider philosophical themes and ideas in works not ordinarily included in the canon of Greek philosophical texts, both to shed light on canonical philosophical authors and also for their own sake. In this case, twelve essays are written by an entirely new list of contributors (the only exception being the editor's contribution). Each contributor explores in some way what various and competing *muthoi* and *logoi* meant for those whose thought they shaped and who in turn shaped them and what they mean to us—the implications of a chosen form of writing, how influence and reception reached across what we mark as different genres, and what answers to these questions reveal about the nature of the ancient intellectual enterprise. Taken together, the essays offer new approaches to familiar texts and open up new possibilities for understanding the roles and relationships between *muthos* and *logos* in ancient Greek thought. A second volume is justified both by the philosophical richness of the works under consideration and by the hope that these further examples of philosophical scrutiny of texts and issues falling outside philosophy's traditional purview will contribute in a meaningful way to the growing body of work that crosses current disciplinary boundaries in order to explore such connections. Which is another way to put the purpose of both volumes: to reinforce, at least implicitly, the recognition that current disciplinary boundaries are our own, and that much fruitful work remains to be done by crossing them.

Story vs. Argument

The Protean nature of myth provides a useful jumping off point. As is obvious from even a cursory survey of recent work in ancient philosophy, the term 'myth' can be used in quite different senses by different scholars.[2] Depending on how it is used, differences between *muthoi* and *logoi* range from weaker to stronger and from more precisely to less sharply defined. This does not mean that any and every approach to *muthos* and *logos* is valid—one could hardly reject the old opposition if that were the case.[3] So while contributors to both this volume and its predecessor were allowed to operate with their own conceptions of *muthos* and *logos* rather than being asked to conform to a single governing sense, most identify a closer relationship between *muthos* and *logos* than the old opposition could ever have accommodated, and even when they do not, the exceptions recast the opposition in quite different terms.[4]

Given the range in which the term 'myth' is used, it seems helpful to posit an initial definition of myth against which other senses can later be marked.[5] A myth in this initial sense is a traditional story, involving personages (typically gods or heroes), formulated and handed down orally over many years, often by nameless creators and retellers, which is taken as true and authoritative by a large portion of a culture's population.[6] As such, a myth shapes and even defines that culture's values and expectations, explaining and justifying features of the social and natural order that are taken to be essential, and may at the same time prescribe or imply structures and rituals that maintain and reinforce that order.[7] Given the conditions of their origin and transmission, key parts of the story are fixed, though other elements may show a remarkable degree of variation. When there is more than one version of a traditional story, one is not taken to refute the other, even though they are inconsistent from a logical point of view. Often, a culture's governing mythology displays a strong syncretistic tendency to absorb conflicting accounts into a larger whole. Much of what is found in Homer and Hesiod originated as stories of this sort, so that the two poets are often taken (at least in textbooks on ancient philosophy) to represent a mythic way of thinking.[8]

In contrast to myth in this sense, a *logos* is the result of a deliberate inquiry by a nameable individual (e g., Anaximander, Heraclitus), involving forces and material entities rather than personages (*to apeiron*, fire). No part of a *logos* is fixed in that every element may be challenged, and where rival accounts are logically inconsistent with one another, at most only one can be true.[9] Its authority therefore depends on its ability to refute rivals and supplant them by offering a more comprehensive explanation of a given set of phenomena. Rather than reinforcing cultural norms, a *logos* is often viewed as challenging them, directly or indirectly. The theories of the pre-Socratic philosophers are typically taken as *logoi* in this sense, accounts deliberately formulated to contrast with traditional *muthoi* and in critical reaction to one another. Crucially, it is communicated in its authoritative form not orally but in writing, whether poetry or prose, so that only a small part of a population—primarily those who are literate—may be influenced by it.

The opposition between *logos* and *muthos* as defined in these ways has often seemed sharpest to scholars considering the origins of philosophy and science. How did the world come to be as it now is? What was the origin of human beings? What is thunder? Myths offered stories or tales to account for such things. Early rational thinkers, by contrast, formulated scientific accounts of nature based on evidence; indeed, the very concept of nature is said to be one of their chief discoveries.[10] Put in this way, the roots of the old opposition go back at least as far as Aristotle. Despite a seemingly generous nod to lovers of myth at *Metaph*. I.2, 982b18–19, Aristotle typically sought to reduce myth to *logos* by clarifying what he took mythologizing predecessors to have said obscurely (*Metaph*. XII.8, 1074a38–b14).[11] Nor is Aristotle's attitude without its contemporary adherents. Thus, in a generally positive review of a recent collection of essays challenging the old opposition, the reviewer nevertheless insists on a fundamental difference between *muthos* and *logos* expressed in terms of story vs. argument. There is, he says, "a distinction between 'traditional' or 'just so stories' and rational expositions that can be checked, revised, and amended in a methodical way."[12]

Whether the distinction can be maintained in this way without question-begging or circularity is not the issue here. What is important is that, while scholars reject the old opposition and its simplistic narrative of progress, many seek to preserve some meaningful distinction between *muthos* as story on the one hand and *logos* on the other even if boundaries can be difficult to draw in practice. Much recent scholarship has sought to do so by identifying nascent "logical" or "rational" elements in mythologists on the one hand, and mythic holdovers and nonrational features in Milesian and other early cosmologies on the other. To what extent, for instance, does Hesiod's account of the generation of the gods display rational or logically sequenced stages? What do early Greek thinkers like Thales and Anaximander retain from earlier creation myths, including Hesiod's but also those of the Babylonians and Egyptians? This approach goes back to the groundbreaking work of Cornford.[13] At least with regard to early theories of cosmology and natural science, work on such questions has played a major role in undercutting any sharp opposition between *logos* and *muthos* even while striving to maintain a difference between the two concepts.[14]

Beyond Cosmology: Pedagogy and Authority

While the engagement by early natural philosophers with mythic accounts of the cosmos is important, a full treatment of the relationship between *logos* and *muthos* must include myth's shaping of ancient Greece's social, political, and moral realities. The influence exerted by traditional stories extended far beyond questions of origins, and led in at least one respect to the rhetoric of *muthos* vs. *logos* we still contend with.

If Plato's claim that Homer was the teacher of the Greeks was decidedly ambivalent, it was nevertheless largely true, and was true in virtually every area of daily life, not just in accounts of natural phenomena. The poetic tradition was pedagogical, a point explicitly recognized by both Aristophanes and Plato. Greek poets, preeminently Homer and Hesiod, taught the Greeks how to be Greek—how to live marry, worship, plant, trade, and die.[15]

At a minimum, ancient stories of origins carried multiple implications about the place of human beings in a world not of their making. This is clearly the case in Hesiod, whose account of the origin of the cosmos and the triumph of Zeus as its ruling deity is also an account of the origin of *nomos* and the human political community (see, e.g., *Theogony* 81–93). As such, it became an essential starting point for many later *logoi*, whether philosophical or otherwise.[16]

Besides what cosmologies may have implied, many traditional stories functioned as morally instructive in more direct ways. One immediately thinks of the lessons derived from destructive rage of Achilles, the dependency of both Odysseus and Telemachus on the support of others, and the courage of Priam.[17] But stories did more than simply hold up positive and negative role models. Greeks growing up with Homer especially were exposed to rich explorations of moral dilemmas, problems of political authority, and the power and peril of language.[13] Such stories provided instruction in ways that were subtle, complex, and pervasive.

Myth's pedagogical function leads to a further dimension of the relationship between *logos* and *muthos*, namely a competition for authoritative status. Already among the early poets a competition for honors and aristocratic patrons was apparent. Hesiod, for instance, claimed superiority over his rivals in virtue of the special quality of his inspiration from the Muses (*Works and Days* 646–63). With the emergence of philosophy and science other rivals arose, including philosophers, lawgivers, historians, and physicians, so that by the Archaic period, competition for authority became a conspicuous feature of the entire Greek intellectual landscape.[19] Xenophanes, for instance, positions himself as a superior authority to his poetic predecessors both by contrasting his own *sophie* over those who celebrate athletic victors (B2) and by criticizing the moral impropriety of Homeric and Hesiodic stories.[20]

It was the competition for authority that gave rise to the rhetoric of *muthos* vs. *logos* in the first place. Greek culture, especially in the fifth and fourth centuries BCE, was highly rhetorical, with both public debates and written controversies. The distinction between *logos* and *muthos* originated in the context of these debates as a rhetorical device used to gain points against a rival: so-and-so's account was "merely" a *muthos*.[21] From the perspective of competing pedagogical authorities, the relationship of *logos* and *muthos* is at least as oppositional as that pictured in the old narrative.

The rivalry between competing authorities was often reflected in the deployment of literary form. Plato made his character Protagoras treat the difference between *logos* and *muthos* as a matter of *mere* form, willing to choose one over the other according to the preferences of his audience (*Protagoras* 320C). But for Plato himself and many other Greek intellectuals, the form employed represented a choice. The form in which a thinker expressed his ideas carried direct implications for one's claim to authority within a tradition or as a rival to it, pointing at the same time to the identity of one's intended audience. Plato's deliberate construction of myth in the dialogues will be treated in the final section of this introduction; two seemingly opposite strategies of deployment can be mentioned here. One thinker might adopt epic meter in order to assume the mantle of authority conveyed by that form and to speak to an audience versed in its subtle cues, even as he sought to undercut or contradict the authority of his poetic forebears.[22] Another thinker targeting a different audience might signal a new authority by rejecting the epic form altogether.[23] In other words, the use by a thinker of one form of writing over another may reflect a deliberate stance with regard to authoritative *muthoi*.

Reception and Revision

A worldview based in *muthos* did not suddenly wither away with arrival of the *logoi* of Anaximander, Anaxagoras, or Aristotle. No doubt many Greeks continued to adhere to the more irrational elements of myth—Euthyphro and Strepsiades must have had many real-world counterparts. But for the population as a whole, including the intellectuals, *muthos* remained a constant presence, permeating Greek culture and society in civic and religious observations, in public and private art, and in theater.[24] Myths of all sorts—local or Pan-Hellenic, cosmogonic/cosmological, those with a more or a less direct pedagogical import—became material to be contended with and material for reworking. As noted above, Hesiod and Homer already show signs of deliberately manipulating mythic materials to suit their purposes. By the classical period, dealing with the mass of story and legend could not be avoided by any serious thinker. The question of reception became urgent.

Properly understood, 'reception' pertains to how materials from one culture or period are incorporated into and appropriated by a later one. One can certainly say that the emergence of the polis created a very different cultural reality from that in which Greek myths arose. Viewed in this light, the question of reception underlies every issue raised in this and the previous volume.[25] But even for the intellectual elite, reception did not mean rejection. Much of what critical thinkers encountered was at least on its surface unsystematic and contradictory. But the task they assumed was not primarily one of making myth consistent. It would be better to say that intellectual elites began to reorient themselves toward both the content and the forms of expression of myth.

Many mythic assumptions were never abandoned even by the intellectuals. The limits of human knowledge and existence, for instance, were always understood within the framework of the distance between mortals and the gods.[26] We have already seen that the stories of Hesiod and especially Homer exerted a profound influence on early moral psychology. Their continuing influence was felt just as strongly in later moral philosophy. Ethical terminology employed by Homer and Hesiod persisted and continued to give shape to later debates about values even as the authority of these two foundational poets came increasingly to be questioned.[27] So too in theater, where tragic playwrights worked to adapt traditional stories to new conditions of civic engagement in the polis. The playwright Sophocles serves as an especially apt illustration of this aspect of reception. As several contributors to this and the previous volume show, he takes over traditional stories to turn them into powerful parables of the realities of his own Athens as he saw them.[28] Equally important are continuities of formal expression: the epic cadences of Homer and Hesiod and the gnomic utterances of the oracle at Delphi provided familiar forms to express various ponderous topics, persisting in essential ways in philosophers, playwrights, and others, along with a continued emphasis on public display and performance.[29] Such continuities count as some of the strongest evidence against the old narrative of a displacement of *muthos* by *logos*. In its place, one can recognize a selective incorporation, revision, and appropriation of mythic elements into larger schemes by its many and various inheritors.

Myth as Narrative Construction

Incorporation and appropriation lead to a final sense of myth, a sense that takes us altogether beyond myth as traditional story. In this sense, a myth is a fictional narrative deliberately created by a single author. It may or may not incorporate traditional elements. It may make up an entire work or appear as an episode within a larger whole. Though a myth of this sort shares many elements with myth as traditional story, the ground has shifted. *Muthos* becomes compatible with *logos*, though with the gain (or perhaps at the cost) of making it subordinate to the rational purposes of a given author. Crucially, a myth in this sense is meant by its creator to be recognized as literally false.

This is a sense of myth employed frequently—though sometimes carelessly—in speaking of myth in Plato. In contrast to those who handed down traditional stories, Plato created "myths" consciously and deliberately, sometimes incorporating old elements into a story of his own devising, but in other cases composing his myths out of whole cloth. More precisely, Plato *constructed* myths.[30] Plato is not, of course, the first or only ancient author for whom this sense of myth is relevant, and both why Plato chose to employ myth and the nature and variety of his mythmaking raise questions that fall outside the scope of this volume.[31] But this much can be said. Some of the myths Plato created were cosmological, others were moral, political, or eschatological; often these purposes were served simultaneously by a single mythic construction.

Many of Plato's myths were, it seems, constructed to appeal to an interlocutor—and by extension, to a reader—for whom *muthos* might hold rather more appeal than *logos*.[32] Not all of Plato's myths were given to Plato's Socrates—some were put in the mouths of characters such as Protagoras or Aristophanes.[33] Indeed, in the sense of myth as a deliberately created fiction, every Platonic dialogue is itself a myth.[34] Further, both Plato and his readers knew his stories were literally false (with the unfortunate exception of those hermeneutically hopeless hunters for the "lost" continent of Atlantis). This is another contrast with those who transmitted traditional stories, who did so because they regarded those stories as true.[35] One could add that, unlike traditional stories, myths in this sense were from their inception written down and were therefore not dependent on oral transmission, regardless of traces of oral culture and performance they may retain.

Finally, myth as a narrative construction offers a possible advantage over argument. The advantage—though it might not seem so to anyone insisting on analytic clarity—might be called narrative indeterminacy. A narrative, unlike deductive argument, may have the posing of a question as its primary aim. It may, in other words, be constructed so as to pose moral and philosophical questions and dilemmas while deliberately leaving them unresolved. This seems especially relevant to the tragic poets. Aeschylus, Sophocles, and Euripides couch their arguments in what particular characters say over the course of an unfolding story. In reading their plays, one must be prepared for the posing of incompatible options without any final resolution, or a surface meaning undercut by the dramatic action.[36] Euripides in particular staged sophistically inspired debates as integral parts of his dramas—imbedding *logoi* within his *muthoi*, as it were—while leaving them without clear resolution.[37] The construction of *muthoi* containing *logoi* points to how sophisticated the relationship between the two became and how carefully any account of them must proceed.

Here one should recall that the deliberate posing of questions and quandaries without resolution has many parallels in ancient philosophers. There are the shorter Socratic dialogues, which typically end with Socrates (though perhaps not Plato) in *aporia*. There are the aphorisms of Heraclitus, the paradoxes of Zeno, the inconclusiveness of *Metaphysics* Zeta, and the arguments leading to a suspension of belief in Pyrrho. All have been taken to intend a deliberate lack of resolution. An indeterminate outcome or ambiguous resolution is in fact common in both narrative and nonnarrative contexts, and so may count as a final, profound continuity with mythic forms of expression.

~

What I hope this introduction has made sufficiently clear is that though the old opposition is deservedly cast aside, useful distinctions between *logos* and *muthos* can still be made, and indeed must be made if the full extent of their ancient interactions are to be understood. But those distinctions are multiple; no one way of distinguishing between *logos* and *muthos* is adequate. By making and refining such distinctions, the old progressive narrative of an almost miraculous progress from irrational myth to rational philosophy can be replaced with more nuanced accounts of various and varied interactions. To provide several compelling examples of such accounts is the ultimate purpose of this volume.[38]

Notes

1. Wians, 2009, 1.

2. An excellent brief but wide-ranging survey of contemporary approaches to myth in fields ranging from psychology, sociology, science, and philosophy to religion is provided by Segal 2004. Greek myth is "anatomized" into three chronological stages in Herron 2017, with an amusing riff on myths as Protean on page 1.

3. The opposition of *logos* to *muthos* was probably formulated in its sharpest terms in Nestle 1940, a book Most 1999b, 31 calls "astonishingly influential" despite its weaknesses and racist undertones. The Greek Miracle is a phrase often attributed to John Burnet in his *Early Greek Philosophy* (e.g., in Waterfield 2018, 69), but I cannot find it in any of the book's four editions. (A miraculous appearance of philosophy is spoken of by Frankel 1962/1973, 255.) Burnet does say "a new thing came into the world with the early Ionian teachers" (Burnet 1930, v), a claim with which many later scholars would agree, even as they all deny the miraculous origins of whatever that was. A Greek miracle was first spoken of with a quite different intent in the nineteenth century by the French linguist Ernest Ronan; see the illuminating history in Laks 2018, 54ff; and also note 13 below. It is worth remembering that Burnet was himself working to discredit two former orthodoxies few modern scholars would wish to revert to: a Hegelian reading of the history of the ancient thought on the one hand, and a Christian Apologist reading that denied Greek originality by

attributing essentials of Greek thought to a "Mosiac philosophy" on the other. Finally, I would note that the phrase "Greek miracle" persists in publications aimed at a more popular audience, e.g., in the title for the catalog of an exhibit of Greek sculpture staged in the first flush of optimism after the fall of Communism that celebrated the birth of humanism and democracy: Buitron-Oliver 1992. The *New York Times* review of the exhibit in its Metropolitan Museum incarnation (March 12, 1993) heaps scorn on its "jingoistic promotional title."

4. In what follows I shall speak of the essays as broadly genetic, complementary, synthetic, or competing with regard to the relationship they identify between *logoi* and *muthoi*, recognizing that more than one label may be applicable (I thank one of the publisher's anonymous referees for the terms used in these comparisons). I should also note that the wide range of figures and themes covered in the essays makes more than one ordering of the volume's contents possible. The arrangement here is loosely chronological, based on the earliest figure mentioned (e.g., Homer, Hesiod, Sophocles) or on the figure who is an essay's main focus (e.g., Anaximander, Aristotle).

5. The definition is my own, based on definitions—and cautions about offering any single comprehensive definition—in Segal 2004, 4–6; Burkert 1979, 1–34; and Kirk 1974, 13–29.

6. Less important here is that a traditional story is a narrative. While traditional stories are narratives, that is not what makes them traditional. The final section of the introduction will consider myth as narrative in a sense quite different from that of a traditional story.

7. As Kirk puts it, a story has "*succeeded* in becoming traditional" (Kirk 1974, 27; his emphasis).

8. The tendency to identify myths with the poems that contained them and therefore to view the poets as mythmakers was widespread in ancient Greece; see Herron 2017, 4. Already in both poets, however, one can see a movement beyond the simple retelling of traditional stories toward sophisticated manipulations of mythic materials. We shall return to this point in a later section.

9. One should not fail to notice, however, that the syncretism evident in traditional stories springs from a felt need for a kind of consistency, even if not that of the philosopher.

10. Burnet, for instance, consistently speaks of the origins of science and "scientific men."

11. Aristotle harshly dismisses Hesiod's mythical subtleties at *Metaph*. III.4, 1000a11–20. For a more accommodative view of myth in Aristotle, see Johansen 1999. Plato could be just as critical of his poetic predecessors, especially in their capacity as educators, but unlike Aristotle he gives mythmaking an important place in the philosopher's toolkit. The very different sense of myth spoken of in connection with Plato's philosophical practice is considered in the final section of the introduction.

12. Mansfeld 2000, 343. And though I hesitate to mention it, a more recent book operates fully—though hardly competently—within the framework of the old opposition (though without citing Nestle, Cornford, or indeed many other important parties to the debate). For a review of this curious effort, see Wians 2016.

13. Cornford 1952, criticized in turn by Vernant 1962/1982, 102–08 for not separating myth and philosophy sharply enough. See further the survey of the issue in Morgan 2000, 30–37 and Buxton's excellent introduction in Buxton 1999.

14. A version of this strategy is pursued by several contributors to this volume, who trace genetic continuities between myth and the non-mythic accounts that emerged from them. Thus, Robert Hahn shows how a rational approach to nature emerged through a process of trial and error as Anaximander and others worked to develop a new and more rational calendar out of a problem already posed in mythic accounts of the cosmos. Luc Brisson uses an explicit genetic metaphor, saying that philosophy grew out of "the loam of tradition." Examining mythic accounts of the origins of human beings, Brisson shows that humans in Greek myth are not the product of an intentional creative act but the distant result of a process that originates in chaos, in contrast to the myths of the origins of human beings in Genesis. For both Hahn and Brisson, a recognizable philosophical stance emerges out of a progressive engagement with mythic predecessors rather than as a discontinuous break marked by unwitting holdovers or partial anticipations.

15. The many ways in which the poems of Homer and Hesiod were didactic are detailed in Herron 2017, chapter 1, and how they came to be authoritative in his chapter 2.

16. Brisson's genetic account makes precisely this point: the origin of the human condition as described in Greek myth had fundamental ethical consequences, demanding "that the place of human being be defined, on the one hand with regard to the gods, and on the other with regard to animals." Lawrence S. Hatab, in a hybrid genetic/competitive account, traces similar consequences for human existence arising from Hesiod's creation story to the tragic values that figure prominently in Sophocles. Similarly, Most 1999a, 343–44 points to the importance and magnitude of their themes for the fundamental conditions of human existence.

17. In the first part of his essay, William Wians shows how the catalogue of ships in *Iliad* 2 subtly draws attention to the withdrawal of Achilles and so prefigures the moral consequences of his destructive rage. Concentrating on *Odyssey* 1–8, Kevin Robb offers a complementary account that shows how the stories of Odysseus and Telemachus taught the values of *hiketeia* and *xenia*. Marjolein Oele shows how the suffering of Priam in *Iliad* books 22 and 24 provided a paradigm of courage arising out of the universal emotions of fear and hope.

18. A point made nicely by Osborne 1997, 24–25.

19. A now classic study of the competition among various claimants to "truth" is Detienne 1967/1996. See further note 21.

20. According to Wians, Xenophanes reveals the competitive nature of his claim to poetic authority by developing a morally motivated logical criticism: mythic cosmological accounts must be wrong, because they attribute shameful actions to divine beings, even as he insists that any account of the gods must fall short of "clear knowledge."

21. On the rhetorical dimension of *logos* vs. *muthos* as part of the larger competitive intellectual landscape, the work of Geoffrey Lloyd stands out. See, for example, Lloyd 1987, and Lloyd 1999, 154–55.

22. Xenophanes's criticism of his poetic predecessors from within the poetic tradition has already been mentioned. Most 1999a, 335 makes the same point more broadly, taking in Xenophanes, Heraclitus, Parmenides, and Empedocles. In his far-ranging essay in this volume exploring how poetry and philosophy may coexist in a few exceptionally rich texts, Long argues that Parmenides deliberately chose poetic hexameter rather than prose to marginalize his poetic predecessors through a parody of traditional epic style and diction. For a different account of how poetry and philosophy function together in the poem of Parmenides, see Rose Cherubin in the first Logos/Muthos volume. She, like Long, sees the use of poetry by Parmenides as much more than window dressing, transforming the poet's traditional duty to promulgate *aletheia*.

23. Hahn's genetic account considers the choice of prose by Anaximander from this perspective.

24. On the pervasive presence of myth in Greek life and thought, see Buxton 1994.

25. In the first *Logos and Muthos*, Catherine Collobert explores three types of philosophical receptions of Homer, one that finds an implicit philosophy in Homer, a second that finds the grounds for a philosophy, the third that investigates the supposed intentions of the poet; Ramona Naddaff traces the permutating image of Helen, who as an Everywoman is always an object of desire and so is never herself, from its first presentation in Homer, through revisions in Sappho, Gorgias, and Euripides.

26. Oele, for instance, shows how the depiction of suffering and courage in the *Iliad* provides a lesson in human finitude, a point reinforced by reference to hope in Hesiod and Aeschylus, particularly in its deceptive form. In the first Logos/Muthos collection, James Lesher shows how the earlier poets were always mindful of the admonition to "think human things"; William Wians in his paper in that collection shows how the *Agamemnon* probes the limits of human as opposed to divine knowledge; C. D. C. Reeve shows the persistence in Pindar, Aeschylus, and Sophocles of the tragic wisdom that recognizes the inescapable vulnerability of human virtue.

27. Robb lays particular emphasis on how Homeric emotive language displayed in quasi-formulaic moral words and phrases became the source for later ethical terminology. Hatab shows how the tragic values in Sophocles had their origins in Homer and Hesiod. In the first Logos volume, Fred Miller, Jr. expresses this as the challenge posed by Homeric psychology.

28. In addition to Hatab's study of tragic values just mentioned, Marina Marren underlines the relevance of tyranny of Oedipus for Sophocles's Athens. Through the image of a character who combines being and seeming and conflates *muthos* to *logos*, the playwright spurs a sophisticated fifth century imperial audience to reflect on the necessary role of *muthoi* in their own lives and in the life of their city. Roslyn Weiss shows how Sophocles's depiction of Antigone builds on the self-righteous, single-minded persona of the Homeric hero, with all of its contradictions, consequences, and ambiguities, and then how many of these same traits are practically reversed in the depiction of Socrates in the *Apology* in his service to Athens. In the first Logos volume, Sara Brill argues that Aeschylus crafted a similar adaptation of a suppliant story appropriate for the justification of authority in democratic Athens.

29. Ruby Blondell makes a special point of the importance of public performance, even as a background for written argument. She traces out a complicated pattern of reaction, revision, and incorporation of the "divine defense" of Helen as found in Homer, Gorgias, and Euripides by picturing each defense being delivered publicly in fifth-century Athens. In the first volume, P. Christopher Smith argued for a rejection of abstract philosophical *logos* in favor of the lived communication of sung poetic speech through an analysis of Cassandra's remarkable speech in the *Agamemnon*.

30. Two papers explore the persistence of mythic elements in Plato. Marina McCoy examines Plato's manipulation of earlier material from Homer, Hesiod, and Herodotus in the story of Gyges that opens *Republic* II, while Pierre Destrée shows how the myth of Er critically incorporates and revises the *Nekuia* from *Odyssey* 11 (along with one of Pindar's odes). The phrase "Plato the mythmaker" becomes the title of Brisson 1994/1999.

31. See here Collobert, Destrée, and Gonzalez 2012, which both in its introduction and in several contributed papers carefully delineates the sense in which one may speak of myth in Plato.

32. Destrée sees the myth of Er as a final appeal to the *thumos* of the still poetry-loving Glaucon, and claims more generally that Plato intends by his myths to provide the deep persuasion and forceful motivation that can be provided only by engaging both reasoning and the emotions (Long makes the same point about Plato's writing style generally). McCoy argues that, through the use of *muthos* in *Republic* II, Plato gives his audience a way to identify mimetically with the shepherd Gyges and to explore their reactions to his actions as a means to self-knowledge.

33. The *eikôs muthos* Plato has delivered by Timaeus should be put in a different category as it is not challenged or undercut as are the myths of Protagoras and Aristophanes.

34. Hatab, for instance, calls the *Republic* as a whole "essentially an anti-tragic *muthos*."

35. The literal and recognized falsity of myths takes us back to the possibility of allegorical intent and a corresponding need for allegorical interpretation, a strategy Plato has Socrates refer to and dismiss with reference to the abduction of Oreithuia by Boreas at *Phaedrus* 229B–E. Such interpretations were motivated by a desire to "save" myths by reducing them to a nonnarrative, rational level. Properly interpreted, it was believed that *muthoi* were not in all cases incompatible with *logoi*, so long as myth submits to supposedly rational constraints. Gerard Naddaf devotes his contribution in volume one to the use of allegory as a rational attempt to save myth.

36. Weiss's analysis of the *Antigone* shows how the playwright raises without necessarily answering a host of questions about the heroine and her motivations—Is Antigone genuinely pious? Is she truly loving? Is her single-minded commitment to her cause meant to be admirable?—with how we are to respond to this larger-than-life character left unclear. Marren emphasizes that the failure of Oedipus to gain self-knowledge can perhaps best be appreciated by interpreters who begin with the ambiguities of the play in performance. In Euripides's *Trojan Women*, Blondell finds the dramatic action undercutting Helen's speech in her own defense, in which Helen claims to be blameless. In the first volume, Paul Woodruff uses the enigmatic action of the plays of Sophocles to reveal a profound reverence for the gods that at the same time expresses a new humanism in the face of divine silence.

37. This is the theme of Michael Davis's paper in volume 1, which explores the seemingly disjointed structure of the *Helen*, the action of which depends on perpetually challenging what characters believe they see and recognize.

38. I want to thank SUNY Press's two anonymous reviewers for their extensive comments and many helpful suggestions, and Larry Hatab for saving me from an embarrassing error.

1

Xenia, Hiketeia, and the Homeric Language of Morals

The Origins of Western Ethics

Kevin Robb

In memory of Walter Donlan

Two social proprieties (*themistes*, established ways, customs, "laws") depicted in the action of the *Odyssey* are, it could be argued, the most prominent in Homer: *xenia*, or "guest-friendship," and *hiketeia*, or "supplication." One or the other, and often both, are found in every book of the *Odyssey*, and widely in the *Iliad* as well. Yet there is an oddity about their modern reception. The scholarly literature devoted to them had remained notably scant, especially in English, until fairly late into the twentieth century.

The reasons are no doubt complex, but a contributing factor may have been that both had long been institutions of Greek oral life, finding their way at some unknown date to an early written text of Homer, but unquestionably emerging from pre-alphabetic Greece. They have a strangeness about them, with features considered "odd" even by sympathetic scholars. Admittedly, both proprieties involved forms of ritualized behavior of a sort commonly found in oral societies, but is alien to modern readers, as it surely was not to the ancient hearers of "Homer." The latter must have participated in, or at least observed, both rituals hundreds of times, especially among aristocrats.

Two works of serious scholarship published in the second half of the last century signaled the promise of change. In 1954 Moses Finley published *The World of Odysseus*,[1] a book that was well-received but was not initially recognized for one of its most original contributions, a short treatment of the supreme importance of *xenia* in Homer and in pre-state Greece. In time, this treatment would become influential indeed, notably for Gabriel Herman in his *Ritualized Friendship and the Greek City*,[2] published in 1987. Herman's book began its life as a doctoral dissertation at Cambridge University supervised by Sir Moses Finley.

In 1973, John Gould published "*Hiketeia*," a rich resource of nearly eighty pages that, like Finley's notice of *xenia*, initially was somewhat neglected.[3] Early in his text, Gould observed that, from Homer to the fifth century and well beyond, *hiketeia* as a social and religious institution "figures prominently both in the traditional, mythological themes of Greek literature and in the historical record." Despite these facts, it was "all the more surprising that it is almost totally ignored in what is written in standard works on the social and religious institutions of ancient Greece and hardly better treated in discussions of Greek literature."[4] Both Finley and Gould would, in time, become powerful catalysts for later scholarship on *xenia* and *hiketeia*, and both lived long enough to see early oversights handsomely remedied.

Gould's treatment emphasized, rightly, the close parallelism between the proper or prescribed treatment of the *hiketês*, Gould's primary focus, and the proper treatment of the *xenos*; both, he notes, were familiar figures in Homer and in later Greek literature and society. Gould identified both as "a ritualizing of behavior" that, among other social functions, "constitutes a powerful factor in keeping the tensions of existence within tolerable limits" in what were, undoubtedly, tense times.[5] Gould acknowledged debts to the anthropologist Julian Pitt-Rivers for his own understanding that Greek *hiketeia* (and *xenia*) belonged to a wider category of "ritualized relationships" of a sort anthropologists had discovered in many societies. Pitt-Rivers in 1968 had published the insightful paper, "The Stranger, the Guest, and the Hostile Host."[6] Gabriel Herman, in turn, preferred the designation "ritualized friendship," as, following him, *xenia* came to be widely known. Such terminology is preferable to the awkward neologism "guest-friendship," but the latter, because much used, is unavoidable. *Xenia* is also sometimes equated with "well-known Mediterranean hospitality," and effectively dismissed from serious discussion.

In recognizing that *xenia* and *hiketeia* are supremely important expressions of moral, social, and political behavior in Archaic Greece (and into even the Christian era, as Herman demonstrated), classicists, and interested anthropologists, are mainly on board. The same cannot be said for all philosophers, however, even historians of ethics. At a recent gathering, some connected part-sentences from Herman's book were read aloud, followed by similar statements from Walter Donlan on the heroic ethos, and were greeted with dumbfounded stares. The quotations from Herman stressed that for the Homeric hero, "the obligation of guest-friendship should be set above all other obligation" and that this was "a part of the natural order of things," a fact of aristocratic life, or the heroic ethos. Furthermore, "adherence to the code of guest-friendship was a supreme manifestation of the hero's free exercise of his prowess. There was, in his world, neither overlord to demand feudal allegiance, nor communal group to claim social responsibility." Nevertheless, with the eventual rise of the polis, "the community tamed the hero, and transformed him into a citizen."[7]

The last remark was in sympathy with Finley's view that "no trace" of the classical polis in a political sense could be found in the text of Homer. That view is controversial, but is repeatedly asserted by Herman, relying on Finley.[8] What is not controversial is that *poleis* were widely dispersed in Hellas by the middle of the seventh century. From the sixth century onward, the surviving literature is increasingly filled with examples of aristocratic *xenoi* with loyalties that were far stronger toward each other than toward their own polis and its laws. That much Herman's book proved with intriguing examples.

In what follows, I propose to concentrate on the first eight books of the *Odyssey* as representative of the whole, and to argue that *xenia* and *hiketeia* dominate much of the action of the major characters, as well as the moral language they use. I will focus on how that language works "emotively" to prescribe adherence to the Hellenic proprieties (and decry the violations), an essential task of epic singers before the advent of written law.

Book 1 of the *Odyssey* deserves close attention because it is especially revealing once the modern reader recognizes that eighth-century Greek listeners would initially perceive the suitors as arrogant, badly misbehaving *xenoi*. Gradually listeners learn that long before the suitors should have departed for other households (*oikoi*) to do their feasting, "going *oikos* to *oikos*," as Telemachus repeatedly pleads (*Od.* 1.375, passim), and the rules of *xenia* required. This loutish behavior in the house of an absent Odysseus has been recognized as a "corruption of *xenia*" scene, the first of many in Greek literature.[9]

The institution of *hiketeia* becomes a theme of the epic starting in Book 5, where a naked, half-drowned Odysseus must become a helpless *hiketês* and supplicate a nameless river-god, or else loose his homecoming and his life. Books 6 and 7 reveal Odysseus, the ragged, helpless suppliant, being transformed back into the proud, handsome *xenos*, clothed in a prince's garments and supremely competent. Book 8 is a triumphant celebration of all the obligations and special joys that belonged to Homeric *xenia*, where at the finest of feasts, with games, dance, epic song, and much wine, the *xenos* is welcomed and incorporated into the group as "spiritual kin."

In a word, *xenia* and *hiketeia* are found everywhere in the *Odyssey*. If they, and the moral vocabulary deployed to support them, were confined to the epos and did not carry over into Greek life in ensuing centuries, then just possibly the proprieties and moralities of Homer were merely stunning literary invention after all. But, of course, the opposite is the case.

Two Definitions

Xenia denotes a highly ritualized, reciprocal relationship in which unrelated persons from different social units voluntarily agree to exchange certain goods and services. The goods are mainly gifts of diverse sorts that are valuable in a pre-money economy; the value of the gift is proportionate to the physical abilities of the giver, but must be, for him, extravagant. The sorts of services involved are diverse but uniformly welcome and socially of great utility. They will be described below as discovered in Books 1 through 8 of the *Odyssey*.

Hiketeia is a highly ritualized act initiated by one person, a suppliant (*hiketês*), who is usually in great distress or need, often a life-or-death type crisis. By a series of precise actions and words that involve ritualized self-abnegation, the suppliant seeks a reciprocal, favorable action from a person in a position to alleviate his need, or provide him with what he seeks. If the suppliant adheres strictly to all the requirements of the *hiketeia* ritual, what I will call "full physical supplication," maximum moral and social pressure is brought to bear on the supplicated person to respond favorably. This outcome is the normal expectation in Homer, and, indeed, will remain so for centuries.[10]

The "great" or spectacular supplications, such as those that open and close the action of the *Iliad*, are uniformly successful in Homer. Thetis, mother of Achilles, successfully supplicates Zeus on Mount Olympus and changes the course of the Trojan War; a defeated King Priam successfully supplicates the victorious Achilles on the plain of Troy and recovers for burial the body of his son, Hector, the last Prince of Troy.

Xenia and the Catalyst of *The World of Odysseus*

In *The World of Odysseus*, Moses Finley early observed that no detail in the life of the heroes "receives so much attention in the *Iliad* and the *Odyssey* as gift-giving, and always there is frank reference to adequacy, appropriateness, and recompense."[11] Not every example of gift-giving in the poems is a component of *xenia*, of course, but when two powerful heroes are involved, many are. Later Finley observes that, however psychologists or economists may try to understand the extravagant gift-giving required by *xenia*, "functionally it took its place with marriage . . . as an act through which status relations were created and what we should call political obligations."[12] His immensely influential treatment of *xenia* is underway, but it will be astonishingly short, roughly six pages in all, with scattered asides added elsewhere.

Arguing that in the permanently hostile environment that is the world of Odysseus alliances were always necessary, Finley details some significant conditions. Beyond alliances created by blood or marriage, political alliances were formed *only* on a personal basis between heads of households (*oikoi*); they were, therefore, largely (Finley implies exclusively) created by the *xenia* relationship. If true, Finley was onto something significant, and an important historical fact had slipped past much of the older scholarship.

To be clear about Finley's claims, he admits there were complex kinship relationships of a sort found in every society, but there are only so many blood brothers and uncles, and not all of these may be available, or desirable. Kinship can also extend beyond bloodlines by means of marriage, always important for forming alliances in ancient Greece, but again, a calculated "dealing out of daughters and assorted female relatives" can create only so many new allies. Here, argues Finley, *xenia* came to play its crucial role in Homer and in Archaic Greece.

He reminds his readers that in a society of self-help, where there are no governmental protections upon which to rely, no police arm to enforce rules of any kinds, a large web of powerful allies is necessary for the survival of any independent *oikos*. Moreover, as indispensable allies for the head of a rich, powerful *oikos*, only *xenoi* would be available in the required numbers. Finley writes:

> Guest-friendship was a very serious institution, the alternative to marriage in forging bonds between rulers . . . Guest-friend and guest-friendship were far more than sentimental terms of human affection. In the world of Odysseus they were technical names for very concrete relationships, as formal and evocative of rights and duties as marriage.[13]

According to Finley, political alliances in Homer's world are forged only between individuals, not political units such as *poleis*, city-states; the polis was, in any case, in the future in Finley's estimation. As a result, in addition to blood kinship and marriage, only *xenia* is available to afford alliances in the numbers and of a sort that these permanently hostile times required. "Pre-eminence lay in the *oikos*, the large noble household with its staff of slaves and commoners, its aristocratic retainers, and its allies among relatives and guest-friends."[14]

Precisely when all this started to change Finley does not say, but he cites Herodotus (1.69) as evidence that one important change had taken place by the middle of the sixth century. He calls attention to the incident in Herodotus where the King of Lydia, Croesus, "sent messengers to Sparta bearing gifts and requesting an alliance." The Spartans, in turn, "rejoiced at the coming of the Lydians and they took the oath of guest-friendship and alliance." As Finley interpreted the Homeric evidence, "Homer knew of no such tie between Argives and Lycians or Taphians or Ithacans–only between individuals, Diomedes and Glaucus, 'Mentes' and Telemachus."[15] *Xenia* was to remain the foundation of political alliances *conceptually* for later Greeks, but in the future the parties need no longer act only as individuals; they can act as heads of political entities, and in their names, speaking for "the Athenians" or "the Spartans," as they forge important alliances.

The most controversial claim, the pre-state, or pre-polis, status of Homeric society, is made in various ways by Finley, but usually, as above, by asserting that the independent household or *oikos* was primary or preeminent in a given locality, notably on Ithaca (where the Homeric evidence does seem to support Finley), not the community. The "community principle" is as yet rudimentary in Homeric society and in the heroic ethos for Finley and scholars in agreement with him.[16] Therefore, as one powerful *oikos* grinds against another in the endemic competition for ever-increasing wealth and power in the turbulent years of the Dark Ages, spurts of local aggression would inevitably bring about the constant tensions that marked heroic existence. Endless conflicts and incessant war were inescapable; so too was the need for allies in the form of *xenoi*, and hence, according to Finley, the great importance of *xenia* to this society.[17]

Also for Finley, the head of the Homeric *oikos* had virtually absolute power over its members if his rules were broken; but there was as yet no entity outside of the *oikos* that exercised any discernible power, or enforceable authority, over it, including "king" (*basileus*) or assembly (*agora*). The kings were little more than local chieftains, and the agora had no power to legislate or enforce. Here again, the Ithakesian evidence supports Finley, especially *Odyssey*, Books 1 and 2.

Difficulties aside, Finley's reconstruction put a welcome emphasis on the alliances necessary in the world of Odysseus. Beyond blood kinship, political alliances relied either on marriage, the strategic "dishing out the daughters" (and any unmarried bastard sons around in the *oikos*, a step down but still usable), or on the far more numerous supply of *xenoi*. The supreme importance of *xenia* in the world of Odysseus emerges as the mechanism that afforded fiercely independent *oikoi* a wide web of necessary alliances, especially before the rise of the polis or a strong civic government.

Absent written records from pre-alphabetic Greece, one tantalizing question will likely remain unanswered and unanswerable: when the emergence of the polis? Whatever that century was, Finley's evidence argues persuasively that the polis emerged from a Hellas in which *xenia* had long flourished. Such a pervasive propriety, known and respected by a whole people, woven into their oldest surviving literature, under the specific protection of their supreme god Zeus himself, Zeus *Xeinios*, was not likely to have been created in a single generation, or century.

Before turning to the *Odyssey*, I propose first to look at the language of Homer as it relates to the emotive theory of ethics that developed in the twentieth century, and especially among some Anglo-American philosophers from the 1930s to the 1950s. Such an admittedly improbable detour may point us to some useful features about Homer's use of moral words.

Homer's Emotive Language of Morals

Recent professional publications in philosophical ethics abound with references to "noncognitivism," a position somewhat better known as "emotivism," that came to prominence the 1930s. The early emotivist position was associated with the writings of A. J. Ayer, notably his short but influential *Language, Truth and Logic*, published in 1936. For Ayer, a statement such as "stealing money is wrong," has no factual meaning; nothing factual about the external world is being asserted. "It is clear that there is nothing said here which can be true or false." Rather, it merely expresses the feeling or attitude that someone, usually the speaker, has toward taking another's money by force or fraud. Such condemning language merely "evinces emotion," as Professor Urmson liked to characterize Ayer's deliberately provocative position, quoting Ayer.[18] Both Stevenson and Hare argued convincingly that moral words, in fact, do a good deal more than Ayer allowed. Some of their insightful analyses may serve to underscore important but neglected—and sometimes even vehemently denied—features of Homer's ethical language.

The surviving texts of Homer (and Hesiod) are unimpeachable evidence that Homer's moral language was used in an historical society, Archaic Greece after 700 BCE, in the largely successful attempt to control human behavior before the rise of written law. Professional singers (*aoidoi*) had developed over the preceding illiterate centuries a very complex moral vocabulary. This vocabulary was demonstrably used, in part, (1) to express attitudes of approval and disapproval (Ayer); in part, (2) to elicit certain stable attitudes in listeners, namely, to alter interests and become guides for living (Stevenson); and, in part, (3) to commend actions, and especially to commend the imitation of certain actions while condemning the imitation of others, also in order to provide guides for living in society (Stevenson and Hare).

Viewed from an historical perspective, the primary Homeric task was to control human behavior effectively with words rather than with force, or force alone. The task of moral language when Stevenson and

Hare wrote (and today still) was not so very different from Homer's day, with one major exception. In a society (Homer's) devoid of law and law enforcement, and with fear of superior force or unrelenting revenge (*tisis*), personal or tribal, as the only effective deterrents to murder and aggression, the task becomes more urgent, or "raw" as Adam Parry liked to say, quoting his famous father, Milman Parry.

The word that loomed large in early emotivist literature was "good," with debts owed to G. E. Moore. In Homer, the neuter adjectives *agathon* and *kalon*, sometimes translatable as "good," play an important role as well. The first modern step of importance toward an emotive analysis of moral language was taken not by a practicing philosopher but by an astute literary critic, I. A. Richards. Ogden and Richards published their influential, *The Meaning of Meaning*, in 1923. In turn, this book did not go unnoticed by the philosopher Charles Stevenson, who in 1944 prominently put a single sentence from Richards on a separate page opposite the Preface of his famous work, *Ethics and Language*: "The peculiar ethical use of 'good' is, we suggest, purely emotive use."[19] That is, whereas good has other uses in English, when used in a moral sense, it has only emotive use or meaning.

In a series of influential writings, Stevenson extended the discussion of "emotive meaning" to other ethical terms, and greatly expanded the concept of "emotive meaning." Referring to ethical judgments, Stevenson would write:

> Their major use is not to indicate facts but to *create an influence*. Instead of merely describing people's interests they *change* or *intensify* them. They *recommend* an interest in an object rather than [merely] state the interest already exists.[20]

A crucially important use of moral words is to change attitudes and behavior in the most effective way possible this side of resorting to force. Thus Stevenson can claim that ethical terms are '*instruments*" (emphasis his) used in the "readjustment of human interests." In this way, "social influence" is exerted, "by means that have nothing to do with physical force." Moral words and ethical language "facilitate influence [to action] . . . They are a means by which men's attitudes may be led this way or that."[21]

The Homeric uses of moral terms conform, I suggest, to Stevenson's analysis. In Homer, the approval that is constantly invoked is that of the community or the group, the established way, what is *themis*, and ultimately, for *xenia* and *hiketeia*, the protecting approval of Zeus himself, Zeus *Xeinios* and Zeus *Hiketêsios* (*Od.* 13.213; *Il.* 13.625, *passim*). In the case of the neuter adjectives *kalon* or *agathon*, both of which can be translated as "good" (and for many other Homeric approval words), there are, indeed, nonethical usages, as, notoriously, is the case for "good" in English. But when they are used in a moral context there is always a detectable "emotive" dimension in Stevenson's sense.

By the end of the eighth century, Homeric language and diction had developed to the point where singers had an extraordinarily large number of ways linguistically to deliver their repetitive (in meaning), simple message. Whatever the metrical requirement for the singer at the moment, in whatever part of the hexameter that needed filling, his formidable arsenal of moral terms and formulas afforded him a way to meet that need, and so express effortlessly, and without at least linguistic monotony, the same essential idea. Homer's many moral words are instruments that effectively alter or enhance attitudes, bringing to bear immense social pressure that results in performing certain actions and avoiding others, all "by means that have nothing to do with physical force," in Stevenson's phrasing.

According to Stevenson, when you say to someone that murder is wrong, you are doing far more than evincing your disapproval of murder; in addition, and perhaps mainly, you are attempting to induce that person to disapprove of it as well. "Your ethical judgment has a quasi-imperative force which operating through suggestion and intensified by your tone of voice, readily permits you to begin to *influence*, to *modify*, his interests."[22]

The reference to a "tone of voice" is especially appropriate to a medium of communication that was sung or chanted by highly professional performers, as was the epical material in ancient Greece. Stevenson adds: "the emotive meaning of a word is a tendency of a word, arising through history of its usage, to produce . . . affective responses in people. It is the immediate aura of feeling which hovers about a word."[23] All of Homer's ethical words accomplish this superbly well, but it is especially true of *aidôs* (and its frequent partner, *nemesis*), perhaps the most powerful of them all, whether used as noun, verb, or adjective, as we shall see.

Stevenson concluded that the statement "this is good" equated, at least roughly, with two components, "I approve of this" plus a "dynamic" aspect, go and "do so as well."[24] Transferred to Homeric moral words, the first component equates with, "your society approves of this; such and such conforms to what the group approves of, the established way, *hê themis estìn*, what is *dikaion*, and so is always 'right.' " This in turn importantly equates with, "this was the way of our ancestors," as authenticated by the direct inspiration of Muses, The Divine Informers. The dynamic or admonishing aspect is the constant appeal, explicit or implicit, to apply by analogy the actions described as right or proper in the poems to the same or similar actions in one's own life, and the life of the community.

As noted, Stevenson admitted debts to Ogden and Richards in such statements as, "the emotive use of words . . . is the use of words to express or *excite* feelings and attitudes."[25] Precisely this use of (moral) words, to arouse feelings of approval for certain actions in Archaic Greece, to instill attitudes of acceptance and compliance for the Hellenic proprieties, and thus to induce contemporary Greeks to "go and do likewise," is the primary purpose behind the moral vocabulary of Homer, so prominent a feature in the poems. It matured in a society that still knew no enforcement arm for what was "right" beyond what self-help could muster, as is clearly still the case in Homeric society. The treatment of homicides, especially an accidental homicide, makes this indisputable.[26] Thus, such inner restraints as the moral words of singers could instill in (especially) powerful male warrior-heroes—hallowed, sacred words such as *aidôs* and *nemesis*—were culturally priceless.

R. M. Hare, a philosopher of the Oxford language school, came to prominence in the 1950s. From the standpoint of Homeric ethics, he adds an insightful emphasis. Hare observed that moral commendation could be quite indirect, and so not immediately recognized as such. Hare offered a sophisticated analysis for how neutral description can create what he called a "synthetic moral principle."[27] Simply stated, the actions or qualities of the "good" person, or a Homeric hero, Achilles or Hector, are narrated as facts in the indicative mood, and as actions that happened long ago, but in such an inspiring way or context (i.e., oral records of ancestral precedent) as to be highly commendatory. Such description then becomes a recipe or prescription for *imitation* by persons in the present time who will aspire to be like the heroic model. The constant but indirect inducement to imitation is the emotive component buried in Homer's seemingly factual narration of past events. Homeric ethics has been, perceptively, described an ethics that is founded on the arousal of moral aspiration. As such, it proved to be hugely successful in a "song culture" society that could neither read nor write.[28]

Examples are found everywhere in Homer, most obviously when authoritative characters resort to the famous *exempla*,[29] the deeds/fames of men of old, *klea andrôn*, in order to alter present behavior. But these are only less indirect instances of what Homeric ethics always does. In this society, the actions of ancestors are the ultimate basis of right action. Or perhaps better, the basis of morality is what each generation was induced to believe were the ways of their "Mycenaean" ancestors, as narrated by singers who were directly inspired by the divine eyewitnesses to all past events, the Muses.

It is time to turn to the *Odyssey* in order to watch epic singers at work at their task. We will look closely at the prescriptive and proscriptive language that accompanies every description of guest-friendship and supplication.

Odyssey I: In the Form of a *Xenos*

The human action of the *Odyssey* begins with the arrival of Athena at the entrance to the forecourt of the house of Odysseus on the island of Ithaka, where she waits. "She was disguised as a friend, leader of the Taphians, Mentes," is the translation of Richmond Lattimore for 1.105. For "disguised as a friend" could be substituted the more literal translation: "in the form/likeness/shape (*eidomenê*) of a *xenos*." The word *xenos* has a notorious range of meanings in Homer, such as friend, guest-friend, stranger, host, among other possibilities, but Athena's action of waiting patiently to be noticed guarantees that the meaning at 105 is a quasi-technical one. The word immediately identifies a waiting stranger as a person who either has, or hopes to have, a guest-friend relationship with a host inside the house, and so to participate in all the protections and privileges (including future reciprocation in his *oikos*) that are associated with the propriety of *xenia*. As the opening gambit of the ritual prescribes, Athena/Mentes "waits at the gate" as we might say; a proper *xenos* does not intrude uninvited into the *aulê* or the house, but waits at some outer entrance, usually at the portico of the forecourt of the house.

Athena/Mentes quickly discovers that the suitors have taken over the functions of the *xenos*-host that belong to Telemachus in his father's absence, while simultaneously they have assumed the roles of *xenoi*, guest-friends, especially in their nightly feasting. The suitors consume food and wine, notably meats, in abundance, having *themselves* slain the ever-valuable work animals (106–112).[30] Peter Jones laudably, if in passing, connects both the offences of the Cyclops and the suitors as a "corruption of the ritual of *xenia*." Richmond Lattimore made a similar comparison, also in passing, in the introduction to his unsurpassed translation of the *Odyssey*. The suitors, he writes, "abuse hospitality," from the first book to the last; they know all the rules that custom requires in treating a *xenos* (citing *Od.* 17.48–487). But, as Lattimore adds, "in action they are a living travesty" of them all.[31]

Sitting dejectedly among the suitors, Telemachus, the all-but-deposed host, is the first to see the *xenos* and also act appropriately; the suitors are occupied with amusing themselves at *pessoi*, a dice-like game, and ignore the *xenos*. But Telemachus, still the proper host, jumps up at once. "He went straight (*ithus*) to the threshold, for he felt great indignation (*nemesis*) in his "heart" (*thumos*) that a *xenos* should wait at the threshold" (119–120).

Nemesis in its various grammatical forms, when used as a powerful term of moral condemnation, refers to the feeling of strong indignation, shading into shame and disgust, that a proper Hellene feels, or should feel, when confronting a violation of a Hellenic propriety. Telemachus, son of the King of Ithaca, is a properly socialized young male aristocrat in this society. Keeping a *xenos* waiting at the gate is a violation of a supremely important Hellenic propriety, and he moves to correct it at once. In contrast, the suitors ignore the waiting *xenos*, although their subsequent actions reveal they know the proprieties required by *xenia*, and are exploiting them in order to impose on the house of Odysseus.

Young Telemachus, carefully continuing with the proper ritual, takes the right hand of the *xenos* and pronounces the greeting: "Hail, stranger-guest (*xeine*), among us you will be welcomed (*philêseai*)," and entertained, as though among *philoi*, as the verb can suggest. Then, after he has eaten, the *xenos* can tell the host of his needs. On hearing such generous, comforting words, the *xenos* knows that, at a minimum, he will be safe, sheltered, fed well, and entertained in this house, to the best of his host's ability.

Still ignorant of the name of the *xenos*, Telemachos leads him inside, but away from the din arising from suitors. The ritual-like actions continue. The *xenos* is formally seated on a better than ordinary chair (*thronon*: a Mycenaean word for fancy, inlaid chairs; the suitors appropriate the same privileged seating, *thronous* at 145), together with a footstool, next to a fine polished table. The point is that the surroundings are aristocratic, and a *xenos* is offered the best the house contains, in what is also a Homeric type-scene. The suitors, in contrast, simply appropriate the best things in the house while ignoring the host, a mockery of *xenia*.

At 136 ff., a maidservant brings a golden pitcher so that host and *xenos* can ritualistically wash together, the water pored over the hands and falling into a special silver receptacle. This act has deep and ancient religious implications in many cultures, including Greek, as symbolic of a cleansing before entering upon something holy, or pure. At 139, a housekeeper, described as "reverend" (*aidoiê*, cognate with *aidôs*)[32] brings bread and other initial food in abundance, distributing it with generous grace.

These highly formulaic verses (136–142), especially the first four hexameters that describe one servant who supervises the hand-washing ritual, and another who provides for sharing initial food, appear later in the *Odyssey*, next in Book 4 (52 ff.; then 7.172 ff.), and elsewhere in Homer in shorter or longer versions. Lines and part-lines, and so various details, can be added or subtracted to a "typical scene," as such scenes were designated in Homeric scholarship, notably by Arend, before Parry. In general, in a type-scene, the same or very similar things happen, in the same or very similar order, in the same or very similar verses or parts of verses. It is a form of composition invariably eschewed by a literate author writing for a sophisticated readership, but of great utility to the improvising oral composer, as Parry persuasively argued in a review of Arend published posthumously in *Classical Philology* in 1936.[33] Such compositions lend themselves to describing ritualized behavior, where certain actions and words follow others in a standard order, while also greatly easing the burden on a singer's memory in improvised performances, as Parry argued. In regard to the latter task, Parry came to believe that the constant deployment of type-scenes was every bit as important as the systems of formulas.

In the two scenes from Books 1 and 4 the repeated sequence of the same hexameters can hardly be missed. That the suitors are, in fact, deliberately imitating or corrupting the ritual of receiving the *xenos* is suggested by a sequence of four verses describing their "arrival" for their nightly feast, immediately after the description of the elaborate arrival scene of a true *xenos*, Athena/Mentes. The pattern of action is the same, although shortened, and with different characters, in the ersatz "arrival scene" of the suitors:

> Then in came the proud suitors, and thereafter
> they sat down on seats and special chairs (*thronous*).

Heralds poured water over their hands
and maidservants heaped high the bread in baskets
and youths (*kouroi*) filled the bowls with wine. (*Od.* 4.145–148)

From the above description, it appears that the suitors have not only taken over the daily management of the *oikos*, but are demanding to be treated as authentic *xenoi* in their nightly feasting. The young host is far from happy about this, but is powerless to evict them. Much later in the *Odyssey* the suitors will even taunt Telemachus, claiming that no man is more unlucky in his *xenoi* (*kakoxeinôteros*) and complaining that he pays too much attention to his other, "worthless" guests, in fact Odysseus disguised as a beggar man (20.376).

There is an instructive parallel scene in the *Iliad*. It is part of a long narration by Nestor of Pylos to Patroclus as he reminds him of the day that he and Odysseus arrived at the house of Peleus, King of the Myrmidons, to recruit fighters for the Trojan War (*Il.* 11.765 ff.). Peleus is busy outside in the courtyard sacrificing a bull, aided by Patroclus and Achilles, who is on his knees. The arriving *xenoi* stand patiently, waiting until at last Achilles, the youngest person present, as was Telemachus on Ithaca,[34] looks up and sees them. Achilles jumps up at once, and rushes over to the *xenoi*. He takes them by the hand, and leads them over to comfortable chairs. "Abundant hospitality [*xeinia*, what belongs to *xenia*] he set before us, as for *xenoi* is *themis*" (precedent, proper, "right,") says wise old Nestor at *Iliad* 11.779.

The addition of the moral formula makes the actions surrounding *xenia* now "typical" in another, and moral, sense; collectively, they are declared to be customary, and so the established way, proper, right, what for this society is *themis*. This may be as close to moral generalization or abstraction (and universalization) as Homeric discourse gets. Although the language remains narrative and descriptive of specific actions, the addition of the moral formula identifies the actions as customary, proper, and so always right; violations are always wrong. The clear intent is to commend as well as to approve this and all similar actions, and the implicit moral command is one of imitation. It fits well the descriptions of Stevenson and Hare of "emotive meaning" for moral terms.

The standard components for such a traditional scene involving an arriving *xenos* are found throughout the poems. Not every step can be found in every instance, but the overall pattern is clear and stable. Also, not every arrival scene involves the arrival of a *xenos*, of course, but the singers could adapt the standard components of typical scenes to the circumstances of the narrative with great skill in performance.[35] The main clue, however, as above, is that a *xenos* always waits to be noticed by a host.

Abundant food is set before the suitors at their own direction; when the feasting is finished, some additional standard components of the *xenia* ritual follow. The guests (but at their own initiation, not the host's) perform songs (*molpê*), and dances (*orchêstus*), "for these [events are] the crown of the feast."[36] Next the suitors (not the host; Telemachus might as well not be in the house) demand *aoidê*, epic song, which requires a professional performer who is also expert on the lyre. The resident minstrel (*aoidos*), the loyal Phemius, complies, but he sings under duress, because the suitor "guests" compel him. That outrageous fact, later relayed by Telemachus to Odysseus, will save the singer's life in the concluding, vengeful slaughter that brings the *Odyssey* to a close.

It becomes increasingly clear that dual procedures of guest-friendship are being played out simultaneously in Book 1. The first, conducted between Telemachus and Mentes, is proper, decorous, and orderly. The other, conducted by the suitors among themselves at their own initiative "is a negative image" of the properly managed situation, and is thus a "caricature of the normal routine."[37] At one point, Athena/Mentes erupts with indignant words:

> What feast is this? What kind of crowd? What need have
>   you for it?
> A festival or a wedding feast? Obviously no meal to which
>   guests contribute.
> With what outrage (*hubris*) do they seem to be feasting in
>   your halls!
> Righteous indignation (*nemesis*) would a man feel at seeing
>   such shameful
> acts, any man of sense who should happen in among them.
>   (*Od.* 1.225–229)

Despite the distractions from the rambunctious suitors, a quiet and proper conduct of the *xenia* ritual is maintained between Telemachus and Athena/Mentes. The delayed questions are finally asked and duly answered: Who are you? What is your name and who are your parents? In the course of this standard questioning, host and guest discover that they are, indeed, ancestral guest-friends (*patrôioi xenoi*) by reason of an established relationship of *xenia* between their fathers.[38]

Here first in the *Odyssey*, and elsewhere in the poems, we discover that guest-friendship is inherited, an important feature of the propriety. It is what, beyond any other feature, identifies its unmistakable likeness to kinship. We can choose our friends in life but not the relatives we inherit; for better or worse, they belong to us by reason of our parents. The same was true of guest-friends; if their fathers, or even grandfathers, were *xenoi*, they are then automatically ancestral guest-friends to each other, *patrôioi xenoi*. The relationship with all of its entanglements, obligations, and rewards is inherited down the generations. "Ancestral *xenoi* do I declare us to be, from old, even as our fathers were," proclaims Athena/Mentes (187–189).

When Athena/Mentes announces her departure, the young host is urgent that his *xenos* accept a valuable guest-gift, an indispensable component of *xenia*, but she shrewdly dodges an awkward situation (no reciprocation would ever come from "Mentes"). She also eludes another offer that is a regular component of guest-friendship, a warm bath. Bathing had both ritualistic and hygienic implications. Agitated, Telemachus urges his *xenos*: "But eager as you are to depart, wait, you must bathe before returning to your ship" (309–310). But she is too quick, and is gone. In the moment of departing, Athena casts strength and courage into his heart (*thumos*), which had been her purpose in coming to Ithaca.

Not everything that belongs to Homeric *xenia* can be found in *Odyssey* 1, but much can be. Some final words from Book 1 appropriately belong to the rightful host, young Telemachus, who is admonishing the squabbling suitors to quiet down, "for it is good (*kalon*) to listen to the singer, especially one such as this, whose voice is like that of gods" (370–371). The adjective *kalos*, when used in the masculine or feminine normally refers to physical beauty in Homer, but in the neuter it can be used to mean that, it is a good or pleasant experience, a good thing, to do X, such as to listen to a singer, as here. But the neuter of the adjective can also be used to say, "*kalon* it is to do X," where what is being communicated is stronger (sometimes said to be the neuter used in a more absolute sense): to do X is fitting, seemly, proper, action; "good" in the sense of "right," and so moral. To do X, by implication, is then always the right action. Whereas there could be many occasions when it may not be pleasant or appropriate to listen to a singer, it would never be right or good to abuse one's *xenos*. Thus, *kalon* and negative *ou kalon* join Homer's formidable arsenal of moral words.[39] We shall encounter many additional examples in Books 3 to 8.

The contribution of *Odyssey* Book 2, with the introduction of the verbal form of *aidôs* (*Od.* 2.63), along with the verb *lissomai*, "I supplicate you" (*Od.* 2.68), belongs more to supplication than to guest-friendship, and can be postponed. Books 3 and 4, on the other hand, constitute a unit as young Telemachus visits first Pylos and then Sparta in search of news of his father; in both instances he is now in the role of a hopeful Hellenic *xenos*, and is graciously received as such by his illustrious hosts. The constant, implied contrast with dysfunctional Ithaca in the treatment of *xenoi*—and with loutish suitor-guests orchestrating the feasting and entertainment, not the proper host—is intended, of course, and needs no further comment.

Odyssey 3 and 4: Telemachus as a *Xenos*

Telemachus's ship arrives at Pylos as a sacrificial feast is underway in honor of Poseidon, patron deity of the city. The feast is being held on the beach; "sandy Pylos" was the Homeric epithet that helped point Carl Blegen to its buried ruins in 1939. As soon as King Nestor and the Pylians spot the strangers (*xenoi*), the Pylians come thronging down, and clasp their hands in welcome. Nestor's son, Peisistratus, takes both *xenoi* by the hands and urges them to sit on soft fleeces arranged on the sand in positions of honor, next to his brothers and his father. The location has moved from an aristocratic *oikos* to a sandy beach, a stately *thronos* has become a beach pillow; the ritualized "arrival scene" for receiving the *xenos* is adapted to the circumstances, as in Homer it always is.

Immediately, Peisistratus addresses the older of the strangers, Mentor, as a guest-friend, thus reassuring the arrivals of their protected status:

> Pray now, guest-friend, to the lord god Poseidon . . .
> and when you have poured and prayed, as is the established
>   way (*themis*),
> give to your friend the cup of honey sweet wine
> that he too may pour [a libation]. All men have need of
>   gods.
> But he is younger, and of like age to myself, so to you first I
>   give the golden cup. (*Od.* 3. 43–50)

The next three hexameters (51–53) are given in the translation of Lattimore.

> So he spoke, and put in her hand the cup of sweet wine,
> and Athena was happy at the thoughtfulness of a just (*dikaios*) man,
> because it was to her he first gave the golden goblet. (*Od.* 3. 51–53)

The quoted hexameters contain two highly important words in Homer's moral vocabulary, *dikaios* and *themis*.

A younger man deliberately offers a goblet of wine to an older man before offering it to a person of his own age, and he is called "just" for doing so? Lattimore has been faulted (by Peter Jones among others) for providing a "wrong translation." Jones adds that the word (*dikaios*) means not "just," but a person "who acted properly," "upright," "correct."[40] Still others have objected that such courtesies belong to manners, not morals; they hardly involve an issue of "justice." The *dik-* stem words are so important for later Greek ethics (*dikaion* will become the common word for "just" and "legal" in later, Attic Greek; *dikaiosunê* for "justice" in Plato's *Republic*) that it will be useful to see how both Lattimore and his critics are, in a sense, right.

Some scholars have believed (and Lattimore believed) that the only word in English that had as much emotional power as Homeric *dikaios* is the adjective "just." Words such as "proper," or phrases such as "a man of decorum," did not—any longer at least—carry the same compulsory force in society. Of course, no Homeric scholar will deny that *dikaios* denoted a male person who observed the Hellenic proprieties. But a skilled translator also wants to find the closest English equivalent in our society to the use and force of a word in Homeric society. What mainly controlled human behavior in Homer's world was custom, a complex set of traditional proprieties (*themistes*); but what mainly controls behavior today is law, and a respect for justice in both a moral and legal sense. Hence the choice of "just" for *dikaios*, while not the most literal translation, was defensible.

Themis,[41] a feminine noun, when used morally fundamentally means "precedent," and hence denotes or identifies what is "of precedent" for this society, or what is customary, the established way. Lattimore translates the common phrase that ends 3.45, *hê themis estin*, as "according to custom." Its moral use in Homer is clear in meaning, although like other moral terms, it has a range of other uses. The plural of *themis* is *themistes*.

Modern English is usually clear about the difference between customs, such as proscriptions about what table utensil to use for dessert, and laws, such as those that prohibit extortion, or murder. The distinction between law and custom could not have been made as clearly in the world of Odysseus, however, because Homeric Greek had no word that corresponds exactly to our word "law," as some nineteenth-century Homeric scholars (e.g., the famous Richard Claverhouse Jebb) argued vehemently.[42]

I propose to mine the remainder of *Odyssey* 3 for additional Homeric quasi-formulaic[43] moral words and phrases, as they are found *in situ*, and happen to turn up in the narrative. Although amounting to many examples in relatively few verses, they are far from a complete list. Such a list would be an important but presently neglected contribution to Homeric ethics. The neglect may, in part, be due to the enormous influence of the late Arthur Adkins, who so effectively and often called attention to the "competitive virtues," *aretê*, *timê*, *kleos*, and the like. These are, as one scholar (Walter Donlan) has noted, much "sexier" than social proprieties that mitigated (somewhat) the heroic world's relentless violence by urging more cooperative behavior. The instances will border on tedium, but there may be no more effective way to demonstrate how often the language of morals, and *xenia*, appear in Homer.

At 3.69, King Nestor decides, with supper finished, to ask his *xenoi* the always delayed questions. "Now is a better [more seemly, (*kallion esti*)] time to interrogate our guests and ask them who they are." The comparative form *kallion* indicates that the more appropriate time, because that is the established way, to delay the *xenos*-questions until after supper.[44]

At 3.137, two tipsy kings summon a drunken agora, "wildly, and in no kind of order (*ou kata kosmon*), as the sun was setting." This is not the proper, established way or time to call men into agora; agoras are summoned at dawn, and the kings are sober. Agoras are also formally gathered and loosened, neither of which happened on this drunken occasion. Hence: *ou kata kosmon*, not according to good order, the latter being always the established way; the phrase equates with "improperly," "unseemly."

At 3.186, King Nestor promises to tell young Telemachus the news concerning his father, "all I have got . . . this you shall know; it is proper (*hê themis esti*) that you should." Telemachus is his *xenos*, and supplicated him verbally (92), "I come to your knees." seeking information. It is *themis*, right, proper, that he should get it.

At 3.331, as darkness falls, Athena/Mentor says to Nestor: "Old Sir, all that you have said was fair and orderly (*kata moiran*)." That is, his words are fitting and proper for the occasion. This phrase is often used when speech is concerned, but not always. At *Od.* 8.166, Euryalos has not spoken well, properly (*ou kalon eeipes*). *Kalon* is being used adverbially here, "not in a seemly way." Plausibly, meter largely dictated the choice of moral formulas with the same meaning?

At 3.334, Athena/Mentor says "nor is it becoming, fitting (*oude eoiken*) to sit about at the feast of the gods," but to go home.[45] The sacrifice, a religious rite, is finished. In effect, "Go, the ritual is ended." Rituals, especially religious rituals such as a mass, like Homeric agoras, have a fixed beginning and end.

At 3.355 ff., King Nestor finishes up a lengthy boast to the effect that he and his sons after him will always treat their *xenoi* as propriety required. Athena/Mentor replies that this was well-spoken, adding: "it is fitting, seemly (*eoiken*) that Telemachus should obey you, since it is much better, more proper (*polu kallion*) that way." Telemachus is younger, and he is learning from the speech of elders, as was right, the established way.

The King's boast concerning his ability to give shelter to his guest-friends is the first explicit mention that this is a function of *xenia*. The *xenoi* had suggested returning to their ship for the night, but the king protests. Zeus forbid that in his realm *xenoi* should sleep on a boat! That will never happen, so long as "I am alive, and my sons after me are left in my palace, to entertain (*xenizein*) our guest-friends (*xenoi*)" (353–354). It seems that the *xenos* might normally expect to be sheltered two or three days; "eleven or twelve days" is a very long stay; and the longest mentioned in the poems, twenty days, is extravagant. The suitors, going on three years, are beyond the pale.

At 3.456–457, Peisistratus (the king's son, not a guest) selects the animal for sacrifice: "they divided her into parts, and cut out the thigh bones, all according to good order (*panta kata moiran*), and wrapped them in fat." The word *moira* means part, share, lot; hence fate, fortune, or even doom. In its "moral" usage, however, *kata moiran*, like *kata kosmon*, describes, and indirectly commends, orderly behavior, conformity to established ways. The heifer was ritually butchered in the proper manner.

When the *xenoi* are about to depart Pylos, Book 3 reveals another component to the *xenia* ritual: *pompê*, escort, convoy–a protected and generous send-off for the *xenos*. Nestor urges Telemachus (324 ff.) to go on to Sparta, adding, "here are horses and a chariot and here are my own sons at your service who will be your escorts (*pompêes*)."

Athena/Mentor addresses Nestor (368 ff.): "give him conveyance" (so Lattimore) with a chariot and your son; give the best you have. These are expensive gifts, and Peisistratus, the King's favorite son as *pompos*, beyond price. In Book 5, when Calypso informs Odysseus that he must build his own raft, he complains (5.174): this is not *pompê*!

Nestor's generosity as a proper host is not quite finished; provisions for a hard journey must be added as well, as a part of *pompê* (479 ff.). So, the reverend housekeeper is assigned a task reminiscent of the arrival scene; she is busy slipping wine and choice cuts of meat into the chariot.

On to Sparta

Sparta, supposedly, is a two-day chariot journey from Pylos. A one-night stopover will be necessary at little Pherae, in the house of Diocles, where conveniently a generous host sets before the *xenoi* all that belongs to *xenia* (3.490). The next day they will be in Sparta, and expect to be received as *xenoi* at the palace of a fabled king, Menelaus, and his even more fabled wife, Helen of Troy.

Arriving the next evening, the hopeful *xenoi* encounter an unexpected gaffe at the gate of the royal compound. They are noticed immediately, but then are kept waiting at the gate. They have arrived at a busy time in the palace. The King's daughter, the only child of Helen, is departing for a long-arranged political marriage; simultaneously, a bastard son is being married off to shore up an alliance at home. An official goes through the halls to ask the King what to do:

> Menelaus, fostered of Zeus, here are certain *xenoi*, two men, and they look like the very offspring of Zeus. Tell me, then, whether we should harness their splendid horses, or send them on to somebody else, who can entertain them. (*Od.* 4. 26–29)

Greatly disturbed, the King tells his trusted official that he had never been such a complete fool previously:

> Surely, we two have eaten much hospitality (*xeinia*) from
> other men . . . Unharness the strangers' horses, and bring
> them here to be feasted. (*Od.* 4. 30–31)

The standard components of guest-friendship duly follow. Maidens of the household bathe the young men and anoint them with oil; the familiar sequence of hexameters of the type-scene follows (4.52 ff.). A servant brings a golden pitcher for the ritual washing of hands; the reverend (*aidoiê*) housekeeper brings initial food that is placed before the *xenoi* on a polished table, and the rest. The King assures the *xenoi* that only after they have feasted will they be asked whose sons they are, but their very appearances suggest that they are sons of scepter-bearing kings.

Later, at the urging ("I come to your knees") of Telemachus for news of his father, King Menelaus recounts what news he has, and concludes (587): "Come now, stay here with me in my palace until it is the eleventh, or even the twelfth day." The King promises that he will give him glorious *pompê*, and splendid gifts of *xenia*.

At this point the action reverts back to the suitors on Ithaca, and Penelope collapses as she learns they are plotting to murder her son. Book 4 closes with this shattering revelation, and the departure scene is postponed to a later book. Book 15 opens with Telemachus anxious to depart Sparta but Peisistratus cautions him to wait for guest-gifts:

> For a guest remembers all his days the man who received him
> as a host receives a guest, and gave him the gifts of guest-
> friendship. (*Od.* 15.55–56)

Odyssey 5 and 6: Virtual Supplication

In Book 5, Hermes the messenger is sent by Zeus to inform the nymph Calypso that she must no longer inhibit the *nostos* of Odysseus. Book 5 is especially relevant because it ends with the first appearance in the *Odyssey* of what may be termed "virtual supplication." The Homeric poems invite a distinction among three variant forms of supplication that I will term "rhetorical supplication," "virtual supplication," and "full physical supplication."[46] The strongest version is full, physical supplication, or *hiketeia* properly speaking, such as that undertaken by Priam to recover the body of Hector from mistreatment by Achilles, or by Odysseus to

Queen Arete. However, two weaker forms (weaker because more easily dismissed) occur often in the poems.

In rhetorical supplication, the weakest of the three, the plea intentionally remains at the level of words alone, as when Telemachus says, first to Nestor in Book 3 (92), and then to Menelaus in Book 4, "I have come to your knees." He seeks news of his father and he is communicating to his host that this is no trivial request, but urgent. His wording, by exploiting the importance of *hiketeia*, sends that rhetorical message. Earlier, in Book 2, in the agora of Ithaca, Telemachus resorted to the language of supplication (68): "I supplicate you (*lissomai*), by Olympian Zeus and Themis."[47] The choice of wording in these and similar instances, by invoking verbally the image of full physical supplication, elevates the importance of the plea, or ratchets up the rhetoric, depending on the circumstance. Such phrasing urges that the plea be taken seriously, but the speaker has no intention of going through the full, physical ritual, although nothing hinders it.

Virtual supplication is more serious, going well beyond rhetoric. In these cases, the sincere intent of the supplicating person is to go through the full ritual, but for some good reason is inhibited from doing so. What is lacking is the element of unbroken physical contact, especially with the knees, without which physical supplication is incomplete. As a result, maximum social and moral pressure is not in play, and the plea is more easily dismissed. Alternatively, the supplicated person may choose to reward sincerity and accede to the plea. Two examples follow in quick succession in the *Odyssey*, one at the end of Book 5 and the other near the beginning of Book 6.

In Book 5, Odysseus departs the island of Calypso on his raft, splendidly clothed by the goddess and so well prepared to become the hopeful *xenos*, but Poseidon sends the storm that reduces his raft to splinters and forces him to swim for his life. When, days later, Odysseus spots land, the only place that is not a sheer cliff is the mouth of a mighty river that flows into the sea. But to swim ashore he must somehow slow the force of the river's strong current that would otherwise push him back out to sea. At this point Odysseus is forced to become a virtual suppliant and address the river-god, to whose knees he cannot, of course, come physically. Words alone must do the job. Not knowing even the god's name, he addresses him respectfully as *anax*, lord:

> Hear me, *anax*, whoever you are. As one greatly in need do
>   I come to you,

> fleeing out of the sea from the threats of Poseidon.
> Reverend (*aidoios*) even in the eyes of immortal gods
> is that man who comes as a wanderer, as I have come
> to your stream and your knees, after many toils.
> Pity me, lord. Your suppliant (*hiketês*) I declare myself to be.
> (*Od.* 5.445–450)

Odysseus, so often called the man of many devices (*polumêtis*), now calls himself *polulliston* (formed from *lissomai*, and found only here in Homer, a *hapax*); he is a self-declared, helpless, prayerful suppliant in great need (death looms), and the proper emotion toward his helplessness in this society would be *aidôs*. This is expressed in the powerful moral word, the adjective of *aidôs*, *aidoios*, used often in Homer where *hiketai* and *xenoi* are concerned, and feelings of *aidôs*, respect and pity, are being commended.[48] Odysseus cannot physically supplicate the god, but with his sincere prayer he does so virtually, and successfully. At once (*autika*), the river-god made his current subside (451).

The language of *aidôs*, whether as noun, verb, or adjective, in connection with the proper treatment of the *xenos* and the *hiketês*, deserves more notice than it is given in discussions of Homer's language of morals, especially by philosophers.[49] Behind the various usages of the *aidôs*-words there is the powerful feeling of reverence, deep respect, and acceptance, for the proprieties of Hellenic life. And the more important the propriety the stronger should be the feelings of *aidôs* concerning it, or so it seems. The same would be true of the shame a person should feel as the perpetrator of a violation, or in witnessing one, when *aidôs* is often coupled with *nemesis*. Thus the verb of *aidôs*, often in the aorist imperative, can commend feelings of awe, respect, deference, or pity associated with the propriety, or equally shame and indignation at its violation.[50]

The next act of virtual supplication in the *Odyssey* is a justly famous one. In Book 6, Odysseus, naked and filthy after his narrow escape from the sea, awakens from deep slumber to the sounds of maiden voices nearby, playing and laughing. The girls, Princess Nausicaa and her maidens, are washing the family clothes in the river and are without male escorts. Odysseus breaks off a few branches, the equivalent of a fig leaf, with which to cover his nakedness, but he must proceed cautiously. Naked and hungry, his need is great, but so is the potential danger. As he emerges from the bushes all the girls flee except Nausicaa. Odysseus ponders whether he should advance directly to her, clasp her knees and supplicate her with full physical supplication, or resort to virtual supplication instead (my designations, of course). Wisely, he remains at a distance. "I come to your knees, as it were [*gounoumai*], my queen," are his artful opening words, thus identifying himself as a self-proclaimed *hiketês*. Clearly, he would have resorted to full physical supplication but for the inhibiting circumstances.

Odysseus's act of virtual supplication, and a long artful speech, are successful. Nausicaa accepts him as a suppliant (*hiketês*, 193), assuring him that he will receive what a suppliant needs. Odysseus had set out a clothed and competent *xenos*, hoping to be welcomed by his next host, but he has been reduced to a naked, near-helpless *hiketês*. To attain what he now needs most, convoy or escort (*pompê*) home to Ithaca, he must be transformed back into a *xenos*. Nausicaa can provide him her brothers' princely clothes, but only her father can transform him into a true *xenos*, and grant him fabulous *pompê*. To her father she must direct him.

Odyssey 7: Transformation from *Hiketês* to *Xenos*

Nausicaa understood without being told that Odysseus seeks *pompê* (6.290,), but she offers some peculiar advice. Go straight past her father in the great hall to her mother, Queen Arete, who will be seated next to the hearth. Then, "with your arms embrace our mother's knees; do this so as to behold your day of homecoming" (6.310–311). Of course, Odysseus understands that she is commending an act of full physical supplication. The ritual act is the centerpiece of Book 7 and is described in detail. I will focus on the emotive language used by the major players.

Odysseus, enhanced by Athena in size and comeliness and dressed in princely clothes, nevertheless is still a suppliant, an outsider, a "comer," a *hiketês*.[51] Rendered temporarily invisible by Athena, he admires the splendid palace briefly, and then strides boldly across the threshold. Although well clothed, Odysseus knows he remains a *hiketês*; the *xenos* waits at the threshold to be noticed. For a guest-friend is always in a sense a suppliant, but a suppliant is not always a guest-friend, as here, at least not yet.

Odysseus makes his way to the great hall where the King and Queen are gathered with the leading men of the island. Odysseus, still invisible, lowers himself in order to grasp the knees of the seated Queen; the ritual also required that his head be lower than hers. At the moment he makes physical contact he is made visible, to the hushed astonishment of those present. The singer's audience is encouraged to visualize a crouched or kneeling man touching the knees of a seated royal woman. Suddenly made visible, his princely clothes would tell them that he was no beggar in rags, and his enhanced appearance that he was a nobleman, but little else. The astonished onlookers fall silent; the Queen neither moves nor speaks as the man, now fully grasping her knees, begins to address her. His position and initial words would reveal that he is commencing an act of full, physical supplication.

His verbal appeal will also be characteristically diplomatic and resourceful by including the King at the outset. Odysseus begins:

> Arete, daughter of godlike Rhexenor to your husband and
> your knees I come, a suppliant, after many toils, and to these
> feasters, to whom may the gods grant . . . (*Od.* 6.146 ff.)

After gracefully asking that those assembled may be granted long life, prosperity, and dutiful children, Odysseus asks the Queen for what he needs. But his choice of an ambiguous verb ("encourage" is a possible meaning) in addressing her may imply, diplomatically, that he knows only her husband can grant his conveyance. His final request, still speaking to Arete, is:

> As for me, speedily *encourage* conveyance (*pompê*) to my
> native land; for long, and far from my own people, have I
> suffered many hardships.

His plea finished, Odysseus lets go of Arete's knees, surprisingly breaking physical contact, and seats himself in the ashes of the hearth,[52] an act of enhanced self-abnegation. A long, hushed silence follows. At last, the oldest man present, the hero Echeneos, described as wise in speech and foremost of the Phaeacian elders in knowing all the ancient proprieties, addresses the King. He uses the descriptive-emotive words and phrases encountered in earlier books, again tautologically; they remain powerful.

> Alcinous, this is not better (*kallion*, more proper), nor is it
>   fitting (*eoike*)
> that a *xenos* should sit on the ground in the ashes from the
>   hearth.
> These others [elders, leading men] hold back, waiting for
>   you to speak.

The King is being politely but firmly told that he has been overly slow in reacting to the suppliant, whose self-abnegation by remaining among the ashes in the most sacred space in the house requires a response. He must not be long ignored.

> But come, raise up the *xenos* and seat him on a chair (*thronos*),[53] silver-studded,
> tell the heralds to mix wine, so that to Zeus, who delights in thunder,
> we may pour libations, even he who walks closely behind reverend (*aidoioi*) *hiketai*.
> And let the housekeeper give supper to the *xenos* from her stores.

What the elder Echeneos describes, of course, is a *xenos* arrival-scene that he urges the King to commence at once. It awaits his word.

Lattimore translates v. 165 as: "and he [Zeus] goes together with suppliants, whose rights are sacred." The verb translated "goes together with" can imply an escort or companion, a protector or a defender who is closely allied to someone. Zeus himself watches over and defends *hiketai* and *xenoi*, who are protected by *aidôs*, almost as though it were a close, physical mist covering them. Gilbert Murray was moved to say that *xenoi* and *hiketai* are "charged with *aidôs*," a happy choice, as is "*aidôs*-filled." Zeus is their ever-ready protector and avenger. His most ancient titles, Zeus *Xenios* and Zeus *Hiketêsias*, appear first in Greek literature in Homer's text, but must go far back into the Dark Ages, if not to Mycenae itself.[54] Lattimore's translation of *aidoios* as "whose rights are sacred" when the adjective is used to describe a *xenos* or *hiketês* conveys well the strong claim these persons had on the actions of another in this society. It does not imply, of course, any sophisticated theory of rights in Homer.

After being reprimanded with traditional, emotive words, the King acts at once. He takes the *xenos* by the hand and raises him up from the ashes and places him on an appropriate seat of honor (*thronos*), next to himself, displacing his own favorite son, Laodamas, a highly symbolic act. The listeners of a singer would know that at this moment, when raised up from the hearth, a recently naked *hiketês* has been transformed into a well-clothed, impressive, and welcome *xenos*. From this moment he will be treated properly as one (172 ff.).[55]

A servant brings water and pours it from a golden pitcher for the *xenos* to wash his hands. The type-scene sequence of hexameters first encountered in Book 1 is repeated here, after which Odysseus is given ample food and wine. Next, Alcinous summons a herald to mix a *krater* of wine and water to serve all present, in order "to make a libation to Zeus who delights in the thunder, and who goes together with suppliants, whose rights are sacred" (180–181, Lattimore). The King announces that the next day will be devoted to the entertainment of their *xenos*, and his imminent conveyance home.

Odyssey 8: At the Table of *Xenia*

The events of the next day for the still anonymous *xenos* are mostly familiar from earlier books, with the notable addition of athletic games that may be peculiar to the unwarlike Phaeacians. Over final wine and male converse Alcinous will ask Odysseus to reveal his name at last (350 ff.). At this final *sumposion* (a post-Homeric word) of the evening that also closes Book 8, the kingly host, presiding "at the table of *xenia*,"[56] makes clear how intimately the pleasures of *xenia* and the reliance on fictive kin are interwoven. Demodocus had been singing of Troy, an episode involving Odysseus himself, and on hearing it Odysseus begins to weep. Only the King observes his tears hidden by a cloak. Alcinous abruptly halts the singer's performance and speaks (*Od.* 8.542 ff.):

> No, let him [the singer] cease, so that all may share in the pleasure,
> guest-hosts and guest alike, since that is more seemingly (*kallion*) by far.
> It is for the reverend (*aidoios*) *xenos* that all of this is done, convoy (*pompê*), and loving gifts, that we give out of friendship.
> Equal to a brother is a *xenos* and a *hiketês* to any thoughtful man,
> one who has any sense left in him at all.

The moment of emotional climax has arrived. The suppliant was transformed into a guest-friend and now into a brother, not in blood, of course, but in true fact; or, as some (Gould) have suggested, "spiritually." Now

Odysseus must reveal his name at last, for he cannot remain nameless after he has been accepted into the group as spiritual kin. "Speak out now, for it is better (*kallion*, more fitting, more seemly) so," demands King Alcinous (549). What is your name and where do you come from? "Every man has a name." It should be noted that the *xenos*-questions have been delayed as the ritual demanded, but obviously can be delayed no longer.

The King continues: Tell us, *xenos*, what your wanderings have been? What cities have you seen and what men known, and who among them were, "cruel and savage and not civilized (*oude dikaioi*), and who were hospitable to *xenoi* (*philoxeinoi*), and the mind in them god-fearing?" (575–576). The King's incorporates into his words the two-hexameter *xenos*-formula usually spoken when a hopeful *xenos* arrives in a strange land. It is not unreasonable to suggest that the compound with *phil-* would evoke in listeners the emotions associated with *philos*, designating whatever belongs to one—what is most dear, steadfast, and reliable—but especially family and kin. And they would evoke the same emotions for Odysseus, now listening to words he had so often spoken in fear and wonder. The King's words are also, of course, graciously self-referential; at that moment, he is the generous *philoxeinos,* and Odysseus the man who is being incorporated into the group as a *philos*.

Alkinous next asks Odysseus why he wept at the mention of Troy, and without waiting for a reply suggests the reason. Did perhaps some kinsman fall before the walls of Troy? Some *esthlos* man, good and true? Your daughter's husband perhaps, or your wife's father, or her brother? Clearly, in this society these persons, kinsmen by marriage, are the persons nearest to a man in life, and second only to his own flesh and blood, as the King specifies at verse 583 (581 ff.).

The King's speculation would be abrupt and puzzling without what had preceded it. Such persons are close kin in truth, although not in blood; but next to blood relations, these are the persons closest in life in Homeric society because they are the most reliable in times of trouble, and in defensive alliances. The clear implication is that Odysseus, as a *xenos*, has now been incorporated into that inner group. The outsider has become the ultimate insider, fictive or spiritual kin. What the King has ritualistically said and done over the past two days has effectively made Odysseus a brother, or kin, in all but blood. It should also be recalled that the *xenia* relationship, like blood relationships, will be inherited down generations; that feature, above all else, marks *xenia* as a form kinship.

Conclusion

Notable scholars have doubted that the society discovered in the Homeric poems was ever a real or historical one. As far as material objects go, "the pins and the pans," of a society in a specific period—or whether it practiced cremation or inhumation, fought in or outside of chariots, and the like—that doubt can be quite legitimate. But it cannot be extended, I think, to Homeric proprieties such as *xenia* and *hiketeia*, or to the powerful Homeric moral words that continued prominently into the historical and literary record of Greece from Hesiod onward.

Moral behavior and its vocabulary, and notably violations, are complex as well as remarkably consistent in Homer. No major break, linguistic or conceptual, is discernible after 700 BCE when the alphabetic record commences. Hesiod knows all about guest-friendship (*Erga* 225–228; 327 ff.), about Muses, the knowledgeable daughters of Zeus (and oral eyewitnesses of past events) who inform the singers (*Theog.* 1–105), about "kings" and the straight or crooked *dikai* they speak—and not the least, about the powerful appeals to *aidôs* and *nemesis*—all in the same language as Homer. The Spartan poet Tyrtaeus, writing maybe fifty years later, or about 650 BCE, can say that it is good (*kalon*) for an *agathos* man to die fighting among those in the front. Homeric wording also abounds in Archilochus, Sappho, and the other very early so-called "lyric" poets; this has been extensively documented in the professional literature.

As Walter Donlan has argued so well, Homeric words that mean good (*kalon*, *agathon*) and virtue (*aretê*) and the other moral terms can narrow in meaning (as *aretê* did for Tyrtaeus), or expand (as did *agathos*) over time, as social and political conditions change, but they remain largely the same words, Homer's words. They belonged to life and not to literature alone when they first emerged into historical daylight ca. 700 BCE. At some period, long before that date, they had become the language of morals for an historical society. but in what century, or just how this developed, in that long span of half a millennium between Mycenae and Hesiod's Greece, we will never have the evidence to know.

The relevant evidence can only start to accumulate with the invention of an adequate recording device, the Greek alphabet with full vowel (minimally five) notation. The earliest scraps are still a handful of inscriptions, most in hexameters and with Homeric wording, dating to around 700 BCE, plus or minus a few decades.[57] With the alphabet's invention, the recoverable history of European morals can commence. Its first great milestone, a gift from Greece's preliterate past, is the text of Homer.

The late Walter Donlan was a colleague teaching at a university not far from my own in Southern California. When one of his colleagues would be lost in the detail of some Homeric passage, Donlan could be counted on to situate that detail in the broader Homeric picture. He had a deep appreciation of the ceremonial and ritualistic character of both supplication and, especially, guest-friendship as part of the heroic ethos. As for the latter, the ethos of the Homeric hero, no one writing in English has understood it better. He was also a most appreciative connoisseur of Homer's language of morals. It is fitting that he should have the last, best words:

> A key feature of the Homeric social system was a highly developed pattern of social behavior between eminent men from different tribal groups: an elaborate etiquette of gift exchange, stylized eating and drinking ceremonial, and modes of polite address. These formed a complex system of guest friendship (*xenia*), which afforded the individual protection in a hostile tribal world [alliances], fostered the expansion of "foreign" contact [travel] and increased the prestige of individuals and their *oikoi*. In addition, the ceremonial aspect [of *hiketeia* and *xenia*] gave a kind of psychological protection to the ideal; everyone took part in the solemn charade which insured the validity of the heroic conventions.[58]

Notes

1. Finley 1978.
2. Herman 1987.
3. Gould 1973.
4. Gould 1973, 21–22.
5. Gould 1973, 55.
6. Pitt-Rivers 1968.
7. Herman 1987, 2.
8. Many today agree with Finley, but for a mustering of some counter evidence, see Raaflaub 1997.

9. Jones 1988, 7: suitors and Cyclops "corrupt" *xenia*; also on 8, 79. So also Lattimore 1965, 17. This theme runs through the later books of the *Odyssey*, where it is even more prominent. See Reece 1993, 10.

10. For *hiketeia* and the "corrupting *xenia*" literature, see Roth 1993, and his references. On the supplication scenes in Aeschylus (and Euripides: found in six of nineteen plays) see Brill 2009.

11. Finlay 1978, 63.

12. Finlay 1978, 103.

13. Finlay 1978, 104–05.

14. Finlay 1978, 111.

15. Finlay 1978, 105.

16. Herman begins *Ritualized Friendship* with the famous encounter between Glaucus and Diomedes that had also been the centerpiece of Finley's treatment. The point for both authors was that the loyalty of *xenoi* to each other was far stronger than either felt toward his "city" (polis as a pre-political settlement), region, or commander. The heroes dramatically refuse to fight each other once they discover they are hereditary *xenoi*.

17. Of course, *xenia* also greatly facilitated travel. See Robb 1994, 52ff.

18. Urmson 1968, 19; 25; 33 (on "evince"); Ayer 1936, 107.

19. Stevenson 1944.

20. Stevenson 1963, 16; emphases in the original.

21. Stevenson 1963, 18.

22. Stevenson 1963, 16, emphasis in original.

23. Stevenson 1963, 21.

24. Stevenson 1963, 25. Similar wording appeared in Stevenson 1937, 23.

25. Quoting Ogden and Richards 1923; see Stevenson 1963, 21n7.

26. For a society of self-help in Homer, the example of homicides, especially an accidental homicide such as that by a young Patroclus, is particularly instructive. Vengeance (*tisis*) must be had by the family of the victim; *poinê* may be offered to them but is usually refused; then either the killer escapes into permanent exile or is killed.

27. Behavior described as "good" is being prescribed or commended for, specifically, *imitation*; see Hare 1963, 23ff; similar analysis appeared in his influential Hare 1952. For Hare, the formal requirements for a moral judgment are three. First, it is prescriptive in intent even if its linguistic expression is not grammatically in the imperative. Second, it can be universalized in the sense that it applies to all similar circumstances. Third, what it prescribes (or proscribes) prevails over all other considerations. These criteria also apply to Homer's use of moral language.

28. The philosophers start complaining about its success with Xenophanes in the sixth century (B11, B12, and especially B10).

29. See Robb 1994, 78–84.

30. The suitors are seated on the hides of animals they themselves (*autoi*) had selected and slain; the point is, the guests and not the host of the *oikos* (or his designated representatives, usually sons, as at *Od.* 3.412ff.) had undertaken the task. On this issue see Pitt-Rivers 1968, 25ff, where the slaughter of the suitors is justified because as *xenoi* they had usurped the role of the *xenos*-host (with much anthropological evidence for the seriousness of that offense in other cultures). The *xenos* must not insult his host's honor by demanding or taking what is *not* offered, or by refusing what is offered (27–28). Pitt-Rivers generalizes: the *Odyssey* "may be viewed as a study in the laws [strict rules] of hospitality [*xenia*]" (13). The brutality of the final slaughter has repulsed some modern ethicists because "disproportionate to the offence."

31. Lattimore 1965, 17: "Their [the suitors] doom seems excessive."

32. Could a slave be designated *aidoiê* because she offers first food to a *xenos*?

33. Parry 1933. Both Milman Parry and Adam Parry were admirers, but felt that Arend had missed the causal dimension, the utility of such scenes to oral singers for improvising verses.

34. As noticed by Gould 1973, 52, 89; Reece, and others.

35. Typical scenes are found for actions that singers had to describe many times, such as battle scenes, or the components of the *xenia* ritual.

36. At 1.152. Constantly to describe the "done" thing is, of course, to prescribe it. So Finley 1978, 84: "But there was *themis*—custom, tradition, folkways, mores, whatever we may call it, the enormous power of 'it is (or it is not) done.' The world of Odysseus had a highly developed sense of what was fitting and proper."

37. I borrow the phrasing from a conversation with the late Walter Donlan concerning the relationship between the dual scenes of *xenia* that play out in *Od.* 1. The one between Telemachus and Mentes is exquisitely proper, but the other with the suitors is its "negative image." In his published work, Donlan applied this language to the dangerous feud between Agamemnon and Achilles, where both men deliberately breach known conventions as tensions escalate. See Donlan 1999, 270. Donlan's point was that something like a dark charade was playing out on Ithaca, with the suitors pretending to be true *xenoi*, and an increasingly shrewd Telemachus pretending, in anticipation of a terrible revenge, to go along.

38. At 1.187; also 175–76. Glaucus and Diomedes made the same fateful discovery.

39. The adjective *agathos* in the neuter, *agathon*, "good," singular or plural, can be used to indicate approval in Homer, e.g., *Iliad* 6. 162, *agatha*.

40. Jones 1988, 29. *Dikaios*, in its moral sense: conforming to the established usages, conforming to the ways of civilized persons, notably Hellenes. At *Od.* 6.120, and often elsewhere, two hexameters (the "*xenos* formula") are uttered when a *xenos* tests the sentiments of unknown local inhabitants. The issue is

whether they receive travelers and strangers hospitably, or not. At *Od*. 14.90, the suitors are said not to woo properly (adverbial *dikaiôs*), in the customary way.

41. *Themis*, when used morally, means: precedent, established way, custom, "right." It is from *tithêmi*, hence, what has been "laid down," established, as precedent or custom. Also see: *Od*. 3.187; 11.451; *Il*. 2.73; 9.33; 24.652. *Themis* is also used without any prescriptive tone, describing what is a fact, but without a moral prescription, e.g., such is the "way" (*themis*, but also *dikê*) of men and women (to have sex together, *Il*. 19.177; *Il*. 9.134). Some scholars speculate that the descriptive "way" for *themis* and *dikê* was the older meaning.

42. See Jebb 1894, 48: "Homer has no word for 'law.'" As I understand *Odyssey* 9, the "lawless" Cyclops living in isolation in their caves are devoid of established, shared proprieties, communal customs (*themistes*). They are not being denigrated because they are devoid of true "laws" that civilized Hellenes possessed.

43. Following G. S. Kirk, I use "formula" loosely for wording that is repeated often and, like some individual words (*megistos* was Kirk's favorite Yale classroom example), behave formulaically by gravitating to the same place in the hexameter (for *megistos*, often but not always to the end of the verse, as at *Od*. 5.185; *Theog*. 49; Xenophanes, B23).

44. *Kallion*, a comparative, when used morally: more fitting, proper, seemly; better so. At *Od*. 3.69 it is more fitting (*kallion*) to question the strangers after they have been fed, as *xenia* required. The word *kallion*, translatable into English as "better," has two senses in both languages, strategical and moral. It was better (strategically) to attack Pearl Harbor on an uneventful Sunday morning. It was better (morally) to question the *xenos* after supper.

45. *Eoiken*, when used morally: it is fitting, seemly, proper, appropriate, "right." The negative *oude eoiken*, it is not fitting, etc., normally reinforces a previously expressed negative sentiment. The positive phrasing is found in the *Odyssey* first at 1.278; next at 1.292, both meaning, appropriate to an occasion, or a traditional amount, as in the number of funeral rites for a dead father or the number of bride-gifts for a much-loved daughter.

46. Some distinction between types of supplication in Homer, setting off full or complete supplication where physical contact remains unbroken, is needed. What I call virtual supplication Gould referred to as "figurative supplication," See his note 17 in Gould 1972/2001, 27.

47. The suitors as *xenoi*, guests, outrageously usurp the proper role of Telemachus as their *xenos*-host, a grievous offence against *xenia*. Such actions justify their death in this and other cultures (so Pitt-Rivers above; T. E. Lawrence—Lawrence of Arabia—living among desert Bedouin tribes could be added).

48. Gould has a persuasive discussion of the relationship of *aidôs* to the *hiketês*, but includes the *xenos*. See Gould 1973, 42–57. Finally, see a brief but insightful discussion of *aidôs* in early Greek ethics by Murray 1924.

49. Murray 1924, 89–90: *aidôs* is a "mere emotion, therefore incalculable and arbitrary, devoid of principle" and so suspect to later philosophers.

50. At *Euthyphro* 12B, Socrates observes that *aidôs* or "reverence," a positive emotion harbors a negative element, the fear of disgrace and a bad reputation.

51. *Hiketês* and its cognates derive from *hikô*, a verb meaning to come to, to reach; hence, a "comer," an "outsider" in search of something—possibly a dangerous person, possibly not. Some etymological speculation concerning the root *hik-* is interestingly reviewed in Brill 2009, 164.

52. Gould 1973, 63ff. has convincingly argued that, in breaking physical contact and moving to the hearth, Odysseus did not impair the full force of physical supplication, because of the sacred importance of the hearth.

53. This word (*thronos*) has been prominent in all the *xenos* "arrival" scenes. Interestingly, in the Linear B tablets the word *thronoi* refers to impressive chairs inlaid with some sort of metal; the *thronoi* in the house of Odysseus are inlaid with silver.

54. About the more remote origins of Homer's moral vocabulary I remain agnostic. No distinctly ethical words have turned up on the Linear B tablets (the one promising candidate from Pylos turned out to be the name of a minor town), but that may due to the fact that the tablets are economic records.

55. The parallels with the supplication scene between Achilles and Priam are especially close, including Priam as a *hiketês* being raised up by the hand by Achilles (even in a "hut" seated on a *thronos*, *Il.* 24.523; 553). Priam, whereas initially a self-declared *hiketês*, is then treated ritualistically as a *xenos*, offered food etc., after his plea has been accepted. See, perceptively, Gould 1973, 32.

56. For the table of *xenia*: four times in the *Odyssey* two notable hexameters appear (once slightly varied, in Book 19) when someone wants to invite an oral eyewitness to attest to a solemn truth. The two verses are notable because of the order of importance of three sacred objects by which the person swears, and because three times the speaker is Odysseus himself. The first appears at *Od.* 14.158–59:

> Now be my witness Zeus, foremost of the gods, and the table
>   (*trapeza*) of *xenie*,
> And the hearth (*histiê*) of blameless Odysseus, to which I have
>   come.

See also: *Od.* 17.155–56; 19.303–04; 20.230–31. In this context, Gould perceptively uses such phrases as "the significance of the common meal in creating solidarity," and "the binding force of the common meal." It is at a very public and lavish table of *xenia* that King Alcinous welcomes Odysseus into his family as kin, equal to a brother, as a true *philos*, together with all his male descendants forever, or so the King believed.

57. See Robb 1994, 23ff.; 44–62; for the *xenos* inscription from Ithaca dated to ca. 700 BCE, see 49–50.

58. Donlan 1999, 30. Donlan writes (15) that for this society "the heroic ethos, with its complicated norms of social behavior, supersedes all other considerations as an impetus to action." Homer's language of morals should, therefore, be considered the font of Western ethics, for we have nothing earlier.

2

The Muses' Faithful Servant
Moral Knowledge in Homer, Hesiod, and Xenophanes

WILLIAM WIANS

> Human beings should think human things . . .

From the beginnings of their literature, the ancient Greeks showed a steady concern and even preoccupation with what human beings could know and what lay beyond their knowing. The contrast as they saw it was between human and divine knowledge. The gods knew all, past, present, and future. Human beings were creatures of a day ephemera, unable to look beyond the narrow scope of their own experience. The contrast figures prominently in epic, lyric, and tragic poets. It surfaces in medical and historical writers. Philosophers took special notice of the separation between human and divine knowledge, as is apparent in many of the pre-Socratics and in Plato and Aristotle, where it both figures explicitly and exerts an influence behind the scenes. For all of these thinkers, the gulf between human and divine knowledge was an abiding feature of how things were.

The difference between human and divine knowledge is most apparent with regard to what can be called factual knowledge. Because they are always present, the gods know more, and usually a great deal more, than human beings of the facts of things—how a dispute arose, the names of those who fought at Troy, the "real" name of some feature of the natural environment. Human knowledge was limited to what a human being could experience directly or in some cases to what one could learn from the reports of others, both of which were subject to severe qualifications of their own.[1] Snell called it a constant ratio of knowledge to experience, "the wider the experience, the wider the knowledge."[2] To the extent that a human being's experience could be enlarged, the scope of that person's knowledge would increase. In virtue of his years of wanderings, Odysseus knew the cities and minds of many men. But no significant enlargement was possible in the ordinary course of things. Far more typical was the twenty-year blank as to Odysseus's whereabouts endured by Penelope and Telemachus. Such ignorance might be made up for to a degree through reports provided by others. Thus, Telemachus learns from Menelaus as much about the fate of Odysseus as any mortal knew after the heroes left Troy.[3] But such secondhand knowledge was limited and unreliable, leaving those in Ithaca prey to false tales of deceptive wanderers. Without direct experience of what was being recounted, the hearer was unable to verify the truth of what was said and so was forced to rely instead on superficial aspects of the report such as the skill and order with which it was told. The gods, in contrast, knew at all times where Odysseus was.[4]

From the great gulf separating the factual knowledge of gods and human beings arose a more urgent problem. It is what I shall call the problem of moral knowledge. This is not a question of what modern philosophers would describe as a "system of ethics," a project to found or identify the duties and obligations humans have toward one another, or the acts or character traits that promote or detract from the overall good of individual happiness and community well-being. Nor is it a knowledge of a certain subset of facts, a specific problem arising within the larger problem of human factual knowledge. Rather, the problem of moral knowledge arises from the limits imposed on human beings by their place in the cosmos, a place in a world not of their own making. Moral knowledge is what Socrates in the *Apology* termed *ta megista* (*Apol.* 22E), those things most needful for a human being to know (including for Socrates, that human knowledge was worth little in comparison to divine knowledge (*Apol.* 23B). It is a recognition of the meaning and significance of human limits for how one should live. To live properly (one should not necessarily say happily), a human being must come to have such knowledge, sometimes with divine cooperation, and sometimes in the face of divine opposition. The problem of human (factual) knowledge directly entails the problem of moral knowledge, so that any sharp distinction between the two is at best misleading. That is why more than one ancient Greek writer would warn "Humans should study human things. . . ."

In addressing the contrast between human and divine knowledge, scholars of ancient philosophy tend to focus on issues pertinent to modern epistemological concerns, particularly on the problem of factual knowledge and the consequent possibility of skepticism. So, for instance, Barnes approaches the question of human versus divine knowledge in pre-Socratic philosophy from the perspective of Lockean skepticism, while Hussey looks for "the beginnings of epistemology" in Homer, Hesiod, and Xenophanes.[5] These and similar studies offer many insights, and I shall refer to them often in what follows. Nevertheless, the moral dimension of the traditional conception of human vs. divine knowledge has, I think, been neglected, and at the cost of misunderstanding a key aspect of the epistemological problem of human knowledge in early Greek thought.[6]

There is no single response to the problem of human knowledge in Greek thought; indeed, one of the main reasons it is worth investigating is because it provokes so many different responses.[7] In this paper, I shall concentrate on Homer, Hesiod, and Xenophanes. The perception of their shared skepticism, along with the attention this aspect of their thought has drawn from modern philosophical commentators, justifies my focus on these three. I shall argue that if their alleged skepticism is to be correctly assessed, recognizing the moral dimension of the problem of human knowledge is essential.

I shall begin, as did the Greeks, with Homer and Hesiod. Especially in their invocations to the Muses, Homer and Hesiod seem to limit the possibility of human knowledge to the narrow compass of direct experience and thus to express a naïve if pervasive skepticism pertaining to all claims to knowledge, including their own. In the second part of my paper, I'll turn to the "enigmatic philosopher-poet" Xenophanes.[8] Xenophanes is often taken to express a nascent philosophical skepticism in his claim that no mortal being, including himself, can know the truth of accounts of the gods. But as we shall see, Xenophanes can be likened to Homer and Hesiod by something more than their seeming skepticism. All three figures can be read as displaying a concern with moral knowledge. The founding observation of my study will be that, while each figure underlines the limits imposed on human knowledge, all three nevertheless proceed confidently, even proudly. In one way, their doing so amounts to a claim of an elevated epistemological status, serving to make the poet the exception to an otherwise comprehensive skepticism, whether more or less philosophical. In another way, their confidence expresses a sense of their elevated moral status—a privileged knowledge that is somehow earned or deserved. It is the latter conviction, I shall argue, that provides the connection between the epistemological problem of human knowledge and the moral lesson each poet seeks to impart.

At the same time, my analysis will offer insight into a key aspect of the familiar so-called rivalry between ancient poets and philosophers, namely the question of the authoritative nature of poetic utterance and performance. The rivalry is not simply a struggle between competing epistemic authorities—between *muthoi* and *logoi* as these terms used to be understood: one an inspired but irrational mythic voice, the other rejecting myth and speaking in reasoned chains of argument.[9] It is also a contest over who can claim the moral authority traditionally presumed by the poets, and why.

Inspiration and Skepticism

The Greek problem of human knowledge first appears in the poems of Homer and Hesiod. Already "at the threshold of literacy" as Most puts it, Homer and Hesiod were regarded as teachers, even divine sages.[10] Homer especially was "the great teacher of the Greeks," as Plato called him (though with a decidedly mixed regard). When early philosophers like Xenophanes (B10) and Heraclitus (B57) or the historian Herodotus go back to Homer and Hesiod, it is because, as Herodotus put it, they taught the Greeks the origins and lineages of their gods. Even, and perhaps especially, those early thinkers who were "radically in revolt against the view of the world provided by Homer and Hesiod" recognized the authoritative status of the two poets.[11]

Against the background of the profound limits of human knowledge, the poet's special status needs justification. If all humans are short-sighted and ephemeral, why should the poet have any claim to exceptional knowledge?[12] How, in particular, could he claim any special authority for what he told about the gods? Put another way, the poet was exceptional, not just because of the extent of his knowledge, but in not being punished for exceeding ordinary human limits. The gods guarded their prerogative jealously. Ordinarily, one who exceeded the limits of human knowledge faced the likelihood of divine wrath (*phthonos*).[13]

The poet who sings of the distant past has not learned of the events he relates through his own experience. Rather, his *muthoi* were inspired by the Muses, who gave him a special knowledge of events he has not witnessed. The Muses are the divine daughters of Zeus and Mnemosyne (Memory). They know everything because they are always at hand and have seen everything. Both Homeric epics and both surviving poems of Hesiod open with invocations to the Muses that put into their hands both the content and the form of the stories about to be retold. The *Iliad*: "Sing, Goddess, the anger of Peleus's son Achilles / and its devastation . . ."; the *Odyssey*: "Sing in me, Muse, and through me tell the story . . ." (tr. Fitzgerald); the *Odyssey*: "From some point here, goddess, daughter of Zeus, begin and tell our story" (9–10; tr. Lattimore).[14] Humans rely on hearsay for knowledge of the past—except for the inspired poet.

Even as their presumed inspiration gave these two poets their authority, it opened the possibility of skepticism. The poet was not present, the gods were; therefore the poet could not know on his own the truth of the things of which he spoke. He therefore had no choice but to accept what the Muses told him about the remote past, particularly the heroic age; the distant future; and the secrets of Fate and intentions of the gods.

Frequently cited in this connection are two invocations in particular, one from Hesiod and one from Homer. In different ways each is a crux for the question of ancient poetic skepticism. The first passage, from Hesiod's *Theogony*, directly underlines the threat of skepticism implied in the poet's dependency on the Muses. Philosophers have been interested primarily in the three lines coming at the end of the passage, in which the Muses speak to Hesiod directly and taunt him with his ignorance:

And it was they [the Muses] who once taught Hesiod his
   splendid singing
as he was shepherding his lambs on holy Helikon,
and these were the first words (*muthoi*) of all the goddesses
   spoke to me,
the Muses of Olympia, daughters of Zeus of the aegis:

> "You shepherds of the wilderness, poor fools, nothing but bellies,
> we know how to say many false things that seem like true sayings,
> but we know also how to speak the truth when we wish to."
> (*Theog.* 22–28)[15]

The taunt of the Muses throws into doubt the veracity of the *muthoi* they will shortly inspire Hesiod to recount. Hesiod accepts what the Muses say—he sings as they inspire him to do—but he has no independent source of verification. The sirens of the *Odyssey*, who also know all, constantly deceive. Hesiod knows that the Muses, with their siren-like ability to deceive, may tell the truth, but they may also amuse themselves by lying.[16]

The second crucial passage is the famous "second invocation" of the *Iliad*. It introduces the so-called catalogue of ships that fills the final third of the *Iliad* Book 2. The invocation has long been a crux for philosophers who look into Homer for something like the beginnings of skepticism. And no wonder. The invocation stresses the limits of unaided human knowledge:

> Tell me now, you Muses who have your homes on Olympos.
> For you, who are goddesses, are there, and you know all things,
> and we have heard only the rumour of it and know nothing.
> Who then of those were the chief men and the lords of
>   the Danaans?
> I could not tell over the multitude of them nor name them,
> not if I had ten tongues and ten mouths, not if I had
> a voice never to be broken and a heart of bronze within me,
> not unless the Muses of Olympia, daughters
> of Zeus of the aegis, remembered all those who came
>   beneath Ilion.
>
> I will tell the lords of ships, and the ships' numbers. (*Il.* 2.484–93)[17]

It is not just that the poet was not present (though, as Hussey points out, the distance of the epic past worked powerfully on the Archaic mentality). The tale to be told exceeds any ordinary human ability.

The poet humbly but powerfully recognizes his limitations and therefore seeks divine aid.[18]

It is not surprising, therefore, that many scholars take the catalogue invocation to imply a kind of skepticism. For Snell, the passage signals the poet's dependency on the Muses. The poet "would not succeed without the Muses" and could not continue without their aid: "It is only natural that the poet found it difficult to picture to himself the forbidding number of leaders and ships, and because of this he calls upon the Muses to assist him."[19] Hussey calls it a cardinal passage for the issue of human knowledge, for here the poet, speaking in his own voice as he tries to relate the number of men and ships, "moves beyond the boundaries of personal or collective human verifiability," opening up "the bare possibility of deception."[20] The lack of direct experience puts the poet and his audience at the mercy of the Muses and raises at least the logical possibility of skepticism.

Given the gap between human and divine knowledge, what is the nature of the difference between the two? Often, the difference between human and divine knowledge is taken to be essentially a difference in the quantity and scope of knowledge, which is to say, a difference in degree and not in kind. Hussey, for instance, says there is no logical barrier in principle to our having the same knowledge as the gods. The difference is in quantity, not quality.[21] In principle a human being could know precisely what a god knows, provided they both have direct personal experience of the event. The difference would instead be reduced to a practical one: the gods have more, humans have less, of exactly the same sort of thing.

There is at least one passage not widely noted in this connection that seems to support this reductive approach to the problem of human knowledge. It comes in *Odyssey* Book 8, when Odysseus praises the singer Demodokos at the feast of the Phaiakians just prior to the rhapsode's recounting of the stratagem of the wooden horse:

> "Demodokos, above all mortals beside I prize you.
> Surely the Muse, Zeus' daughter or else Apollo has taught you,
> for all too right following the tale you sing the Achaians'
> venture, all they did and had done to them, all the sufferings
> of these Achaians, as if you had been there yourself or
> > heard it
> from one who was." (*Ody.* 8.487–92)[22]

Odysseus knows that Demodokos speaks as one who was there because he, Odysseus, *was* there. While this passage serves as a bit of wry self-praise by the poet of his craft (cf. 8.479–81), it could also be taken to imply that the difference between human and divine knowledge is only a matter of degree. The rhapsode was inspired, but an eyewitness to the events would need no divine aid. Presumably, a human participant in the destruction of Troy could have recounted the same facts without the aid of the Muses (though likely without Demodokos's poetic skills), just as Odysseus, after praising Demodokos for an inspired knowledge of events that Odysseus himself had witnessed, proceeds to take the place of the inspired poet and tell his own story for the *Odyssey*'s next four books.[23]

If the difference between human and divine knowledge is one of quantity and not quality, philosophical skepticism is not a threat. Both the Phaiakian king Alkinous and Penelope in Ithaca know that travelers may lie to take advantage of an audience that has not as a matter of fact experienced what the liar reports. While this does make them properly skeptical of travelers' tales, it doesn't make them skeptics. A genuine skepticism grows out of something deeper, a limitation or insufficiency that cannot in principle be overcome.

Remarkably, both Hesiod and Homer seem untroubled by the threat of skepticism, even as it is they who raise the issue. Both regard their poems as truthful.[24] This is clearest in the case of Hesiod. He recognizes that the Muses may tell lies that resemble the truth, yet in the continuation of the invocation just quoted he proceeds not just confidently but even proudly:

> So they spoke, these mistresses of words, daughters of the
>   great Zeus,
> and they broke off and handed me a staff of strong-growing
> laurel bay, a wonderful thing; they breathed a voice into me,
> and power to sing the story of things of the future, and
>   things past.
> They told me to sing the race of the blessed gods everlasting,
> but always to put themselves at the beginning and end of my
>   singing. (*Theog.* 29–34)[25]

Hussey makes an important point: the Muses do not lie to their faithful servants ("Should the Muses, *per impossibile*, deceive Homer about the Trojan War . . ."; Hussey 1990, 15). But this leaves the nature of faithful service still to be determined. The Muses, as Hesiod says, will tell the truth when they wish to. And so the question returns, why has the poet been granted the privilege to know? Why, again, was the poet an exception? To answer these questions and to determine what constitutes faithful service, we must go back to the difference between factual knowledge and moral knowledge.

Faithful Servants

The poet will not be deceived (though characters in a story, human or divine, often are) because he is, in some relevant sense, a faithful servant. His service, I will argue, consists in devoting himself to imparting the moral lesson of the story. Events of the heroic past, the generations of the gods, Fate—these are not merely items of factual interest, but amount to knowledge of the greatest ethical import. To relate their full import requires a kind of experience ordinary humans cannot in principle have. Only with divine aid can the poet recite the names and actions of the participants in a story that will teach humanity's place in the divinely ordered cosmos and our proper attitude given our place. The gods who produced the Trojan War and the prolonged homecomings of the surviving warriors teach us the lessons of these stories by inspiring the stories sung by the poet. The one exception to the traditional gulf between human and divine knowers is the very figure who taught listeners about the gulf and its moral significance—the divinely inspired poet.

In one way, faithful service amounts to praising the Muses and singing their glory.[26] The divine order of the cosmos depends on a *dikê* of distribution of *timê* to all the gods. By placing the Muses "at the beginning and end" of his song about the blessed gods (as the Muses charge Hesiod to do in final two lines of the quote above), Hesiod properly honors them and their essential role in what he relates. At the same time, the poet conveys the economy of divine *timê* to human beings, showing in the process the origin of *nomos* and *dikê*, an awareness of which is crucial to how his audience ought to live.[27] The poet has been chosen not randomly or for idiosyncratic divine reason; rather, by his readiness to convey fundamental moral and constitutive aspects of the cosmos he has proven himself worthy to be medium and messenger.[28]

The most important evidence for my position comes from two extended scenes in the *Iliad*. The relevance of the first for the moral import of the story has been noted before, but bears repeating in connection with my theme. The second passage will put the supposedly skeptical second invocation in quite a different light.

The moral center of the *Iliad* is Achilles and his implacable wrath. The wrath of Achilles has exceeded all limits and bounds. It is his wrath that causes him to withdraw from battle; his wrath that leads to death of his companion Patroclus; his wrath that leads to the slaughter of Trojans in revenge of Patroclus; a wrath that finally breaks when Hector's father Priam comes as a supplicant to retrieve the desecrated body of his son.

We know Achilles is wrong to indulge it because of the story within the story in Book 9. This comes during the embassy sent by a chastened Agamemnon to Achilles, and could be said to provide a model for the moral lesson of the *Iliad* as a whole. The embassy consists of Odysseus, Ajax, and Phoenix, an older kinsman of the great warrior sent by his father as an advisor and mentor. Odysseus tries to manipulate Achilles by appealing to his greed and his sense of honor; he is unsuccessful. The old man Phoenix, who has tended Achilles as a son, tries to reach Achilles by means of a story. It is the story of his own youth, when his own rage turned him against his father. His punishment was to go childless, and now he implores Achilles to be persuaded to relent in his anger. Like Odysseus, he too is unsuccessful, and events are set in train that will lead to the destruction of Patroclus, Hector, and Achilles himself. The point is that one should listen to such stories and learn from them one's proper attitude. Just as Achilles is meant to learn from the story of Phoenix, the audience is meant to learn from the story of his wrath entrusted to and told by the poet.[29]

This insight helps us understand the invocation preceding the catalogue of ships in *Iliad* 2 and the moral significance behind the catalogue itself. Even serious students of Homer are prone to endure rather than enjoy the long recitation.[30] However, those scholars who limit themselves to the ten lines of the invocation quoted above in order to attend only to its epistemological implications miss the lesson implied by the *muthos* surrounding it. The poet says that he cannot tell the numbers of ships and men without divine aid, but it is not just the recounting of the names in the catalogue that is important. The catalogue points to the moral order (and more immediately, the disorder) of the poem. Taken as a whole, it intimates the chief moral lesson of the poem in a way that powerfully connects with the apparent skepticism of the invocation with which it begins.

We can begin with a general observation. Here in the final third of Book 2 (one might say already in Book 2) comes the grandest moment for the human combatants, a scene cinematic in its sweep. In terms of the narrative, it is the moment before the battle is joined, while armor is still gleaming and bodies still whole. The scene is also deeply ironic—we are witnessing the height of human glory mere hours before it is shattered by the duplicitous gods. Homer's profession of ignorance in the second invocation should be understood against this crushing irony. His knowledge at its unaided best is, like any human power, woefully limited, subject to the same limitations faced by any human endeavor—the inscrutable intentions of the gods. The knowledge with which he is graced is gained by the rest of humanity only through experience of harsh reality—this is how by the end of the *Iliad* Achilles and Priam will have learned it—or is conveyed to his audience by the poet acting as medium. Through him his audience is taught by the gods to know its limits, just as in the invocation the poet recognizes this own limitations and in so doing proves himself worthy as the Muses' faithful servant.

The lesson is prepared for in what happens immediately before the invocation. In the preceding thirty lines (2.455–83), the poet has described the assembled forces of the Greeks in a series of stunning images. The images are all of disorder. The soldiers are like an obliterating fire consuming a vast forest; like multitudinous nations of birds, flying in clashing swarms above a meadow; like multitudinous nations of insects flying in every direction. Chaos reigns until their leaders under the command of Agamemnon, who is described with a series of godlike epithets and is aided by Athena, begin to impose order. Before the second invocation, in other words, the poet could not create order out of the masses of men on his own. After the invocation, the situation has changed. Immediately after recognizing his dependency on the Muses, the poet finds a voice and begins to recite the numbers of ships and to identify their warlord leaders (2.493). Just as the goddess Athena helped Agamemnon impose order on the Achaians, so too the Muses enable the poet's ensuing ordered recitation and its message.

The recitation of the ships takes place in two phases, each culminating with a passage that speaks of the Myrmidons and their leader Achilles. The first culmination comes 180 lines after the invocation. After identifying the Myrmidons and their home in Greece, the poet takes particular notice of their lack of order:

> Of all these and their fifty ships the lord was Achilles.
> But these took no thought now for the grim clamour of battle
> since there was no one who could guide them into close
>   order. (*Il.* 2.685–87)

The cause of the disorder was, of course, the rage of Achilles. He now sits away from the incipient action, brooding over the loss of the woman Briseis, though the knowing poet reminds us that he will soon rise up (2.694).

The lack of a leader need not be an insuperable barrier to order, however. Two bands of warriors provide instructive contrasts to the leaderless Myrmidons. The very next contingent to be named, the men from Phylake and Pyrasos, had lost their leader Protesilaos; but now Podarkes, who is no less than the son of Ares, "set them in order" (2.704). A few lines later the men of Thaumakia are said to long for their leader Philoktetes, whose foul-smelling wound has caused him to be exiled on a desert island. But they too do not go leaderless, for Medon, the bastard son of Oïleus, "set them in order" (2.727). The lesson—shown but not stated—throws into relief the rage of Achilles as a force of disorder, both now and in the ominous hint of his return to action.

So too in the second and greater climax of the catalogue, which comes 260 lines after the catalogue began. Here again Achilles's rage as a force of disorder is signaled. Perhaps as a sign of the importance of what is to come, the poet for a third time—though much less often commented on—invokes the Muses:

> These then were the leaders and the princes among the
>   Danaans.
> Tell me then, Muse, who of them all was the best and the
>   bravest,
> of the men, and the men's horses, who went with the sons
>   of Atreus. (*Il.* 2.760–62)

Readers may feel some surprise that the naming of horses, too, requires the Muses' inspiration.[31] There are, after all, only four, so it can hardly be that their number exceeds any human ability to recount them. The need arises instead from their special status in the larger order. As the next five lines reveal, these are immortal horses bred by Apollo, the so-called mares of Eumelos who have been entrusted to Peleus's son Achilles, and so lead us again to the moral center of the poem:

> Among the men far the best was Telamonian Aias
> While Achilles stayed angry, since he was far best of all of them,
> and the horses also, who carried the blameless son of Peleus.
> But Achilles lay apart among his curved sea-wandering vessels, raging at Agamemnon. . . . (*Il.* 2.768–72)

While he rages, his men idly mark time, playing with discus and spear and bow, the chariots covered, the magnificent horses left to feed and rest.[32] The men, we are told, "forlorn of their warlike leader/ wandered here and there in the camp, and did no fighting" (2.773–79). The brooding Achilles remains as the source of discord to come. "But the rest went forward," we are told in the very next line, bringing an end to the catalogue of the Greek forces.

The poet of the *Iliad* is not a skeptic, not at least about the tale he tells. He is a medium for a story that tells of the limits imposed by the gods, a story taught by poets inspired by gods. Just as the god-like Agamemnon put into order the teeming Greek hordes prior to the invocation, so too do the gods inspire the poet with the skill to recount in order their vast numbers. To understand the poem's moral lesson, one must attend to more than its logical content. The structure of the *muthos*, inspired by the gods, is the key.

Book 2 concludes with a much briefer catalogue of the forces of Troy and their allies. They are alerted to the movement in the Achaean camp by all-seeing Iris, who, in disguise and sent by Zeus with a dark message, inspires Hector to muster the Trojan forces. Despite the multitudinous speech of scattered nations, the Trojans and their allies are marshalled in order. They do so round a nearby hill, called the Hill of the Thicket by mortals, but which the gods know to be the burial mound of the nymph Myrina, just as only they know the ultimate fate of Troy and the combatants now assembling.

The Poet-Philosopher

We may turn now to Xenophanes. Here we will discover the same pattern seen in Homer and Hesiod: an insistence on the limitations of human knowledge, with a consequent appearance of skepticism; followed by a confident exposition that seems to exceed the limits the poet himself had set for what a human being can know. The difference will come in the grounds for this assurance.

Xenophanes of Colophon is probably the earliest of those thinkers born in Ionia who set themselves up explicitly as critics and rivals of Homer and Hesiod. Yet going back at least as far as Aristotle, Xenophanes has been subject to neglect or outright derision as a significant philosopher. When Aristotle comes to Xenophanes in the *Metaphysics*'s survey of predecessors, he dismisses him as an unsophisticated thinker who said nothing clearly (*Metaph.* A.5, 986b21–27). Many centuries later, Friedrich Nietzsche is equally dismissive in his little book on the pre-Socratics, calling the Colophonian a religious mystic, a rhapsodic "teacher of ethics," and a forerunner of the Sophists.[33]

A similar attitude is shared by many more recent commentators. Against a minority of defenders like Barnes,[34] many see Xenophanes as not really, or not entirely, a philosopher. He employs reason as his authority, but haltingly, prompting Hussey to accuse him of employing two quite different methods, one an a priori speculative method for his "theology" and another more empirical method for his thoughts about nature, an inconsistency a more systematic philosopher would avoid.[35] And though Xenophanes offers some noteworthy (and frequently noted) remarks about natural phenomena (e.g., about the rainbow and fossils), he retains the poetic form abandoned by philosophical forerunners like Anaximander, who chose to write in prose, earning Algra's ambivalent label cited at the start of this paper, "the enigmatic poet-philosopher."[36]

My approach to Xenophanes will be based on three facts, none of which in itself is controversial. First, Xenophanes is one of the first Greek thinkers to object to literature on moral grounds, challenging traditional stories of the sort found in Hesiod and Homer for depicting the gods anthropomorphically. For Xenophanes, such stories were not only intellectually suspect; they were morally bankrupt as well.[37] Second, Xenophanes advanced what was apparently the first monotheistic conception of the divine in Greek culture. He describes one god, unlike human beings in every way, who sees, knows, and hears all, moving all things with its mind alone. Third, like Homer and Hesiod, Xenophanes was a poet. By the form of his writing as much as through his theology or epistemology he places himself as their successor.[38] For Snell, Xenophanes is a rhapsode praising the god-given wisdom he has received, who like Hesiod, has raised himself above the ordinary level because he has a special truth to impart. Hussey draws attention to the "Homeric vocabulary and conceptual equipment of Xenophanes' (Hussey 1999, 18). Though a sharp critic of his predecessors, Xenophanes remains within the poetic tradition of the inspired teacher of moral lessons.[39] This connection should influence how we interpret his more philosophical remarks, particularly his fragments bearing on human and divine knowledge. About these there is considerable controversy.

First, a note of caution. The literary remains of Xenophanes are highly fragmentary, amounting to about forty quotations and references that have come down to us from many diverse sources written over many years and from various viewpoints and motives.[40] It is not clear whether Xenophanes wrote a unified work "On Nature" as many pre-Socratics are said to have done. Several groups of fragments I shall consider do seem to cohere as if they were part of a larger argument. Nevertheless, putting fragments into any sort of continuous passage is speculative.

In his most famous fragment bearing on human knowledge, Xenophanes strikes a now familiar skeptical chord. He claims that a human being can never state the truth of things, nor would he recognize it as true if he were somehow able to say it:

> And of course the clear and certain truth (*to saphes*) no man has seen (*iden*) nor will there be anyone who knows about the gods and what I say about all things. For even if, in the best case, one happened to speak just of what has been brought to pass still he himself would not know. But opinion (*dokos*) is allotted to all. (B34)[41]

For Snell, B34 echoes the catalogue of ships in its denigration of human ability to know while sharpening the contrast between human and divine, so that humans have only *dokos*, "semblance" or "appearance": "Xenophanes feels that human knowledge is in its very essence deceptive." Hussey resists this last point, but does take B34 to be the denial of "the entire framework, taken for granted by Homer and Hesiod, of generally accepted truths about the gods." No man can have certain knowledge of the truth concerning these things, not even the seer. For this reason, B34 can be read as an attack on the poets or any other supposed sage claiming inspiration from the gods. Lesher calls B34 a "master fragment," reflecting on the entire body of his philosophical thought, comparing it to Heraclitus B1 and Parmenides B7. Rather differently, Broadie takes B34 as expressing the "voice of traditional piety" in its strict separation of human from divine, though she quickly adds it is not simply that voice: "Xenophanes's new account of the divine never purported to give out the truth about god as god would see it."[42]

Like Homer and Hesiod, Xenophanes limits human knowledge to that which a human being directly experiences, whether individually or collectively. Yet, again like Homer and Hesiod, Xenophanes proceeds confidently, developing a radical reformulation of the concept of divinity. There is undoubtedly a tension here. He denies to mortals any certainty about the gods, yet advances a new theology.

One might speculate that in some lost portion of the poem containing his new theology, Xenophanes invokes for guidance the very god whose nature he delineates. Snell goes so far as to assert that Xenophanes received a "revelation" of a single, unitary god, but gives no evidence; the question is still debated.[43] Perhaps relevant to this point is B1, which compares men speaking of gods at a drinking party to those inspired. But the fragment leaves Xenophanes's own attitude toward such alleged inspiration obscure.

One cannot rule out that there was in Xenophanes some suggestion of inspiration or even an invocation to the Muses; but I want to offer a different suggestion, supported by the fragments we possess. In particular, I want to consider two other passages bearing on the possibility of human knowledge.

I will begin with B18. The passage is consistent with the limiting human knowledge to what is directly experienced, but broadens the notion of experience so that it extends over time:

> Indeed not from the beginning did gods intimate all things to mortals, but as they search (*zetountes*) they discover better. (B18)

Many scholars find in this passage an announcement of a new empirically based approach to knowledge. For Snell, it is a declaration that humans can acquire knowledge through their own efforts: "For the first time man's own initiative, his industry and zeal, become crucial for the acquisition of knowledge" (140). Hussey reads it as an endorsement of progress, relying on what is observable, with minimal reference to the gods.

Xenophanes's use of fossil evidence and his naturalistic explanation of the rainbow are striking, and must qualify as examples of "empirical research" in some rudimentary sense. But surely one must be careful in applying modern ideas like a belief in progress to a thinker at the very beginning of philosophy. These ideas must also be fitted into the larger context of Xenophanes's thought, which is as we saw deeply colored by the poetic tradition. Conspicuously, B18 speaks of the seeking done by *mortals* and uses the theologically charged *hupodeiknumi* which could suggest a slow and deliberate unveiling by the knowing god rather than empirical discovery produced by human researchers. In any case, it is hard to see how empirical research or diligent investigation could yield any increase in positive knowledge of the gods, even if such research suggested that a rainbow was not the direct result of divine action.

The second passage I will consider is the fragment B35, which is often joined to B34 as its direct continuation:

Let these be accepted, certainly, as like (*eoikota*) the realities (but . . .). (B35)

Because human knowledge is limited to that which is directly experienced, many scholars take Xenophanes to be a fallibilist. His own claims about the god cannot be known to be true, but they can be accepted as probable, or at least plausible. As the most recent extended treatment of B35 argues, this sense is conveyed by the word *eikôs*, a form of which appears in B35.[44]

There is, however, another connotation conveyed by *eikôs*, one that connects to the concern over the limits of human knowledge in a way different from fallibilist interpretations. Something is *eikôs* if it is fitting or appropriate. This is very much like an old sense of the English term "'like," and in the dual sense still detectable in the probabilistic "seem" on the one hand and the moralistic "seemly" and "unseemly" on the other. Thus, *eikôs* can carry the sense of being seemly or fitting at least as strongly as it carries the sense of probability: an opinion is *eikôs*-probable only if it is *eikôs*-fitting.[45]

Specifically with regard to the fragments pertaining to the problem of human knowledge, I would argue that a need for fitting expression is evident. In religious contexts especially it is important that one's words be *eikôs*, fitting and appropriate for their subject matter. One must be careful in one's ignorance not to inadvertently say anything impious, for it is as hard to detect error as it is truth. The limitations of human knowledge mean that one's account can be no more than probable. But this places a duty on the poet as well: the account must be fitting to the divine subject. Traditional stories about the gods and their supposed inspiration reveal themselves to be improbable just because they are impious. By avoiding saying what is shameful, Xenophanes properly elevates god and separates the divine from human. In doing so, he offers not just a probable account, but an account that is fitting to the divine subject matter.

The concern that philosophical speech about the gods to be fitting is apparent in later philosophy. Among the pre-Socratics, both Empedocles and Parmenides have prologues that echo back to Hesiod's invocation of the Muses. In a gesture Broadie calls "a methodological dependence of divine assistance," she takes both of these philosophers to be entirely sincere: "Piety entails the admission that only god unaided can fittingly celebrate god."[46] An argument to this effect is found in Plato. In *Republic* Book Two, Plato's indictment of the stories of Homer and Hesiod opens by charging that many poets make an "improper representation" (*eikaze kakôs*) of gods and heroes. All such stories are, in Plato's terms, lies. Faced with this limit to human knowledge, Socrates and Adeimantus conclude by insisting that human speech about the god must therefore strive to be seemly and proper. And though mentioning the *Timaeus* raises a host of questions that cannot be addressed here, a similar pious dimension seems to be in the background of Timaeus's *eikôs muthos*, beginning with an invocation asking that the god ensure that the account be appropriate, given the limitations of both what can be known and those who are conducting the investigation.[47]

It is not necessary for me to claim that similar ideas in Xenophanes were ever part of a continuous argument. It is sufficient to say that even if they were worked out over many decades of his long life and come from several different compositions, the fragments of Xenophanes bearing on human and divine knowledge stand as a consistent and intelligible response to the poetic tradition. Xenophanes, it might be said, initiates a line of thought linking the limits of human knowledge with a concern that our accounts about the divine be suitable, just because our knowledge is limited.[48]

Human knowledge is limited. From this the poets derived a moral prescription against seeking knowledge of things beyond the human. Yet, while the gap between human and divine was a belief widely held in the thought of the earliest philosophers (Xenophanes, Heraclitus, Pythagoreans, and Parmenides), it produced no similar warning or prohibition. Recognizing the limits of human knowledge did not discourage them from the investigation of the highest things, nor did it stop them from urging their auditors to continue with such investigations on their own. What is the source of their confidence?

At least with regard to Xenophanes, the resemblance between the activity of the philosopher and that of the divine mind seems relevant.[49] Like Homer and Hesiod, Xenophanes is intent to impart a knowledge of human limits. Despite this, he like they speaks of things beyond ordinary experience. But Xenophanes advances a conception of a divinity that is not jealous of our search, if we piously strive to make our account fit and appropriate to its divine subject matter. Just as the god of Xenophanes moves all things by mind alone, our reasoned search for knowledge mimics the essence of divine activity and offers a route to an account that is both probable and fitting. Blind faith in divine inspiration is replaced by divinely modeled rational activity. The truth of an account about the gods may never be known with certainty. But the moral probity of what is said provides a criterion by which its adequacy may be judged. Xenophanes's epistemology, theology, and ethics converge in a life guided by reason focused on god unlike human beings in every way—except in the essential activity of the divine mind. Though echoing the voice of traditional piety, Xenophanes speaks as a philosopher.

Notes

1. Even firsthand knowledge, including that of including eye-witnesses, faced profound qualifications because of limited viewpoint, the influence of desire, and willful ignorance of what was apparent. I have explored these limitations in Wians 2009a, from which several ideas in these opening paragraphs are borrowed.

2. Snell 1953, 137, also cited at Wians 2009a, 182. Fränkel developed a similar account of knowledge in Homer by direct personal experience in Fränkel 1962/1973 and Fränkel 1974, so that it is possible for Hussey 1990, 13, to speak of—and proceed to criticize—a "Snell-Fränkel thesis." See further the next note.

3. Similarly, Hussey 1990, 14–15 (who argues that Snell's position can be true only in a severely restricted form) points to the encounter between Achilles and Aeneus at *Il.* 20.203ff, where the warriors know already each other's lineage through reports repeated over generations, to suggest that direct experience can be supplemented by a collective human experience.

4. The omniscience of the gods requires a qualification One must distinguish between the gods a Greek believed in and the gods who function as characters in a story. There are episodes in both the *Iliad* and the *Odyssey* in which a god as a character in the story lacks knowledge of specific events or circumstances. Hera deceives Zeus so that she can work against Troy. Ares and

Aphrodite enjoy an adulterous affair while her unknowing husband Hephaistos attends a festival of the Aithiopians. Even Zeus himself has to be reminded by Athena that Odysseus is a virtual prisoner of Kalypso at the start of the *Odyssey*. These cases don't seriously challenge the claim that the gods are all-knowing. Characters in a story, whether human or divine, may act under the burden of a limited perspective, especially when it suits the poet's narrative purposes. But while a character may be deceived the poet certainly is not, nor is there any hint that the Muses share in anything less than divine omniscience. In a similar way, the omniscience of the God of the Jewish Bible is not seriously undercut by his apparent surprise at discovering the theft of the fruit of the tree of knowledge while walking in the Garden of Eden to enjoy the evening breeze. In writing this note, I have tried to come to grips with insightful comments by Rose Cherubin, who subjected an earlier version of this essay to a careful and through criticism. The paper as a whole is better for it.

5. Barnes 1979; Hussey 1990.

6. An exception to this neglect can be found Lesher 1999 and Lesher 2009 (though I would not go as far as he does in speaking of the "pessimism" of the poets).

7. As Snell remarks, Greek thinkers "would find themselves embroiled in a heated debate" about what is meant by divine knowledge and its human counterpart and what is considered the limits and the trustworthiness of human understanding." I explore Aristotle's response to the traditional contrast in Wians 2008.

8. So-called by Algra 1999, 59.

9. Reasons for casting the contrast in other and less sharply defined terms are surveyed in the introduction to this collection.

10. Most 1999a, 336–37, 342–46. Hadot 2002, 18–19 emphasizes the presumed power of the poet's words to heal, transform, and enlighten.

11. The phrase comes from Hussey 1990, 11.

12. Another exception to the ordinary limits of human knowledge is that of the seer (*mantiké*). I consider two examples of prophetic knowledge in Wians 2009a.

13. See Lloyd-Jones 1971, chapters 3 and 4, for pertinent comments on the pervasive envy of the gods.

14. I shall return to the question of the importance of the form that the inspired story takes particularly in connection with the catalogue of ships in *Iliad* 2.

15. Translations of Hesiod are those of Lattimore 1959.

16. Snell makes a different point to which we shall return: the Muses' boast, followed as it is by an inspired account of the generation of the gods, amounts to an implied contrast between Hesiod and other singers. While they sing unworthily of heroes and battles, he has been chosen and singled out to sing of "the total aggregate of concrete reality," standing halfway between divine

knowledge and human folly (138). Why he has been singled out is what we shall attempt to establish.

17. Translations of passages from the *Iliad* are those of Lattimore 1951. For reasons I will explain in the next note, I have inserted a blank line before the final line of the quoted passage.

18. I take the tenth and final line to indicate that the poet's prayer has been answered and that inspiration is forthcoming, which I indicate by inserting a blank line that is not present in Lattimore's original. Cp. the question asked at line 1.8 of the proem: "What god was it then set them together in better collision?" which (I take it) is then immediately answered.

19. Snell 1953, 137–38.

20. Hussey 1990, 17.

21. Hussey 1990, 36–37.

22. Translations for the *Odyssey* come from Lattimore 1965.

23. Odysseus's narration of his own story does not, of course, show that humans can have knowledge unaided in all areas of possible knowledge. The passage is mentioned by Most 1999a, 343 as evidence that Homer (and also Hesiod) took the content of their poems to be true. We shall return to this point shortly.

24. A point also made by Most 1999a, 342–43.

25. In line 31 I have replaced Lattimore's "olive shoot" with "laurel bay," conforming with the otherwise largely uniform practice of translators of the Greek *daphnês*. The laurel was the symbol of priestly and poetic inspiration and authority.

26. I owe several ideas in this paragraph to Rose Cherubin.

27. I take this to be equivalent to Snell's speaking of the total aggregate of concrete reality referred to in n.16 above. See also Hadot 2002, 19, who speaks of the poet's inspiration as allowing both the poet and his audience to attain a cosmic vision.

28. A foreshadowing of the privilege Hesiod is granted comes in the opening lines of the *Theogony*, which relate a vision of the Muses on Helicon that no ordinary human being would be permitted to share (1–9). Chreubin suggests a comparison with the youth in the poem of Parmenides, who has been brought on the road to the goddess by *themis* and *dikê*, a road far from the usual human paths.

29. See the sensitive analysis in Edwards 1987, 224–29.

30. Snell calls the catalogue "that most sober section of the *Iliad*" (136). Kirk 1985, 169 describes it as "somewhat daunting" to modern readers "who are not connoisseurs of ancient political geography."

31. Kirk regards mentioning of the horses as "awkwardly and gratuitously appended" and the brief invocation at 761–62 as "inappropriate to what will follow" (Kirk 1985, 240 and 243). Despite his lengthy commentary on the catalogue, he does not address the implied moral lesson.

32. At a much later point, their weeping for the dead Patroclus prompts Zeus to regret that immortal creatures have been placed under wretched human beings; 17.426ff. Still later, one of the horses, Xanthos, is granted knowledge and voice by Hera to foretell Achilles's death; 19.404ff.

33. Nietzsche 1962, 74–76. In the portion of his *nachlass* translated into English by G. Whitlock as *The Pre-Platonic Philosophers* (Urbana/Chicago: University of Illinois Press, 2001), 76–80, Nietzsche treats Xenophanes at greater length and in less strident tones, though his overall characterization is consistent with his remarks in the *Tragic Age*.

34. Barnes 1979, 82–99 and 136–51.

35. Hussey 1990, 37–38.

36. See above, note 8. Most 1999a, 350 calls (with perhaps some deliberate exaggeration) the retention of the poetic form after the invention of philosophical prose a "grievous scandal."

37. It should be noted, however, that though he is often credited for being the first such philosophical critic, Xenophanes's moralizing was part of a larger movement in Archaic thought, including figures such as Archilochus, Theognis, Solon, and Hecataeus. See also next note.

38. Most 1999a, 335 makes the same point about the poetic form employed by several pre-Socratics, including Xenophanes, Heraclitus, Parmenides, and Empedocles. Homer and Hesiod had in fact many successors by the sixth century. Theogonic and cosmogonic poems had been written by Epimenides, Musaios, Linos, and an anonymous Titanomachy. See further West 1966, 12ff.

39. Fragments B1 and B2 clearly show Xenophanes as seeking to impart virtue into the body politic. Lesher 1992 is especially good in bringing this out. So too Broadie 1999, 212: his aim was not to expound a new theory of physics, but was to speak "as a matter of moral and civic leadership." Most 1999a, 351–53 sees in the retention of epic meter by Xenophanes a sign of his intention to surpass Homer and Hesiod in moral and political virtue. Also relevant is the likelihood that Hesiod's *Theogony* was recited in public apparently as part of a cultic or religious occasion; Algra 1999, 49 and notes 9–11.

40. Fragment 21a (Lesher) speaks of five books of *silloi*, "a vehicle for caustically humorous moralizing" (Broadie 1999, 209), and he is credited with many elegies as well.

41. Translations of Xenophanes are from Lesher 1992.

42. Broadie 1999, 212. Hussey reads B34 as distinguishing between knowledge that no single man may have, and the "probable" opinion that can be constructed (*tetuktai*, a crucial term in the continuation of B34) out of collective human experience.

43. Snell 1953, 141–43. One could imagine fragment B18, quote below and which speaks of revelation over time, as being connected to a lost invocation

to the Muse for guidance, followed by B34 as the explanation as to why divine help is needed. See further Bryan 2012, 52, note 148.

44. Bryan 2012, chapter 1.

45. Bryan does not consider this sense at all. She is faulted for this omission in Mourelatos 2014, 174–75. In his textbook on the pre-Socratics, Hussey seems to have this sense in mind when he describes Xenophanes's innovative approach to theological speculation (Hussey 1972, 14). See also Robb in the volume.

46. Broadie 1999, 208–09.

47. See further Morgan 2000, 273–74 on Timaeus's myth as both likely and fitting.

48. It is perhaps for this reason that Xenophanes praises his own *sophiē* in B2. In B1, after the tables of the banquet are cleared, the guests look forward to morally uplifting tales of virtue. But these, he cautions, ought not to be tales of divine strife.

49. A connection also noticed in Broadie 1999, 211.

3

How Philosophy is Rooted in Tradition

Stories Describing the Appearance of Man and Woman in Ancient Greece

Luc Brisson

As far as the origin of human beings is concerned, we in Europe and America are accustomed to the twofold story of Genesis. Its elements, which complement one another more or less well, tell how a unique, omnipotent god first created the world and then man and woman in his image: "God created man in his image, in the image of God created he him, man and woman created he them" (Gen 1:27). A bit later, however, we read: "Then God made a deep sleep fall upon man, who fell asleep. He took one of his ribs and closed up the flesh. Then, out of the rib he had taken from man, God fashioned a woman and brought her to the man" (Gen. 2:21–22).[1] There follows a story that tells how the first man and the first woman disobeyed their creator, and how they were expelled from Paradise and punished: to work in the case of man, and to give birth in pain in the case of woman. In both stories, the origin of human beings depends on a deliberate act of creation, that is, production of man and woman by an omnipotent God in his image and out of nothing.

In the Greek world, human beings are not the product of an intentional act of an omnipotent god. They appear as the end result of a process of differentiation: out of a primordial chaos in which everything was mixed, with the gods as the first to appear, from whom human beings will distance themselves, acquiring an inferior status. In other words, one cannot speak of an origin of human beings in general, in the sense of an absolute starting point. We shall see how matters stand in Hesiod, the Orphics, and in Plato's Aristophanes as depicted in the *Symposium*.[2]

Hesiodic Myths

My goal in recalling these Greek myths is a broad one. Convinced as I am that philosophy grows in the loam of tradition, I would like to show, all too briefly, how in my view the story of the appearance of human beings has fundamental consequences in the field of ethics.

The starting point of any inquiry into the origin of human beings in ancient Greece is Hesiod, hence the *Theogony* and the *Works and Days*, written around 700 BCE.

As is implied by the myth of the races invoked in the *Works and Days* (109–201), there were several races of human beings before ours, the term "race" designating generational groups of human beings who are born together and disappear altogether at same time.[3] Under Kronos, there was first a golden race who lived like gods, who did not work, and whose death resembled a sleep (109–26). Inferior to the first race, the human beings of the silver race appeared, who also seem to have lived under Kronos; but Zeus made them disappear (127–42). Then Zeus made the race of bronze appear: violent human beings who thought only of war, and who succumbed in fratricidal combats (143–55). Zeus then brought to light a fourth race, that of the heroes who fought beneath the walls of Troy (the tale recounted in part in the *Iliad*) and of Thebes (the story told in the tragedies of Sophocles; *WD* 156–73). Finally came our race, the race of iron, which is to be annihilated by Zeus (174–201). It is probably this race that is the subject in the myth of Prometheus as told in the *Theogony* (535–616), and the myth of Pandora as told in the *Works and Days* (42–105).

The goal of these myths is to explain why human beings, after their defeat in quarrels that opposed them to the gods, became distant from them, gaining autonomy but seeing the conditions of their lives deteriorate.[4] Because they are mortal, they will have to reproduce sexually to perpetuate the human species and work the earth in order to provide the food that will allow them to eat, two demands that imply the existence of suffering on earth.[5] This mythical set contains four sequences.

First Sequence: Bloody Sacrifice

It is impossible to identify the place of the action or to situate the story in time, although it is to be placed under the reign of Zeus. The first mythical sequence, telling of the ruse hatched by Prometheus, manifests all the ambiguity of the situation of human beings with regard to the gods, an ambiguity that will be removed by bloody sacrifice.

> . . . [W]ith eager spirit he [Prometheus] divided up a great ox and, trying to deceive Zeus's mind, set it before him. For he set down on the skin before him the meat and the innards, rich with fat, hiding them in the ox's stomach; and then he set down before him, the ox's white bones, arranging them with deceptive craft, hiding them with gleaming fat. (*Theog.* 536–41)[6]

It should be noted that: (1) human beings, who were not distinguished by sex before the reign of Zeus, already exist; (2) they are not very different from the gods (with whom they share their food); (3) they can take sides in the conflicts that oppose the gods; and (4) they are powerful enough to oppose the current king of the gods, with the help of Prometheus, who is a Titan and therefore a god. In fact, the antagonism of human beings to Zeus is a continuation of the hostility of the Titans and their descendants toward Zeus who has seized power by dethroning his father Kronos, a Titan. Indeed, Prometheus is the son of Iapetus, one of Kronos's brothers, and his mother is a daughter of Oceanos, another of Kronos's brothers. In Greek mythology, Prometheus plays the part of a trickster, a swindler, and cheater. However, he cheats and swindles not for himself, but for the sake of human beings, whose benefactor he thus becomes. In this specific case, Prometheus tries to favor human beings by giving them the best share of the animal.

This dialogue then takes place between Zeus, who has become aware of the fraud, and Prometheus:

> Then the father of men and of gods addressed him: "Son of Iapetus, eminent among all rulers, my fine fellow, how unfairly you have divided up the portions!" So spoke in mockery Zeus,

who knows eternal counsels; but crooked-counseled Prometheus
addressed him in turn, smiling slightly, and he did not forget
his deceptive craft: "Zeus most renowned, greatest of the
eternally living gods, choose from these whichever your spirit
in your breast bids you." (*Theog.* 542–49)

This first fraudulent distribution, which was to favor human beings, is ambiguous, for as an archetype of bloody sacrifice, it establishes a clear separation between gods and human beings in the very act of the sacrificial meal:

And ever since then the tribes of human beings upon the
earth burn white bones upon smoking altars for the immortals.
(*Theog.* 556–57)

Before the ruse plotted by Prometheus, gods and human beings could receive any piece of the ox. Yet in the traditional bloody sacrifice that reproduces the distribution carried out by Prometheus, the sacrificed animal is systematically divided into two sets. The flesh that will be eaten goes to human beings, for human beings need to eat to survive, while the bones and the inedible fat, which will rise in smoke toward the gods, go to the latter.

Second Sequence: The Theft of Fire

To punish Prometheus's trickery in favor of human beings, Zeus decides to punish them by depriving them of the fire of his lightning:

So spoke in rage Zeus, who knows eternal counsels. And
from then on, constantly mindful of his wrath after that, he
did not give the strength of tireless fire to the ash trees for
the mortal human beings who live upon the earth. But the
good son of Iapetus fooled him by stealing the far-seen gleam
of tireless fire in a hollow fennel stalk. It gnawed deeply at
high-thundering Zeus's spirit and enraged his dear heart,
when he saw the far-seen gleam of fire among human beings.
(*Theog.* 561–70)

By no longer making the fire of his lightning descend upon the earth, Zeus lowers human beings to the level of animals, insofar as human beings must henceforth eat their meat raw. To spare human beings the disastrous consequences of this punishment, Prometheus intervenes once again. Since Zeus no longer makes fire descend upon the earth, Prometheus steals it. Prometheus's gift, which is a theft committed at Zeus's expense, is once more ambiguous, for it establishes a new separation between the gods and human beings. The theft of fire allows human beings to acquire an autonomy they did not have when they depended on fire from heaven, but this autonomy is a definitive separation of human beings both from the gods and from the animals. The appearance and definition of human beings are thus presented in the context of a process of separation and distinction from the gods.

THIRD SEQUENCE: THE GIFT OF WOMAN

To avenge the theft of fire, Zeus gives human beings the gift of woman which seems magnificent, but will prove itself to be a trap (*Theog.* 570). At first glance, woman is a magnificent being:

> For the much-renowned Lame One [Hephaestus] forged from earth the semblance of a reverend maiden by the plans of Kronos's son [Zeus]; and the goddess, bright-eyed Athena, girdled and adorned her with silvery clothing, and with her hands she hung a highly wrought veil from her head, a wonder to see . . . (*Theog.* 570–75)

Yet this beauty is an evil:

> Then, when he had contrived this beautiful evil thing in exchange for that good one [fire], he led her out to where the other gods and the human beings were, while she exulted in the adornment of the mighty father's bright-eyed daughter; and wonder gripped the immortal gods and the mortal human beings when they saw the steep deception, intractable for human beings. For from her comes the race of female women: for of her is the deadly race and tribe of women, a great woe for mortals, dwelling with men, no companions of baneful poverty but only of luxury. (*Theog.* 585–93)

Two essential elements emerge from this story. (1) Whereas no description of the origin of human beings can be detected in Hesiod, one does find a description of the origin of woman in the sense of an absolute beginning; and (2) It is woman who, by her very ambiguity, ultimately allows a definition of the status of the human species which, in order to reproduce itself, implies sexual union. In other words, it is not woman *qua* human being who is fashioned by Hephaestus, but woman as a means, and as it were an instrument of reproduction, and hence of the survival of the human species through sexual union. Thus the difficulty, not to say the impossibility, of placing woman on an equal level with man in this context.

However, normal—that is nonviolent—sexual union implies seduction. To seduce a man and thus bring him to unite with her with a view to producing children, woman makes use of lies and artifices. This is why woman is associated with deceitful words, which seduce by their lies and artifices:

> . . . and Pallas Athena fitted the whole ornamentation to her body. Then into her breast the intermediary, the killer of Argus [Hermes], set lies and guileful words and a thievish character, by the plans of deep-thundering Zeus; and the messenger of the gods placed a voice in her and named this woman Pandora (All-Gift), since all those who have their mansions on Olympus had given her a gift—a woe for men who live on bread. (WD 76–82)

What is more, as Hesiod also points out, woman is associated with a man's work and the transmission of the wealth produced by this work. He who does not marry does not have to work as much as a married man, and keeps all his possessions; yet no one cares for him in his old age, and above all, his possessions will be distributed among strangers at his death. He who marries, in contrast, will have to work for his wife and children, if he is lucky enough to find a serious wife; otherwise, things will be terrible for him.

FOURTH SEQUENCE: THE OPENING OF THE JAR

Things get worse, however, when woman becomes the instrument of the ultimate vengeance of Zeus in the context of another ambiguous event that seals the fate of human beings, viz., the opening of a jar containing all evils:

For previously the tribes of men used to live upon the earth
entirely apart from evils, and without grievous toil and distress-
ful diseases, which give death to men. But the woman removed
the great lid from the storage jar with her hands and scattered
all its contents abroad—she wrought baneful evils for human
beings. Only Hope remained there in its unbreakable home
under the mouth of the storage jar, and did not fly out; for
before that could happen she close[d] the lid of the storage jar,
by the plans of the aegis-holder, the cloud-gatherer, Zeus. But
countless other miseries roam among mankind; for the earth
is full of evils, and the sea is full; and some sicknesses come
upon men by day, and others by night, of their own accord,
bearing evils to mortals in silence, since the counselor Zeus
took their voice away. Thus it is not possible in any way to
evade the mind of Zeus. (WD 90–105)[8]

Previously, all evils remained enclosed within a jar. By opening it Pandora frees them. Yet a life given over to unremitting evil would be unlivable. This is why Pandora closes the lid over hope, which remains at the bottom of the jar in the house, the place of woman. There is hope only because there is evil, but without the possibility of escaping evil there is no hope.

The gods, who are immortal, have no need of hope, any more than animals do, who do not know that they are mortal. The episode of the jar thus allows a definitive definition of man's place within the continuum of living beings: the ambiguity of his fate, divided between happiness and misfortune, situates him at a level lower than the gods, with whom he nevertheless maintains relations by means of bloody sacrifice, but he differs from them by his mortality, which demands sexual reproduction, the use of fire, and work. At a higher level, he distinguishes himself from the animals, which have no relation to the gods, and do not use fire.

The fact that woman gives birth makes clear man's mortality in the face of the immortality of the gods. Only sexual union allows the perpetuation of the human species: immortality being no longer indi-vidual becomes specific. Since woman remains at home, and since her children, who cannot yet work, must be fed, it is she who, in a way, forces man to work the land to harvest grains. The human species can thus perpetuate itself, but on the condition of establishing between men and women relationships that generate the suffering associated with work and death. Woman, who remains at home, suffers when she gives birth, while man, who goes outside, loses a part of his life by working. The struggle against death entails the pains of childbirth in woman, and the fatigue of work in man. Through marriage, woman is for man the only means to have children and to ensure a certain kind of immortality—not for the individual, but for the human species.

In this new world inaugurated by Prometheus's fraud, all is ambiguous and ambivalent. The sacrificial meal inaugurates a relationship between the world of the gods and that of human beings, but only by establishing a radical separation between them. Likewise, woman, through her beauty, recalls the omnipresence of evil, for she is associated with death, illnesses, and suffering, and she demands endless work from man, a merciless struggle of all against all. In short, it is—it must be repeated—a woman, Pandora, who seals the fate of man. She is, if not alien to him, at least distinct, fashioned as an instrument for ensuring the survival of the human species. This is why she is kept in private, excluded from the public sphere.

Later, in the fifth century BCE, the tragic poet Aeschylus develops another theme in his *Prometheus Bound*: that of the hero's punishment. In the tale Hesiod recounts, he speaks only of the punishments inflicted on the human beings who profited from Prometheus's fraud and theft. In Aeschylus, Zeus punishes Prometheus himself by tying him to a rock, where an eagle comes to eat his liver as it regenerates.

Orphism

It seems that in the *Orphic Rhapsodies*, based on a theology that was later than Hesiod's *Theogony* by a century or two (their composition is dated toward 500 BCE),[9] one finds a myth concerning man akin to the myth of the races in Hesiod, a myth Proclus evokes in his *Commentary on Plato's Republic* (*In Remp.* II 74.26–75.30 = OF 140 Kern = 159 Bernabé). Once again, the succession of the human races corresponds, for the Orphics, to a distance from the gods.

The appearance of a new race of human beings presupposes that the Titans were struck by Zeus's lightning, who thus wanted to punish them for having eaten his son Dionysus, whom Zeus had chosen as his successor. Zeus could not use the very limbs of the Titans, who had been hurled into Tartarus, to produce a new race of human beings; only the smoke and vapors rising from their lightning-struck bodies could serve for this production.

Whatever the chosen process may be, it is important to note that the idea that man comes from the Titans goes back a long way, and there is nothing specifically Orphic about it. In the *Homeric Hymn to Apollo* (verse 335), one learns that human beings, like the gods, have issued forth from the Titans, while in *Orphic Hymn* [37] that is devoted to them, the Titans are considered as being at the origin of all mortal creatures, not merely human beings. Yet this process is not described in either text. According to Dio Chrysostom (*Discourse* XXX, 10), human beings took their origin from the blood spilled by the Titans during the war they fought against the gods. According to the *Orphic Argonautica*, they come from the seed of the Giants who fell from the heavens. In short, the production of the third race of human beings is associated with divinities who, because they wish to contest the order Zeus wants to impose, are on the side of evil. Here we find once again the theme of opposition to the gods, though without any mention of sexual differentiation, and no insistence on the misery of man.

Plato's Aristophanes

I shall end with a tale that pertains to the same context, but is distinct insofar as it seeks to explain the sexual behavior of human beings. This is a myth told by the character Aristophanes in Plato's *Symposium* (189d–193e),[10] a dialogue the dramatic date of which Plato situates in 416 BCE, though written in the first half of the fourth century. Ancient human nature, whose origin is not mentioned, contained three genders: male, androgynous, and female. These human beings, who exhibited the form of an egg, were twofold beings. They had four hands, four feet, two faces placed opposite one another, and most importantly two sets of sexual organs, the second set placed on what now constitutes the human being's rear end. In the case of the male, the two sexual organs were masculine; in the case of the female, they were feminine; while in the case of the androgyne, one was masculine and the other feminine. In addition, the circular appearance of these beings indicated their origin: the male was an offspring of the sun, the female of the earth, and the androgyne of the moon, which is in an intermediary position between the sun—compared to which it is a species of earth—and earth, compared to which it is a species of sun.

Like the Giants Ephialtes and Otos, who tried to scale the heavens to attack the gods, these human beings rebelled against the gods. To punish them without exterminating them, Zeus decides to cut them in half. Having done so, he calls upon Apollo to heal the wounds he has opened, the last scar of which is now the navel. However, this punishment leads the human race straight to its ruin, as each half tries to find its complementary half, with such zeal and constancy that they began to die off from hunger. This is why Zeus intervenes once again, by transporting the sexual organs of each of the resulting halves to the front of their bodies. This new operation makes possible an intermittent sexual union which, while it allowed each human being to find its complementary half, gives them the time to look after other needs, and especially those absolutely essential ones constituted by nutrition and reproduction.

A safe distance is thereby established between the complementary halves of human beings, who are no longer either permanently joined or disjoined, for their intermittent reunion makes bearable a separation that is in effect for the rest of time. As one can understand by reading Aristophanes's speech, this "safe anthropological distance" is inseparable from a "safe cosmological distance" between heaven and earth, as well as from a "safe theological distance" between the gods and human beings. Eros therefore appears as the only god capable of enabling human beings to temporarily rediscover their ancient unity; it is precisely in this that his power resides, which also extends to such pairs of opposites as those constituted by heaven and earth, gods and human beings. And since these reunions can take place in man only through sexual union, Aristophanes is led to establish a complete typology of the sexual life of human beings (*Symp*. 191d–192b), in which there is a place not only for "heterosexuality," but also for "homosexuality," both masculine and feminine.

In each case, the wish is the same: to unite definitively with one's complementary half (*Symp*. 192e–193b). In this conclusion, one finds themes similar to those that characterize the myth of Prometheus in Hesiod and the Titanic race in Orphism. (1) There is no absolute origin of human beings. (2) Relations between the gods and human beings were much stronger in the distant past. (3) This proximity engendered tensions and struggles, and it is the gods who win. (4) The result was a lessening of the strength of human beings, who are henceforth opposed as mortals to the gods, who are immortal. (5) Mortality imposes two things upon human beings today: (a) they must unite sexually to perpetuate; and (b) they must work or occupy themselves with political affairs, with woman being relegated to the private sphere. (6) The entire problem consisted in maintaining a proper distance between the gods and the animals. Once again, the origin of mankind is not considered as a question of creation, but as one of localization within a continuum of living beings. Mankind is defined by its position with regard to the gods and to the animals.

Consequences at the Level of Ethics

One can derive a few common points from the analysis of these three testimonies. These myths concern not precisely the origin of human beings, but the origin of the human condition, which demands that the place of human being be defined, on the one hand with regard to the gods, and on the other with regard to animals.

The Mythical Scenario. Let us recall the development of the scenario of the inauguration of the human condition:

1) Mankind does not appear suddenly out of nothing.

2) Several "races" of human beings exist before our own.

3) Human beings of the previous races had a life more similar to that of the gods; they seem to be exempt, if not from death, then at least from suffering and work.

4) They were more powerful than current human beings, and at any rate powerful enough, if not to attack the gods, then at least to confront them by obtaining the support of other gods. In fact, man does not oppose the gods, but takes sides with one group of gods against another.

5) The origin of our race is linked, one way or another, to the Titans (and sometimes to the Giants as well) who confronted Zeus and his siblings.

6) Our race, which is therefore mortal and weaker than the preceding ones, appears as the result of a process of separation, which implies a division into a hierarchy.

7) The symbol of this separation is bloody sacrifice, in which the separation between mortal men and immortal gods is recalled by the distribution of the parts of the victim: a) to the gods go the bones and fat which are not eaten, and b) everything else, especially the meat and edible entrails, goes to human beings. The gods have no need of food to survive, whereas it is a necessity for human beings.

8) Fire prevents man from falling to the level of beasts who eat their meat raw, use no technology, and offer no sacrifices to the gods.

9) Sexual reproduction enables the human species to ensure its survival. Sexual reproduction implies a clear distinction between men and women, their proper roles and their functions.

10) Fashioned in order to ensure the perpetuity of the human species, woman is in a way alien to man, or at least distinct from and inferior to him.

11) Man must find food to feed his wife and children, which is why he is constrained to work.

12) The human condition is associated with evil as a result of the first woman's opening the jar, but hope subsists and makes life bearable.

As I have said, the appearance of human beings in Greek mythology is progressive, and akin to a process of increasing differentiation. It implies a growing hierarchizing between human beings, on the one hand, and animals on the other. Finally, fire enables human beings to establish relations with the gods (through sacrifice), among human beings (through work), and to distinguish themselves from beasts, but it also marks the definitive separation of human beings from the gods and the need for work. In addition, human beings of our time are always weaker than those of previous races, and above all they are mortal. It is woman who, because she can ensure the survival, not of the individual, but of the species, is the most important marker of the human condition. It should therefore be emphasized that myths in ancient Greece describe the origin not of mankind, but of the human condition.

Ethical Consequences. This has two important consequences from the viewpoint of ethics. In *Genesis*, God creates man in his image, which implies that every man, even the most degenerate, handicapped, impoverished, can claim a dignity equal to that of any other man, for he is, like any other man, a creature of God. In ancient Greece, by contrast, human beings, who are inferior to the gods but superior to animals, appear like some kind of fruit, and have in themselves no value given in advance; it is up to them to make the best of what nature has given them, and to develop it. Nothing justifies their value *a priori*. A man's value depends on what nature has given him at the outset, and on the success he has encountered by developing his natural gifts. In this perspective, a human being's value is established as a function of his rank in a social hierarchy recognized by all, whatever the means of achieving it; this can explain why, for instance, neither Plato nor Aristotle condemned slavery.

In one passage from *Genesis*, woman is derived from man, which places her, if not on an equal level, then at least at the same anthropological level. In ancient Greece, by contrast, woman is fashioned from earth by Hephaestus, independently of other human beings. There is therefore a gulf between man and woman, which implies a radical ontological difference. Hephaestus fashions woman not as a different human being, but as a solution to a problem raised by the emergence of a new stage in the human condition that demands sexual reproduction. There can therefore be no question of equality or equivalent dignity between men and women. One will have to await Plato who defines human beings by their soul rather than their body in the *Republic*, to reduce this distance. If the essential element in every human being is the soul, then men and women are on a level of ontological equality, with the residual difference being explained by the body with which that soul is associated.

To conclude, the status accorded to human beings in general and to women in particular by ethics, and not merely by popular ethics, depends on the myth that describes whence man and woman derive. This shows, once again, that the most rigorous and rationalistic philosophy, including that of Plato or Aristotle, depends more or less directly on a religious or mythical tradition, whatever the chosen term may be. This amounts to saying that philosophy is rooted in tradition, that is, in the values and the beliefs shared by all members of a community or by most of them.

Appendix

An attempt has been made to interpret as a myth of the origin of mankind the tale of the appearance of the Titanic race, based on a single item of information transmitted by a *Commentary on Plato's Phaedo* now attributed to a certain Olympiodorus, whose identity is still a matter of debate. Born between 495 and 505 CE, Olympiodorus is thought to have died shortly after 565. A disciple of Ammonius at Alexandria, he succeeded to the chair of philosophy around 541. The essential part of his activity was situated in that city, and there are many indications that allow us to suppose that although a large part of his audience was made up of Christians, Olympiodorus never converted to Christianity. However, he was able to display his differences from the beliefs of his auditors.

It is not known when Olympiodorus wrote his *Commentary on the Phaedo*. Yet he had before him a third version of the commentary by Damascius, which differed from the other two. This is why the commentary by Olympiodorus cannot be confused with that of Damascius, as L. G. Westerink has shown.[11] For his part, Damascius took much of his inspiration from the commentary of Proclus, in which the latter must have taken up the teachings of his master Syrianus. Yet as Damascius does not hesitate to criticize Proclus and Syrianus, Olympiodorus shows genuine originality not only with regard to Proclus and Syrianus, but also to Damascius. Nevertheless, one may suppose that this Neoplatonic Olympiodorus is the same as the author of a commentary on the *Katâ enérgeian* of Zosimus.

The passage that concerns us is found at the very beginning of the Commentary, where Olympiodorus enquires into Socrates's condemnation of suicide (61c–62c). Olympiodorus will comment on this condemnation by invoking several kinds of arguments, particularly the one qualified as "mythical," which appears in this form:

> The mythical argument [against suicide] is as follows: in the Orphic tradition we hear of four reigns. The first is that of Uranus, to which Kronos succeeds after emasculating his father; after Kronos, Zeus becomes king having hurled down

his father into Tartarus; then Zeus is succeeded by Dionysus, whom, they say, his retainers the Titans tear to pieces through Hera's plotting, and they eat his flesh. Zeus, incensed, strikes them with his thunderbolts, and the soot of the vapors that rise from them becomes the matter from which men are created. Therefore suicide is forbidden, not because, as the text appears to say, we wear the body as a kind of shackle, for that is manifest, and Socrates would not call it an esoteric doctrine; but it is forbidden because our bodies belong to Dionysus; we are, in fact, a part of him, being made of the soot of the Titans who ate his flesh. (*In Phaed.* I, par. 3-4, transl. Westerink)

In a previous article I explained why I thought the explanation presented by Olympiodorus implied an alchemical interpretation of the Orphic myth.[12] In addition, this commentary differs from all other Neoplatonic commentaries concerning the condemnation of suicide, for it deals not with the soul, which defines man for Plato and all Platonists, but with the body. Suicide concerns the body, not the soul; and according to Olympiodorus, one must not attack the human body, for the human body comes from Dionysus, a god considered in a positive way. This, then, is a myth that concerns not the origin of mankind, but the respect due to the human body.

Notes

1. Translations are from The Holy Bible, 21st-Century King James Version. Gary, SD: Deuel Enterprises, Inc., 1994.

2. I shall not enter here into the question of whether the myth Plato gives to his character Aristophanes has roots in ideas derived from the historical Aristophanes. Nor I shall take into consideration the many tales of human beings born from the earth, most of which belong to myths of autochthony, for in such myths it is not the origin of human beings that is at stake, but a territorial claim, with the descendants of the human beings who emerged from the earth claiming exclusive ownership of the territory from which their ancestors emerged. See further Loraux 1979.

3. Vernant 1974/1990.

4. Vernant 1974/1990, 177-94.

5. Both the need to work and the need to reproduce sexually are aspects of the Genesis myths, though the reason for these necessities is different.

6. Translations of Hesiod are taken from Most 2006.

7. In any case, one should note the contrast between woman as a gift-trap and the Genesis account of woman as a gift-companion to man. But in Genesis, Eve succumbs to the temptation to eat the forbidden fruit and shares it with Adam. They were expelled from Eden, and their actions had consequences on the rest of humanity: for men working by the sweat of his brow, and for women, bringing forth children and being ruled by her husband. On this issue, there are many similarities between the two stories.

8. Translation by Most, slightly modified.

9. West 1983. Numbering of fragments are those of Kern 1922 and Berubé 2005.

10. Brisson 2002, 73–85.

11. Westerink 1976.

12. Brisson 1992.

4

Muthos and *Logos* on New Year's Day
Trial and Error in Anaximander's Seasonal Sundial[1]

Robert Hahn

It is well-known to all readers of Copernicus's *De revolutionibus* that his innovative astronomical hypothesis emerged serendipitously from the practical task of reforming the calendar.[2] The calendar that was then in use was off by at least nine days, and in a system of indulgences where a person's salvation rested quite literally on the performance of certain prayers and rituals on a specified date, the reformation of the calendar was indispensable to the path of the faithful. The required ritual was to be performed when the time was right, but just when was "when?" Could it have been calendar reform, *ceteris paribus*, that motivated Anaximander of Miletos to invent a *seasonal* sundial, and serendipitously to foster his own innovative astronomical hypothesis?

In this essay I shall: (A) explore the issue of calendar reform, the idea of a *seasonal* sundial, and its specific *muthos* and *logos* connection to New Year's Day for Anaximander; (B) reconstruct Anaximander's sundial, exhibiting the trial and error that was required to make it; and (C) illuminate the context of Anaximander's sundial and prose writings in light of Archaic architectural prose treatises and the analogous success of their trial-and-error experiments that they discussed in their books.

The Calendar and New Year's Day

I take it as established since the time of Cornford's 1952 publication of *Principium Sapientiae* that Anaximander's cosmological thought is fundamentally a naturalistic and rational version of Hesiod's *Theogony*, and that Hesiod's cosmic reflections are Hellenized versions of the Babylonian mythological cosmogony enumerated in the *Enuma elish*.[3] Cornford sought to clarify the mythical and ritual origins of Greek philosophy. Against a prevailing view in the early twentieth century that Greek philosophy began *ex nihilo*—the Greek Miracle—Cornford's *Principium Sapientiae* makes the case that Anaximander's thought emerges from this earlier context, is rooted in it, and belongs to a continuous sequence of the development of this historical thought.[4]

In order to explain the present world order, which is not now as it had been in the "beginning," the *Enuma elish* tells of the creation of the world and the stages that subsequently led to our world today. Since it was recited during the New Year's festival in the first month of the year, the month of Nisanu, and tells the story of the beginning of the world, the *Enuma elish* celebrates New Year's Day. After all, if the world has a beginning, it was created on *some* day, and in the annual procession of days, that "first" day coincides each year with some day assigned in the calendar. So, what day was it? When was New Year's Day? For the ancient Babylonians it was the first day of Nisanu—New Year's Day—a month that began in close relation to the vernal equinox.[5] But we have no evidence that the Babylonians made a *seasonal* sundial, a device that would have identified the day of the vernal equinox. From the secure evidence we do have, the Babylonians seem to have determined the equinox mathematically, confirmed roughly by observations.[6]

In the *Enuma elish*, Marduk triumphs over Tiamat, the female goddess who presides over disorder. Marduk slays Tiamat and separates out the sky and earth, regulates the place and movements of the stars, fixes the year and months, and apportions privileges and destinies. Cornford argued that in Hesiod's Hellenization of the Babylonian myth, Zeus triumphs over Typhon, the creator of disorder, the hundred-headed snake, the dragon with a myriad of fearful voices; in slaying Typhon the corpse gives rise to the winds in the space separating sky from earth.[7] But in a way highly relevant to the emergence of *logos* from *muthos* and the complex relationship between them, the beginning of the world according to Hesiod's *Theogony* is revealed in two accounts, one mythological and anthropomorphized, and the other more abstract and general. While the one account involves the triumph of Zeus over Typhon, as Marduk slays Tiamat in the Babylonian epic, in another passage of Hesiod the beginning of the world is marked by *chaos*, the yawning gap, the dark abyss, before *Eros* comes into being to account for creation of the things in our world.[8] In both accounts, however, Hesiod's narrative is genealogical.

In contradistinction, Anaximander's narrative is strictly natural and rational, a point defenders of the Greek Miracle were quick to make. Anaximander's cosmos begins with an undifferentiated *apeiron*, a separation out of the hot and cold and the wet and dry in a world of perpetual change. The heavens come to attain a structure in this process, with the cold and wet moving to the center and the hot and dry moving to the extremities. But, Cornford argued, in all three accounts there is an original and primordial unity that is the common origin of all things, and from which elements separate out; there is perpetual motion; and there is a constant struggle against and uniting of opposites.[9] Thus, from the time of Cornford's *Principium Sapientiae*, the ideas underlying Anaximander's thought are shown to be derived in continuity—rather than miraculous intervention—through Hesiod from the mythical cosmogony of the *Enuma elish*, a work that was generated as a reflection on the New Year's festival. And since we know that in Anaximander's book(s), he discussed the very *beginning* of the cosmos and the stages that led to the present world order, his natural and rational narrative in prose was perforce a reflection upon and celebration of New Year's Day.

But just when was New Year's Day in Archaic Miletos? How did the Milesians know when that day had arrived? It was announced in relation to the vernal equinox. The new moon following the vernal equinox marked the new month of Taureon (= att. Mounuchion) the first month of the Milesian year, the first day being New Year's Day.[13] But how could Anaximander and his compatriots have been sure that the spring equinox had already arrived? Surely a seasonal sundial could have secured this result. Perhaps, then, it could have been through the making of a *seasonal* sundial—an invention made through a *logos* not *muthos*, constructed carefully through trial and error—that Anaximander solved practically the challenge of the *muthos* of the New Year's Day festival, to know when to celebrate New Year's Day, and thus when to acknowledge the very beginning of the cosmos that he identified and explored in his book. Could the challenge of calendar reform have led unexpectedly to Anaximander's novel astronomical hypothesis, where, for the first time, the cosmic picture envisions the sun most distant from us, behind the moon, and the moon behind the stars that already are so very far from us—a vision of immense depth in astronomical space? This astronomical hypothesis was as new in Anaximander's day as Copernicus's hypothesis had been in his own day, also an unexpected consequence of calendar reform.

The calendars in Archaic Greek cities exhibited both diversity and disarray.[11] We have evidence for lunar calendars of "months," for solar calendars of "years," and civil and festival calendars codependent on both.[12] Lunar calendars, as a matter of fact, do not coincide with solar calendars, and many inscriptions that do survive indicate proposals of intercalary calculations to bring these calendars into agreement.[13] Moreover, not only were the calendars in constant need of adjustment but throughout the Greek world New Year's Day was celebrated at different times of the year—*but always following a seasonal marker such as a solstice or equinox*. The very idea of a "calendar" then, posed for the Archaic Greek communities a problem of the "One over Many," a search for some underlying unity of days to provide for the demands of social and ritual regularities. This problem was on a par with two others that were addressed contemporaneously in Archaic Greece. One innovation dating to Archaic times is the invention of coinage,[14] a solution to a problem of the One over Many, a way to identify a standard against which the vicissitudes of value could be reckoned. Coinage identified and certified a standard of quantity and quality, and although born in Lydia in the second half of the seventh century BCE, it soon was embraced in Miletos as the existence of electrum, gold, and silver staters prove in the first-half of the sixth century BCE. A second contemporaneous example of a search for One over Many arose in the new enterprise of monumental stone architecture when the success of temple building required a "module," a basic architectural unit in terms of which the other structural dimensions could be reckoned as multiples or submultiples in order to produce the desired aesthetic effect.[15] The Archaic architects of the great Ionic temples of the sixth century selected as their module "column-drum diameter," the very same module that Anaximander selected—having identified the shape and size of the earth with a 3 × 1 drum[16]—to construct his model of the cosmos, and to measure the distances to the heavenly wheels (stars, moon, and sun).[17]

To think about ancient calendars, then, is a formidable task. The making of a calendar required an astronomical vision, a grasping of the motions in the heavens, most especially for the Archaic Greeks of the moon and the sun. The cycle of the moon extends for twenty-eight to thirty days, unlike the solar year that was more than three-hundred-and-sixty days. The comparative shortness of the lunar cycle, and the easy observations of the moon in a region that experiences more than three-hundred mostly cloudless days per annum, were familiar to the entire population. But the careful plotting of the days that defined the months by the reappearance of new moon, or even full moon, was not commensurate with the cycle of the solar year. If a society made their "year" to consist in twelve lunar cycles, then within the normal life span of a person the New Year celebrated during one lunar month marking the beginning of one of the seasons would later appear in a different season altogether. Thus, societies that tried to make their calendar to accord with the lunar cycles had to improvise in a variety of intercalations to have it accord with the seasons that were incremental to a solar reckoning and the agricultural realities that were assigned and dictated by it. Not surprisingly, therefore, we have evidence of Luni-Solar calendars, and they too boast a great antiquity.

In Athens and Delphi, we have evidence for the New Year beginning with the first new moon after the summer solstice; in Boeotia and Delos after the winter solstice; in Sparta, Rhodes, and Crete after the autumnal equinox. In Chios, the New Year began after the vernal equinox.[18] Miletos posed a problem for historians that has now been corrected. New Year's Day for the Archaic Milesians had been thought to follow the autumnal equinox.[19] We now know, based on a fifth century BCE vase from Olbia inscribed with the Milesian calendar, that the New Year began with Taureon, the month that begins following the vernal equinox. Olbia was a Milesian colony, and it was customary for the calendars of colonies to be identical with those of the metropolis, that is, the founding city.[20] In any case, the key point for our discussion is that the New Year was customarily fixed in relation to a solstice or equinox, and so was determined by a *solar* calendar.[21] Of course, there are times during the year when a new moon appears preciously close to one of these solar markers. With cloudy weather, and/or even the difference of a day when the solstice or equinox arrives, the whole calendar ran the risk, without a careful determination of the equinox or solstice, to have been set back a full month, and thus cast into further disarray. To resolve the problem of New Year's Day, then, was to resolve the problem of the year itself, and the festival, sacrificial, and prayer calendars that were required by the Olympian religion.

The importance of the reform of Archaic calendars reflects plausibly a theme in Greek society and religion—announced in the surviving literature—of great import and relevant to the emergence of *logos* from *muthos*. The Greeks prized a peculiar meaning of "time" that they understood by the term *kairos*. We might render this term *critical time*. For it was not enough to know what to do, that something needed to be done, but what was prized most highly was knowing precisely *when* to do it. The meaning of goodness, of excellence, was tied inextricably to the notion of critical timing. And in a manner analogous to the indulgences that were required of the faithful who hoped to attain salvation in the time of Copernicus, the Greek tradition provides cautionary tales of the sorry consequences that befell a man who was unable to know when to perform the required task at the required, critical time. In the *Pythian Odes*, Pindar reminds his audience that ". . . in the hands of men, the fitting moment (*kairos*) has a brief limit of time . . ." and the sad result occurs when a man misses this moment.[22] In the *Electra*,[23] Sophocles relates Orestes's surmise of striking at just the right critical moment (*kairos*) to avenge the death of his father Agamemnon. In the *Republic*,[24] Plato has Socrates emphasize the importance of critical time (*kairos*) in doing one's work well, to realize his own nature (*eu prattein*) and so become happy. In the *Philebus*,[25] Plato has Socrates award first-prize in the assessment of essential ingredients of the good life to measure, measurement, and critical time (*kairos*), not the Forms. And in his *Histories*, Thucydides echoes the same theme, in reflecting on the Athenians' dealings with the Spartans,[26] and again when Pericles stepped onto a high platform to begin his funeral oration,[27] or yet again when the Athenian army was stranded on the Peloponnesus facing grave hardships;[28] it was not enough to know the right thing to do but, moreover, knowing the critical moment (*kairos*) to do it that would separate success from doom and gloom. Finally, we have evidence in festival and sacrificial calendars that identified the required rituals to be performed if a man was to propitiate divine wrath or discover divine inclinations.[29] Such calendars suggest an analogous relation to the calendars that regulated indulgences in the time of Copernicus.

In all these instances, we are reminded that for the ancient Greeks it was not enough to know the right thing to do if you did not know the critical time to do it. But this is just the point: *When* exactly was the right time? In the realm of the faithful, with the calendars both diverse and in constant disarray throughout Greece, it could not have been easy for a practitioner of Olympian religion to know just when "when" was. A *seasonal* sundial would have been most welcome; it would have contributed to the triumph of order over disorder, as Zeus slew Typhon, as Marduk slew Tiamat, in the very beginning of the world, on New Year's Day. Was Anaximander's invention of a *seasonal* sundial—analogous to the resolution of "One over Many" challenges in the invention of coinage, monumental architecture, and his own hypothesis of the *apeiron*[30] as that which from which the world began—motivated to reform the calendar and to ensure the knowledge of New Year's Day, the day the cosmos began and about which he wrote in his book, the first philosophical treatise in prose? Was his motivation, in other words, not to break (miraculously or otherwise) with mythological thinking, but rather an attempt to preserve the goal of such thinking by placing it on a more secure foundation?

The Development of Anaximander's Sundial: Trials and Errors and Experimental Techniques

We have two reports that Anaximander made a *seasonal* sundial. One report comes from Diogenes Laertius;[31] on the authority of Favorinus, Anaximander discovered the gnomon and set one up on the sundials in Sparta to measure the solstices and equinoxes, and it also had hour indicators. Another report comes from the *Suda*;[32] Anaximander discovered the equinox, solstices, and hour indicators . . . and he introduced the gnomon. The discovery or introduction of the gnomon is made in the same report as the discovery and measurement of the sun's turnings (solstices) and the point when there is equal day and equal night (equinoxes). And it is of great importance to note also that in the very same passage Anaximander is credited with making a map of the world and also a model or drawing of the cosmos. Diogenes Laertius credits him with making a *perimetron* of the earth and sea and also a *sphairos*, while the Suda mentions *gês periodon* (a work on the map of the earth) and a *sphairos*. And in two other passages, Agathemerus credits Anaximander with making a *pinax* of the *oikoumenê*,[33] and Strabo mentions also the *pinax* that was perfected further by Hecataeus.[34] So, what we have are reports that Anaximander invented a *seasonal* sundial connected to some introduction or invention of a gnomon, and in the same passages, supplanted by other reports, Anaximander made a map of the earth and some kind of model or drawing of the cosmos. The case I propose to make plausible is that they were all integrally connected; indeed, all these ingredients plausibly came together to make one and the same thing—a seasonal sundial, map, and model with a specially measured gnomon set in the center, perhaps in Sparta. Let us explore these ideas.

In *Anaximander and the Architects*,[35] I attempted to reconstruct Anaximander's sundial following the suggestion by Sharon Gibbs in *Greek and Roman Sundials*.[36] Gibbs suggested that the markings found inside the

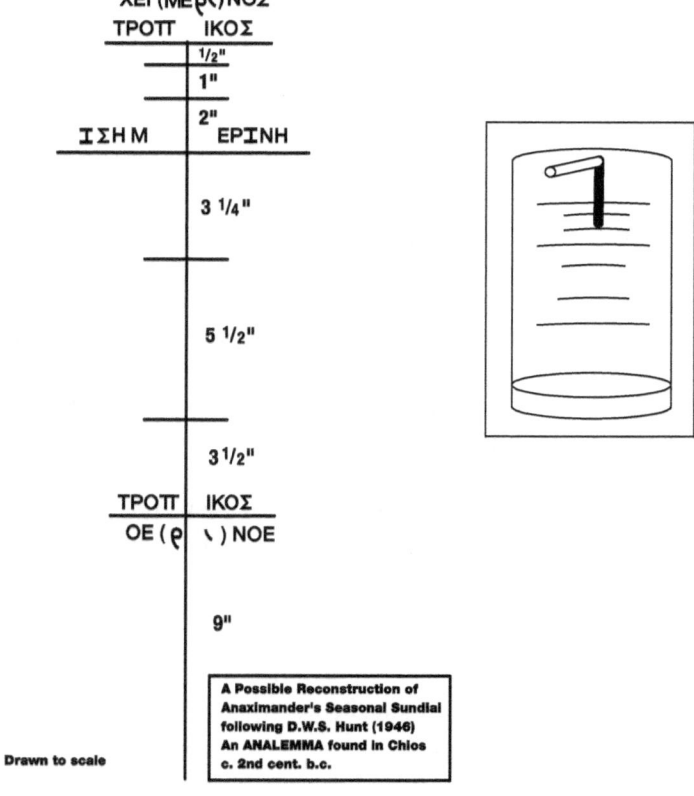

Figure 4.1. A possible reconstruction of Anaximander's sundial with the gnomon set horizontally pointing southward and casting shadows on the north wall of a well in Chios.

north wall of a well on Chios, although too late to be Anaximander's design, displayed the essential ingredients of a "seasonal" sundial. With a gnomon, pointing south, set *horizontally* into the north wall of the well, the deepest shadow in the well marked the summer solstice and the shortest shadow marked the winter solstice. Having reconstructed the markings in the well, it was clear also that the "equinox" shadow was not midway between the two but rather closer to the winter solstice marker.

I am in agreement with Gibbs that these are relevant markers for the sundial attributed to Anaximander. But, after working for a number of seasons with students in Greece making sundials, I became convinced that this proposed design was mistaken. While it is true that, as Gibbs shows, the earliest surviving Greek sundials date to Hellenistic times, and their designs are either hemispherical or conical, it seems more fitting for Anaximander to have used a gnomon set *vertically*, not horizontally; and in the process of reflecting upon a design appropriate both to Anaximander and to the sixth century BCE, I now propose a new hypothesis of the design Anaximander plausibly made.

In light of a review of the reports mentioning together the gnomon, the sundial, the map of the earth, and the model of the cosmos, let us begin again by thinking of Anaximander's sundial face as a column drum. Why? Because Anaximander had described the earth as a flat disk, analogous with it,[37] it seems clear that he realized that the shadows cast on the column drum would be analogous to the shadows cast on the Earth itself, a microcosm of the macrocosm.[38] And furthermore, as will become clearer, the sun-shadow markings would provide clues for the *map* with which Anaximander is also credited, since some sundial markings were key to the making of a "frame" for it. And since the shadows marked by the sundial were caused by the sun, the most distant heavenly wheels in Anaximander's cosmos, a visualization could be inferred by means of those shadow markings. *The sundial, then, holds the key to connecting the earthly map and the cosmic map.*

Let us be clear about what a prepared column drum looked like, the image that so greatly impressed Anaximander and members of his Archaic community. Below is, on the left is a reconstructed column drum from the Archaic temple of Apollo at Didyma (note the round *empolion* in the center, and the *anathyrôsis* band along the circumference), on the right is a column drum from the Archaic temple of Hera in Samos, Dipteros II, where the *empolion* is rectangular, not circular, but the *anathyrôsis* band runs around the circumference of the drum.

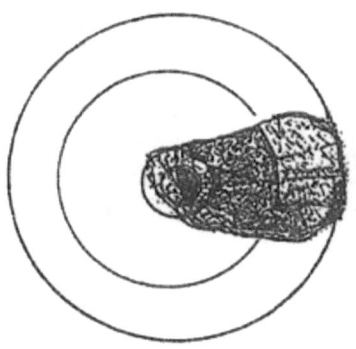 

Figure 4.2. Drum fragment from the Archaic Didymaion exhibiting *anathyrôsis* and a round *empolion* (*l*), and next to it (*r*) a drum exhibiting *anathyrôsis* found in Samos from Dipteros II.

Let us also be clear on how the drum would be installed, and thus the purpose of *anathyrôsis* and *empolion*. The drum would have had "bosses"—stone extrusions—on all four sides, in the process of production, and ropes would have been placed around the bosses so that the drum could be lowered into place. A wooden, and sometimes metal, dowel would be placed in the drum as it was lowered—this is the *empolion*—ensuring that both upper and lower drums would be installed perfectly, the new drum sitting on the smoothed band (like the one around a doorway, hence called *anathyrôsis*). Thus, the concentric circles on the drum face ensured that the center was equidistant from the center, and the smoothed surface running around each drum ensured a perfectly smooth fit. Once the drums touch, there is no more movement for fear of chipping the drums. After installation, in the stages of finishing, the bosses would be removed.

Let us now explore this sundial construction further by imagining that in the center of a column drum where the architect's *empolion* would be placed, Anaximander placed a gnomon, set vertically.[39] Let us now imagine plotting the *shortest shadow each day*, which we can call "local noon." The sun reaches its zenith each day at local noon; it is highest in the sky when it is due south, and consequently casts the shortest shadow of the day off a vertically-placed gnomon. If we make a line perpendicular to those shadow markings, we not only create a

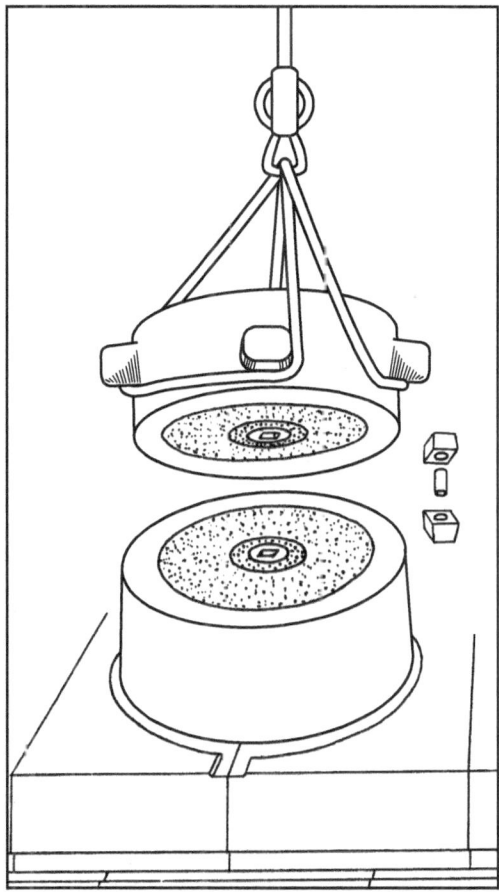

Figure 4.3. Column-drum installation—*anathyrôsis* and *empolion* are exhibited as well as drum bosses and use of rope with lifting device, after Orlandos. The *anathyrôsis* and *empolion* technique allowed for each drum to be lined up perfectly, the circumference equidistant from the center, controlled by inner circular rings.

diameter by bisecting the (column-drum face) circle but the line will be due East-West. Thus, the local noon shadow markings will appear in the "northern half of the semi-circle" of that circular column-drum face, perpendicular to a straight-line diameter bisecting the column-drum face running East-West. To realize the geometry of this astronomy requires careful observations, confirmed over the course of time.

Now that we have in mind what a prepared column-drum face looked like, and the basics of its installation, let us take a look at how a drum would look with a gnomon in the place of the *empolion*. Since Anaximander imagined the shape and size of the earth by analogy with a column drum, the shadows cast on the drum by the gnomon would be analogous to the earth itself; the markings enabling Anaximander to make a map. The underlying principle is geometrical similarity; the sundial/column-drum has the same shape and markings as the earth itself, with which it is similar.

The *shortest* of all the short shadows over the course of the whole year marks the summer solstice, and the *longest of the short shadows* marks the winter solstice. When we identify the equinox by modern methods, it is plainly clear that the short shadow on the day of the equinox is *not* midway between the shortest and longest "local noon" markers—it is closer to the shortest of the shadows (i.e., it is closer to the summer solstice marker, and not closer to the winter solstice marker as it is when the gnomon is set horizontally). So, it remains for us to consider how Anaximander might have reckoned exactly *when* the equinox occurred, if indeed he had done so.

Now, let us turn for a moment to begin a consideration of Anaximander's map. This is complicated, first of all, because Agathemerus and Strabo report that he made a *pinax* of the *oikoumenê*, while Diogenes says

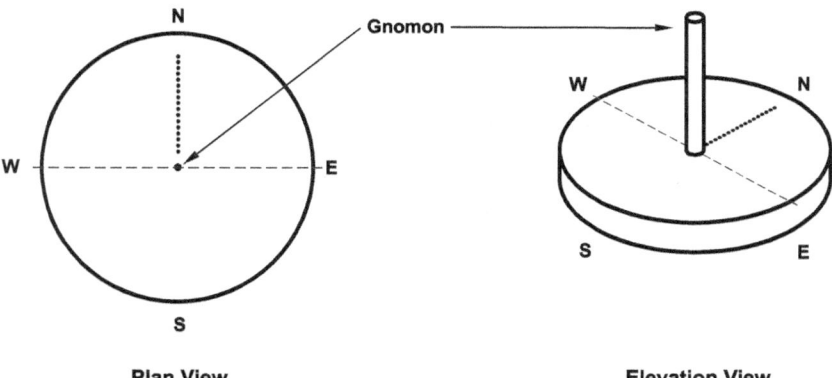

Figure 4.4. Circle/column-drum face bisected East-West with many local noon points running North-South.

Muthos and *Logos* on New Year's Day

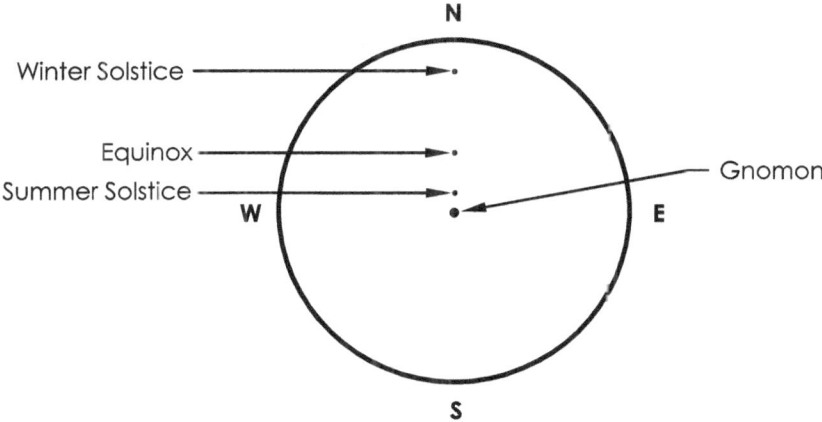

Figure 4.5. Circle/column-drum face with only three shadow points: Summer Solstice, Equinox, and Winter Solstice.

that he made a *perimetron* of the earth and seas.⁴⁰ The complication is that, on the one hand, he made a map of the inhabited earth, and on the other, he made a map of the Earth that would certainly include the uninhabitable realms, and so quite a different map.⁴¹ But for the moment, let us just consider some outlines on the column-drum face to supply the reference frame for the map. A conventional approach has taken its lead from Heidel, namely, that to make a map one needs to make a "frame," and this is made by constructing a rectangle using the rising and setting points of the sun, against the horizon, on the summer and winter solstices, and the equinox.⁴² Heidel took up Aristotle's explanation in the *Meteorologica*⁴³ of just these markers to make an earthly frame, and in a simplified form, below, this idea is illustrated.

The key element that has been neglected in the discussion is the reckoning of the *center* as well as the outside frame. Once considered, the whole picture is transformed. And so the question remains: How did Anaximander conclude where the center was on this flat-disk Earth? How did he determine where *he*, the observer, was on the flat disk? And how did he reach those conclusions? The answer to be explored here is that his sundial revealed it to him, and in turn he revealed it to his community in a book that almost certainly discussed it.

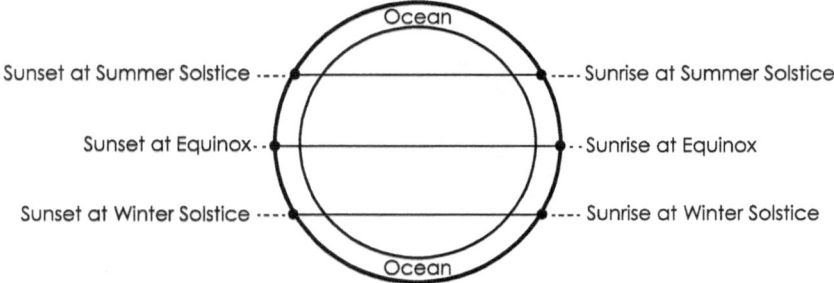

Figure 4.6. Anaximander's Earth with Sun risings and settings on Solstices and Equinox.

So what did Anaximander's sundial look like? The earliest surviving Greek sundials date to Hellenistic times and are either hemispherical or conical. These sundial shapes make sense if the designer is imagining a spherical Earth and a domed-shaped heaven, but not for Anaximander who imagined the shape of the Earth as a column drum and the Earth and heavenly wheels forming a great tree, though encompassed within a spherical canopy.[44] Are there any ancient artifacts that offer a clue? There is an artifact, usually taken to be a sundial but whose identity is uncertain, dating to the first century BCE and found in Qumran, along with the Dead Sea Scrolls. The scientific interpretation of this "sundial" has been the subject of considerable debate, but the conjecture here is that Anaximander's "sundial" had a very similar appearance, whether or not the identity of the artifact in Qumran is eventually definitively revealed.[45]

Having already plotted the "local noon" shadows cast by a vertical gnomon, let us take those distances as radii and make concentric circles with the gnomon at the center (i.e., the gnomon hole would have been round like the *empolia* in Archaic column drums from Didyma![46]): the smaller circle was made by taking as radius the distance from the gnomon to the shortest of the short shadow markers (= summer solstice marker), and the second was made using the radius from the gnomon to the longest of the short shadow markers (= winter solstice marker). The "frame" of Anaximander's map consisted in these concentric circles plus the rectangular dimensions emphasized later by Aristotle. Anaximander's sundial, then, looks much like a column-drum face prepared by the

Muthos and *Logos* on New Year's Day   109

Figure 4 7. Artifact, possibly a sundial, found at Qumran, first century BCE.

Archaic architects but, perhaps, without *anathyrōsis*,⁴⁷ unless one wishes to preserve "Ocean" running around the outside of Anaximander's map, a tradition that Ionian cartographers embraced, according to Herodotus. Indeed, Herodotus ridiculed the early map-makers who made Ocean running round the circumference *apo tornou*, as if it had been "turned on a lathe" (or "traced with a compass").⁴⁸ We know from archaeological reports that Archaic drums in Samos *were* turned on lathes, and it is perfectly plausible that not only the sundial circumference, but also the inner concentric lines were turned on a lathe.⁴⁹ Thus far, then, the reconstruction conjectured is that Anaximander's sundial looked just like a column drum, with at least two concentric circles to represent the solstices, and a third between them (but not uniformly) marking the equinox. The original sundial might even have displayed *anathyrōsis*/ Ocean. Indeed, the winter solstice circle might be coincidental with the inside-circle of the *anathyrōsis*/Ocean band. There may also have been quite a number of examples Anaximander's sundial design, and some of them might have displayed only markers for solstices, while others had also the equinox marking, and even hours. Some versions may have had only two or three concentric circles, and thus it seems quite plausible that the archaeologists might have missed identifying Anaximander's sundial because it would have resembled closely a prepared column-drum face.

Next, let us consider the reports that Anaximander "discovered" or "introduced" the gnomon, according to Diogenes Laertius and the *Suda*. Scholarly opinion has dismissed the reports on the grounds that we have evidence for the use of the gnomon much earlier by the Babylonians, and perhaps also by the Egyptians.[50] But, let us try to see these doxographical reports in a different light. Anaximander did *something* with a gnomon that was judged to be "original." Can we make any sense of this? The report in Diogenes is that Anaximander set up his gnomon "*epi tôn skiotêrôn*" in Sparta. I take this to suggest that there was a place in Sparta where other "sundials" (= shadow-catchers) were already set up,[51] and almost certainly they indicated some sort of "hour-markers." And the proposal here is that Anaximander's innovation was to mark the *solstices* and the *equinox(es)* and from those markings to "frame" his map.

Let us now turn to some considerations about the length of *his* gnomon. Since the numbers 9 and 10 had special meaning for Anaximander,[52] it seemed like a promising starting place to consider that his

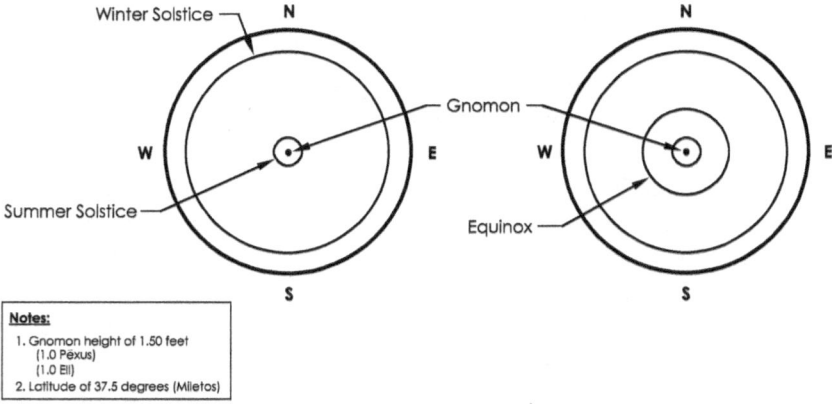

Figure 4.8. Anaximander's sundial with two concentric circles, Summer and Winter Solstices (*l*); Anaximander's sundial with three concentric circles, Summer, Winter Solstices, Equinox (*r*).

gnomon was 9 or 10 feet (or ells) in length. When shadow-lengths were calculated, both '9' and '10' feet or ells could be ruled out since, then, Anaximander would have needed a "field"—literally a horizontal surface more than 30 feet in diameter to contain the measurements of the winter solstice shadow. It is of course possible that Anaximander's "sundial face" was an "open-field," but it seemed increasingly doubtful. not only because the working hypothesis now under consideration was that the sundial face had concentric circles (far more difficult to produce precisely on a 30-foot field!) but also because it is difficult to imagine any way to fix the position of a vertical rod 9- or 10-feet tall in the windy conditions of Greece. The gnomon must remain motionless if the sundial is to be useful. Moreover, because it seemed plausible to imagine the sundial as part of a model, perhaps the earliest example of what we have come to call a planetarium, such a tall gnomon could be ruled out. If the sundial was also connected to the map and model, a much shorter gnomon would have been required. So let us continue our reconstruction comparing gnomon sizes of 1 ell, 1 foot, and .5 feet, and the resulting local noon shadows that would be cast corresponding to them for Miletos and Sparta. By modern-day measurement, with Miletos at 37.5 degrees North latitude, and Sparta at 37.31 degrees North latitude, we can see that the inscribed circles for summer and winter solstices would have been virtually identical in both locations. Using a gnomon of 1.5 feet (= 1 ell), the shadow length on the summer solstice in Miletos was 0.374 feet, and in Sparta using a gnomon the same size, the shadow would be 0.369 feet. Had the gnomon been 1 foot in height, the same comparative shadow lengths would have been 0.249 ft. in Miletos and 0.246 ft. in Sparta. And if Anaximander had used a significantly smaller gnomon, let us say of .5 feet, the difference of marking the summer solstice radii (0.125 feet in Miletos and 0.123 feet in Sparta) would have amounted to a mere 2 thousandths of an inch (0.0024 inches)!

Of course, the gnomon would need to have been very slender and have had a very sharp point to deliver these exacting results, and the shadow marks would have had to be made by most careful observations. And had the gnomon height been *shorter* still, the inscribed circles identifying the seasonal markers would have differed from Miletos to Sparta by even less. Now, if it is neither practical nor likely that such refined measurements could be produced on a stone dial face—given the limits on sharpness of the gnomon point and the width of the inscribed circle line possibly made by means of a lathe or caliper, then for all practical

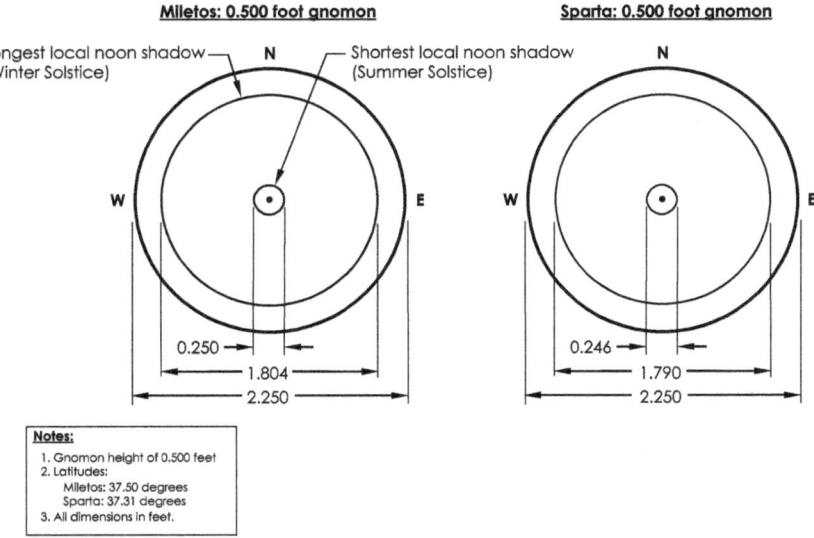

Figure 4.9. Anaximander's sundial comparative: Miletos and Sparta.

purposes the circles inscribed on column drums in Miletos and Sparta would have been virtually identical. Thus, it is tempting to propose that this is what the gnomon reports plausibly mean: Anaximander *brought with him to Sparta his own gnomon* whose seasonal markers he had already measured in Miletos. Moreover, he brought with him to Sparta measured strings to make exactly the (radii of the) concentric circles that he determined in Miletos. The use of measured string or rope is the usual measuring technique of the architects when, with great precision, they laid out the building plans of the great Ionic temples. Thus, Anaximander could make not only a "replica" of his Milesian research in Sparta, but moreover he could *test* his understanding, and of course have others marvel at his "scientific predictions." Understood in this light, Anaximander's gnomon was yet another display of the principle of "One over Many," and this one born from careful observations, not *muthoi*. Thus the finished appearance of Anaximander's sundial, then, is more or less the *same* as a prepared column-drum face—both might well have exhibited concentric circles on a flat disk.

Now let us follow through the consequences of this proposed interpretation of the doxographical reports. Since it is certainly plausible that

Muthos and *Logos* on New Year's Day 113

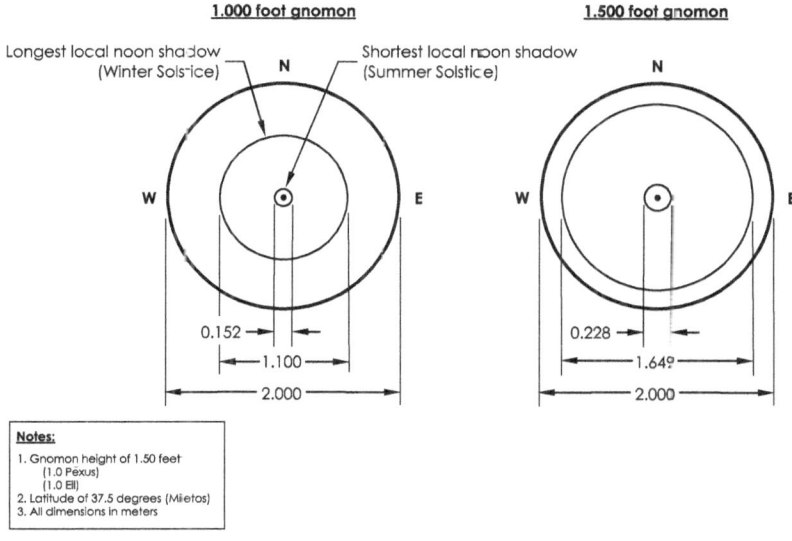

Figure 4.10. Anaximander's sundial with diameter measurements for 1.000-foot and 1.500-foot gnomons in Miletos.

Anaximander visited Naucratis since the Milesians alone of the Greeks were granted the privilege of establishing a colony in Egypt (. . . or even if he did not, he could have sent *his own gnomon* with a compatriot—perhaps Thales?) when Anaximander repeated his sundial experiment in the Nile Delta with the *same* gnomon (and the *same* string length that he verified for both solstices and equinoxes in Miletos and Sparta) he would have realized that the measurements were significantly *different* at this more southerly location. In Naucratis, the markings for the summer and winter solstices, and hence the concentric circles, appear *much closer* to the gnomon. Thus, Anaximander would have been aware that the circles appear much closer to the gnomon as he traveled south. What could this result have plausibly meant to Anaximander? Well, unlike the uniform results he experienced when he traveled east and west, from Miletos to Sparta, the results were quite different as he traveled south and north . . . *although he brought with him the same gnomon!* There is a report that Anaximander founded a colony, Apollonia, on the Black Sea.[53] There can be some doubt about his founding a colony because, had he done so, we should have expected him to be known as "*Anaximandros tou Apolloniou*" and not "*Anaximandros tou Miletou*" as he is known. But the report allows us to consider further that he was perhaps a much-traveled man and may likely have traveled northward to the Black Sea region. Had he made measurements there with *the same gnomon* he would have seen also that the summer solstice circle is significantly *larger* than at Miletos, and as he traveled south the concentric circles would become increasingly *smaller*. Could Anaximander have believed that the center of the Earth was *south* of Naucratis, and indeed south of Heliopolis? If he reached this conclusion, then, Anaximander's map may well have identified ancient Cyene (= modern day Aswan), not Delphi the *omphalos*, as the center of the earth. The key reason that can be produced that would justify such a conclusion is that if Anaximander realized that the summer solstice circle got smaller as he (or his compatriots taking his gnomon to make measurements) traveled *south*, he might have inferred that he was moving *closer to the center* of the *flat*-disk earth, and would get closer and closer still had he ventured farther south from Naucratis in Egypt. Such a train of reasoning would require that he grasped that *his* location on the earth, revealed by the outlines of the "earthly map" that in fact appeared by the shadows on the column-drum sundial face, was always *on* the circle—indeed, on the *north part of the circle!*—marking the summer solstice. When he reached the center of his projected earthly map, there would be *no* summer shadow cast on the summer solstice, and thus he would be *at the center* (*en mesôi*).

We have no independent evidence that Anaximander imagined the center of his flat Earth in southern Egypt. The plausibility that he may have thought so rests entirely on whether he realized that *his* location was always on the (northern or upper part of the) smallest concentric circle on the drum face that he inscribed in making his map, and furthermore that Miletos, Sparta, and Delphi were significantly north of center but located between the concentric circles marking the summer and winter solstices. All map-makers, ancient or modern, have to make an arbitrary judgment about where to set the "center" in making their map. Perhaps Anaximander might well have selected as the center of his map a location significantly south of Delphi?

While it is true that such opinions would be very strange for a Greek in the Archaic period, we need only recall that Anaximander held other startlingly nontraditional views. He was first of the ancients, according to Aristotle,[54] to hold that the earth remained aloft at the center of the cosmos *held up by nothing*; he maintained, according to Hip-

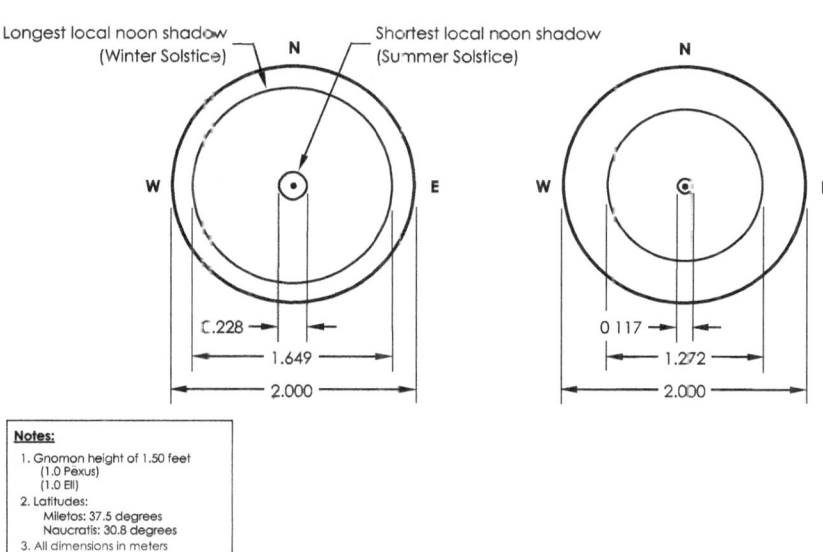

Figure 4.11. Anaximander's sundial comparative: Miletos and Naucratis (emphasizing smaller solstice circle diameters in Naucratis).

polytus (*Ref.* I, 6, 4–5), against the view of a crystalline sphere where all celestial objects are fixed at exactly the same distance from us, that there was such depth in space that the sun was immensely farther from Earth than the immensely distanced moon; and from Ps.-Plutarch (*Strom.* 2) we learn that Anaximander claimed that humans were descended from some kind of fish! If we keep in mind how "nontraditional"—shall we say "revolutionary"?—were Anaximander's ideas, the possibility that he held that southern Egypt was the center of the flat-disk Earth cannot be simply dismissed.

The reports from Diogenes Laertius and the *Suda* placed together the sundial, the map, and a "*sphairos.*" The term "sphairos" refers plausibly to a "model" of some sort. So, perhaps *they were all one thing* set up in Sparta! Had the gnomon been 1 Greek foot, Anaximander would have needed a column drum of roughly 4 feet in diameter to contain both solstice circles and still have "ocean" running around the circumference; had he selected instead a gnomon of a "pêchus" (= 1½ feet = 1 ell), he

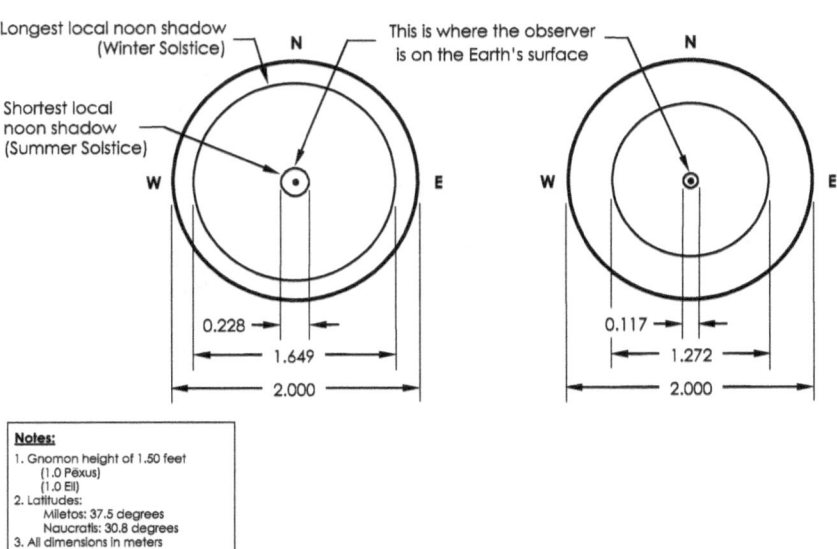

Figure 4.12. Anaximander's sundial comparative: Miletos and Naucratis (emphasizing the observer's location on the Earth's surface).

would have needed a column drum of roughly 6 feet (i.e., 2 meters).[55] This idea of a column drum, perhaps in the proportion of 3:1 with a diameter of roughly 6 Greek feet (or 4 ells) seems like a particularly attractive hypothesis because such a size would have been more or less identical to the architect's module, judging by the Ionic temples in Didyma, Ephesos, and Samos.[56] And had Anaximander's gnomon been .5 feet, the dial face needed to be only 2 feet in diameter, easily turned on a potter's wheel. And the seasonal markers at Miletos and Sparta would have been for all practical purposes indistinguishable.

Diogenes's report is that Anaximander set up his gnomon in Sparta.[57] The proposed design—resembling a column drum—might have been seated on a slender stand, perhaps resembling a column itself but much narrower than the drum itself. It is plausible that the drum face had three concentric circles marking the summer solstice, winter solstice, and the equinox. Traveling from Miletos, he would have known beforehand the exact distances—the radii—to each of the concentric circles, by means of measured strings. Of course, the sundial would have been "testable" in front of the whole community. Moreover, the circumference of the drum would have contained markings for the rising and setting of the sun on the solstices and equinox, and on the drum face a "map" of the earth might well have been inscribed that had at its center south of Naucratis, and certainly far to the south of Delphi. Finally—the *sphairos*—we can imagine that two "wheels," possibly made of bronze, representing the path of the sun, could have been attached (at the drum sides), one depicting the sun at summer solstice and the other the sun at winter solstice, and both wheels would have been continued *under* the earth, one of Anaximander's truly awesome cosmic speculations. By supposing that the column-drum sundial would have been supported by a slender column, the sun wheels could be shown to continue "under" the earth. These bronze "wheels," now hypothesized, would certainly not have been made to scale, since the sun-wheel orbit is at least 54 earth diameters. There would have been no way to make such gigantic wheels unaffected by wind; or had they been made to scale, the sundial would have been so tiny that reading the shadows on the dial face would have been quite impossible. So, these bronze wheels, while not made to scale would have conveyed that the sun-wheel goes *under* the earth; and the earth stands in the middle. This, then, was the "sphairos," the map, and the sundial, made possible by the use of a uniform gnomon whose shadow-casting properties had been studied by trial-and-error care—a product of *logos*, not *muthos*—all mentioned together but not connected explicitly in these very late reports. Below is a reconstruction of the proposed model "set up" in Sparta.

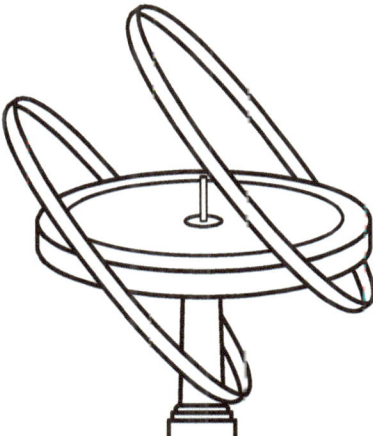

Figure 4.13. Scale model of Anaximander's Sundial with Summer and Winter Solstice "Sun Wheels."

Now the time has come to consider the problem of the equinox. Scholarly opinion has been doubtful about Anaximander's measurement of the equinox, and the reason commonly proposed is this: a knowledge of the obliquity of the ecliptic is required to identify correctly the time of the equinox, and that discovery belongs not earlier than Oinopides of the fifth century BCE.[58] The "obliquity of the ecliptic" is the angle between the planes of the ecliptic and the celestial equator. On the celestial sphere, it is the angle at which the ecliptic intersects the celestial equator. Now the ecliptic is a great circle on the celestial sphere that represents the apparent path of the Sun in its motion relative to the background stars. This great circle is known as the "ecliptic" because eclipses can occur when the moon crosses it. The celestial equator is the great circle on the celestial sphere obtained by the intersection with the sphere of the plane of the Earth's equator. When the sun lies in the plane of the celestial equator, day and night are everywhere of equal length, and this occurs exactly and only two times each year. The "equinox" then is the instant at which the Sun crosses the celestial equator; the Sun is then vertically overhead at the equator, and day and night have equal duration at every point on the Earth's surface. The apparent annual path of the Sun on the celestial sphere is inclined to the celestial equator and intersects it at two points. The term "vernal equinox" and "autumnal equinox" then, are applied to these points.

Thus, the objection has been that Anaximander could not have measured the equinox because he could not have known the obliquity of the ecliptic. This objection proves to be rather beside the point. For we need to imagine the astronomical picture that developed from Anaximander's approach to the gnomon and circular but flat-faced sundial, reflecting his conception of the Earth as a column-drum-shaped cylinder and not a sphere. By means of the sundial construction that has been proposed, Anaximander could have identified the equinox to the day, but the case that he could have known it to the minute cannot be established. Let us enumerate the argument.

We have now considered, speculatively of course in the absence of any Greek sundials that survive prior to the Hellenistic period, how Anaximander may have made his sundial, how he plotted the shortest shadows each day and made concentric circles to identify the solstices, and how he made marks on the circumference of his sundial (mimicking the markings obtainable from the column-drum Earth itself) to indicate

Muthos and *Logos* on New Year's Day 119

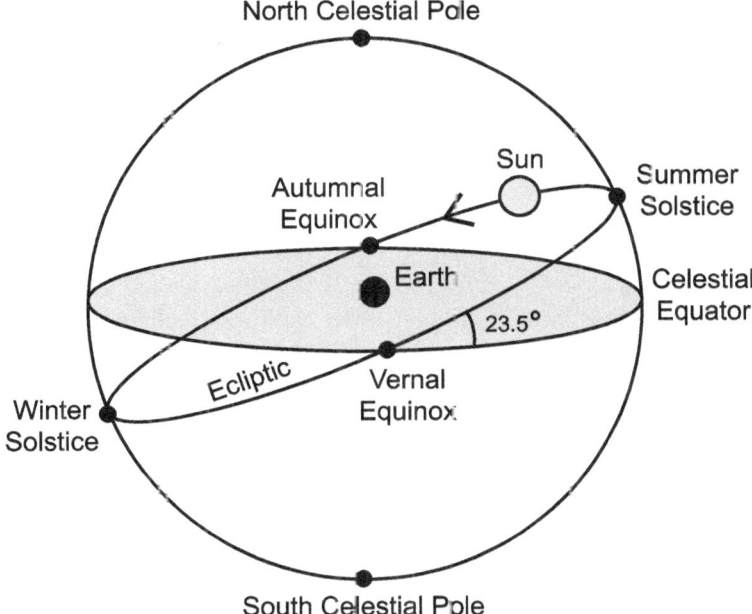

Figure 4.14. The Celestial Sphere and the Obliquity of the Ecliptic: Identifying the exact moments of the Equinoxes.

the rising and settings of the sun on the solstices. Now, in order to identify *the day of the equinox*, Anaximander had to "bisect" the angle formed by the lines connecting the rising (or setting) of the sun on summer and winter solstices. Bisecting the angle merely confirmed his construction at the outset on the sundial face. At that earlier stage, Anaximander made a line perpendicular to the north-south line of the shortest shadow markings of the day throughout the course of the year. The line perpendicular to this North-South line not only makes a diameter that bisected the circular drum face but at once it identified the cardinal directions of due East-West, the rising and setting points of the sun on the equinox itself. Bisecting an angle in a circle was simple and straightforward to the tradition of Archaic architects who routinely worked the geometry of the drum faces they were preparing for installation in the colonnades of the temples, and aligned their temples along cardinal directions. If Anaximander needed a first or second opinion on bisecting an angle, he could have consulted the architects working in his own backyard. Thus, as he sited the sun rising (or setting) on the East-West line he would have known the exact day *when* the equinox would take place. On that day, identifying the shortest shadow mark, Anaximander would have been able to produce the third, intermediary concentric circle by means of that radii measurement.

According to two doxographical reports, Anaximander's sundial also had "hour indicators."[59] Of course this is possible, but we must first get clearer about what kind of "hours" these could be. Anaximander might have been familiar with the same sources known later to Herodotus, indicating that the Babylonians had divided the day into twelve hours.[60] And if he proceeded with this view in mind, he approached the sundial face taking as his starting line the diameter made by the East-West line, and the North-South line perpendicular to it formed by the shortest shadow markers thereby creating a right-angle. He could have bisected each angle a series of times to achieve the "twelve parts." Without committing to the number of "hour-markers" that Anaximander's sundial displayed, it seems most likely that Anaximander's technique of "hour constructions" consisted in bisecting a series of angles.

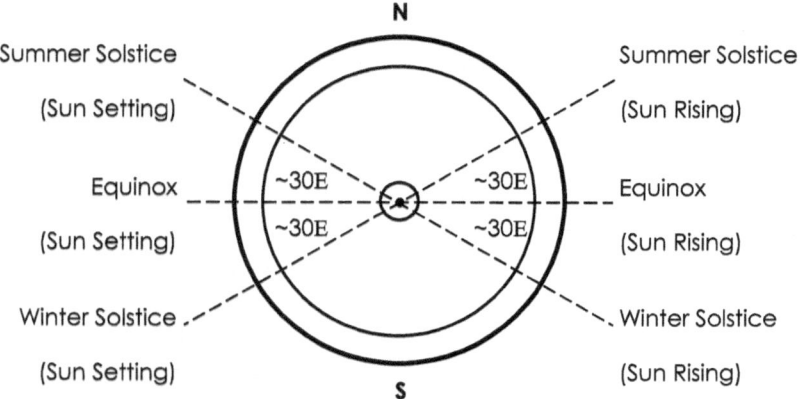

Figure 4.15. Anaximander discovered the Equinox by bisecting the angle between the Summer and Winter Solstice risings, and the Summer and Winter Solstice settings.

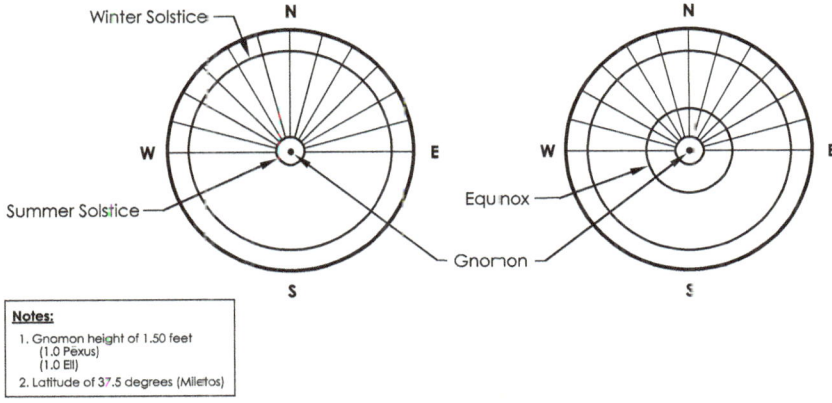

Figure 4.16. Anaximander's sundial with two concentric circles, Summer and Winter Solstices, and hour-markers (*l*); Anaximander's sundial with three concentric circles, Summer, Winter Solstices, Equinox, and hour-markers (*r*).

Thus, had the sundial displayed also "hour indicators," additional radiating lines would have appeared. This result could have been achieved in a straightforward way by the simple geometrical technique of bisecting each angle, that is, by the same technique by which he calculated geometrically the equinox.

The key summary points, then, in arguing plausibly that Anaximander identified the "equinox" are twofold: (i) the base line of a sundial displaying hour-markings is a diameter bisecting the circle running due East-West, and that line identifies the day of the equinox when the sun could be observed visually rising due east and setting due west, and (ii) calendar reform in either Miletos or Sparta depended upon the identification of the equinox—the vernal equinox in the case of Miletos, and the autumnal equinox in the case of Sparta, where the New Year was announced by the new moon following that seasonal marker. The report that places Anaximander in Sparta setting up a *seasonal* sundial is the crown jewel that suggests he recognized that the one device he invented in Miletos could be installed in Sparta to resolve comparable problems of calendar reform.

It is also possible to imagine that the sundial, even the version set up in Sparta, was much smaller. From the reports we have about the Archaic architects, we know that they were capable of making miniatures.

There is a famous story that Pliny relates of the architect Theodorus who supposedly made a miniature of a chariot drawn by four horses that could be hidden behind the wing of a fly![61] Since, as we shall turn to discuss now, the architects—their techniques and their projects refined by trial and error—influenced significantly by Anaximander's cosmic thoughts and writings, their model-making miniatures might also have encouraged him to produce smaller versions of the sundial in Sparta or elsewhere.

The *Logoi* of Anaximander's Prose Book: Trial and Error and the Architect's *Logoi*

We have already considered (in part I) how Cornford's *Principiium Sapientiae* affected significantly the course of studies on Anaximander. Rejecting "the Greek Miracle," Cornford showed how Anaximander's thought was part of a continuous history accounting for the origins of the cosmos, embedded in a tradition of religious belief and ritual. But curiously enough, in rejecting the view of those "discontinuists" like Burnet, who had claimed in addition that the origins of empirical and experimental science could be properly traced to Anaximander,[62] Cornford insisted that there was no tradition of observation and experiment to be found in the researches of the Milesians.[63] From our study reconstructing Anaximander's seasonal sundial, it should now be clear that while Cornford seems persuasive about the continuity of Milesian thought traced through Hesiod and the Babylonian epic, he was mistaken in his sweeping remarks about the perceived absence of observational and experimental endeavors. By correcting Cornford's error in this domain, we can see better how Anaximander's rationalized cosmos evolved. Correcting the balance of this story requires a review of the architects' *logoi*—of observations and experiments—the source of prose writing prose at the same time and in the same place. These architectural technologies illuminate Anaximander's *rational* accounting. In order to become clearer about this rational accounting, let us review the bigger picture of recent scholarship on *logos* and *muthos* in early Greek philosophy.

Throughout the course of the twentieth century, scholars of ancient philosophy, including luminaries such as Cornford,[64] Nestle,[65] Snell,[66] Kirk-Raven,[67] and Guthrie[68] formed something of a chorus in proclaiming "Greek philosophy" to be demarcated by a narrative *from muthos to logos*. That chorus, although sounding different notes, fostered a single euphonic theme, namely, that the literature of "philosophy" promoted a rival form of discourse—rational discourse—over and against mythic storytelling. And, no doubt, these older assessments do indeed capture a central theme in early Greek philosophy. But studies in the past fifty years have called this old formulation into question. These new studies, and I should like to include mine among them, have suggested a much more complex range of interactions, reactions, tensions, and ambiguities emerging between literary and philosophical forms of discourse. One challenge to the older formulation arises when we try to get clearer about the *context* in which *rational* discourse first appears in prose writings. This study concerns some of the rationalizing discourse initiated by Anaximander of Miletos, and is set within a cultural context that has been, until recently, almost entirely neglected, namely, the context in which the *muthos* of the temple deities—the gods and goddesses—was forced into marriage with the *logos* of monumental temple building. In this new marriage, the architects building temples to Hera, Artemis, and Apollo in Archaic Ionia came to discover and command nature's hidden order, through trial and error no doubt, and the language of prose was more aptly suited to communicate these rational discoveries. Anaximander's prose book needs to be reviewed in this light.

Anaximander of Miletos is credited with, among other things, writing the first philosophical book in prose. Scholars in the first half of the twentieth century focused upon this quintessentially important innovation. But the shortcomings of these earlier studies were that they fixed upon Anaximander's prose work as the abandonment of *muthoi* and *muthoipoieia* without offering a plausible motivation for Anaximander's rationalizing. On the one hand, there were those who found no need to explain Anaximander's motivation because they accepted the Greek Miracle; on the other hand, there were those who embraced narratives of continuity and interconnections to explain Anaximander's innovation but still failed to explain why he rationalized the older stories—the Babylonian New Year's Day festival celebrating the triumph of order over disorder, Hellenicized by Hesiod. The appeal to the architect's monumental temple technologies and prose writings finally supplies a context, a proximate cause that helps us explain Anaximander's rational accounting. The trial-and-error work—the building of gigantic temples out of hard stone—that literally transformed for the Archaic Greeks both the visual horizon and capacities of human understanding, created an audience ready to hear about *thaumata*, architectural and philosophical.[69]

Prose now became introduced as an appropriate medium to communicate the details of cosmic speculations, and offered a new vehicle to create a distance from the dactylic hexameter of the older narratives.

To see the motivation and rationality of Anaximander's prose book more clearly yet, we need to ask again about the context in which he wrote it. Who else was writing prose treatises that could help explain Anaximander's purposes, audience, and competition? Until recently, the most formidable proposal came from Martin West, who, in *Early Greek Philosophy and the Orient*,[70] proposed the usefulness of setting alongside Anaximander's book the prose writing of Pherecydes of Syros (c. 7th century BCE) who relates the marriage of Zas and Chthonie. But West also acknowledged that Pherecydes was the *theologos*, while Anaximander was the *phusiologos*, and so had different agendas and purposes. A more promising hint comes from Xenophon in his *Memorabilia*.[71] There, Xenophon has Socrates ask the sophist Euthydemus, who has made a collection of technical treatises, whether he is planning to become an architect. The sarcasm would be pointless unless architects were accustomed to learning from other architects by means of written prose books. From Vitruvius in *The Ten Books on Architecture* we know about the early history of architectural writing dating back to the mid-sixth century BCE.

The case has been made already in *Anaximander and the Architects* for the usefulness of setting alongside Anaximander's pioneering book in prose the only other tradition of prose writings produced contemporaneously in Ionia where Anaximander published (548 BCE) and flourished.[72] Those contemporaneous prose treatises, now lost, were attributed to the architects building monumental temples. Theodorus, the architect of the temple to Hera on Samos (c. 575 BCE), and Chersiphron and Metagenes, architects of the temple to Artemis in Ephesos (c. 560 BCE), were credited with writing prose treatises. In the opening of Book VII of *The Ten Books on Architecture*, Vitruvius mentions the wise and useful provision of the ancient architects to record their thoughts in treatises, that is, prose books.[73] Vitruvius names Theodorus, Chersiphron, and Metagenes as publishers of books that communicated the rules of proportions for the temples they built[74] and mentions some technologies associated with the challenges of monumental building.[75] What are we to make of this? Why did they write the books? What else was in them?

It is a worthy and not unlikely conjecture that these architects discussed the various technologies required by monumental stone architecture—quarrying, transporting, installing, and finishing the stones—in addition to the real possibility of producing plans and models. Pliny the Elder relates that when Chersiphron's temple collapsed under the enormous weight of its marble, Theodoros was called from Samos to Ephesos to help.[76] Moreover, Kienast's recent work shows that Theodorus had already addressed the same problem. Kienast explains why a second temple to Hera in Samos (Dipteros II) was begun forty-three meters to the west of the original Dipertos I, a mere twenty-five years or so after the first gigantic temple was begun.[77] The limestone Dipteros I was collapsing under its own weight. The new temple, Dipteros II, had a channel built underneath the perimeter of the colonnade and filled with sand, a technique designed specifically to prevent the temple from listing and sinking. So given the possibility that Theodorus supervised the rebuilding of his own Samian temple (and Pliny's testimony is garbled) and/or was called to Ephesos when the architects there encountered similar problems, perhaps Theodoros published his book to serve as a guide for would-be temple architects throughout the Greek world. Moreover, in keeping with the *agonistic* culture that gave birth to the Olympic Games, his purpose may also have been to display his excellence. In Book X.11, Vitruvius recounts the clever *inventions*—machines—by Chersiphron and Metagenes to deliver weighty blocks of stone from the quarries to the building site many kilometers away. Thus, it seems possible that the architects' books contained drawings of models and technological innovations, or at least prose descriptions of them. Placing Anaximander's prose book alongside these architectural books, we can see more clearly the real possibility that his book also contained diagrams, numbers, and proportions in the discussions of the map, the sundial, and model of the cosmos.[78]

Vitruvius VII.1 informs us that the architects' prose books contained the temple "proportions." What does this mean? In order to produce a very carefully imagined aesthetic effect when working on gigantic scale, the comparative sizes of the architectural elements had to be determined in advance. In "The Proportions of Intercolumniations and of the Column,"[79] Vitruvius emphasizes that the key to the temple's proportions is the module, one basic unit in terms of which all the other architectural proportions are to be reckoned either as multiples or submultiples. The success of monumental architecture, then, required a *module*, the identification of "One over Many," a familiar formula for describing a focus in early Greek philosophy, the search for some basic unity, some substance, that underlies all diversity. According to Vitruvius, the module for the Ionic temple builders was "column diameter." Thus, the Ionic column height is reckoned as 9 or 10 times the (lower) column diameter; the distance between the columns in the colonnade, the proportional size of the entablature—architrave, *kyma*, *geison*, *sima*—are all reckoned in terms of the column-diameter module, and these details are discussed in *Anaximander in Context*,[80] and reviewed in a fresh light in *Archaeology and the Origins of Philosophy* over the debate of where exactly on the column is "lower" column diameter measured.[81] Since the column tapers as an optical corrector to create the visual sense that the column looks straight from the distance, and so the width of the column is not uniform throughout, it becomes a question for the architect-excavator of just where on the column the module of column-diameter is to be located.

Anaximander identified the size and the shape of the earth with a column drum—*to de schêma autês (sc. tês gês) gyron, strongylon, kionos lithōi paraplêsion*[82]—at the very time when column-drum construction was introduced into Ionia by the architects.[83] He reckoned the size of the whole cosmos—the distances to the stars, moon, and sun—in earthly proportions, and that means earthly column-drum proportions. He reckoned the size of the cosmos in terms of his module. It can hardly be mere coincidence that Anaximander adopted a modular technique and selected the very *same* module that the architects used, working in his own backyard, when building their temples.[84] The adoption of a modular technique, and most especially the architect's module, shows that Anaximander was making use of an architectural technique. The question of whether or not Anaximander played a more engaged role, interacting with the architects and their projects, must remain unanswered at this time, though it is tempting to suppose that, as a practical problem-solver, he did.

With this architectural and modular technique, Anaximander measured the cosmos in earthly proportions, that is, column-drum proportions. He appealed to architectural and building techniques because he came to view the cosmos as built architecture; just as the temple was built in stages, so was the cosmos. There can be no doubt that Anaximander visited the temple building sites and that he observed carefully their techniques as they worked. His prose book attains a cultural meaning in the context of the prose books by the architects. Since we have secure evidence that Theodorus began building the temple to Hera shortly after 575 BCE,[85] and Chersiphron and Metagenes began building the temple to Artemis around 560 BCE,[86] and both are credited with writing prose books that by all indications suggest provided rational prose accounts of their techniques, it seems plausible to suppose that Anaximander's rationalizing prose book in 548 BCE followed their lead.[87] The architects produced *thaumata*, and discussed in prose books the stages by which the house of the cosmic powers was built. Analogously, Anaximander discussed in his prose book the building stages of the house that *is* the cosmos—the greatest *thauma* of them all.

The architect's work was to a great extent one of trial and error. This was especially true prior to the end of the seventh century BCE when there was hardly any monumental *stone* architecture in eastern Greece, and the tradition of monumental building had been lost for centuries since the fall of Mycenae. The architects learned to constrain their aesthetic imaginations by the realities of *physis*, of nature, whose ways made only some architectural dreams feasible. They must surely have tested their imaginations and their theories by countless trials and errors at the building sites. In the context of architectural prose books that detailed the "proportions" of the temples, it seems plausible that Anaximander's book displayed also trial-and-error experimentation in coming to grips with the realities of *phusis*. The seasonal sundial with which Anaximander is credited is a result of such trial-and-error experimentation; it signals a grasping, command, and display of nature's hidden order. The reconstruction of Anaximander's seasonal sundial supplies a narrative *from muthos to logos*, true enough, but only if we see it in the context of the burgeoning empirical science of architectural experimentation that forged a union between the gods of the *muthoi*, on the one hand, and *logoi* of building technologies, on the other.

The reports about the ancient architects credit them with many inventions—the rule, the lever, the lathe, the set-square among other tools.[88] Some of these tools and techniques were introduced from Egypt,[89] but the architects no doubt adapted them to suit their own purposes. Anaximander most certainly did *not* invent the gnomon, whether or not he introduced it into Greece. But, the doxographical reports by Diogenes Laertius and the *Suda* make new sense once we see how the sundial was constructed and the likelihood that Anaximander journeyed with his gnomon whose shadow-casting properties he knew beforehand, as he traveled west to Sparta from Miletos. Indeed, the results he (or one of his compatriots) recorded south of Miletos, in Naucratis or north of Miletos in Apollonia on the Black Sea, could have made sense—a troubling sense I might add to anyone who believed the Earth was flat— to Anaximander only when the pattern of shadows was produced using the *same* gnomon: in this case, the gnomon was Anaximander's *One over Many*. Whether or not these discrepancies urged him to conclude that the center of his flat Earth lay far to the south of Miletus/Sparta/Delphi—all along more or less the same line of latitude—and not as a central Greek tradition supposed was at Delphi, we can only wonder.

Anaximander is credited with writing books of several titles, including *On Nature, Map of the Earth*,[90] *Introduction to Geometry, On the Fixed Stars*, and *A Celestial Model* (Sphairos). These titles must be regarded with reserve, but the secure evidence we do have points to these themes as genuinely Anaximander's. It is possible that Anaximander's prose book discussed these themes in separate parts of one single work. So what exactly did Anaximander "write?" What did he do, that is, what did he make? The testimonies overlap in such a way to make it impossible to distinguish clearly between his writings and his deeds. At all events, the alleged titles and the other tertiary testimonies, taken together, allow us to form a picture that Anaximander wrote in prose, and made a map, a cosmic model, and a sundial. The inclusion of a title as "Outlines of Geometry" makes sense once we get clear that geometrical techniques were needed to make the sundial, map, and model.[91] If we reflect on the case for architectural prose books, it seems clear that the architects first built their temples and only then recorded their deeds in writing. Had Anaximander followed their lead, *as he followed their architectural methods*, it seems even more plausible that his writing recorded his own achievements—map, sundial, and cosmic model. Just as the architects were inventing and writing about their inventions, so also we should come to see Anaximander as inventing and writing about his inventions, in the *agonistic* spirit of the time.

To grasp Anaximander's literary contribution, then, we need to see his prose book(s) in the light of the prose books written contemporaneously by the architects. In those prose treatises, we are presented with the results of their *logoi* born of trial and error. These architectural prose books were the impetus, the proximate cause, of his rationalizing writing; they formed the new, immediate horizon in terms of which he, and his Ionian community, thought of written treatises. The evidence we have suggests that we should expect to find proportions, numbers, and perhaps even drawings, in the architects' books, and thus we should expect also to find proportions, numbers, and drawings in Anaximander's book(s). The focus of the architects' books was the various stages of the building of a house that displayed and expressed the cosmic powers. The focus of Anaximander's book was the stages by which the house that is the cosmos was built. For Anaximander, the cosmos had a beginning. The first day was New Year's Day, and whether or not Anaximander held along with his fellow Milesians that this day recurred at the first sighting of the new moon following the vernal equinox, or as did the Spartans following the autumnal equinox, or even the Athenians who identified the beginning of the year following the summer solstice, Anaximander lived in a world where New Year's Day followed one of the seasonal markers. The seasonal sundial, whether or not it was explicitly motivated by calendar reform, did indeed produce a result that contributed to it. His sundial revealed nature's hidden order; revealed the seasonal solar markers; and produced an imagined vision of the most distant heavenly structure, the sun that cast the shadows he recorded. The seasonal sundial offered a most welcome clue to identifying New Year's Day, the annual return in nature's great cycle that marks the beginning of the cosmos. In the fragment from Anaximander's book that survives thanks to Simplicius, we are told of a cycle that recurs perpetually:

> He [Anaximander] says that *it* is neither water nor any other so-called elements but some other *apeiron* nature, from which come into being all the heavens and the worlds in them . . . and the source for coming-to-be for existing things is that into which destruction, too, happens, according to necessity . . . for they pay penalty and retribution to each other for their injustice according to the assessment of time.[92]

That cycle had a beginning. Anaximander's rational account of the cosmos began on New Year's Day.

Notes

1. I would like to acknowledge gratefully the following colleagues who discussed, read, or made suggestions to this project: Anton Bammer, Hermann Kienast, Kathleen Lynch, Duane Roller, Nancy Ruff, Richard Schuler, Barbara Tsakirgis, and William Wians. An earlier version of this essay was presented to the annual meeting of archaeologists at the Classical Association of the Middle West and South, April 2004. The responsibility for what appears here is mine

alone. I would also like to acknowledge that the second section of this essay draws heavily on Hahn 2010, 148–65, though there are variations and even divergences from this earlier publication.

2. Copernicus 1543; English trans. 1939, 509. At the end of his "Preface and Dedication to Pope Paul III," Copernicus writes "For many years now under Leo X when the Lateran Council was considering the question of reforming the Ecclesiastical Calendar, no decision was reached, for the sole reason that the magnitude of the year and the months and the movements of the sun and moon had not yet been measured with sufficient accuracy. From that time on I gave attention to making more exact observations of these things and was encouraged to do so by that most distinguished man, Paul, Bishop of Fossombrone, who had been present at those deliberations."

3. Cornford 1952, 159–224 where the whole argument is set out in all its intricacies. See also Thomson 1955, vol. 2, 140–72 where the same thesis is championed. See also this volume's introduction and the paper by Brisson.

4. The idea that Greek philosophy did not develop out of some continuous tradition but rather emerged without sufficient cause, see Burnet 1920, 10: "the Greeks were born observers"; Heath 1921, 6: "the Greeks were a natural race of thinkers"; Frankel 1962/1973, 255: "pure philosophy . . . came into existence suddenly and without a cause . . . as if by a miracle."

5. For a description of the New Year's festival see Thomson 1955, vol. 2, 86–89.

6. Rochberg 1995, 1925–940.

7. Hesiod *Theogony*, 820–85.

8. *Ibid*. 117ff.

9. Cf. the elegant formulation of, and agreement with, Cornford's argument in Vernant 1965/2006, 372ff.

10. Trumpy 1997, 89–94.

11. Cf. Pauly-Wissowa s.v. Kalender; Thomson 1955 vol. 2; Samuels 1980, Bickerman 1982, Trumpy 1997, Hannah 2005.

12. For the most recent summaries, see Hannah 2005, 42ff.

13. Trumpy 1997.

14. Herodotus 1, 94 tells that coinage was invented in Lydia. Cf. the thoughtful discussion about the very idea of coinage in Thomson, vol. 2, 194ff.

15. Cf. Hahn 2003, 105–18.

16. Diels-Kranz (henceforth D-K) 12A10, Ps. Plutarch.

17. For the distances to the sun and moon wheels, cf. D-K 12A22 and D-K 12A21. Cf. also Hahn 2003, 145–49 and esp. Hahn 2011, 73, Fig. 3.5.

18. Hahn 2011, 111, but Thomson repeats Rehm's mistake identifying Miletos's New Year with the autumnal equinox.

19. Rehm 1914 set the standard reasoning that the Milesian New Year began with the month of Boedromion that was coincidental with the autumnal

equinox, and later changed after the time of Alexander the Great to Taureon, i.e., the vernal equinox. This view is accepted by Samuels 1972, 114–15. Bickerman 1968, 20 seems to suppose that the Miletos year began eight months after the Athenian year, which would put the New Year in later winter, theoretically in February or early March.

20. Trümpy 1997, 89–94.
21. Thomson 1955, 111ff.
22. Pindar, Pythian Odes, 4.286ff. cf. also Isthmian Odes, 2.22.
23. Sophocles, Elektra 1291ff. Cf. also 1368.
24. Plato, Republic, Book II, 374C.
25. Plato, Philebus, 66A.
26. Thucydides, 1.42.3.
27. Thucydides, 2.34.8.
28. Thucydides, 4.27.4.
29. The festival calendars were lunar calendars. Cf. Hannah 2005, 42ff.
30. Recently, there is a new argument that Anaximander's *apeiron*—"Unlimited" or "Unbounded"—conjuring an "abstract" principle and perhaps not a material stuff, really should be read *apeira phusis*—"Unlimited Nature" as his source and substance monistic principle. Cf. Couprie and Kočandrle 2013; also Kočandrle and Couprie 2017.
31. Diogenes Laertius, II, 1–2; D-K 12A1. ". . . he was the first to discover a gnomon, and he set one up on the sundials in Sparta, according to Favorinus in his Universal History, to mark solstices and equinoxes; he also constructed hour-indicators. He was first to draw an outline of earth and sea, but he also constructed a celestial model."
32. *Suda s.v.*, see also Kirk-Raven-Schofield (henceforth KRS) 1983, 100. "He was first to discover the equinoxes and solstices and hour-indicators . . . he introduced the gnomon and in general made an outline of geometry. He wrote "On Nature," the "Circuit of the Earth" and "On the Fixed Stars" and a "Celestial Model" and some other works.
33. Agathemerus, I,1; D-K 12A6.
34. Strabo, I, p. 7 (Casaubon); D-K 12A6.
35. Hahn 2001, 205ff; conjectured reconstruction illustrated on page 209.
36. Gibbs 1976, 6–7, and 94n12. Gibbs is referring to an archaeological report by D. S. Hunt who discovered in 1938 this *analemma* in a well on Chios. Hunt's report gives only a verbal description which, I believe for the first time, was illustrated in my 2001 study.
37. There is plentiful evidence for identifying the shape of Anaximander's Earth with a flat cylinder, expressly analogized with a column drum: D-K 12B5, 12A11.3, 12A10.
38. There is a long tradition of scholarship that emphasized the importance of "microcosmic-macrocosmic" thought to the Pythagoreans. Cf. Burkert 1972.

But it is clear that this kind of reasoning, akin to "analogy" was made use of by Anaximander, whether or not, as one tradition would have it, he played some role in "teaching" Pythagoras.

39. In preparation of column drums for installation, the *empolion* is a wood or metal dowel that is inserted in a hole in the center of a drum and allows the new drum to be aligned with the previous drum or base as it is lowered into place. Cf. Hahn 2001, pp 7–8, 154–56, 162, 196.

40. Agathemerus D-K 12A6, Strabo D-K 12A6, and D. L. 12A1. *Pinax* and *perimetron* and [*gês*] *periodos* almost certainly refer to the same thing: a map.

41. Cf. Clay 1992 for a consideration of a map with uninhabitable regions over and against the *oikoumenê*.

42. Heidel 1937, esp. 2–59. This also was my point of departure in Hahn 2001, 208ff.

43. Aristotle *Meteorologica* II.6,

44. D-K 12A10. Ps. Plutarch reports that the original fire surrounded the cosmos *like bark around a tree*. The cosmos contains with in a great tree, the heavenly wheels analogously forming "rings" in this tree. This is a departure from the position I took in 2010, chapter 6, when I sided with the position that the whole cosmos was a great tree. I am still convinced that Anaximander imagined that the whole cosmos was alive and growing like a great tree, but the canopy I am now more persuaded was spherical as suggested by our visual experience.

45. Photo by the author, with placement of wooden gnomon added for effect. See further Glessmer and Albani 1999, 442: "It could have been used to handle the discrepancy between 365.25 days and a calendar year of 364 days. It allows the determination of the cardinal points and fixing a calendar whose seasons are as near as possible to the signs of sun, moon and stars."

46. For an example of a column drum from the Archaic temple to Apollo at Didyma, cf. Hahn 2003, 91, fig. 2.3.

47. For a discussion of the architect's technique of *anathyrôsis*, and its implications for Anaximander's cosmic picture, cf. Hahn 2001, 149–62 and 194–95.

48. Herodotus II 109.

49. Cf. Johannes 1937.

50. According to Herodotus II, 109, the Greeks learned from the Babylonians of the celestial sphere and the gnomon and the twelve parts of the day. Cf. also KRS 1983, 103.

51. *Ibid.*

52. Cf. Hahn 2003, 85–89; 2001, 173–74, 184–85.

53. D-K 12A3, Aelian *V.H.* III, 17.

54. Aristotle, *de Caelo* B 13, 295b10ff.

55. For a discussion of the lengths of a "pous" and "pêchus" cf. Herodotus II 149; and Hahn 2003, 92.

56. Cf. Hahn 2003, 100–21.

57. D-K 12A1.

58. Cf. Dicks 1970, 45 and 174. Dicks is the most prominent of the naysayers; and Dicks 1966 for the full argument.

59. D-K 12A1 *hôroskopeia*, D. L.; *hôrologia*, in the *Suda*.

60. Herodotus II, 109.

61. Pliny, *Natural History*, XXXIV, 83.

62. Burnet 1930, v. "The early Ionian teachers . . . first pointed the way opened which Europe has followed ever since."

63. Cornford 1952, 159ff. Referring to claims that Ionian natural philosophy was "pre-eminently scientific" Cornford writes: 'We found that it was not in fact anything of the kind, but a dogmatic structure based on *a priori* premises" (p. 159). Cf. also Vernant 1965/2006, 372 in assessing Cornford's view: "It knew nothing at all of experimentation; nor was it the product of the direct observation of nature."

64. Cornford 1912.

65. Nestle 1940.

66. Snell 1953.

67. KRS 1983.

68. Guthrie 1962.

69. Aristotle identifies the experience of *thaumazein* with the origins of philosophical thought, *Metaphysics* A.

70. West 1971, 27, 55.

71. Xenophon, *Memorabilia*, 4.2.8–10; cf. Hahn 2001, 55ff.

72. Hahn 2001, ch. 2.

73. In the edition of Morgan 1914, 195.

74. See Morgan 1914, 198 where Theodorus, Chersiphron, and Metagenes are mentioned in the context of their published books that discussed proportions of the temple's structures.

75. Morgan 1914, 288, where Vitruvius mentions some technological achievements, for example: (referring to Chersiphron's invention of a device to move large blocks from the quarry to the building site) "Using four-inch timbers, he joined two of them, each as long as the shaft, with two cross pieces between them, dovetailing all together, and then leaded iron gudgeons shaped like dovetails into the two ends of the shafts as dowels are leaded, and in the woodwork he fixed rings to contain pivots, and fastened wooden cheeks to the ends. The pivots, being enclosed in the rings, turned freely. So, when yokes of oxen began to draw the four inch frame, they made the shaft revolve constantly, turning it by means of the pivots and the rings." Cf. also X.12 where Metagenes's invention is described, adapting his father Chersiphron's invention, to convey the architraves to the building site from the quarry.

76. Pliny *Natural History*, XXXVI, 90.

77. Kienast 1991. The old theory, mentioned by Tomlinson 1976, 127, that Dipteros I was destroyed by fire, has now been disproved.

78. Netz claims that the first geometrical diagrams do not appear until the middle of the fifth century in the "rolls" of Hippocrates, Anaxagoras, and Oinopides based upon later reports that mention diagrams in them. But Netz also focuses on geometrical diagrams which are not "practical diagrams" of buildings, for example, but where the diagram is a thing in itself.

79. Vitruvius III.3.7.
80. Hahn 2003, 105–18.
81. Hahn 2010, ch. 1.
82. D-K 12A11.3.
83. Hahn 2001, 149–62.
84. Hahn 2003, 105ff; Hahn 2001, ch. 4.
85. Kienast 1991, 24. Pottery dating to 575 BCE was discovered buried under the foundation as part of a "foundation ceremony." Thus Kienast can conclude that the construction started shortly thereafter.
86. For the dating of the Ephesian Artemesium 'D', Cf. Hahn 2003, 110ff, esp. note 168, and also Hahn 2001, 77ff.
87. Hahn 2001, 47–49.
88. Hahn 2001, 62, and esp. note 73.
89. For the transmission from Egypt of inspiration to build multi-columned temples and the know-how to do it, cf. Hahn 2001, 66–69; Hahn 2003, 73–78.
90. Here I have translated *gês periodos* "map" of the Earth.
91. Cf. the *Suda*, D-K 12A2.
92. Simplicius *Physics* 24, 13; D-K 12A9.

5

Tragic Values in Homer and Sophocles

Lawrence J. Hatab

> Then let this be our defense—now that we've returned to the topic of poetry—that, in view of its nature, we had reason to banish it from the city earlier, for our argument compelled us to do so. . . . Nonetheless, if poetry . . . has any argument to bring forward that proves it ought to have a place in a well-governed city, we would be glad to admit it.
>
> —*Republic* 607b–c

In the *Republic*, Socrates condemns tragic poetry (including Homer) because of its immorality and threat to rational composure. In this essay I want to accept Socrates's invitation to poetry's "defenders" who might "speak in prose on poetry's behalf" (*Rep.* 607d). I will do so not by arguing for a moral sense in poetry that could satisfy Socrates, but by granting much of the terms of his analysis and showing how poetry is not "immoral" but expressive of a different kind of valuation, which I am calling "tragic values." In my discussion, the tragic pertains to indigenous limits in human existence, inescapable limits on life, knowledge, control, achievement, and agency. Yet these limits can be shown to permit, even constitute, a defensible kind of valuation, of finding meaning and worth in human existence. In fact, I argue that with tragic valuation, whatever is good or worthy in life is necessarily informed by finite limits, such that without these limits it would not *be* good or worthy.[1]

I will focus mainly on Homer and Sophocles, and in gathering both poets around the notion of the tragic, I take a cue from Plato, who in the *Republic* calls Homer a tragic poet (*Rep*. 598e, 605d). From the formal standpoint of poetic genres, this seems odd, but I believe that Plato was advancing the material point that both epic and tragic poetry present a view of *life* that ultimately limits human aspirations and that stands in the way of a moral reformation guided by the order of reason. I believe that, in the main, Plato's account of the Greek poetic tradition as a tragic worldview was indeed accurate. The question is whether a tragic world must be renounced as the antithesis of a moral life. I begin with some background material on the pre-Platonic worldview.[2]

The World-Order in Hesiod's *Theogony*

Early Greek myth and religion did not exhibit any transcendent realm beyond earthly life, but rather the sacred manifestations of all the forces and meanings in the lived world. The divine realm was divided into Olympian "sky" deities, marked by beauty and intelligence, and Chthonic "earth" deities of the underworld, marked more by violence and brutish passion. Human beings live on the earth's surface, in between these two realms and subject to their competing powers. In religious practices, both sacred regions were honored in rituals, at times conjointly. Moreover, Olympian gods often had Chthonic counterparts.[3] So these divine spheres were not separated from each other; their interpenetration was a part of Greek religious experience. Human life, therefore, dwelled in the ambiguity of sacred tensions: passion and moderation, natural drives and culture, malevolence and benevolence, death and life.

Hesiod's *Theogony* presents an organization of this worldview by telling the story of "how the gods and the earth first came into being" (*Theog*. 108) and the nature of their relationships. Right away we notice that this is not a typical creation story, because the gods do not create things and they, themselves, simply "come into being" (*genonto*)—we are not told from where. There seems to be no prior cause above or before the world-order; rather the gods simply *appear* (call it a sacred phenomenology). If there is any "priority" in the *Theogony* it is the first sacred appearance, *Chaos* (*Theog*. 116), which should not be taken as disorder but as a "yawning gap" (derived from the verb *chainō*). The best we can say is that what is "first" is not a cause or even a privileged form, but a differential "between," out of which the earth and sky deities divide.

So, priority is not given to some positive state of being, but to something indeterminate. Moreover, the sequence of generation shows a similar precedence: Earth and Night come before, and give birth to, Sky and Day.[4] And beneath the earth there is a great empty gulf, *Chasma*, (related in meaning to *Chaos*), in which no direction or bearing can be found, but which gives the "sources and limits" of all things (*Theog.* 736ff). *Chasma* is described as "abhorrent" even to the gods, and yet it is also called *deinon* because the gods view it with awe as a kind of wondrous monster.[5]

Other indications of the priority of negative limits can be found in the *Theogony*: Night, in addition to generating Day, gives birth to "hateful" Doom, "black" Fate, Death, Sleep, Disgrace, and Woe (*Theog.* 211–12); also to Nemesis and "hard-hearted *Eris*," or Strife (*Theog.* 223–25). Most significantly, Night bears the "ruthless, avenging Fates"—*Klōtho* (Spinner), *Lachesis* (Disposer of Lots), and *Atropos* (Unturnable)—who "give mortals at their birth both good and evil to have," and who relentlessly "pursue the transgressions of mortals and of gods" (*Theog.* 217–21). We realize that both humans *and* deities are subordinate to terrible forces of fate; the gods in Homer are not omnipotent, especially when it comes to death. In the *Iliad*, the gods certainly control much of the heroes' actions and destiny, but in the epic, fate (*moira*) is more of an impersonal force usually associated with death and catastrophe. And the gods cannot intervene if a hero's time has come to die.[6]

The early generation of Strife (*Eris*) in the *Theogony* is significant for understanding the actual narratives in epic poetry. In Hesiod, Strife is indigenous to, and pervasive throughout, Earth (*Works and Days* 11ff). The course and structure of the world-order in the *Theogony*, in fact, unfolds by way of vivid violent battles between the progeny of Earth, which can be organized around the Chthonic-Olympian division. Olympian Zeus is ultimately victorious, yet the result is not the destruction of Chthonic forces but a threefold apportionment of power: Zeus (Olympus), Poseidon (Sea), and Hades (Underworld). Each god will have its own domain of power, which will be respected by the others. Indeed, this apportionment accompanies Zeus being *elected* king by the other gods (*Theog.* 883–85). Such an apportionment of *relational conflict* (strife within familial offspring) can help illuminate pervasive elements in Greek myth, religion, and poetry that turn on the tension between culture and nature, between Olympian and Chthonic forces, a tension that is not resolved into one side or the other. There is "order" in Greek myth, but it involves exchanges of shared power among different forces. Zeus is not an absolute ruler but a focal point for "a balance of powers that is vulnerable to the turbulence of competing divine wills."[7]

Homer

Both Homer and Sophocles focus on heroic values and their tragic character, although there are significant differences between epic and tragic poetry, as we will see. In any case, given the way life is depicted in Homer and Sophocles, it may seem difficult to locate there much of a sense of morality in our sense of the term. Yet we can begin by considering the term "moral," not in terms of familiar principles of "right and wrong," but first in terms of valuing in a broad sense, of articulating what is worthy and unworthy, better or worse in human affairs, particularly what is worthy of praise and blame, which opens up the social element necessary for valuation.

In Homer, the praiseworthy is in most respects different from later moral outlooks, even to the point of being blameworthy in those systems. Rather than being egalitarian, Homeric values are aristocratic; rather than reducing to harmony and peace, they celebrate competition, strife, and power; rather than stemming from an inward, reflective self, they embody the outward field of action, circumstance, worldly success, and social recognition. In Homer the word *agathos*, or good, exhibits a variety of meanings, for example: right feeling (*Il.* 9.341); discerning, well-balanced (*Od.* 3.266, 14.421, 16.398); well-born, noble (*Il.* 14.113, 21.109); skilled in war (*Il.* 1.131, 6.478); brave (*Il.* 4.181, 9.341); daring (*Il.* 13.238, 284, 314). The word *aretē*, which is commonly translated as "virtue" for later writers, is better rendered "excellence," meaning superior performance (cf. virtuosity) or high station. The wide range of uses shown in *aretē* is applied to horses in a race (*Il.* 23.276, 374). Some meanings of *aretē* are applied to humans: manly valor (*Il.* 8.535, 13.237), skill in manly pursuits (*Il.* 23.571), majesty and rank (*Il.* 9.498, 23.578). Homeric values and virtues, therefore, have more to do with performance than some inner state of "character." Indeed, valuation in the *Iliad* mostly concerns war and strife, and there is no evidence that such values are fundamentally called into question in the text.[8]

Within this field of epic values is an intrinsic fatalism that is manifested in two forms: (1) the divine management of heroic life—in the course of events generally, and even to the point of psychological intervention in heroic behavior; and (2) the pervasive force of death and ruination that ultimately cannot be mastered by mortals or even by the gods themselves. Homeric fatalism gives us a first look at what "tragic valuation" might mean: (1) what is worthy cannot be attributed to full self-sufficiency; and (2) what is worthy is intrinsically caught up in limits and loss.

MORTALITY AND HEROISM IN HOMER

The most crucial feature in epic poetry is the horizon of death that limits human existence (in *Il.* 16.855, death is described as the *telos*, the end/limit of life). Humans are typically called "mortals," those who know that death is their ultimate fate (*Od.* 13.59–60), as opposed to the immortal gods. Death is a natural part of life (*Il.* 6.146–49) and is depicted as the departure of the *psuchē*, or "life force," out of the living body.[9] There is a place for the departed *psuchē* in Hades, but this can hardly count as an afterlife in any meaningful sense.[10] Hades is the god of the underworld, and his name means the "unseen one." As depicted in Book 11 of the *Odyssey*, the realm of Hades is a shadow-world with none of the features of a living existence, a kind of ghostly, sleep-like condition that held no attraction for humans: Achilles tells Odysseus that he would rather be a poor laborer on earth than king of all the dead (*Od.* 485ff). Even the gods find Hades loathsome (*Il.* 20.64–65). The dead cannot be said to have any kind of personal life: Hesiod calls the dead in Hades *nōnumnoi*, nameless and unknown (*Works and Days* 154); Homer says they are without mind or perception (*Il* 23.104; *Od.* 11.475–76); death is at times associated with "forgetting" life (*Il.* 16.776) or "covering over" life (*Il.* 16.855), or being done with the cares of life (*Il.* 23.73). The only sign of life for the dead is when they appear to the living, and then only as a phantom (*eidōlon*) that has no real substance (*Il.* 23.65ff; *Od.* 11.204ff).[11]

What are we to make of Hades, a "place" that is really "no place" when compared with life? The departed *psuchē* in Homer is not a "soul" apart from a body, but a visual *image* of a hero, indeed an image reflecting the specific circumstances and moment of a hero's death (*Od.* 11.40–41); and it is an image that cannot be "grasped," as illustrated by the *psuchē* of Odysseus's mother that flits away like a shadow when he tries to embrace her (*Od.* 11.206). I think it is useful to adopt a phenomenological approach to these renditions and the way they function in the poetic narrative. With Hades and the phantom *psuchē*, we can say that the absence of death is given a vivid *presence*, a life-*lacking* presence that is more than nothingness and less than life, a counter-*image* to life that in fact is more striking and more telling than an abstract nothingness or absence. In other words, the *meaning* of death as the absence or lack of living features is "placed" on the other side of life.[12] Odysseus's experience of the loss of his beloved mother is "embodied" in her image that both attracts and eludes him. At the same time, the *value* of life is sharply enhanced against this repellant counter-image.[13] This is especially true in the context of Homeric poetry, where the normally stark divide between earth and Hades is bridged when a living hero encounters Hades and the phantom dead. It seems right to say that the significance of Hades has more to do with the *living* than a straightforward description of a place called Hades.[14] In this way, the counter-image of Hades helps to shape some of the central themes in the life-narratives of Homeric poetry, the most significant of which is the heroic ideal.

The heroic ideal can be organized around the following tensions: (1) Humans are essentially mortal and subject to fate (*Il.* 6.488–89, 21.99ff). (2) Although the hero's ultimate fate is death, he can achieve the worldly compensation of honor and the quasi-immortality of glory and fame (*Il.* 22.297–305).[15] (3) Honor, glory, and fame can be achieved by risking one's life and facing death or defeat. (4) The courage to face death and risk life isolates and alienates the hero from normal existence, but it also elevates him above the rest of humanity. The heroes are often called god-like and god-favored, and they are honored by others as protectors and defenders.[16]

The *Iliad* is built around the figure of Achilles, who faces an existential dilemma. He knows that he is fated to die young in battle if he fights the Trojans; if he leaves the war, he will live a long life, but without the fame and glory attaching to death in battle (see *Il.* 9.410ff). Each of these seems to be a real option for Achilles, so when in the end he joins the fight, he has *chosen* a fated death. The entire epic is thoroughly charged with death, not only the hundreds of deaths depicted in battle scenes (often in gruesome detail), but particularly in the looming death of Achilles. His horses speak to him of his coming death (*Il.* 19.407ff); and Hektor, before he dies, foretells to Achilles his imminent death at the hands of Paris and Apollo (*Il.* 22.355ff). Achilles replies (365–66) that he will accept death whenever the gods bring it to completion (*telesai*). So it is clear that Achilles knowingly and willingly gives up his life for heroic glory.[17]

We can say that heroic values are incongruous with what is *normally* most desirable in human life: the importance of such normal values is vividly portrayed in the epics through the voices of female family members and children, and the appeal of these values to the heroes themselves is displayed in their emotional and often poignant conversations with family members (see *Il.* 6.390–502; *Od.* 6.180ff).[18] And, in both epics, particularly in the *Odyssey*, heroes experience the alienation from home life as part of their noble exploits. Homeric heroes, therefore, are not reckless thrill-seekers who spurn normal values. They encounter the dilemma of *conflicting* values: the benefits and importance of heroic achievement measured against the comforts, pleasures, and significance of home life—and all of this in the midst of mortality and fate.

Homeric poetry presents a much more nuanced account of heroism than simply the idea that heroes achieve their excellence and stature "despite" an indigenous mortality and fate. We notice in the text a reciprocal relation between mortality and heroic values. The heroic ideal (and its larger importance for the community) can be seen as *informed* by mortality. The clearest example of this is found in Book 12 of the *Iliad*. After praising the virtue of fighting for one's country, Hektor asks a hesitant warrior: "Why are you so afraid of war and hostility?" (*Il.* 244). For us this is a strange question, but the heroic rationale is presented a short time later (*Il.* 310ff), when Sarpedon says something to Glaukos right before they go into battle. His speech amounts to encouragement in the face of the heroic dilemma: Why, he asks, are they honored above other men and looked upon as gods? Why do they have wealth, land, status, and all their privileges at home? Because the people honor and admire their courage in defense of country. So if they want to preserve their status, it is necessary (*chrē*) for them to fight. But what about death? Sarpedon poses a hypothetical: If they were ageless and immortal, they would not have to strive for glory, which is the source of their station. The meaning seems clear: If there were no death or danger, there would be no *need* for valor and its rewards. If a hero values aristocratic privilege, he must also value the possibility of death. Mortality and noble values, therefore, are structured together with reciprocal force. Accordingly, Sarpedon returns from his hypothetical back to mortal reality and closes his speech with these remarkable words: "But now, seeing that countless fates of death stand close around us—fates that no man can escape or avoid—let us go forward and gain glory for ourselves, or give it to others" (*Il.* 326–28).

Here we find exemplified the starkest sense in which human life dwells *between* Olympian and Chthonic forces, between the deathless gods and lifeless Hades. Both realms together give humans the attraction-repulsion dynamic that constitutes a *mortal* life, its virtues and limits.[19] The apportioned sphere of mortal existence between immortal life and Hades is delineated in the following way: (1) The *aversion* of both humans and deities to the realm of the dead highlights the beauty and value of life.[20] (2) The *exclusion* of humans from Olympian immortality assures the maintenance of this disclosive structure by forbidding mortals an escape from death.[21]

The Justice of Strife

Heraclitus tells us that justice (*dikē*) is strife, that the way of things and their meaning are structured by conflicting tensions, that "peace" would actually amount to nothingness or meaninglessness.[22] We can call this a formal account of the material narratives of conflict and its cultural significance in Greek poetry. Divine strife is evident in Homer, but in a specific manner. The original battles of the gods (as depicted in Hesiod) are in the past and have been resolved by the apportionment of divine powers, an arrangement that sorts out the various norms at work in the *Iliad* and *Odyssey*.[23] But an essential feature of Homeric poetry is the apparent need the gods have for witnessing and enjoying the spectacles of heroic conflict.[24] Indeed, the gods instigate most of the conditions and terms that prompt the mortal struggles they love to watch.[25] Such elements in Homer have often been the source of consternation for readers of this picture of divinity, which seems to suggest that human life is just a plaything for the pleasure of the gods. Yet I think we should begin with a principle of charity that assumes serious intent and cultural value in epic narratives, at the very least in order to understand why Homer remained such a lasting source of education and exemplification. We should appreciate the rich portrayal of human action and divine observation as a serious and complex worldview that turns on the alluring, yet tragic character of earthly existence.

The overall narrative of gods and mortals in Homeric poetry suggests that the experience and witnessing of heroic conflict are a primary source of meaning for both humanity and divinity. The gods do not suffer from mortal limits; they are ageless and deathless, they do everything with ease and generally live a life "without *heteros*, without cares or sorrow" (*Iliad* 24.526). With their brutal struggles behind them, they nevertheless still need to witness and engage the drama of human affairs. Zeus says that he cares about the heroes, even though they die (*Il.* 20.19–25). He tells the other gods to go among the Greeks and Trojans, to aid either side as they wish. He will stay on Olympus and delight his heart in gazing upon the events.

Like a theater audience, the gods find great pleasure and excitement at the sight of human exploits, without having to suffer their real consequences. They experience both joy and sorrow over the fluctuations of human fortune, even to the point of laughing and weeping. Yet, unlike a theater audience, the gods also leave their abode to intervene in and influence events in the human drama. It is evident, then, that the tragic structure of meaning-amidst-limits is at the heart of epic poetry, because even the gods in their non-tragic condition seem to need the vicarious experience of mortal limits and conflict; and the gods sustain their own conflicted patterns in their engagement with human events.

We should surely concede that the epic worldview (as something more than mere "literature") presents an ambiguous array of human and divine values, which at the very least makes understandable the later complaints and criticisms of many Greek writers. Aside from the supposed "immoral" behavior of the gods—the target of Xenophanes and Plato, among others—the conflict *among* the gods in their engagement with mortal exploits presents irresolvable burdens on human "piety." That is to say, honoring or obeying "the gods" in a pluralized, conflicted sacred arena means that one and the same course of action can find both favor and disfavor among different gods.[26] Homeric heroes confront the *double* strife of their human contests that are also caught up in divine contests. Book 13 of the *Iliad* offers a clear model of this situation: The brothers Zeus and Poseidon are of "divided purpose" (*amphis phroneonte*) in their respective support for the Trojans and the Greeks, and accordingly they are "fashioning grievous woes for mortal warriors," who are thus caught in an unbreakable "knot" of strife and war (*Il.* 345ff).[27]

What follows from the conflicted pluralism of early Greek religion is a kind of ethical ambiguity that might frustrate us, but that should be taken on its own terms as a lasting motif in Greek poetry: Heroic values give grandeur to mortal life, but in an environment constituted by strife between mortals, between deities, and between mortals and deities. Homeric "piety," therefore, cannot mean mere subservience or acquiescence to the gods or fate. The *global* network of multiple sacred forces shows that *resistance* to the gods and fate is not an irreligious disposition but an intrinsic consequence of this network when it come to the *local* circumstance of a hero's particular actions or allegiance to a divine sponsor. Obedience or subjugation to one particular god entails resistance to another. A hero can actually challenge, even fight a god, as in the case of Diomedes in *Iliad* 5 (and in this fight he was aided by another god). The formula *daimoni isos* (god-like or equal to a god) occurs frequently in the *Iliad* as an indication of heroic virtuosity, often in a direct contest with a deity.[28] In any case, Greek polytheism exhibits intrinsic plurality, divergence, ambiguity, and disharmony. Yet humans simply dwell within this mixture without deeming it deficient.[29]

Heroic achievement, then, cannot help but be an ambiguous virtue within the overall sacred order. Human life is both fated and free; it is neither autonomous nor slavish. The inaptness of any such binary code is another telling mark of the "tragic" that must be addressed when trying to assess Greek poetry and its depiction of life. Homeric limits on human agency figure *in* agency, and so they are not perceived as utterly alien to self-determination. Epic language exhibits extensive use of middle voice constructions, which function in-between the active and passive voice, in the sense of *performing* an action that is not self-generated or fully self-controlled.[30]

Homeric Behavior

Given the competitive environment of the Homeric world, it is no surprise that the predominant value is power, especially for the gods but also for the heroic ideal of achievement in the midst of contention. In such a setting the many traits that might seem immoral for later moralities—pride, aggression, rank, and powerful emotions—should be taken as a different kind of morality. Moreover, the epic self lacks a strict sense of interiority because the primary standard of value is performance in an external field of action. Such a standard helps us understand the near-obsessive concern for honor (*timē*) in the manner of praise and reward. Honor too must be externalized, thus the fixation on tangible prizes and the spoils of victory. Excellence is measured only by public signs of recognition. The wrath and withdrawal of Achilles may indeed be excessive, but they were brought on by Agamemnon's seizure of Briseis, Achilles's captured concubine; and this was surely an offense to heroic honor. Without an "internal" sense of worth, it would do no good to ask Achilles to "swallow" his pride, because his sense of worth is thoroughly informed by public measures and markers.[31]

The baseline competitive structure in the *Iliad* issues another value: respect for one's opponent. Victory requires a competitor, and a worthy one at that, because the value of victory is measured according to the level of an opponent's ability, and thus to the possibility of one's own defeat. "Defeating" a feeble or disabled opponent would lack significance (and conversely, "upset" victories are thrilling). Worthiness in the *Iliad* has a competitive measure that is not reducible to any particular agent or side in the conflict. Both the Greeks and the Trojans are displayed in a worthy light; and both sides are favored by (different) deities. There are many instances of admiration and respect between mortal combatants in the midst of vicious fighting. In Book 7, as Ajax prepares to do battle with Hektor, the following prayer is voiced:

> Father Zeus, most great and glorious, watching over us from Ida, grant Ajax victory and glorious renown; but if you love Hektor too and care for him, give to both of them equal might and glory. (*Il*. 202–05)

After their brutal and exhausting fight, Hektor proposes to Ajax that they stop their battle and agree to a postponement, so that they can "fight again until the divinity chooses between us" (291–92). Then they exchange gifts! The effect of this moment, Hektor says, is that both the Greeks and the Trojans will be able to say: "The two of them truly fought in the rivalry of heart-consuming strife, but then they made an agreement and parted in friendship" (*Il*. 301–02).

Another feature of heroic behavior that runs afoul of later moral assumptions is the absence of autonomy or a strict sense of responsibility.[32] In addition to divine management and instigation in the course of events, the gods will often intervene and alter the motives, emotions, and capacities of the heroes themselves.[33] Agamemnon even describes his seizure of Briseis as the result of a divine seizure: "I am not responsible," he says, because Zeus and the fates "caught my heart in fierce delusion (*atē*) that day, when in my arrogance I took from Achilles his prize. But what could I do? It is god that brings all things to completion" (*Il.* 19.86ff). Yet the heroes do not seem to rebel against such intercessions as diminishments of their worth or to bemoan ruinous consequences as "unfair" or wretched enslavement to cruel deities. Once again, the Homeric self seems to be a middle-voiced confluence of fate and freedom, of noble achievement in the midst of forces larger than their own efforts. Indeed the overall economy of life for mortals in Homer is unpredictable, beyond human control and comprehension; important turns of fortune come to pass "as the god's heart pleases" (*Od.* 8.570–71: *philon epleto thumō*). But rather than call this a woefully chaotic world awaiting rectification in later writers, we can say that the poet tells stories that help mortals *make sense* out of the fact that life does not always make sense (which it often does not, to be sure).[34]

ODYSSEUS

The figure of Odysseus in the *Odyssey* is remarkable. He embodies the heroic tension of glory and alienation from home in the most acute manner. After the war he embarks on the long journey back to Ithaca and Penelope, a journey packed with danger, death, challenges, and the typical mix of assistance and hindrance from the gods. One of the continuing descriptions of Odysseus is a man who endures great suffering. Yet the word for endurance, *tlēnai*, can also mean resolve and daring. Odysseus exhibits great courage, resourcefulness, and intelligence in the face of his troubles on the way home.[35]

Odysseus is called *polutropos*, a man of "many ways," which can also mean "many turns," to capture the shifting personas and behaviors he displays in the varying contexts of his journey. He is also called the man of many "wiles" (*kerdea*) and "tricks" (*doloi*), and his ventures are permeated with a host of deceptions in speech and performance. The term summing up such traits is *mētis*,[36] or cunning, which to us can seem morally questionable. Yet *mētis* contains much ambiguity because it can also mean wisdom, skill, craft, and planning—an ingenuity needed for overcoming an adversary or natural hazard. The capacity for *mētis* is not questioned morally in the poem because it is a skill required of Odysseus in his many circumstances of challenge and danger. Without *mētis* he would not have succeeded in his quest. To the dismay of many later critics, *mētis* is even affirmed as a divine virtue. After Athena recounts Odysseus's renown for cunning, crafty counsel, and artful stories, she notes that they are both well-versed in this manner, and she says "I among all the gods am famed for cunning (*mēti*) and wiles (*kerdesin*)" (*Od.* 13.291ff). Concealing truth, therefore, is affirmed as a virtue, but not as an absolute value; rather, it is a capacious virtue for success in certain contexts of activity in the face of obstacles and threats. Moreover, *mētis* can be linked to the overall absence of substantive identity in the figure of Odysseus, as shown in the Cyclops episode, where Odysseus gives his name as "No one" (*Outis*) and is referred to by Polyphemus as "not one" (*mē tis*).[37]

The most important feature of the *Odyssey* is what I take to be the dramatic core of the poem: the affirmation of mortality in the course of homecoming. We have noted how heroic values are informed by death and alienation from normal values. Odysseus's arduous journey is obviously a condition of alienation, but it aims for a restoration of the values of home life that heroes also hold dear. Yet since Odysseus survives his ordeal and is restored to his homeland, shouldn't we take his story as something other than tragic when compared with Achilles? If the question is posed in terms of mortality the answer is clearly, No. In Book 5, Odysseus is being held captive by the beautiful goddess Calypso, and is longing to return to Penelope and Ithaca. Calypso surprises him by saying she will release him for his journey home (he is not told that she was commanded to do so by Zeus). Calypso, however, has enticed him to stay by offering to make him "immortal and ageless all his days" (*Od.* 5.136). She enhances the offer by foretelling how much suffering he will have to endure on the way home, and by reminding him how much more beautiful and glorious she is than his mortal wife. While conceding that she is finer in form than Penelope, Odysseus nevertheless turns down Calypso's offer. Despite the vital benefits and pleasures of this proposal, he still longs to return to Ithaca. As for the pains and perils of his journey, he says: "I will endure it, having in my breast a heart that endures suffering. For before now I have toiled and suffered much amid the waves and in war; let this trouble be added to those" (*Od.* 5.221–24).

This is a stunning moment in the poem. With the condition of mortality and limits in the Homeric world, Odysseus is offered release, so that Sarpedon's hypothetical immortality is now a real prospect. Yet Odysseus refuses and thus *chooses* to trade an ageless and deathless existence for his mortal life with Penelope, along with the sufferings that will accompany his return to that life.[38] And it should be noted that Odysseus makes this choice *after* he had witnessed the grim reality of Hades.

This episode in the narrative is noteworthy in being the utmost possible affirmation of mortality, because it is a deliberate refusal of immortality. And my claim for the importance of this episode in the poem can be borne out by the text, because it is highlighted right at the start of the narrative in Book 1.[39] The gods are surveying the situation of Odysseus's story and the Calypso scene is cited first (*Od.* 11ff). The captivity of the hero is marked by his suffering at being kept from home. Calypso is trying to beguile him into forgetting Ithaca, but Odysseus, "in his yearning even just to see the smoke rising from his own land, longs to die (*thaneein himeiretai*)" (*Od.* 1.57–59). We might read this simply as despair, in the sense that he just wants to be put out of his misery. But in context I think it is more plausible to read this as a powerful forecast of the meaning and import of his coming choice: In yearning to return home he must also yearn for mortality. Homecoming in the poem is far more than simply a return to home-life; it is also a recollection and reclamation of mortal finitude.

In sum, Achilles and Odysseus both embody from different angles the tragic structure of significance and value. Both encounter the coincidence of death and meaning in their lives. If we keep in mind that normal values of home and hearth are part of the epic world, then Achilles and Odysseus can be understood in their tragic dimension, in terms of what they must sacrifice for meaning. Both live for the heroic ideal, but Achilles is the one who perishes and pays the ever-looming price for heroic action: he sacrifices normal life for glory and fame. Odysseus does not pay this price in the war, but he sacrifices immortality for the heroic return to normal life. The two epics together can be said to celebrate the value of heroic deeds *and* normal life in one sweeping narrative. And both spheres of value are affirmed in the face of death and fate; indeed these spheres are *informed* by the force of mortality and limits.

Limits and Care

We have seen how tragic limits constitute various values in epic poetry. In this section I want to show how elements of care are expressed in Homer, and how these elements are related to limits.[40] In Greek, as in other languages, care has a double meaning: The words *kēdos* and *kēdō* mean both "caring" (caring-for, carry-about) and "cares" (worries, troubles). Likewise, the word *meletē* and its variants mean both attentive care and anxiety. It is clear that this double meaning is not accidental because it fits well a basic feature of human existence: We care about and for things *because* of the worrisome limits in life. Positive aspects of care are caught up with negative cares.[41] We have also seen how epic poetry involves a tension between heroic values and normal home life. Human care in everyday practices is indicated and described throughout the *Iliad*.[42] Yet a rich sense of care functions in other ways in the poem, sometimes even bridging the difference between heroism and normal life.

The anger of Achilles can be said to have caused cares through his not caring (refusing to fight).[43] Yet we have seen that Achilles was not without reason in being offended by Agamemnon, and what was most offensive was that Agamemnon dismissed Achilles's complaint by not caring about it (*Il.* 1.180). Later on, Patroclus, a caring man, carelessly comes to his death, which reawakens care in Achilles, not only for Patroclus, but for the other Greeks as well (*Il.* 18.100–03). Close friendship and love between fellow warriors is a central ingredient in the *Iliad*. Achilles deeply loved Patroclus; his grief over Patroclus's death and the fact that he was not there to protect his friend caused Achilles to set aside his anger at Agamemnon, take up his allegiance to the other Greek warriors, and join the fight against the Trojans—knowing he will die in the process (*Il.* 18.96ff). Not only can glory outweigh death for a hero, so too can devotion to comrades.

The final book of the *Iliad* shows a dramatic conjunction of heroism, death, and care. Even though death does not lead to any positive condition, mortals perform rituals of care for the dead—hence the problem of Hektor's corpse lying *akēdēs*, uncared-for (*Il.* 24.554). In lines 33ff., Apollo rebukes Achilles for his excessive rage, his defilement of Hektor's body, and his lack of pity for the father Priam (extreme postures that are ever-present possibilities in the midst of war). He says that the fates gave mortals an enduring heart, so that after a loss, after mourning and grief, mortals can "let go," "let be" (*methenke*). He tells Achilles that his actions have achieved nothing noble. Later (*Il.* 477ff.) Priam, with help from the gods, goes to Achilles and begs for the release of Hektor's body. He asks Achilles to think of his own father, upon which both men weep. Achilles agrees to the release, mentioning mortality and limits, that no one escapes woe, which nevertheless should not be allowed to overwhelm humans (this speaks against his own actions earlier)—and significantly, Achilles's own mortality looms with his forecasted death soon to come. We noted that mortality in Homer highlights by contrast the value of life. The scene depicting Achilles and Priam goes further to show that an engagement with death can bridge enmity with a shared compassion stemming from a shared mortality.[44]

Book 24 concludes the epic, not with an end to the war, but with an intervention of care, indeed care that expands beyond kinship, that shows kindness (*charis*) to the outsider.[45] The final scene concerns mourning and funeral rites. Care for the dead in this way is also care for the living, as an active, meaningful response to the ultimate limit of death. Here mortality and care coalesce.[46] Some have read the final book of the *Iliad* as a repudiation of heroic conflict and violence, or a final vision of a different kind of life. But this seems a stretch, especially since the war will resume. Rather, it can be said that Book 24 issues a poignant *part* of an overall worldview, that even with (or because of) violence, strife, and cares, there is care in human life.[47]

Oedipus and Tragedy

Sophocles's Oedipus plays are a model for the way in which tragic poetry continues, yet alters, the fatal limits of epic heroism. Oedipus's fate looms in the background without divine personification, and his actions are not prompted by any divine intervention, because they stem from a fully individualized, free agency.[48] In addition, Oedipus differs from Achilles and Odysseus because the epic compensations of glory and home-life in the face of mortality are now lost in a catastrophe of ruination and disgrace. With Oedipus, epic values concerning heroic achievement and the household seem not to be in tension at first because of his successful reign at Thebes. Yet for Oedipus both spheres are permeated by a terrible *violation* of these values, a violation that has been ordained by fate and in fact *brought about* by Oedipus's attempt to resist his fate. In fact, I want to argue that Oedipus's fate is actualized by his *moral* resistance to the awful prospect of patricide and incest, a resistance on behalf of the mix of values sketched above. If this is true, then the Oedipus story is a striking extension of the limit-conditions and ambiguities marking epic poetry: It is no longer simply the limits of epic values of heroism and home life in the midst of finitude; now there seem to be limits *in* these values, to the point of being complicit with their violation. In other words, the Oedipus play depicts, in part, *moral* tragedy.

With Oedipus, epic ambiguity and an alienating tension between heroism and the home are extended to a remarkable degree. His story embodies the living coincidence of a host of contrary features: success and failure (his own advance led inexorably to his decline); knowledge and ignorance (everything he thought he knew about himself and his station was wrong); power and powerlessness; home and homelessness (Corinth was not his true home, and his true home was his ultimate alienation); convention and taboo; guilt and innocence. With Oedipus, epic ambiguity and the tension between heroism and the home are pushed to the extreme.

I want to highlight those elements of the play that bear most on my overall topic. In *Oedipus Tyrannus* it must be said that no familiar moral script can be satisfied in this story, not in the sense that there are no human values affirmed in the narrative, but that there can be no over-arching moral reading of the text.[49] Human values are shown to be intrinsically checked by what they want to hold off. It is not just that life is limited by death and loss; what is *worthy* in life cannot ultimately be traced to any preserve of its value, even in the older senses of divine immortality or human fame. Even though I think that the Oedipus story can easily prepare the attraction of Plato's moral critique of tragedy, nevertheless I want to say that the text need not evoke moral horror or moral pessimism. The play embodies, in an admittedly stark way, the tragic structure of meaning-by-way-of-its-limits that I have been working with.

In making my case it is important to challenge the idea that the play is any kind of morality tale, or even a warning against impiety. The prophecy that Oedipus will murder his father and marry his mother is surely not the kind of sacred message that would prompt reverence or even resignation. In the face of the oracle, what would "piety" mean for Oedipus's parents? Would it mean that Jocasta waits to knowingly marry her son after he kills her husband? We have noted that resistance to the gods is not out of line in the overall economy of Greek religion. Since the prophecy predicts the most awful violation of basic human norms, the original resistance of the parents can be said to stem from understandable moral horror; so too the flight of Oedipus from Corinth when he hears about the oracle there. And the herdsman, who spares the child Oedipus from death by giving him to a Corinthian, does so out of compassion (OT 1178).[50] Yet these acts of *moral* resistance to the fate at hand are in fact what bring its horror to fruition. How could this fate have come about at all if the parents "accepted" it at the start, or if Oedipus accepted it at Corinth? One could say that if they were "pious" from the beginning the prophecy would *not* have come to pass.[51]

A similar complexity must also apply to Oedipus's character traits, which are often taken to be the cause of his downfall. Well, what are these traits? In almost every way, Oedipus is a model of Greek excellence: strong, brave, intelligent, and a responsible leader. We can find no dismissive criticism of these traits *as such* in the play. Oedipus's mental prowess is distinctive in his heroic posture, especially with his deliverance of Thebes from plague by solving the riddle of the Sphinx, who would devour anyone unable to solve the puzzle (who but a heroic type would want to engage the riddle under such circumstances?). Also worthy is his genuine concern for the welfare of Thebes as its king. At the beginning of the play Oedipus is described as famous and god-like. An elder tells him: "you saved all our lives . . . [you] are our master and greatest power; we are all in your care" (*OT* 39–41). And none of the benefits of Oedipus's rule would have come to pass apart from his resistance to fate. This is why those moments in the text that speak against Oedipus's "hubris" must be considered carefully.

The choral speech that rebukes Oedipus (*OT* 863ff.) extols reverence for fate (*moira*), its justice (*dikē*), and the authority of its oracles—this against a man who would arrogantly speak or act contrary to sacred law. An important line (*OT* 873) is disputed by scholars; it is often translated as "hubris begets a tyrant." Some prefer a corrected text that would read "hubris grows from tyranny." I side with the latter reading because the former lacks sense in the context of the play.[52] First of all, *tyrannos* in Greek does not automatically connote a negative appraisal, but simply kingly power not assigned by law or by inheritance (*basileus*).[53] Moreover, as Oedipus says about his reign: "I never asked for it; it was given to me by the city" (*OT* 383–84). In this case *tyrannos* was achieved by merit and cannot be the effect of hubris. Yet hubris, as an excess, can be seen as a *potential* effect of *tyrannos*, which lacks the kind of grounding in the other forms of kingship and may rely more on self-effort and its possible excesses.

Nevertheless, the choral complaint about hubris is hard to pin down. The problem cannot be traced simply to kingship, because it was awarded to Oedipus for saving the city. If it is simply Oedipus's traits in general, the city's salvation would then be stained. In the narrative context of this choral speech, hubris is more likely a matter of Oedipus and Jocasta doubting or resisting the oracle's authority. Yet again we face the strange prospect of what "piety" would call for here, because within the overall story the city received great blessings from Oedipus's flight from the prophecy. Moreover, at the moment of this speech in the play, the full details of Oedipus's situation have not yet been revealed. Later on, after everything has been filled out, the chorus speaks in a revised tone about a fatal ambiguity for all concerned (*OT* 1186ff.). The "high-flying" hubris in the first speech is now the "high-aiming" success of Oedipus's deliverance of Thebes and his glorious rule. The fatal truth is now described as sad and pitiable, and simply a "reversed life." Finally, the chorus sees Oedipus's fate and downfall as not simply his own but indicative of the human condition as such: "O, the generation of mortals. Our lives add up to nothing." Human happiness is thus only apparent, and to Oedipus they say: "You are our model (*paradeigma*), your fate is ours" (*OT* 1186–194). This collective notion can also refer specifically to the political setting wherein the success of Thebes under Oedipus was likewise caught up in his tragic limits.

I do not think that the text can support a moral rebuke of Oedipus. In the *Colonus* play (*OC* 270ff., 960ff.), Oedipus twice defends himself as morally blameless, since the prophecy preceded his birth, and he actualized the offenses in ignorance of the true identities of Laius and Jocasta. Even the unwitting killing of his father was defensive in nature because he was struck first (at a road-crossing involving a typical aristocratic jousting of the "After me! No, after me!" variety). Yet despite Oedipus's moral innocence, he nevertheless takes "responsibility" for his actions and their terrible consequences by accepting disgrace and exile, and by gouging out his own eyes, a powerful gesture of shame and self-withdrawal. As he says of this ambiguity: "Apollo! It was Apollo who brought about my miserable sufferings. But it was my own hand that did this [the gouging]" (*OC* 1329–332) In this way the early Greek middle-voice confluence of fate and freedom is pushed to a remarkable limit, with Oedipus taking responsibility and punishment for a terrible offense that both was and was not his own doing. In the play, the self and an external fate are *correlative*—neither without the other, each inert without the other.[54]

Finally, the most notable of Oedipus's traits that brought his transgression to light was his passionate desire for the truth. Even when it is becoming evident that his inquiry will implicate him, he says to Jocasta:

"You will never persuade me not to learn the truth. . . . I have to know who I am. . . . That is my nature, and I could never be someone else or fail to learn what I was born to be" (*OT* 1065ff.).

To sum up the masterful tragic structure of Sophocles's play: Oedipus's fate was to enact a horrible transgression of human values. Various actions counter to this fate were morally motivated, yet they wound up bringing this fate to completion. Likewise, Oedipus's estimable qualities and achievements were caught up in this paradox. So we can say that the tragic outcome was caused by normally worthy characteristics: compassion, standing up for family values, heroic rescue, responsible leadership, and a passion for truth. Moreover, the great achievements and their vital benefit to Thebes would not have come about without this resistance to fate, without this self-contaminating path of life.[55] In other words, excellence and ruin were *both* caused by Oedipus's resistance to his fate. Such a daunting mix of blessings and curses, with no resolution of its tensions, surely leaves us in breathless suspension, or as the chorus says, "without a foothold" (*OT* 878). It is no wonder that the tragic character of Greek poetry incited criticism from later Greek writers.[56] But there is more to the story than rootless disorientation.

Oedipus at Colonus portrays the last days of the exiled king, his noble departure from life without anger or resentment. Once again, ethical care is displayed in his daughters' guiding and caring for (*hēmera*) their blind father (*OC* 1612) as he makes his way to the place where Hades will open up for him. His life there reaches its "end" (*teleutaion bion*), to be hidden (*kruphthēnai*) in the earth, concealed (*krupsōn*) in Hades (*OC* 1654–655). The end is fearsome, with dark forces opening up the earth to receive Oedipus, who yet gives worship to the earth and sky (Chronos and Olympus) before his death. Near the end of the play, the chorus urges the daughters to end their grief, because Oedipus "resolved the end of his life in happiness and blessedness (*olbios*)" and because "no one can escape misfortune" (*OC* 1720–723). The story of Oedipus, though in many ways disturbing, is surely an impressive model of coming to terms with the tragic limits of life.

Plato and Greek Poetry

To Plato's credit, he fully recognized the tragic sense of life in Greek poetry, and he responded to it authentically by taking to heart its dark themes, moral ambiguities, and what it would mean to call the tragic the last word on life. He wanted to advance a different worldview and set of values that could bring more hope and order to the human condition. The critique of poetry in the *Republic* had nothing to do with "aesthetics" or a censorship of "the arts." Greek poetry was not an "art form" but a world-disclosive source of meaning, and in Plato's day epic and tragic poetry were still primary vehicles for cultural bearings and education.[57] Socrates calls Homer the primary educator of Greece; his poetry has been ordering "our entire lives" (*panta ton autou bion: Rep.* 606eff.). Plato's critique had to do with truth, the transmission of cultural values, and pedagogical authority.[58] He was waging a momentous *diaphora*, or contest (*Rep.* 607b), against established meanings on behalf of new standards of truth and morality.[59]

Plato's critique of traditional poetry was fundamental because it challenged both the material and formal elements at the heart of epic narratives and tragic drama. The material element can be summed up as the depiction of a tragic worldview; the formal element can be located in the psychological features of poetry's composition, performance, and reception—each of which involved forces that surpassed conscious control and blocked critical reflection. For Plato, the formal and material nature of traditional poetry represented a powerful and ingrained cultural barrier that had to be overcome to clear the ground for two new ideals: rational inquiry and an overarching justice governing the world and the soul (*Rep.* 602d–604a; 605a–c).

Epic and tragic poetry present a world that is unstable, unpredictable, mysterious, and fatally ruinous of human possibilities. Here mortality is the baseline limit of life, and death is portrayed as repulsive in its darkness (*Rep.* 386–92). The poets tell "false stories" (*pseudeis muthous*), where heroes come to grief and surrender to powerful emotions, where the gods act immorally, fight each other, cause evil and ruin, punish the innocent, change form, disguise themselves, and lie (*Rep.* 377ff.). With respect to the gods and morality, one particular description from Homer is disturbing to Socrates: Zeus bestows good fortune to the good and bad alike, as he wishes (*Od.* 6.188–90).

One thinks of Oedipus as the paradigm case of tragic life: a noble man faced with a ruinous fate, who resists out of moral motives, and yet in this very resistance actualizes his fate. One might also think of Socrates in this vein, a man who compares himself to a tragic hero (*Phaedo* 115a), and who is destroyed following a divine calling to practice philosophy. The *Republic* displays a wealth of meanings, but I think that the dialogue is essentially an anti-tragic *muthos* (a term applied to the account of the polis at *Rep.* 376d).[60] The full course of the dialogue can be called a narrative about the possibility and desirability of a just life in a world that resists justice. The internal virtue of justice is defended by Socrates against Thrasymachus and the cynical implications of the Gyges myth (Books 1–2). The long digression about the polis is meant to clarify the picture of a just soul and its advantages, and the digression unfolds to meet the daunting task posed to Socrates in Book 2: Prove not only that the just man is worthier but also *happier* than the unjust man, that he will flourish in some way—and this in terms of the toughest case imaginable, pitting the unjust man thought by everyone to be just against the just man thought by everyone to be unjust (*Rep.* 361). This task is reiterated in Book 10 as the point of the entire conversation (612). And the rectification myth of Er (*Rep.* 616–18) performs the climax of Socrates's project. Immortality serves an essential function in overcoming the limits on rationality and justice in earthly life. That the poets and their tragic stories figure prominently at both ends of the dialogue, therefore, cannot be an accident. Traditional myths were fully expressive of obstacles blocking the path of Socrates's mission. He wants to tell a *better* story than the poets, one that can overcome the possible tragedy of a just life. And one cannot help but remember the fate of Socrates, whose death at the hands of Athens *would* be tragic without the kind of rectification suggested in the *Republic*.[61]

The formal element in Plato's critique concerns the psychological structure of poetic production, performance, and reception. The traditional view was that poets were inspired receptacles for the sacred power of the Muses, a "revelation" more than a "creation."[62] This matter of absorption in a force beyond the conscious mind was also implicated in the objections to *mimēsis* in the *Republic*. In Greek, *mimēsis* referred not only to representational likeness but also to psychological identification in poetic performance and audience reception, where actors, reciters, and listeners were "taken over" by the poetic imagery and its emotional power.[63] What really mattered to Plato in the *Republic* was not mimetic representation, because the example of painting is described as merely an *analogy* for the genuine matter of concern, mimetic identification with poetic language (*Rep.* 603c). And Socrates confesses (*Rep.* 605cff.) that even the "best of us" can become enchanted by poetry and swept away by the *pleasure* of empathic union with the sufferings of tragic characters—an effect that ruins the "manly" ideal of silencing and mastering grief (*Rep.* 605e).[64] In Books 2 and 3, the censoring of poetry was qualified and seemed restricted to the context of educating children. But later, poetry's power threatens the reflective mental control of sophisticated adults as well, and for this reason *all* mimetic poetry (epic and tragic) are to be banned from the ideal polis (*Rep.* 595a). The "falsehood" in traditional poetry is not really a matter of epistemology, but rather its effect on people's souls and how they live. As Socrates puts it, poetry creates falsehood *in* the soul, which is not simply false "words" (*logoi*) or beliefs, but a morally "false life" (*Rep.* 382b–c).

The material element of Plato's critique is that tragic poetry is expressive of, even a stimulant for, a way of life and a world view that are morally problematic.[65] The gods can be responsible for evil outcomes (*Rep.* 379a–c, 391d); the repulsive character of Hades (Socrates cites relevant passages we have discussed) could dissuade people from noble actions that risk death (386aff.); the death of loved ones is taken as a profound loss that prompts strong lamentation and grief (*Rep.* 387dff.);[66] and justice and happiness are often decoupled, so that the unjust prosper and the just come to ruin (*Rep.* 392b). This critique comes in the discussion of educating the city's guardians who in some respects possess characteristics of Homeric heroes. Perhaps times had changed, but surely Homeric heroes had not been dissuaded from noble deeds by the repulsion of death. Indeed, as I have argued, the fearsomeness of death and passionate grief over loss did not bring on pessimism, despair, or flinching from risky deeds; rather, mortality tended to magnify the value of life's attractions and define the significance of noble action.

In any case, Plato seems to want death and Hades transformed from a repulsive to an attractive prospect that can surmount the finitude of embodied existence with a substantive soul delivered from earthly limits. The moral context of this proposal is clear in both the *Phaedo* and the *Republic*, in that a belief in an immortal existence tied to one's moral character in life will stand against both fear of death and license to indulge any and all carnal desires. In the *Phaedo* Socrates concedes that "most people" believe that the soul is scattered and lost when departing from the body at death (80d). Yet he aims for an alternative view that specifically rejects the old picture of Hades. After death, the soul will depart to a place that is "noble, pure, and invisible," which is the "true

Hades" (*Adiou hōs alēthōs*), the abode of the "good and wise god" (*ton agathon kai phronemon, theon*) (80d). So little is death now repulsive that the invisible purity of Hades has been the aim of philosophical knowledge all along, and that philosophy has been in fact "the practice of death" (*meletē thanatou*) (*Phd.* 80e–81a).

In a similar fashion the myth of Er at the end of the *Republic* offers an alternative to tragic limits with a script of rectification for departed souls that rewards and punishes them based on their past deeds and their own responsibility for having *chosen* the course of their lives. Socrates specifically contrasts this myth with the tale "told to Alkinous," which is a reference to the stories recounted in Books 9–11 of the *Odyssey*, the last of which described Odysseus's journey to Hades. Socrates's tale is told by Er, who is described as a "brave (*alkinou*) man" (*Rep.* 614b), which seems to be a jab at Homer.

In Homer, Hades was morally neutral, because the human *psuchē* is neither punished nor rewarded for its deeds.[67] With Plato, the afterlife is morally informed for human souls, where the consequences of injustice and a lack of philosophical wisdom when choosing what life to lead block the soul's happiness.[68] Such a script provides an answer to the task posed to Socrates in Book 2: A life of justice, even if ruined in earthly life, will reap benefits after death (*Rep.* 614c–619e). And the reincarnation scheme described in Er's tale has souls choosing the types of lives they will pursue next, and this choice is clearly a break with older conceptions of mixed responsibility in the midst of divine management and fate: "the responsibility is with he who chooses; god is not responsible" (*Rep.* 617e). In general terms, Plato completely alters earlier (Homeric) conceptions of the self (as externalized, pluralized, and fated) by describing the fully realized self as inward, unified, and autonomous (*Rep.* 443cff.).

The moral problem for Plato is the vulnerability of life to tragic limits on human aspirations, particularly the aspirations of a philosophical life, as in the case of Socrates. There are some elements in the Er myth that are similar to Christian rectification when it comes to the shared problem of *moral* tragedy, the possibility that virtue not only can be ruined in life, but perhaps bring on its own ruin (if the crucifixion or hemlock were the last word). Platonic rectification shares with Christianity a certain triumphalist picture: the ultimate victory of the Good over its Other. In the Er story, unjust souls are beset by "savage men" who bind them, flay them, and lacerate them on thorn bushes before being thrust into dark Tartarus (*Rep.* 615eff.). In the *Gorgias*

(*Gorg.* 525c), the incurably wicked suffer from their assigned pains for all eternity (*ton aei chronon*).

In the Er myth there are also specific revisions of some early poetic tropes we have witnessed. The "ruthless, avenging Fates"—Lachesis, Clotho, and Atropos—now administer the process of souls choosing their next lives, and the Fates are decidedly less dreadful: dressed in white, singing songs, with garlands of flowers on their heads (*Rep.* 617c). Most notable, however, is the soul of Odysseus, the last one to choose a life. The Er story has Odysseus repudiating a heroic existence: Since his soul's "memory of its former suffering had relieved it of its love of honor (*philotimias*)," it gladly chose "the life of a quiet, private man who kept to himself away from public struggles" (*bion andros idiōtou apragmonos*) (*Rep.* 620c). Was Odysseus spotlighted for revision in this manner because of the troubling fact that in Homer he deliberately chose to reject immortality in favor of a mortal, heroic life? In Socrates's account, Odysseus takes an opposite course that can be paraphrased as a reformulation of Achilles's outlook: "I would rather lead a quiet, ordinary life than be king of Ithaca." And this new Odysseus can stand as a dramatic paradigm for Plato's attempt to deconstruct his poetic tradition.[69]

Conclusion

If the tragic sense of values in Greek poetry is disturbing, it cannot be because certain esteemed moral norms are rejected or doomed to meaninglessness; if that were the case it would be relatively easy to dismiss tragedy as nihilistic or inattentive to important human values. What may actually be disturbing, then, is that Greek poetry does affirm the importance of certain values while simultaneously acknowledging their intrinsic limits—either in terms of irresolvable conflicts between differing values or irredeemable limits on human happiness in a finite world marked by negative forces. In other words, the difficult message of tragic valuation is this: Whatever is good in life cannot ultimately be preserved, guaranteed, or immunized from otherness, cannot be tracked all the way down in the nature of things. Yet if negative limits actually figure in the very *meaning* of life and its values, then the aim to overcome or transcend tragedy may be an unwitting gateway to nihilism. That is why some philosophers, especially Nietzsche and Heidegger, have celebrated Greek poetry as anything but deficient modes of thought.

Notes

1. A source for material in this essay comes from Hatab 2008. There I explored features of Greek poetry to flesh out Nietzsche's examination of "noble" morality in relation to a later "slave" morality. Some points are also drawn from Hatab 1990.

2. I am using the following translations of Greek texts (occasionally modified): *The Iliad*: Lattimore 1951; *The Odyssey*: Murray 1995; Hesiod *Theogony*: Evelyn-White 1914; Sophocles, *Oedipus the King*: Meineck and Woodruff 2000); Plato, *The Republic*: Grube 1999.

3. See Burkert 1985, 199–203.

4. Homer speaks of the priority of Night and its power over both gods and mortals (*Il.* 14.258–59).

5. Similarly, the *Iliad* speaks of *Okeanos*, which is at the limits (*peirata*) of the earth, and which is rendered as the deep-flowing and brimming origin (*genesin*) of the gods (*Il.* 14.300ff.). In Plato's *Theaetetus* (152e), Homer's account of *Okeanos* puts him in the company of past philosophers (excepting Parmenides) who gave priority to becoming over being.

6. Witness Zeus bemoaning his inability to prevent the fated death of his beloved Sarpedon (*Il.* 16.430ff.).

7. See Allan 2006, 8.

8. See Adkins 1982. For a thorough examination of value terms in Homer, see Yamagata 1994, especially chs. 10–11.

9. See Claus 1981.

10. For a study of how positive conceptions of an afterlife emerged in Greek culture (e.g., in Pythagoreanism and Orphism), see Bremmer 2002, chs. 1–3.

11. Christiane Sourvinou-Inwood notes some instances that imply comprehension and awareness in the dead. See Sourvinou-Inwood 1996, 76ff. She argues that such instances reflect newer beliefs in Homer's time mixed in with older beliefs from the Mycenaean age. In the *Odyssey* (10.492–95), it seems that only the seer Tiresias is granted thought and understanding (*noon, pepnusthai*); all other souls simply flit about as shadows.

12. See Vernant 1991. Also Kerenyi 1973, 269–70.

13. An excellent study of such themes is Griffin 1980.

14. See Redfield 1975, 177ff.

15. Epic poetry in large part was the vehicle for recounting and sustaining heroic glory; *kleos*, literally "what is heard," meant a report of fame bestowed by singers of poetry. The *Iliad* itself speaks of this function, as when Helen says to Paris that in their dire situation they "will be subjects of song for future generations" (*Il.* 6.357–59). The *Odyssey* mentions singers telling of the famous deeds of both mortals and gods (*Od.* 1.338).

16. See *Iliad* 22.392ff. and 430ff.

17. Regarding Achilles's claim in the *Odyssey* about preferring the life of a laborer over kingship in Hades, some have read this as a retraction of his choice and even a renunciation of the heroic code. For a discussion, see Schmiel 1987, 35–37. Schmiel sees no grounds for this reading. I think it is easy to see the same Achilles in the *Iliad* and the *Odyssey* when viewed in light of the value of life marked against death. Achilles, still a hero, is saying that even a lowly life is preferable to the non-life in Hades.

18. See Griffin 1980, ch. 4. Indeed, the course of both Homeric epics is animated by the value of the home: The *Iliad* begins with the breakup of a household and the *Odyssey* ends with the restoration of a household.

19. See Griffin 1980, 162. A rich image of the mortality-immortality divide unfolds in the *Odyssey* (5.333ff.): The goddess Leukothea sees Odysseus struggling at sea on a raft. She offers him an "immortal veil" that will preserve him. But when he has reached land he must hurl the veil back into the sea, while turning away his face.

20. A vivid instance of this disclosive structure is given in Book 3 of the *Iliad* (428ff.): Paris has just confronted death in his duel with Menelaus, and will shortly do so again. In the interim, Helen pleads with him to avoid this mortal threat. Paris rebukes Helen, but asks her to make love with him, telling her that *never before* has his love and desire for her been as strong as *now*

21. Although the heroes are praised for being *god-like*, they are always warned against over-stepping their limits. When Apollo is challenged by a warrior, he says: "Take care and fall back; strive no longer to be like the gods in mind, because never the same are the race of immortal gods and humans who walk the earth" (*Il.* 5.440–42). We should note that Apollo's famous maxim, "Know thyself," was not a call for self-discovery, but a reminder of one's limits, that one is not a god—more akin to "Know your place" (Burkert 1985, 148).

22. Fragment 80, Kirk, Raven, Schofield 1983, 193.

23. See Muellner 1996, chs. 2–3. Allan 2006, 14 maintains that *dikē* in epic poetry applies to the unstable balance of divine powers. Against the idea that there is moral "progress" in the course of Greek poetry (from divine "immorality" in the *Iliad* to the emergence of 'justice" in the *Odyssey* and Hesiod), Allan maintains that there is more commonality throughout than change (p. 1). In the *Iliad* there *are* patterns of moral justice (punishment and reward for wrong-doing and right-doing), but not a consistent or intelligible pattern because of contextuality, differing divine aims, and the inscrutable will of the gods (pp. 2–4, 10).

24. See Griffin 1980, ch. 6.

25. The substantive role of the gods in Homer has at times been downplayed by scholars in favor of human and literary matters. But both the *Iliad* and the *Odyssey* depict the clear prominence of the gods and their causal powers. For a helpful account, see Heiden 1997.

26. This is precisely why Socrates (in the *Euthyphro* 7bff.) rejects the definition of piety as doing what is loved by the gods.

27. The global ambiguity of human prospects is personified by Zeus distributing the "gifts" of weal and woe to mortals and sometimes blending these as a "mixed lot" in the overall course of a life (*Il.* 24.525ff.).

28. Muellner 1996, 12.

29. See Versnel 2011.

30. See Peradotto 1990, 129ff.

31. Achilles's posture cannot be entirely problematic because the opening lines of the story describe his anger and withdrawal from the war as fulfilling the will of Zeus (*Il.* 1.5). His anger (*mēnis*) cannot be attributed simply to a human foible because the word *mēnis* in all other cases is attributed to the gods, as a response to violating a balance at the heart of cosmic order. On this matter see Muellner 1996, chs. 1–2.

32. See Adkins, 1960. See also Miller 2009, 29–50.

33. Some examples: Ares "enters into" Hektor and "fills his limbs with force and fighting strength" (*Il.* 17.210–12); "Poseidon . . . striking both of them with his staff, filled them with powerful valor" (*Il.* 13.59–60); ". . . not without a god does he rage so" (*Il.* 5.185).

34. See Gould 1985, 1–33.

35. Allan 2006, 16–25, argues against the idea that the *Odyssey* exhibits an advanced morality over the *Iliad*, particularly with respect to human responsibility. There remain many moral ambiguities and divine interventions in the *Odyssey*. In the opening lines (*Od.* 1.32–35), Zeus supposedly rebukes humans for blaming the gods for their woes, since human recklessness is to blame. But Allan points out a *kai* in the lines that is commonly untranslated: humans *too* are to blame.

36. See Detienne and Vernant 1991.

37. *Od.* 9.366 and 450ff. See Peradotto 1990, 147ff.

38. See Wians 1996; also Segal 1994, ch. 2. At *Odyssey* 7.258, Odysseus says that Calypso was not able "to persuade my heart."

39. The episode is also referred to several times in addition to the main account in Book 5: see *Od.* 7.253ff., 9.29ff., and 23.333ff.

40. For much of this section I am indebted to the article by Lynn-George 1996. He shows how the force of care "persists, even through annihilation, permeating the poem as a value of central significance" (p. 1).

41. In Heidegger's *Being and Time*, this double meaning of care (*Sorge*) is central to his phenomenology of existence.

42. In *Iliad* Book 6 (390–502), where Hektor and Andromache talk of her worries about his pending battle, there is a long, detailed, and vivid account of family matters, activities, and affections. Hektor shares his wife's attachment to these things, but duty and fate call him to fight.

43. Lynn-George 1996, 1–3, for this and the following two points.

44. See Herrero de Jáuregui 2011, 37–68. The ground of the argument here is that Priam's visit to Achilles's abode is metaphorically a visit to Hades, owing to a host of descriptions that match or suggest traditional features of a journey to the realm of the dead. With respect to Achilles, for a nuanced account of his bearing at the end of the *Iliad*, as well as a comprehensive analysis of his character in the overall epic, see Dean Hammer 2002, 203–35. See also Woodruff 2015, especially p. 602.

45. Lynn-George 1996, 13 and 16. Although concern for kin is strongest in the *Iliad*, there is also shown care for, and obligations toward, non-kin such as guests, suppliants, and beggars. See Gagarin 1987.

46. Lynn-George 1996, 21.

47. Lynn-George 1996, 24–26.

48. For the mix of human and fated forces in Sophocles, see Woodruff 2009, 233–54.

49. For a classic refutation of a moral reading of the play, see Dodds 1966.

50. It should be said that the child was to die not from direct killing, but from exposure, which was a gesture to fortune as the actual cause of death.

51. But then the prophecy would be an empty fiction. It is possible that the play's message is the foolishness of believing in sacred fatedness at all. But advancing secularism would seem to be a facile, flat alternative to the rich ambiguities in the drama.

52. See Meineck and Woodruff 2000, xxii–xxiv and 64.

53. See Anderson 2005.

54. For an important and philosophically sympathetic treatment of moral ambiguity in early Greek literature, see Williams 1993, with particular attention to Oedipus on pp. 68–72.

55. Heidegger interprets the Oedipus figure in terms of the "violence" to familiarity done by creative thinkers, who have to sacrifice home-like life for the "homelessness" of new ventures. The home-homeless factor is also examined in terms of the word *deinon* (meaning both wondrous and terrifying) used in the famous choral ode in *Antigone* (332–75). See Heidegger 2000, 111–14, 156–78.

56. It should be said that Aristotle's *Poetics*, in which the Oedipus play is a model tragedy, can be read not simply as an analysis of aesthetic form, but as a recognition of moral limits in human life. See Nussbaum 1986, ch. 11, Kosman 1992, 64–66. I take up this matter in Hatab 2008, 226–31.

57. Poetry was commonly thought to bear "wisdom," and in both writing and public speech poets were typically quoted or cited as "witnesses" for important beliefs. Plato himself frequently cited poets in the dialogues, either to challenge or enlist their authority. See Stephen Halliwell 2000, 94–112.

58. See Havelock 1963, ch. 1.

59. Socrates tends to deflate poetry by limiting its effects to pleasure. But poetry portrayed itself as delivering knowledge and truth along with pleasure (see *Iliad* 2.484–87, 9.186–89 and *Odyssey* 12.188). On poetry and truth see Detienne 1967/1996, ch. 2. See also Lesher 2009, 13–28.

60. Note that in the *Laws* (817b), philosophers are called "counter-artists" to the tragic poets and thus their "antagonists."

61. This dialogue can be called a theodicy of sorts, a response to the "problem of evil," of why ruin could befall a good person. One thing in tragedy's favor is that it does not face such a problem because pure "goodness" is not posited as the ultimate principle of reality.

62. See the Prologue to Hesiod's *Theogony* 98–108.

63. See Havelock 1963, ch. 2; Halliwell 2002, 1–33; and Prier 1989, 169–79. References to *mimēsis* in acting and spoken performance can be found in *Ion* 533ff., and *Sophist* 267. In the *Ion* (533ff.), the power (*dunamis*) of poetry is depicted as a chain of magnetic rings, which transmit a compelling force of attraction from the Muses to poets to rhapsodes to audiences. For a treatment of Plato's engagement with poetry as oral performance, see Yamagata 2005.

64. Plato concedes that tragic art can bring pleasure, but this is precisely the mimetic force that can infect souls in real life and tempt them to accept moral limits. In the *Laws* (2.569dff.) it is said that justice must coincide with happiness and pleasure, injustice with unhappiness and misery. That is why the arts must be carefully managed, to assure that pleasure is coupled with proper themes and effects.

65. See Halliwell 1996.

66. In Homer a common construction has a hero moving on "after having taken his fill of lamentation" (e.g., *Il.* 24.513), a usage stemming from the verb *terpō*, which connotes the pleasure of satisfying an appetite. Compare *Phaedo* 117cff., where Socrates's friends lose control and begin to weep at his coming death. Socrates chides them, saying he had sent the women away precisely for behaving in this "offensive way." He tells them to "keep quiet and be strong."

67. Sourvinou-Inwood 1996, 66. Those subject to punishment in Hades (Tityus, Tantalus, and Sisyphus), are demigods who violated the "cosmic order" with respect to fundamental elements of food, sex, and death (pp. 66ff.).

68. See Bernstein 1993, chs. 1–2.

69. Deneen 2000, ch. 2 gives a detailed account of the Odysseus reference in the *Republic*. He aims to show how Odysseus now stands for the Socratic philosophical ideal. See also Howland 1993.

6

Sketches of Oedipus in Sophocles's Play about Tyranny

MARINA MARREN

What has Oedipus to do with Athens? To answer this question, we have to understand the question first: What has Oedipus to do with tyranny? I offer a philosophical analysis of the philological, historical, and dramatic dimensions of Sophocles's tragedy in order to show how an image of tyranny grows out of the play. Oedipus's metaphorical blindness to the repercussions of his own actions, I argue, is not dissolved (as is commonly assumed), but sealed at the end of the play, when Oedipus deprives himself of sight.

I base my case that Oedipus is a tyrant on an analysis of the philological and literary evidence, which I present in section I. In section II, I elucidate the problematic relationship between sight, foresight, and insight by offering remarks about the significance of the visual images in the staged performance of the play. I probe the mettle of Oedipus's self-proclaimed perspicacity in section III, where I explain that Oedipus seeks power not to do good, but to hide his weakness. In section IV, I argue that Oedipus's defiance in the face of any, even divine, power renders him monstrous. I make sense of Oedipus's encounter with the Sphinx (Sophocles's metaphor for Oedipus's blindness to his own monstrosity) in section V. The reader will find the arguments about Oedipus's incapacity for self-knowledge and the philosophical implications of this view of Oedipus in section VI. In section VII, I address the question of Oedipus's responsibility and of the role of fate. In section VIII, the central argument about Oedipus's tyranny expands to include reflections on what it would mean for the audience in ancient Athens to see Sophocles's Oedipus not as a glorious king, but to understand the message of the play as a warning issued to the bellicose city. Section IX presents the philosophical implications of seeing Oedipus as a deeply flawed character and indicates what follows from this conclusion for the contemporary study of the play.

Introduction

Sophocles gave us an extraordinary play. In *Oedipus* we have a poetic image of a "wholly unpoetic man" (Benardete 2000, 75). Sophocles's Oedipus is an image of a complete merging of actual and seeming; of a complete coincidence between the meaning of the speeches and the poetic turns of phrase. Oedipus represents a total dissolution of the *muthoi* into *logoi*.

We often take Oedipus-like characters (in drama and in life) too literally. That is, we take the tyrants at their word—for what they give themselves out to be. To see why it is the case that Oedipus is a tyrant, we need to put his words together with his actions. The *logoi* and the *dramata* draw their deeper meaning from the world of myth. We do not seek to separate the *logoi*—the speeches of the play and what these speeches reveal about the nature of tyranny, from its *muthoi*—its poetic and mythic elements. We do not seek to use the poetic art didactically, because that would rid poetry of its perennial, aesthetic power. Instead, we aim to understand the meaning of the speeches in relation to the *poetic action* rooted in a mythic tale.

The philosophical import of the drama is potent owing, precisely, to the non-expository character of artistic expression. In our analysis of *Oedipus*, we do not shy away from the artistic images, but let them be the ground from which the philosophical reflection gains its amplitude. If drama, poetry, and myth are simply taken as a "package" for a philosophical *logos*, i.e., for the outside wrappings of an argument or of a certain "teaching," then, I insist, the philosophical import of the dramatists remains misunderstood.

A survey of the secondary sources on Sophocles's play makes it apparent that insufficiently careful consideration given to the historical or the artistic dimension of the piece (a consideration that addresses these aspects in a programmatic, rather than in a philosophical or a literary register) leads to presenting a caricature of Oedipus. Consider the strangely ingrained view that *Oedipus* is about "a brave man . . . bent on avoiding evil [. . .], a restless intellect, devoted at all costs to self-knowledge" (Woodruff 1999, xxii). The idea that "modern readers are attracted to Oedipus also because he is a ruler devoted to the welfare of his people, whom he sees as his children" (ibid.), is even more disturbing in its blind misrepresentation of the figure of the tyrant and the implicit agreement with the notion that to be ruled is to be parented. Equally strange is the common view, espoused by authors like Bernhardt Zimmermann (2000) and Bernard Knox (1998) that, as the play unfolds, Oedipus gains genuine knowledge of himself. In regard to the question of self-knowledge in *Oedipus*, I follow Seth Benardete (2000) who sees Oedipus's defiance strengthened and his capacity to know himself proportionally undermined as the play draws to an end. I analyze the relationship between Sophocles's artistic imagery and Oedipus's tyranny in consultation with commentaries by Walter Burkert (2000) and Jean-Pierre Vernant (1996). Although my conclusion about Oedipus's capacity to understand himself differs from Bernard Knox's, I am in agreement with Knox's view that Oedipus's tyranny is a commentary on the tyranny of Athens (1998, 61). Psychologically astute artistic appropriations of the piece by André Gide (1950) and Jean Cocteau (1934) also place emphasis on the question of tyranny. These pieces attune the reader to the variations on the tyrannical motif voiced in Sophocles's original. Perhaps it is because *Oedipus* is most of all a play—a performance meant to be seen, heard, and understood from the perspective of the audience—that the commentators, like Ortrud Gutjahr (2010) who studies drama, offer insightful interpretation of the play.

I. Painting the Background: Philology, Semantics, History

The title *Oedipus Tyrannos* is first given to the play at the Library at Alexandria long after Sophocles's time, between the third and second century BCE.[1] This way the play could be differentiated from *Oedipus at Colonus*. It came down to us in a Latinate translation as *Oedipus Rex*, the king. The title, which was meant to expedite indexing, became convention. In the play, Oedipus is referred to as a tyrant on several occasions. I recognize that *tyrannos* does not necessarily have the same negative connotation for the Archaic Greeks as "tyrant" does for us. However, as Victor Parker (1998) argues, *tyrannos* does refer to an unjust ruler by the time that Sophocles is composing. I take this designation as a key to prove one thing: king Oedipus is a tyrant. Tiresias says about Oedipus that he is in τυραννεῖς (the word appears at line 408 and is a verbal form of τύραννος)—referring to his ruling power over Thebes. Oedipus's own earlier tirade against Tiresias exhorts us to long for τυραννί, for a power over others for which, Oedipus thinks, he is being envied (380).[2] In an exchange with Creon, suspecting him of treason, Oedipus recants desiring τυραννίδα (541), a friendless and aidless tyranny. Creon, too, his subsequent poetic history notwithstanding,[3] claims disinterest in being a τύραννος (588). Oedipus, whether ruling in Thebes or in Corinth (940), rightly looks like a tyrant to the Corinthian messenger (925). The Corinthian is certain that Oedipus is neither a son of Merope and Polybus of Corinth, nor of Laius and Jocasta of Thebes. Oedipus is a babe off Mount Cithaeron (1026) or, to put it in the language of another tyrant, "a bastard from the basket."[4] Since the messenger thinks that Oedipus does not belong to the illustrious kingly lineage of either polis and since the custom calls the outsider who rises to power (whether he is welcomed by the citizenry or not) *tyrannos*, the Corinthian's motif in calling Oedipus a tyrant is benign. Oedipus's motive in saying that Laius, whose royal lineage in Thebes unbrokenly descends from Cadmus, had ruled by τυραννίδος (line 128), is unclear.[5] The chorus's meaning in their description of Oedipus's character—ὕβρις φυτεύει τύραννον—at line 873, could not be more condemning. "Hubris begets a tyrant."[6]

This play of meanings, revealed by the term "*tyrannos*," happens both at the level of Sophocles's play and in the history of the word's usage. As to the former, the stylized form of Sophocles's art vitiates both precipitous and final judgments passed on the meaning of the play. The context, the exchanges, the puns and metaphors, the characters and their moods, the events—all these things matter in figuring out the place of tyranny in *Oedipus*.[7] So do the other customary terms for rule—ἀρχή (rule) and βασιλεύς (king)—to both of which the characters resort. The instances of βασιλεύς, a name used for hereditary kingly rule, are sparse. The first occurrence of βασιλεύς is at line 257, where Oedipus is speaking of Laius as ἀρίστου βασιλέως or "noble king." The term appears once more at line 1202 when the chorus, reminiscing about Oedipus's rise to power in Thebes, calls him βασιλεύς. Cognates of ἀρχή, on the other hand, come up more often, at lines 259, 585, 627, and 628 to name a few. An especially interesting juxtaposition of governance and tyranny (ἦρχον and τυραννίς) happens at lines 591–92 when Creon questions the incentive for desiring tyranny (τυραννίς) in view of the restraints that governing (ἦρχον) places on one's personal wishes and affairs.[8] We learn from Sophocles's *Oedipus at Colonus* and *Antigone* exactly how unfit Creon's unbending character is for rule. Once he ascends to the Theban throne, Creon, too, is tyrannical in his actions. I am presenting, here, a simplified view of Creon's character. Although Creon's own tyrannical tendencies can be traced in the plays that Sophocles composes, these tendencies are better understood if each play (*Antigone*, *Oedipus*, and *Oedipus at Colonus*) and Creon's role in each is given individual consideration. Finally, the term *wanax*, which designates kingship for Mycenaeans (1600–1100 BCE) and is appropriated by the Homeric Greeks as ἄναξ, occurs in *Oedipus* at line 80. At that point in the play, not a mortal but a divine power is invoked by Oedipus himself when he calls on ὦναξ Ἄπολλον (Lord Apollo).

Although Sophocles's play describes the form of rule that is commonplace in Archaic Greece (the power concentrated in the hands of a single individual), Sophocles's own world is governed by the decrees of a democratic assembly. Sophocles's choice to refer to Oedipus's reign as that of a *tyrannos* bespeaks the author's concern with the fate of the Athenian polis. We should recall, also, that Athens bore the strain of Hippias's tyrannical cruelty only thirty years prior to Sophocles's birth.

Outside of Sophocles's play, the historical meaning of *tyrannos* is well accounted for by Parker's philological study of the word. Parker shows that *tyrannos* did not always carry the negative, let alone sinister, connotation. The term suffers marked shifts in meaning. Parker insists that its first appearances in literature, in Simonides, for example, simply refer to non-hereditary, but by no means illegitimate, rule. By the time Aeschylus, Sophocles, and Euripides write their tragedies, the meaning of the word changes to signify the corrupt and unjust actions that we, today, readily understand as being tyrannical. Since the three tragedians are composing at the time when the term is no longer identified with righteous rule of an ἄναξ or βασιλεύς, Sophocles's choice to call Oedipus a *tyrannos* is all the more telling.

His usage does not fail to speak, among other things, to the poet's own history. Sophocles, a general himself, saw the Athenian Empire expand its territory during the early days of the first Peloponnesian war

(445–440 BCE) just as well as he could see the signs of Athens's demise. Both the conflicts within the Athenian state and the growing success of the anti-Athenian Peloponnesian allies were crippling Athens's strength toward the end of the war (circa 407–406 BC). [9] The final battles of the Peloponnesian war against the alliance led by the Spartans (431–404 BCE) destabilized the Athenian polis. A posthumous recipient of cultic recognition, Sophocles did not live to witness the aftermath of that war, nor an Athens under the tyranny of the Thirty. However, he witnessed and put on stage a kind of thirst for power, a paradigm of a tyrannical blindness, attributable to both the Peloponnesian and the Delian parties at war.[10] The first performance of the play, hypothesized to be between 428–425 BCE, follows closely the dissolution of the peace treaty between Athens and Sparta and the first year of the war, 431 BCE, that proved ruinous to Athens.[11]

II. Vision and Blindness

The 2015 Freiburg Theater performance of *Oedipus Tyrannus* begins before the Sophoclean beginning. From the start, the play seeks to expose Oedipus's monstrosity. A grown man appears on the stage. Patches of film cover his eyes. The man is naked, save for a linen cloth wrapped around his hips. He descends a flight of stairs, then stumbles and falls to the ground. His convulsive movements and helplessness bring to mind some sickness, some physical or psychological ailment. The weakened body is picked up by a stalwart man who carries the afflicted, as if he were disfigured or disabled, and then holds him still while newly arrived characters cover up the nakedness with clothing. Now, a woman, tiptoeing, approaches the dressed man, whose sightless face is intermittently invoking antipathy and pity. She removes the film that hinders eyesight.

She is Jocasta, and now Oedipus can see.

Now Oedipus can see the hall and audience before him—a multitude in the dark. It is as if under his gaze we, the spectators, are transformed into the many mono-gendered, helpless Thebans of the feeble age.[12] Now Oedipus can see, and yet . . . does he have foresight? Once more, much later in the play, Jocasta will shock Oedipus into another sighting—a show of ugliness, disease, and weakness that not the others, but Oedipus himself has been and is. Oedipus, from that moment on, will "gaze in darkness on forbidden faces" (lines 1243–344).[13] Does Oedipus regain the power over the horrible circumstances of his life when he denies himself the capacity to look upon the world?

Sophocles plays with the metaphor of sight as a treacherous power, turning the question about human capacity to see into a maddening, persistent idea. What kind of a joke is it? What sort of a bizarre aberration? To have the capacity to see and yet to fail to see the truth of the most important things? To see the figure of a woman, but not what guides and moves her; not her dreams nor her intentions. To see a man, but not his loves and not his pains. To see an animal, yet not to see its life—never to penetrate by means of sight and grasp the essence of its being. To see all things lifeless and alive. Only to see, but not to know them.[14] Is this our predicament? Is this the predicament of human sight—to glide over surfaces and always past whatever depth that they bespeak? Or is it Oedipus's only? The capacity to see—does it entail, also, the potential to become Oedipus-like? Are all of us subject to seeing things merely for their surface appearances—for those surfaces, which with such expedient delight (itself but a desire of a viewer) hold images projected unto them?

III. Power and Weakness

Oedipus desires to see the Theban supplicants as powerless children (59); Tiresias and Creon as ill-meaning conspirators (535);[15] Jocasta as a haughty blue-blood (1062–063);[16] himself as an offspring of a goddess Fortune, born to embody the course of the waxing and the waning moon (1080–084).[17] Those around him Oedipus sees as either completely powerless or as challenging his power. The invocation ὦ τέκνα, which means children, deeds, or progeny, appears in line 1; and ὦ παῖδες οἰκτροί, pitiable children or youth, is the phrase that Oedipus applies to his subjects in line 59 (the word, παῖς, also refers to servants or slaves). Sophocles's diction portrays Oedipus as if he were a father-figure for the Thebans, who are as helpless without his rule as children are without their real or adopted parents.

Benardete relies on examples from Plato's dialogues, the *Odyssey*, and the *Iliad* to question why it is the case that in the communal political imagination of the Archaic Greeks, the idea of ruling as shepherding, rather than fatherhood, is at work (2000, 354–75). Benardete underscores the peculiarity of Plato's recourse to the identification of ruling with shepherding when he observes that the "notion of king as shepherd of his people (*poimena laōn*) is almost confined to the Homeric epics; indeed in the *Odyssey* it is applied to the last representatives of the former generation" (367). It looks as if a father and a shepherd—these two ancient metaphors for rule—split up to assert themselves in the domains of political and religious leadership. In Christian narratives, we find solidified the relationship between flock and its shepherd. The image of a patriarch, who validates his kingly rule by way of a recourse to the inheritance of a divine power, congeals in the realm of political government.

Contemporary political history offers chilling examples of rulers who sapped the strength and political maturity of the citizenry by propagandizing themselves as father-figures in power. Reciting the biography of Joseph Stalin (pseudonyms: "Soso" and then "Koba" Jughashvili) Radsinski makes a sinister remark: "we all were, to some extent, his children." Radsinski observes that Stalin's early pseudonym, Koba, is borrowed from an 1882 novel by Alexander Kazbegi entitled *The Patricide*. Stalin is hardly the first tyrant to cultivate his patronizing image. Russian Tsars were most commonly referred to as "tsar batjushka" or "tsar, the father." Stalin fills the role vacated by the murdered tsar and becomes the nation's father.

Contemporary cinematic imagination portrays the terrors of tyrannical, father-like ruling figures. Consider the character of Colonel Kurtz in Francis Ford Coppola's *Apocalypse Now*. Kurtz is as a rogue. He is deranged. He is a vicious tyrant. Yet, his sheltered subjects think Kurtz to be divine. Kurtz's "subjects" are treated in the film as his children. Curiously, the lyrics for the film's theme song, "The End," were written by Jim Morrison in an attempt to re-instantiate the Oedipus myth.[18]

Oedipus's desire to see himself as an agent of supreme power, even as an all-powerful force of nature, is fueled by an incapacity to admit his own powerlessness. In the face of the Theban misfortunes, Oedipus has no power; he cannot stop the plague. And his "own reason for driving out [the] . . . infection [is] . . . the killer [who] . . . could kill again" (138–39). Not to benefit the Thebans, but to help himself—this is Oedipus's primary goal. Oedipus reverses the order of priority when he says, "As I serve this cause, so I serve myself" (141).[19] Of course, it is in serving himself that Oedipus is most ineffective. Whether it is his fear, his anger, his despair and anxiety, his suspiciousness, or his arrogance that drives Oedipus out of the Corinthian land and sets in motion the events predicted by the oracle at Delphi, were Oedipus able to take pause and overpower the excess of his own emotions (777–78), there would have been no scheming phantoms to combat, no killer to track down, no monster to dismantle.[20] Oedipus's human origin makes him powerless in seeing through the ages back to the moment of his birth—a moment that would verify the place and parents to which he was born. Oedipus lacks the strength of self-assurance. He cannot see past the passing insult of a drunk (779). He trusts the creeping doubt. Why not reign in anxiety and anger and leave Corinth having made peace with what has happened, with his (adopted) parents, with himself? Here issues one of Sophocles's warnings: it is not what we know, not even what we (granted the genius of innovation) *can* know, it is what we do with the things that we find out about that matters.

The arc of Oedipus's overzealousness about power, which issues from the kind of powerlessness that we, too, being human, share with him, for Oedipus defines the way in which events unfold. Even at the very end, Oedipus has to be held back by Creon from an attempt to "take control of everything" (1522).[21] Another Sophoclean wisdom: the realization of the truth that there are things, and many of them, which human beings cannot control, often stirs up the desire to negate the fundamental weakness and to act as if one were a limitless, inhuman being.[22] Perhaps it is this weakness about which the chorus grieves: "Oh, what a wretched breed / We mortals are: / Our lives add up to nothing . . . Does anyone harvest more of happiness / Than a vacant image . . . Oedipus, your misery teaches me / To call no mortal blessed" (1186–196).

IV. Humanity, Divinity, Monstrosity

Despite our attempts to run from ourselves or to defy our mortal limits, we cannot be gods—immortal and all-mighty. What we can be, when the limits of humanity are transgressed, is monstrous.[23] Among the gods of ancient Greece incest and patricide are common.[24] But human beings are not gods. Both the myth about Oedipus and Sophocles's play press hard on the point of tension, which shows the incongruity of grafting back onto a man (if even onto a king) the being and the deeds of gods. We may entertain a notion that history presents such examples as when, to preserve a line of kingship, familial ties are turned into amorous ones. We may further argue that Nietzsche's insight into the ancient Greeks' relationship with their gods is right and that, for the Greeks, some mortal transgressions are absolved in divine misdoings.[25] Nonetheless, if in an effort to relieve the psyche of its guilt not only an incestuous Pantheon is generated, but also the human being is identified with the divine, then neither of the two orders remain true. The human order vanishes when the divine is used to indiscriminately justify all of our transgressions instead of to question them.

The myth that Sophocles's play enacts—the myth that tells of incest and of patricide—stands in for a metaphor of absolute, and therefore impossible, inhuman power. Killing Laius, his biological father, and taking his place when having children with Jocasta, his biological mother, Oedipus in his fantastical, mythical act seeks to negate the truth of human nature. This truth puts limits on our power. The first and necessary limit is defined by birth. We do not give to ourselves our own existence. Our lives do not originate from us. We are brought into life by other human beings. To rewind the biological time, to be one's own progenitor is not a possibility, but is that not a dream of absolute control over one's life? A nightmare. An irony is that in attempting to avoid this nightmare, Oedipus also shows that his parents mean precious little to him. Unless, of course, by parenthood he understands just that—a biological connection, a blood line that strengthens his connection to the Corinthian throne. Gutjahr traces Oedipus's controlling impulse and relates it to Hölderlin's view of the play. Gutjahr explains that on Hölderlin's account Oedipus "places his knowledge as absolute and, thus, trespasses into the region of God's knowledge. In this transgression he [Oedipus] negates his human existence, which, for Hölderlin, constitutes Oedipus's hubris" (2010, 81, author's translation).

Oedipus is terrified of the oracular pronouncement (788–94). Does this terror account for Oedipus's failure to pay his dues to Merope and Polybus? Does his fear explain Oedipus's all but gloating at Polybus's death (970–74)? Oedipus's actions, guided by fear, highlight the strangeness of his attitude to matters of familial affection. There is something sinister about Oedipus's callousness in the face of Polybus's death, no matter the excuse of being relieved at not having killed him. Oedipus is not weeping for the dead. The deaths come as a "great comfort" (987). It is the "living that scare [him]" (987).[26]

There is something perverse about Oedipus's anger at dismayed Jocasta and about the terrible parting words to his daughters (lines 1255–267 and 1490–1503, respectively). Benardete describes Oedipus's anger as a "passion for homogeneity" (2000, 78). Despite this equalizing or homogenizing passion, this blind and blinding impulse, the abyssal contradictions in Oedipus's life do not get erased. They deepen. The resolution is not—cannot—be attained by means of "*thumos*" (82). Although "Oedipus cannot stand opposition [and] . . . must overcome everything that resists him (cf. 1522–523)" (78), he does not end up as a good-natured victor. Instead, Oedipus is a tyrant: paranoid and perverse. Oedipus's passion demands, as Benardete puts it, that "everything . . . be reduced to the same level or eliminated until he alone as the city remains" (78). For all of its intensity, Oedipus's ravaging anger is helpless to resolve the strange contradiction that he is—an intimate outsider (a Theban citizen by birth, Oedipus thinks himself a foreigner to the city).[27] At first a benevolent stranger in Thebes (219–220),[28] Oedipus ends up being most abominably estranged (a cast out polluter).[29] He is a blood heir to the throne, yet he usurps the power (Oedipus is king Laius's son and he is also Laius's murderer, 451–62). Both in the polis and inside the home, in life of psyche and in public life (1319–320), Oedipus is, paradigmatically, a tyrant.

In support of my view of Oedipus's tyranny, I turn to Benardete, who argues that Oedipus embodies the "movement . . . from the question of who killed Laius to that of who generated Oedipus [as the movement] . . . that goes more deeply into the family [at the same time as it] . . . goes more deeply into the city as well. Oedipus violates equally the public and the private with a single crime. He is the paradigm of the tyrant" (2000, 73). In view of Oedipus's paradigmatic tyranny, it is unclear why Knox chooses to deny Oedipus the "classic pattern of *tyrannos*" (1998, 59). In support of his claim Knox writes: "He does not defy ancestral laws, outrage women, or put men to death without trial" (Ibid). But of course, Oedipus does all of these things. Oedipus commits incest, drives Jocasta to suicide, and murders Laius, taking his place as a ruler of Thebes. Arguably, although less obviously, Oedipus does also "plunder his subjects, distrust the good and delight in the bad [and] . . . live in fear of his people" (ibid., 60). The famine of the Theban plague can be seen as the result of the first—Oedipus's paranoid and megalomaniac tendencies—as that of the second; and the supplicants' excessive obsequiousness and pusillanimity can be interpreted as the upshot of the third of Oedipus's transgressions. Oedipus, indeed, "is not equipped with [the] . . . armed bodyguard which is the hallmark of the *tyrannos*" (ibid.). However, all other signs of tyranny, of which Knox absolves Oedipus, are applicable. As the play draws to an end, Oedipus's life takes a turn for the worse in a manner described by Herodotus in the *Histories*, where Herodotus considers tyranny in Croesus's life (I.32 and I.86–89). Croesus, Herodotus lets it be known, is the direct descendent of the proto-tyrannical figure, Gyges, the Lydian.

V. The Sphinx

As an assassin of the Sphinx, Oedipus faces the tyranny, which he is incapable of seeing in himself.[30] The Sphinx is a symbol of an unassailable power, which draws its strength from none other but human nature. The Sphinx's riddle, which has destroyed many a man, is about human beings. Oedipus—the man who is so afraid of his foretold future as to insure that the abominable events come to pass—annihilates the Sphinx. Oedipus frees his way to Thebes and, thereby, to his mother's bed. He helps to forge the chain of his own enslavement to the promised horror. Perhaps Creon is right about Oedipus's punitive "justice—[when he cries out:] . . . you hurt yourself the most" (675)! Would Oedipus have been as dear to the city, if it were not for his victory over the monster? Would he have been given the kingly throne and wife, the queen Jocasta, to go with it, if the Thebans were not downtrodden and in despair over the terror of the Sphinx?

The Sphinx, which in ancient Egyptian means a "living image,"[31] remains for Oedipus a picture of his debilitating blindness, not of his "enlightening knowledge" (γνώμῃ κυρήσας, 398).[32] Oedipus transfers his condition—an untimely three-leggedness or an evening darkness that descends at noon—onto the Sphinx's riddle and gets the answer right.[33] I am indebted to Benardete, who sees that Oedipus solves the riddle not because of some extraordinary power of detection, but because he simply (and perhaps unwittingly) inserts himself into the question that the riddle asks (2000, 75). Not only Oedipus's physical state, but also the image that his name evokes—two-footed (δίπους)—is a give-away to the solution of the fairly straightforward riddle. The Sphinx is as an indicator of Oedipus's uniqueness, that much is true, but this uniqueness does not have a positive character. The fact that no one but Oedipus is able to solve the riddle establishes a special link between him and the Sphinx. If there are heroic undertones in Oedipus's so called "victory" over the monster, they are tinted by the unsavory connection between the monstrosity of the Sphinx and that of Oedipus. Gide (1961) offers a similar understanding of Oedipus's monstrosity when he discusses Oedipus's murder of Laius and the relationship between the murder and the appearance of the Sphinx.

Oedipus's solution to the riddle is neither metaphorical nor poetic. It is literal and simplistic. Oedipus sees the world as if it were an image of himself. He sees all of humanity as if it were his own reflection. According to that image, a human being's progress is defined by impaired movement, by escape and, at the same time, by a human being's birthright to the physical dominion and lordship over the earth. At bottom, the Sphinx's question asks about the relationship between human infirmity and our need to draw on the earth's plenty. The question is about our weakness and the resultant impetus to provide for the store of power. Oedipus answers the Sphinx's question, but does he understand what it implies?[34] Does Oedipus reflect on his own quest for power—the search that originates in his fear of not belonging to a place, to a family, to a royal bloodline? Does Oedipus realize that his lust for power has fear at its root?

The riddle, which asks about human nature is, in every case, also a question about a particular human life. It is not sufficient to guess at one without reflecting on the other. Oedipus collapses his own persona with the universal view of humanity. He does not see the riddle as an occasion to reflect on himself. He does not see the monster as the riddle that she is for him.[35] For all of Oedipus's flights, his thinking remains, somehow unrealized and motionless. Knox draws attention to Oedipus's "speed of action" (1998, 16–17). I argue that regardless of Oedipus's swiftness or perhaps, because of it (because of the swiftness of his facile conclusions decisions, ideas, and actions) Oedipus remains unskilled in the task of thoughtful reflection and, thus, he remains fundamentally unchanged or unmoved. Sallis, in his discussion of Plato's Meno, gives examples and explanations of epistemic obstinacy (1996, 90–91 and 95). Both Sallis's analysis of the Meno as well as analyses of Oedipus presented here, show that an incapacity to be moved toward genuine knowledge has to do with the characters' literalness or their simplistic attitude toward poetic images and metaphors; toward the mythic fabric of the world.

Oedipus's image, which we can but he does not distinguish from himself, stresses the uncertainty that is at the basis of our longing for a better life. We always fall short of a perfect coincidence between our dreams for happiness and our being in the world. Having a world and being aware of it comes at the expense of living in perfect harmony and unity with it. Vernant, too, reflects on our inalienable strangeness; on the perpetual displacement and non-coincidence that are at the core of human life (1996, 91). We long to round out the eternal incompleteness, which rises from the fissure of the self-aware being. This is an impossible task. A human being is only complete in death, but having attained such a completion, we cease to be ourselves.[36] Oedipus's double blindness—a blindness that is both human (necessitated by the finitude of our perspicacity and understanding) and tyrannical (fueled by the desire to have infinite power over things) in kind—bars him from any genuine attempts at self-discovery. His search for knowledge is reactionary.

VI. Knowledge, Reflection, and Self-Knowledge

Although the knowledge of oneself cannot be complete, the search for that knowledge has to start somewhere. For Oedipus, the starting point is fear. What sets Oedipus on his ill-fated flight from Corinth? Is it his desire to learn about who he is? Not exactly. That sends him to the oracle, which gives no answer to the question about Oedipus's origin or his past. A drunken guest of Merope and Polybus's blurts out an insult when he says that Oedipus is "not [his] father's son" (πλαστὸς ὡς εἴην πατρί, 780). Whether or not Oedipus descends from Polybus, it is the Corinthian family that raised him. The prospect of being a bastard may be shocking. Nonetheless, even if Oedipus is not the son of Polybus and Merope by blood, he is still their adopted son. Maybe, to Oedipus, the blood relation is what matters most. If Oedipus is not Polybus's offspring, then the kingship does not have to go to him by hereditary right. Moreover, Oedipus will no longer be "held in highest esteem [and be as] . . . [a] prominent man."[37] If he is not a rightful son of Polybus, then he cannot be a rightful βασιλεὺς, either. Vernant comments on Oedipus's unease in the face of his possibly lowly origins and stresses the significance of Oedipus's initial inability to accept the fact that he is not the blood relation of Polybus and Merope (1996, 106–07). Knox further observes that "Oedipus's misgivings about his birth express themselves as a fantasy that he is in one sense or another of the line of Laius" (1998, 56). Oedipus runs from being a τύραννος in Corinth, only to become one in Thebes. However, while in Corinth Oedipus's tyranny would have been simply the result of his adoption,[38] in Thebes, he is a tyrant, not because his bloodline deviates from Laius's, but because he kills the rightful king, marries his wife, and brings the plague as a punishment unto the tormented city that helped him rise to power.

Oedipus's so-called search for self-knowledge goes no further than a reaction to an offense. Oedipus does not stay with his Corinthian parents. He chooses not to turn to them for their advice and their judgment. Oedipus flees from what he knows to be his homeland. This flight sets into motion the monstrous unfolding of his life's events. As a mutilated child, Oedipus has no choice but to be saved by the Theban shepherd and be delivered to the court at Corinth. But as a man he has a choice not to close out the circle that prophecy has etched into his life.

On the point of choice and fate, I agree with Knox that *Oedipus* is not a "tragedy of fate" (1998, 3). To say that it is, is too simplistic and hasty an interpretation. It labels the play instead of understanding what is at stake in it. However, Knox's claim that "'fate' plays no part at all" (6) leans too heavily in the direction of seeing human agency as perfectly autonomous. This latter view does not coincide with the ancient Greek understanding of the world and of a human being's place in it. If fate is interpreted, rather, as an essential passivity and receptivity at the heart of human nature, then the interaction of the active and the passive forces in Sophocles's play can be put into its proper context. Knox's remark that "Sophocles has chosen to present Oedipus's actions not as determined but only as predicted, and [that] he has made no reference to the relation between the predicted destiny and the divine will" (38) is helpful in thinking about the role of fate in Sophocles's play and, also, in our lives.

The words of oracles, are they not also riddles?[39] Both Oedipus and Jocasta take the oracular pronouncements too literally and apply them selectively. Oedipus could have conjoined the first oracle given to him with the insult from the drunken guest to suppose that he cannot sleep with his mother in Corinth, because not only Polybus's but also Merope's identity as his alleged parent is questionable. Oedipus does not pursue this line of thought.

In turn, Jocasta waits for her son to come back, announce himself as the descendent of the Theban throne, and then kill Laius. Since this does not happen in the exact way she must needs imagines, she dismisses Apollo's prophesy on the grounds of it being false (720–23). Jocasta and Oedipus lack the interpretive imagination necessary to put together the actual events of their lives with the fulfilled prophesied events, which they experience but do not recognize for what they are.

Prior to the fulfillment of the prophecy, Oedipus does not have to flee from Corinth, and yet he does. Oedipus fails to face his strange and cruel fortune, his fears, and his anger. He cannot find the strength to face himself. Not even at the end.[40] The closer that he gets to seeing what he did; how all-encompassing a lie the life he lives is, and that the path he took to manifest the prophesy that he was given is complete; the more reluctant Oedipus is to accept the fairly apparent truth. "A terrifying thought / What if the blind prophet can see?" (747–48)—an inkling of a realization is replaced quickly by denial: "Laius was killed by several thieves / Then I could not have killed him / How can one be the same as many?" (843–45). To be known as a murderer of an unknown and unimportant man or to have killed a father and a king? But Oedipus is not choosing the lesser of two evils. His mind is only bent on circumventing one—the grave one, the one that has been prophesied to him. Precisely that from which he ran, that of which he was most afraid, befalls Oedipus, but when it does, he cannot recognize the crime for what it is. Oedipus keeps evading, instead of facing, the horror and its truth.

Believing the first prophecy given to him, Oedipus shuns the oracle related by Creon. Then he dismisses and suspects Tiresias of having conspired with his wife's brother (705). Maybe it is because Creon, not Oedipus himself, has heard the oracle's pronouncement that a shadow of suspicion falls over and obscures the truth, but note the strange coincidence: before Oedipus has done anyone any harm, he trusts the oracle completely.[41] After he has committed murder and incest, Oedipus refuses to figure out how and why it is no other but himself from whom Apollo means to free the citizens of Thebes. It may have been the years spent in power in the city—the city and the power that were "handed" (δωρητόν, freely gifted, 384) to him—that taught Oedipus to favor suspicion, hubris (964–65), "prosperity, tyranny, and outstanding prowess" (πλοῦτε καὶ τυραννὶ καὶ τέχνη τέχνης, 380) over trust and clarity of mind, but it is obvious that for all of his self-professed mindful knowledge (γνώμη, 399), his thoughts are paranoid, his reactions are overbearing, and his denial is only suspended when his kingly lineage is at stake. "Even if I find my mother was a slave / Descended from slaves, you would still be noble" (1061–062) he sneers at Jocasta. Shortly thereafter, Oedipus gives another paranoid response: "however low my birth / That woman with her feminine conceit / Is ashamed of my humble origins" (1077–079). This sentiment, nonetheless, bids Oedipus to press ahead and threaten torture (1153) in exchange for truth about his birth. Knox makes a very interesting point about "Oedipus's deep-seated feeling of inadequacy in the matter of birth" and about him feeling 'legitimized by [the] . . . connection" to Laius (1998, 56). Knox cites lines 258 through 68, where Oedipus first remarks that Laius's wife and bed are now his and then says that he will fight for Laius "as if" (265) he were Oedipus's own father. In these lines, Oedipus, effectively, admits that he is sleeping with his mother. Believing that he shares Laius's cause, Oedipus is in denial about the identity of his father's murderer.

Although all pieces of the puzzle are laid out before him, Oedipus fails to put them into the true picture of events. He seeks to hear the solution to the mystery from someone else. He is no longer a self-reliant solver of the Sphinx's riddle (of course, he never has been, only having transposed his own image onto the question of the Sphinx). He is an anxious, angry man, who flirts with terror and succumbs to paranoia, sometimes believing that the end is near, sometimes behaving as if it were impossible that guilt is his. Instead of finding himself, Oedipus is still running from the answer. Instead of finding it out, he leaves the truth to be delivered by an eyewitness to the fateful event, which he himself has seen, and in which he himself took part and action.

How can one be blind to that which one has done and witnessed?[42] How can one fail to recognize oneself? Or are these both unfair questions? Is it not the case that oftentimes we do not realize the import of our own words and actions? Is it not the case that recognition of ourselves as unfair, cruel, weak, but also as happy, caring, and giving takes time to manifest? Does Oedipus realize the possibility of seeing who he is, or is his coming to the point of being witnessed—being discovered for his deeds—the continuation of his ceaseless flight?[43] "From now on you must gaze in darkness / On forbidden faces" (ἀλλ' ἐν σκότῳ τὸ λοιπὸν οὓς μὲν οὐκ ἔδει / ὀυοίαθ', οὓς δ' ἔχρῃζεν οἵ γνωσοίατο, 1273–1274)—the faces, which for Oedipus will always be the same. These are the images of people from whom he will not ask forgiveness. He will not take the chance of being denied pardon for his crimes. Instead, he will seek mastery: "If I could stem the stream of sound. . . . Sweet oblivion, where the mind / Exists beyond the bounds of grief" (ἀλλ' εἰ τῆς ἀκουούσης ἔτ' ἦν / πηγῆς δι' ὤτων φραγμός . . . τὸ γὰρ/τὴν φροντίδ' ἔξω τῶν κακῶν οἰκεῖν γλυκύ, 1386 and 1388–1390). It may look like Oedipus is making peace with his abominable fate, but it is a false image.

Although he pines for what could have been his life, Oedipus does not give himself a chance to live out any but the stifled, sightless life he has. He is his own judge. He deals out his own punishment.[44] The self-inflicted blinding, the exile, even the castigation of himself as a polluter and a criminal—all this is his own decree (223-51). Gutjahr, explains that

> Oedipus appears as a tyrant, who bases his thoughts and deeds on himself alone. He, thus, shows himself as being reckless in both the divine and the human perspective. As a statesman, he bears a double responsibility: on the one hand, he must respect the divine ordinance given in the form of religious commandments and mores, on the other hand, his duty is also to care for the maintenance of the political order and the welfare of the citizens. . . . Oedipus ignores both of these principles. (2010, 82-83; author's translation)

Indeed, it turns out that Oedipus's concern with his own identity and safety takes precedence over his worry for the fate of Thebes. In fact, that worry is less and less pronounced as the play unfolds. Benardete attributes Oedipus's incapacity to live up to his role as the king to his excessive and vicious anger. He explains that in his management of the affairs of Thebes, Oedipus's

> anger . . . expresses his private devotion to public justice, though the same anger once brought him to kill Laius and his retinue (807). Oedipus cannot stand opposition. He must overcome everything that resists him (cf. 15–23). He fails to see any difference between his indignation at an injury to himself and one to the city (629, 624–43). (2000, 78)

However, it is not clear that the identification that Oedipus makes between the city and himself is beneficial for the Thebans. It is unclear whether at the end, when Oedipus is found out and cast out, the Theban plague has lifted. At the end, we face, again, Oedipus's misery, but what do we know of Thebes?

Oedipus's spirit of opposition bids him to treat himself in the very same way that he promises to treat the murderer in hiding and the accomplices who are silent about the killer's whereabouts. There is neither acceptance nor forgiveness in Oedipus's heart. There is but negation. Oedipus embodies the impulse of negation. Fantastically, he rounds out the whole that has to be forever incomplete, if our being is to remain human. Not to see the horror come to pass—the horror, which was only looming at the outset, but which became the truth of Oedipus's life, because he could not suffer himself to face it. Not to see the stranger as a fellow man. Not to see his own deformity (both physical and psychic) in the Sphinx's riddle. Not to see the Thebans as anything but children, incapable of having power over their lives. Not to see that even those he wronged are capable of being forgiving. *Not to see*—that is Oedipus's driving force, not, as has been strangely argued, a quest for knowledge. Unless, by "knowledge" we mean ideas and views spurred by the impetus to move further away from the knowledge of oneself.

As I understand it, Sophocles's *Oedipus* is a play about the danger of thinking that humans possess absolute knowledge or that knowledge resolves the tensions, incongruities, and ambivalences at the heart of human existence. Thus, I disagree both with Zimmermann and with Knox when the former claims that Oedipus is capable of self-knowledge through the gradual revelation of oracular pronouncements (2000, 27–28) and when the latter states that "careful reflection and deliberation [or] . . . great intelligence" (1998, 17 and 18) are attributable to Oedipus's character. Both of these views are confused. Aristotle's remarks on vice, excellence, and deliberation help clear up the confusion. In Book VI of the *Nicomachean Ethics*, Aristotle states that "deliberation is not rightness in every sense. For someone who lacks self-restraint [like Oedipus does,] or someone of bad character [like Oedipus] will, as a result of reasoning, hit upon what he proposes that he ought to do, so that he will have deliberated rightly, despite the fact that he gets something extremely bad" (Sachs, 2002, 112, 1042b20). The thinking process might make sense and look intelligent, but if the disposition and character are lacking in excellence, the attained result will not be good. I find questionable even Oedipus's capacity to deliberate well, let alone his aptitude for careful self-reflection.

Knowing one's progenitors, knowing about one's misdoings, does that amount to self-knowledge? Hardly. Reflect, realize, interpret, and accept that which has happened; this—in his defiance and denial—Oedipus does not do. But it must be done. Otherwise, we follow in Oedipus's footsteps and fall for misinterpreting ourselves and misusing what we know.

VII. Passivity, Receptivity, and the Role of Fate

It is not up to Oedipus to know everything about the causes of his life's events. It is not in his, nor in any human being's power, to master chance and fate.[45] Not us, not Oedipus; the human being does not command omnipotence. Self-knowledge is not the same as knowledge of the whole. The former is, at bottom, incomplete; the latter is impossible. In his denial and in his fear of himself, Oedipus strives to master the dependence, the passivity, the non-sui generic nature of the human being.[46] This denial makes his soul a fertile ground for the transformation from a tyrant *in potentia* into an actually monstrous being. Oedipus changes from being suspicious (778) to being paranoid (573–74 and 618–19); from being angry (781) to being hateful (671–73). He does not suffer this metamorphosis in such a way as to allow himself a possibility of being freed from his enslavement to the tyrannical visions and dreams. Intensification of his passions transforms them, but does not purify him. His paranoia turns into a willful delusion as Oedipus extinguishes his sight. Oedipus wants to see nothing that his actions did not already bring about. Even as he suffers the closing of the circle of his fate, Oedipus yearns to shake off the passivity in the act of undergoing and to be the one who not only acts and undergoes, but also the one who inflicts and suffers all of life's troubles upon himself. Himself a rising tyrant, Creon remarks about Oedipus, "Your submission is as painful as your rage. It's in your/nature" (763–64). At the outset of the play, Oedipus's pain is not his own, it is not an emotion to be related. Pain, there, is an inflated universal pathos which, in reality, cannot be felt. Oedipus calls out, "My poor children . . . I know you are all in pain[,] . . . but at least that pain is only yours. / None of you can know the anguish that I feel" (57–61). Nothing about Oedipus's suffering has changed at the end. Even at the close of the play, his pain does not relate him to others, but shuts him off from the world, as he despairs—"no one but me is able to endure my pain" (1415).

Is Oedipus as singular in his professed capacity to embody the universal (nature of the human being and human suffering) as he makes it out to be? Is he the sole cause of what befalls him? No. Oedipus's curse is also a curse that was issued to Laius. Can Oedipus dispel it in denial? Can he escape from it? He did not. Oedipus, born to Laius, is a son born to a king who was forewarned that he should have no male offspring. Laius is a refugee king, who in his lascivious desire rapes a boy—the son of Pelops.[47] To have no son or to die at his hands—that was the punishment allotted for the crime of the boy's rape and abduction. But Laius did enjoy Jocasta. She did bear him a boy. Jocasta. A bereaved mother. A queen, who saves her kingdom and her life at the expense of Oedipus's.

How is it possible that Jocasta does not know? "And our son? / He did not last three days. / Laius yoked his feet and had him thrown away" (717–18). Does she not see the scars on Oedipus's ankles? Oedipus asks her: "Tell me what Laius / Looked like. How old was he?" (740–41). She replies: "He was dark, about your size" (742) and yet she does not question whether the physical signs point to kinship. Instead, Jocasta, once again, chooses to save herself and her place at the Theban throne. This time she does it by marrying a man young enough to be her offspring.[48] "But this is spectacular—your father's dead!" (937). Does this befit a queen? Is this an utterance of a sensible human being? Jocasta is rejoicing at the death of her husband's father. Is this not very odd? Yet even stranger is the queen's insistence that "many a man has slept with his own mother / In a dream. But these things mean nothing" (981–82).[49] She pacifies her husband's reeling mind . . . with this assertion?! Whereas Oedipus seeks to master all events in his life by fleeing from the terror that permeates it, Jocasta lets things be—"Why be afraid? Chance governs human life, / And we can never know what is to come. / Live day by day, as best you can. / You must not fear this marriage to your mother" (977–80). But her indifference is as self-contradictory as is Oedipus's attempt at mastery.[50] The queen only speaks of letting things go, but she does the opposite. She holds on. Jocasta makes sure to remain in Thebes—with Laius or with Oedipus—but to hold on to power.

VIII. *Oedipus* and Ancient Athens

Is the setting of *Oedipus*, Thebes—a foreign place, made all too familiar in mythic tales—a warning against hubris; against a "monstrous waste" (πολλῶν ὑπερπλησθῇ μάταν, 874), issued to the Athenians at war?[51] Or is it an encouragement to war-bound Athens? Although Thebes, historically, is an ally of Sparta, Thebes is not simply a poetic copy of the Spartan polis. As rendered by the poet, Thebes is not a particular image of a historical city. Instead, it is a reflection on the universally recognizable ugliness of tyranny and hubris, which both foster war as easily as they proliferate therein.

The universal themes expressed in a poetic paradigm are bound to evoke responses that are as enthused with patriotism (if the play is understood as inciting pro-Athenian moods) as they are with readiness for conquest (if it is seen as an anti-Spartan piece). Yet, if *Oedipus* is understood as a reflection on the dangerous, self and state-undermining character of domestic and political tyranny, the tragedy can also be interpreted as a piece that questions, precisely, both the excessively patriotic and the expansionist ambitions. Knox offers a careful discussion of the play in relation to the Athenian political situation (1988, 53–106), and then proceeds to warn the reader that the "play could not have been an attack on *tyrannis* as an institution, for not only was *tyrannis* universally detested, it was also, by the beginning of the Peloponnesian War, a dead issue" (58). I disagree. I propose that the metaphors and images of tyranny in Sophocles's piece make it all the more pertinent to the Athenian viewers. The citizens of a state that believes itself to be a democracy, while being singled out by some of its own as well as by the foreign individuals as a tyrannical empire headed for expansion, view *Oedipus*. The tragedy invites the Athenians to consider tyranny in all of its apparent and incipient horror. Commenting on tyranny in Athens, Knox, himself, refers us to Thucydides's recitation of the speeches by Pericles, Plutarch, Cleon, and the Corinthian enemies of Athens, who make it "clear . . . that the idea of Athens as the *polis tyrannos* was a commonplace both at Athens and elsewhere in the second half of the fifth century" (60–61). In an apparent contradiction to his earlier claim, Knox concludes, "Oedipus's peculiar *tyrannis* is a reference to Athens itself" (61). If it is and if we understand Oedipus as an unreflective and a monstrous tyrant, whose hubris, paranoia, and *thumatic* sensuality get the better of him, then that reference to Athens portrays the polis in a particularly unattractive light.

At the beginning of his analysis of the play, Knox points out the "identification of the [Theban] plague with Ares," the god of war (9). The divinity's wrath calls to mind the terrors and pestilence of all war as well as, specifically, of the Athenian war and plague. Thucydides records the terror and the devastation that the war and the plague inflict upon Athens in the *History of Peloponnesian War* (II.17 and II.34–37). The opening scene of *Oedipus*—an image of a city downtrodden by the plague—would have been all too familiar to the Athenians who were themselves the plague survivors.[52] The outbreaks of the Athenian plague began in 430 BCE. The plague came back again a year later and again in 427–426 BCE. Dating Sophocles's play between 428–425 BCE makes the opening stanzas all the more poignant; they would have brought to mind recent events. "Some furious god hurls pestilence and plague"

(28)—this would have been the refrain transposable from the dramatic Thebes right into war-bound Athens.

Whereas, the memory of the plague that the first scene evokes is recent, the myth of Oedipus, which guides the plot, indeed, is old. Odysseus, as Homer's epic tells us, sees Epicaste (Homer's Jocasta) as a ghost in Hades (XI.271–80). Thus, the Oedipus myth does not exclusively relate to the Athenian audience in fifth century BCE. However, it serves as a reminder of the swift and terrible change of fortune that can befall a city and its leaders. Sophocles's iteration of the myth portrays the inevitable failure of the ruling family, which has dark secrets (be it Oedipus's murder of a stranger on the road to Thebes or Jocasta's compliance with Laius's plan to expose their baby), yet delays to confront them. The price that the city pays for the failures of its rulers is devastation.[53] We are not sure at the end of *Oedipus* if the plague's curse is lifted. At the end of the play, is the calamity resolved? The chorus sings, "Amazing horror!" (1297), casting doubt on our hopes that the fate of Thebes will turn for the better. What about the fate of Athens? It did not. What about ours?

IX. *Oedipus* Today

If *Oedipus* is as dark a play as I have argued here, then how is it tragic? If Oedipus is simply wicked and that is his character's failure, then, as Aristotle would affirm, what happens to him is "neither pitiable nor fearful" (Benardete and Davis, 2002, 1053a5). However, Sophocles's play does not portray Oedipus as a monster. It is the analysis of the play that shows the monstrosity of Oedipus's choices and actions. My interpretation follows closely the transformation that Oedipus undergoes. Oedipus—at first an anxious and defiant royal youth—turns into a destructive tyrant.

In *On Poetics*, which offers Aristotle's sustained analyses of tragedy, we read: "tragedy is an imitation, not of human beings, but of actions and of life . . . they [tragedies] include characters because of actions [and] . . . without action, tragedy could not come to be" (Benardete and Davis, 2002, 1450a16–26).[54] If we pay attention to the characters of tragedy, it is because through these stylized, paradigmatic images of human beings, we are drawn to accounts of their (and, if we are reflective, also our) actions. Characters are dispensable. A tragedy, like a good detective story, relies on putting together into a plot, which moves or "guides

[our] ... soul" (ψυχαγωγεῖ, ibid., 1450a34) that which has happened. On these grounds, Davis speculates that an alternative title of Aristotle's work could be: *On the Art of Action* (2002, xiii). Davis goes on to weave together theater and life saying that "actors and acting ... have something to do with action; poetry ... somehow [is] ... at the center of human life" (ibid.). The study of tragedy is the study of paradigmatically rendered human action. This study leads, by way of a meditation on the plot, which Aristotle says is "like the soul of tragedy" (Benardete and Davis, 2002, 1450a40),[55] to the detection of an ethos or a way of life, which transpires in our actions, in the things we say—in the deeds and speeches that outline the contours of our souls.

It would appear that Sophocles's work, in all of its metamorphoses, itself a changeling born from myth, continues to command our attention because it is a tragedy *for us*.[56] It is our tragedy. It is a tragedy of not realizing the import of our actions—not least because each action is set in a certain context by the next. It is the tragedy of having to act despite the fragile ground of deliberation and decision.[57] It is the tragedy of being blinded by our passions; the tragedy that jests: "He was perfect [. . .] He only had to live."[58] Even if, upon reflection, Oedipus is despicable, *that* he is so, is tragic. It is tragic that there is such blindness as Oedipus's, which is a permutation, albeit monstrous, of the necessary human finitude and the resulting shortsightedness. To put it in Benardete's words, "The knowledge of man's mortality is the knowledge of universal motion made tragic" (1981, 139). To be alive is to be in motion. Yet, all motion, for a human being, at some point, comes to an end and there is nothing that can be done to stop that. However well-tested, this simple truth does not forestall attempts at immortalizing individual existence—in works of art and literature, in actions great and terrible, in monumental and monumentally inane constructions erected to commemorate an imprint left by a transitory life.

It is tragic that Oedipus's destructive blindness, which rises in defiance of being finite, has come and will still come to pass. Benardete renders his understanding of such spiritual and epistemic blindness formulaically as the "incompatibility of Oedipus the bound with Oedipus the knower" (ibid.). Oedipus, who is held captive to his temper (343–44, 669–72, 777–78, 1255–262) and who is bound to his destiny by his fear (795–800) does not add up to a wise and perspicacious knower, who with the power of his mind alone saves Thebes by defeating the Sphinx. "Unwittingly," says Benardete, "tragedy puts together in Oedipus complete virtue and complete vice" (1981, 139). Sophocles's *Oedipus* may be a drama in which tragic blindness (of a character) points to the blindness of tragedy (its allegedly non-philosophical character). However, *Oedipus* may also be a very well made theatrical piece which, if it is allowed to take a hold of its audience, avails the spectators of a double *desis* and a double *lusis*. The first (*desis/lusis*) pair is at the level of the literary work. It is the quickening and the unraveling of the plot.[59] The second is at the level of philosophical reflection. It is the analysis of what has been woven together—of the play which is experienced as a complete whole—and the consequent understanding of the significance of the exact arrangement of the parts that, on the first go, do not seem to fit.[60] In his later reflections on the play, Benardete acknowledges the double structure.

> I had not understood originally. There is this double level of self-ignorance. . . . Sophocles wrote a play which has a very queer character to it; he traps the audience in a way that puts them in this funny position like that of Oedipus. They cannot possibly understand what's going on, but they think, because they're already familiar with the story of Oedipus, that they know what's happening. (2002, 123)

Oedipus's curse, on this interpretation, is not his fate, nor the fact that he knows it, but that he thinks he knows *exactly* what is going to happen and then interprets events, draws conclusions, and acts based on this supposed knowledge. It is uncanny, is it not, that our familiarity with the myth of Oedipus, with his life-story, speeds us along the trajectory that mimics Oedipus's blind belief? It is this—the unwavering and unexamined commitment to the initial opinion about the state of things—and not knowledge that is the quintessential mark of Oedipus. If we stop at the immediate portrayal of the king, who falls from power to disgrace, and if we fail to make sense of the play's many incongruities (*pace* Benardete), then we, at least as far as Sophocles's theatrical piece is concerned, walk in Oedipus's footsteps.

However, can *Oedipus* even be understood unless the blindness of the characters is taken on by us as ours? For Oedipus, the transformation is complete. For him, the self and the other (let alone another self), private and public, particular and general, individual and universal—are all comingled into an amorphous sameness. Because there is no poetry and all is literal for him, for Oedipus, there is no knowing, there is no learning, and there is no loving.[61] All three, when genuine, are wedded to the enterprise of reflection. We distance ourselves from the immediacy of life and, thereby, recognize its metaphorical and mythical dimension. Paradoxically, such recognition of the poetical and theatrical quality of life is a prerequisite for any serious attempt at surveying it past the apparent surface. The change of state—from surface understanding to a reflection on oneself—for Oedipus, remains impossible. The moment that the difference comes in "It all comes clear! . . . I am exposed" (1182–84), Oedipus folds it back into the amorphous sameness: "*Light*, let me look at you one *last time*" (1183, italics mine). Oedipus is unchangeable. Yet the meaning and the import of the play promises a metamorphosis. *Oedipus* holds a possibility of change that can take place for us.

Notes

1. See Sheehan 2012, 1 and 115–18, where he explains how the Alexandrian Library handled the ancient Greek materials, including Sophocles's plays.

2. ὦ πλοῦτε καὶ τυραννὶ καὶ τέχνη τέχνης / ὑπερφέρουσα τῷ πολυζήλῳ βίῳ. O wealth, and tyranny, and supreme skill / these are exceedingly envied in life. This translation is mine. However, I use Meineck and Woodruff's 1999 translation throughout. Where translation differs from Meineck's and Woodruff's text, assume that the English is my own.

3. Consider Creon's character and actions in Sophocles's *Antigone* and his *Oedipus at Colonus*.

4. This is how Daniel Plainview refers to his adopted son H. W. at the end of *There Will Be Blood*.

5. At line 799 Oedipus calls Laius τύραννον and at line 1043 Oedipus, again, refers to Laius as τυράννου.

6. Meineck and Woodruff translate the line as "hubris grows from tyranny" (1999, 36). This reverses the order of generation, making out hubris to be the offspring of tyranny and not the other way around. In the original, ὕβρις can be read as a feminine noun that appears either in the nominative singular or in the accusative plural. The verb, φυτεύει, is in the third singular present indicative active, and τύραννον is in the singular masculine accusative. Since the latter cannot be a nominative subject, it is more likely that τύραννον is an object of ὕβρις, and not the other way around.

7. See Davis 1999, where he describes tragedy as a "metaphorical analysis of a metaphor [during which] . . . [t]hings that at first look accidental in retrospect become absolutely necessary" (93).

One of the play's many puns occurs at line 924. Given the context, Oedipus's name can be understood to mean "see" or "know" where. Oedipus—Οἰδίπους—contains οἶδα, which is the perfect tense of the aorist εἴδω. Both verbs are the cognates of ὁράω. The meaning of the verb changes from "seeing" in the aorist, to "having knowledge" (in the sense of "having seen") in the perfect tense. Cf. Liddell and Scott 1953, 483 and 817. See, also, Sallis who notes that "in Classical Greek, εἴδω was obsolete in the present active and was replaced by ὁράω" (2012, 134n8).

Benardete comments on the lines 924–26 and says that Oedipus is "an *oide-pous* (knows-a foot)" (2000, 76). Benardete goes on to connect the more common interpretation of Oedipus's name—swollen foot—to "hubris [which] makes man rise to heights he cannot maintain and hence plunges him into sheer compulsion, where he wields a useless foot' (873–79). The swollen foot that is Oedipus finally trips him up" (77).

8. εἰ δ᾽ αὐτὸς ἦρχον, πολλὰ κἂν ἄκων ἔδρων. / πῶς δῆτ᾽ ἐμοὶ τυραννὶς ἡδίων ἔχειν. If I am myself a ruler, I would have to do many things against my will. / Why should tyranny be to my liking?

9. Cf. Zimmermann 2005, 65.

10. Woodruff reports that Sophocles was venerated as a hero and associated with Asclepius's cult (1999, xn.4). On the history of Asclepius's arrival to Athens, see Burkert (1998, 139, and 155). Whereas Burkert places the arrival of the cult following the events of the plague in 429 BCE, Wickkiser cites 420–419 BCE as the date of cult's acceptance in Athens (2008, 36 and 62). Burkert himself cites 420 BCE in the English language version of the text (2000, 114). Edmunds corroborates the later date by indicating the year 420 BCE as Asclepius's introduction to Athens (1996, 163).

11. Zimmermann contests both the date of the play, placing its production between 436 and 433, as well as the possible reflection of the Athenian disaster in Sophocles's drama. However, he does not give a reason for his choice of thinking that the plague, which terrorizes Thebes, is simply a familiar trope like the one used in Homer's *Iliad* (2005, 66). I follow Woodruff's as well as Knox's dating of the play.

12. Benardete makes a terrific observation about the ages and the physical state of Oedipus's supplicants. He comments on lines 16–19: "Children incapable of going far, priests weighed down with age, and a group of unmarried men stand before him. Oedipus is the only man *(anēr)*, in the strict sense, who is present. Two of the groups are weak, the other is strong. Together they represent an anomalous and defective answer to the riddle of the Sphinx, for the aged appear as priests, and the two-footed men appear as bachelors. The supplicants of the city are either below or beyond generation: the children have not yet reached puberty, the youths have not yet become fathers, and the priests are presumably impotent" (2000, 71–72).

13. It is unwholesome, according to Oedipus's own admission, for him to want to look upon the faces of his mother-bride and of his sibling-children. The trope of looking at the things that are forbidden comes up both in Herodotus's *Histories* (Book I.8-16) and in Plato's *Republic* (Book II.359c-360b). The story has to do with the adventures of a certain Gyges and an ancestor of Gyges, respectively.

14. Seeing and (or as) knowledge is a theme that recurs in ancient Greek drama. Wians examines the relationship between knowledge, ignorance, sight, and lack thereof (2009, 181-98).

15. ξυμφυτεῦσαι τοὔργον εἰργάσθαι. To have labored planting this deed along, at line 347; as well as λῃστής τ' ἐναργὴς τῆς ἐμῆς τυραννίδος. And an obvious thief of my tyranny.

16. θάρσει: σὺ μὲν γὰρ οὐδ' ἐὰν τρίτης ἐγὼ/μητρὸς φανῶ τρίδουλος, ἐκφανεῖ κακή. You, take courage, though I discover my mother to be thrice enslaved, you will not be revealed as base.

17. ἐγὼ δ' ἐμαυτὸν παῖδα τῆς Τύχης νέμων / τῆς εὖ διδούσης οὐκ ἀτιμασθήσομαι. / τῆς γὰρ πέφυκα μητρός: οἱ δὲ συγγενεῖς / μῆνές με μικρὸν καὶ μέγαν διώρισαν. τοιόσδε δ' ἐκφὺς, I am, myself, a child of Fortune, dispensing good and giving, will not be dishonored. I come from that mother. The months, my siblings, mark the waxing and the waning [moon]. Such is also I, by origin and nature. Also Woodruff, in his introduction to *Oedipus Tyrannus*, comments on the opening lines of *Oedipus* saying that the "Elder treats him [Oedipus] . . . like a god" (1999, xviii).

Given the examples from the anthropological history (Egyptian pharaohs, shamanism), a community leader's identification with the supernatural forces or with the forces of nature is not obviously or necessarily deplorable. Nonetheless, we find instances in which such identification coupled with utter disregard for the divine point to psychological disorders and the malignancy of character in those who rule. Consider the Persian tyrant Cambyses and the Roman tyrant Caligula. Their tyrannical trait takes on a form of a desire to embody that which is not in the power of human beings to manifest, subdue, or overcome.

18. Cf. Densmore, who sheds light on what is at stake in Morrison's understanding of the myth (2009, 88).

19. See, also, Xenophon's *Hiero*, III.10-13. The work postdates Sophocles's play. However, Xenophon's insistence on the fact that tyrant lives in constant fear for his own life retrospectively illumines Oedipus's concern for his.

20. θαυμάσαι μὲν ἀξία, / σπουδῆς γε μέντοι τῆς ἐμῆς οὐκ ἀξία. [That] was worthy of wonder, however, of my anxiety it was not. Alternatively, [that] was worthy of wonder, but it did not warrant how my mind then raced.

21. πάντα μὴ βούλου κρατεῖν. You wish to [take] power [over] everything.

22. See lines 964-69, where Oedipus denies the need to pay heed to the divine oracles and lines 1080-085, where he claims to have supernatural powers and identifies as an offspring of a divinity.

23. Despite referring to Oedipus as "wise" Nietzsche claims that it is an "unnatural abomination" to be as "wise" as Oedipus is (Kaufmann, 2000, 68). Nietzsche's question: "How else could one compel nature to surrender her secrets if not by triumphantly resisting her, that is, by means of something unnatural?" (68–69) gives away the answer, which hinges on an understanding of Oedipus's character as being transgressive, hubristic, and defiant in the face of the natural as well as of the human limits.

24. See Vernant's discussion of incest in relation to the play (1996, 95). See also Burkert's comments on incest in Near Eastern religions (2000, 13–14 and 7–20). For a general discussion of oriental influences on ancient Greek mythic and religious consciousness, see Burkert (1984). He offers especially interesting remarks about the purification rights (57–65).

25. I am referring to Nietzsche's description of the "Olympian world" in chapter 3 of the *Birth of Tragedy* (Kaufmann, 2000, 43). Consider also Vernant's explanation of the difference between approved and prohibited incestual relationships among the ancient Greeks (1996, 100).

26. Compare this line to Xenophon's *Hiero* II.20, where Hiero is convinced that a tyrant's worries do not subside with the deaths of those whom he fears.

27. Compare Oedipus's rage to Daniel Plainview's self-professed misanthropy in *There Will be Blood*: "Are you an angry man, Henry . . . I hate most people."

28. ἀγὼ ξένος μὲν τοῦ λόγου τοῦδ' ἐξερῶ / ξένος δὲ τοῦ πραχθέντος. This I will speak, although a stranger / stranger to that which has come to pass.

29. Although, in Homer's *Iliad* (XXIII.678–80), Oedipus dies in Thebes.

30. Sphinx appears at lines: 35 ἀοιδοῦ or singer; 130 Σφίγξ; 391 ἡ ῥαψῳδὸς . . . κύων or that singing bitch; 507 πτερόεσσ' . . . κόρα or the winged girl; 1199–1200 γαμψώνυχα παρθένον χρησμῳδόν or prophetic girl with crooked talons.

31. El-Shahawy gives this description of the monster (2005, 117). The author's text translates "Sphinx" as "lebendiges Abbild," which I, in turn, translate as the "living image."

32. Oedipus's self-assured attack aimed at the blind Tiresias and at the prophet's devotion to religious rituals is misguided. We could read back into Oedipus's speech the repercussion of the following saying: "Boy, I got vision, and the rest of the world wears bifocals" (*Butch Cassidy and the Sundance Kid*). Oedipus's foresight, however, is prodigiously ineffective.

33. See a succinct description of the riddle and the Sphinx's possible genealogies in Zimmerman (1966).

34. Benardete understands Oedipus's confrontation with the Sphinx differently. He sees in it Oedipus's failure to guess 'not the *eidos* of man, which the Sphinx had posed as a riddle, but his *genesis* [which is] the riddle of man" (2000, 81)

35. Although I disagree with Gutjahr's (2010, 60) presentation of the Sphinx as an amalgam of both Laius's and Oedipus's transgression, Gutjahr's

analysis suggested to me the idea that the Sphinx could be seen as an image of Oedipus's own monstrosity.

36. Notice that the sense of perfection, completeness, but also death is preserved in the ancient Greek word "τελευτάω." For instance, ἀποτελεῖν (*Timaeus* 37d), means a "brining to completion," whereas, the adjectival form, ἀτελεῖ (30c), means "incomplete." The various forms of the verb τελέω usually signify completeness, rather than perfection. Nonetheless, we also find related adjectival forms such as τελήεις, which mean not only "complete," but also "perfect." For the latter use, see the *Iliad* I.315, "ἔρδον δ' Ἀπόλλωνι τεληέσσας ἑκατόμβας" (they accomplished perfect hecatombs to Apollo, translation mine). The Liddell & Scott, *Greek-English Lexicon* cites both τελειόω and τελεόω as to "make perfect, complete" (1770). Herodotus uses τελευτήσαντι (*Histories* Bk. I.66) when he describes the death of Lycurgus.

37. ἡγόμην δ' ἀνὴρ/ἀστῶν μέγιστος τῶν ἐκεῖ. I had [a reputation] of a great man among the townsfolk there (775–76).

38. See the first section of this paper.

39. Knox offers an interpretation of the oracular pronouncements (1998, 34–38 and 44–45). Also, Herodotus's *Histories* gives an excellent example of how Croesus, the Lydian, misunderstands the oracles that he is given and how acting on this misinterpretation accelerates the downfall of his empire (History, I.47–56 and 77–92).

40. Benardete confirms this view of Oedipus's incapacity to change (2000, 80–81).

41. Oedipus has grounds to suspect the veracity of Creon's words. Creon could have bribed the oracle. We realize this when we read Herodotus, who explains why the people of Lydia accepted Gyges as their ruler. Herodotus points out that the Lydians are ready to rise up against Gyges who murdered their king Candaules and sought to take his throne. However, the magnificent sacrifices and gifts that Gyges sent to the Delphic oracle changed things in Gyges's favor (*Histories* I.14). The oracle accepted the offerings and "pronounced Gyges king of Lydia" (I.14), but warned that the fourth generation of Gyges descendants would suffer retribution and pay dearly for the ancestral violence.

The oracular pronouncements in ancient Greece were subject to manipulation. Burkert writes, "private worship [of a sanctuary] could bring considerable income to a priest through offerings and sacrifices, and with some gift and luck or through the grace of particular god, a flourishing enterprise could come into being" (1987, 31–32).

42. Benardete's diagnoses Oedipus's peculiar, untreatable spiritual blindness: "Oedipus . . . does not regard *nous* as a third faculty distinct from hearing and sight" (2000, 81).

43. Even the nonhuman others are invoked by Oedipus for their capacity to remember. ὦ τρεῖς κέλευθοι . . . ἀρά μου μέμνησθ'. O three paths . . . do you remember me (1398–401)?

44. ἐγὼ/κάλλιστ' ἀνὴρ εἷς ἕν γε ταῖς Θήβαις τραφεὶς / ἀπεστέρησ' ἐμαυτόν. I / the finest man raised by Thebes / Have robbed myself (1379–381).

45. Reinhardt discusses fate in the play and sees it not as a deterministic trajectory of one's life, but as a sudden, unpredictable agent, which points to the non-coincidence between being, appearance, and the tragic incongruities that result from this non-coinciding (1933, 110–12). Cf. Zimmermann's discussion of the relationship between being and appearance in *Oedipus* (2000, 21–34). See, also, Kirkland's note to Dodds's argument that the contemporary understanding of determinism does not correspond to the ancient Greek view of freedom and necessity (2014, 65n2).

46. Davis makes a similar point in his *Ancient Tragedy and the Origins of Modern Science* (1988, 4).

47. Dethroned by Antiope's sons, Amphion and Zethus, Laius flees to Phrygia and finds shelter at the court of king Pelops. Laius rapes Pelops's son, Chrysippus (Dynes and Donaldson 1992, 133). This act, undoubtedly, is enough to hold Laius in contempt of the guest-friendship custom and of Zeus, the god of *xenia*. Pelops, the father of the accursed Thyestes and Atreus, himself has a violent history. Pelops suffers death at the hands of his own father, Tantalus, who tries to feed the dead boy to the gods. Tantalus is punished and Pelops is later restored to life by Zeus. Pelops's physical loss is but a shoulder, which Demeter unwittingly swallows in her distress over the loss of Persephone. Pelops is given an ivory shoulder replacement by Zeus (Zimmerman, 1966, 197).

48. Xenophon's Hiero guesses that some partners in royal, especially in despotic families, enter into marriage for the sake of distinction and power, not out of love (*Hiero* I.33–34).

49. Zimmermann is also perplexed by Jocasta's "argumentation acrobatics" (2000, 26).

50. See Gutjahr's explanation of the way in which Oedipus's and Jocasta's dark "family secrets" bear on the analysis of the play (2010, 59).

51. Sophocles's Thebes is a poetic and a mythical rendition of the actual Thebes. Burkert says as much in his "Mythen um Oedipus" (2000, 8–9). The ancient Greek Thebes should not be confused with the ancient Egyptian Thebes. Both cities appear in Homer's *Iliad* Books IV.406 and IX.383, respectively.

52. In the opening scene, Oedipus rules over the dying and the dead and, thus, he does the opposite of what Achilles advises Odysseus to do in the eleventh book of the *Odyssey* (489–91).

53. Consider Socrates's remarks about Diotima in the *Symposium*—the dialogue about *eros* and its extraordinary power—in the context of the Athenian plague. Diotima "when the Athenians made . . . a sacrifice before the plague . . . caused the onset of the disease to be delayed ten years" (201d). If we believe that the priestess forestalled the plague, then we have to note, also, that the onset of the postponed disaster would have weakened the Athenian forces at the very beginning of the Peloponnesian War.

54. ἡ γὰρ τραγῳδία μίμησίς ἐστιν οὐκ ἀνθρώπων ἀλλὰ πράξεων καὶ βίου . . . ἀλλὰ τὰ ἤθη. συμπεριλαμβάνουσιν διὰ τὰς πράξεις . . . ἄνευ μὲν πράξεως οὐκ ἂν γένοιτο τραγῳδία

55. οἷον ψυχὴ ὁ μῦθος τῆς τραγῳδίας

56. See, for example, renditions of the play and of the myth by Seneca (*Oedipus*), Corneille (*Œdip*), Voltaire (*Œdip*), Schiller (*Die Braut von Messina*), Kleist (*Der zerbrochne Krug*), Platen (*Der romantische Ödipus*), Hoffmansthal (*Ödipus und die Sphinx*), Pannwitz (*Die Befreiung des Ödipus*), Gide (*Œdip*), Cocteau (*La Machine infernale*), and Eliot (*The Elder Statesman*).

57. Vernant confirms that also the Athenian audience of Sophocles's times saw in *Oedipus* the fundamental lack of the complete determinability of human action (1996, 88–90).

58. Seneca 1983, 17–18.

59. Cf. Davis's introduction to Aristotle's *On Poetics*, where he claims that "[t]ragedy is distinct in being simultaneously synthetic or genetic–*desis*, and analytic or eidetic–*lusis*. On one level, then, the movement from *desis* to *lusis* is simply linear—there is a point in the play where things begin to unwind. On another level *desis* and *lusis* are the same" (2002, *xxviii*).

60. Davis explains that "[l]*usis* in its deepest sense is not a part of the plot but a second sailing—a rereading which makes visible what was implicit from the outset but could never have been seen without first having been missed" (2002, *xxviii*).

61. Benardete says about Oedipus that "the ordinary imprecision of speech always betrays Oedipus. Speech in his presence becomes literal and as univocal as mathematical definitions. [. . .] He is the wholly unpoetic man, and hence it seems not accidental that in *Oedipus Tyrannus* alone of the seven plays we have of Sophocles the word *muthos* (speech, tale, false tale) never occurs" (2000, 74, 75). Reinhardt holds that the multivalent character of Oedipus's speeches is available for the interpretation of the viewer or the reader, but it is not accessible to Oedipus himself (1993, 117–18). The blind literalness of the protagonist's speeches, from the audience's perspective, is transformed into what Vernant refers to as the "tragic consciousness" (1996, 114, 117).

7

Helen and the Divine Defense
Homer, Gorgias, Euripides[1]

RUBY BLONDELL

Almost all the texts that have reached us from ancient Greece were created not for solitary reading but for performance. In other words, they were envisaged as communications between a speaker and audience, in a concrete setting, framed by the conventions of a particular genre. In many cases, this external or performative context of utterance is complemented by an inner or dramatic context—the fictitious situation in which imaginary persons are speaking, listening, and so on. In this paper, I want to look at the differences both these contexts make, individually and together, to our interpretation of the argument that I call the divine defense: the claim that one is not responsible for one's actions if they were caused by a god.

I shall focus on the three principal occasions when this argument is used to exonerate Helen of Troy. In Euripides's *Trojan Women*, Helen herself blames Aphrodite for her own elopement (940–41, 948–50). Her speech is routinely labelled "sophistic," in part because a similar argument is made on her behalf by the bona fide Sophist Gorgias, in his *Encomium of Helen*. Yet the argument is not "sophistic" as such. It appears in its essentials as early as Homer, when Priam reassures Helen that he blames the gods, not her, for causing the Trojan War (*Iliad* 3.164–65).

Despite differences in verbal expression and detail, the logical content of these three iterations of the argument is basically the same: Helen is not guilty because her elopement was caused by the gods, or more specifically, by Aphrodite.

The gods were, of course, heavily involved in Helen's elopement.[2] Zeus begot her specifically to make men fight over her beauty and, at the Judgment of Paris, Aphrodite offered "marriage to Helen" as a bribe. Yet our sources agree that she left her husband willingly, driven by her own desire. In such cases, divine influence on human behavior does *not* normally remove human responsibility.[3] Thanks to the overwhelming power of Aphrodite and her son Eros, sexual misdeeds put considerable pressure on this fundamental outlook (often called "double determination"). Nevertheless, the human agent remains responsible for behavior inspired by such divinities.[4] Women were considered innately susceptible to this kind of influence, but that was not, in the larger cultural purview, a reason for excusing them, but the opposite: a reason for blaming (and controlling) them. Even in the later fifth century, when causation and responsibility started to come under philosophical scrutiny, blaming the gods for one's own misdeeds remained problematic, and it never became acceptable in ordinary thought.[5] On its face, then, the divine defense of Helen, as used in these three texts, is specious. Yet the context of utterance—both internal and external—is fundamental to its precise import in each case.

The texts in question come from different periods, belong to different genres, and might be performed in a variety of venues and locations. For convenience, however, I shall imagine all three performances taking place in fifth-century BCE Athens. Athens is, of course, the native home of tragedy; Homer in general, and rhapsodic performances in particular, carried enormous cultural weight there;[6] and Gorgias's *Helen*, though it could have been delivered anywhere the sophist's travels took him,[7] seems especially well-suited to Athens,[8] where he was a familiar figure.[9] All three genres were performed, at least sometimes, in large public spaces such as the Theater of Dionysus. Oratory and epic were also performed in less formal venues,[10] but for purposes of comparison I shall envisage public performance before large audiences in all three cases.

In each case, the performer is a single conspicuously dressed man—a rhapsode, orator, or dramatic actor—competing with other similar performers, for fame, glory, and substantial material rewards. All three strive to entertain their audience with a verbal and visual display, often at festivals.[11] All three perform in large public spaces, which would minimize the importance of subtle facial expressions and call for a loud voice and large, histrionic gestures in order to reach the members of a large and possibly noisy crowd.[12] All three perform a dramatic role from a memorized script composed in high style.[13] Each speaks—albeit in rather different ways—with an authoritative voice.[14] And in each case the notional audience consists of privileged males, namely Athenian citizen men and youths with the leisure, taste, and opportunity to attend, gathered together in a public space with a view to enjoyment, and eager to express their approval (or otherwise) of the performance.[15]

In other ways, however, these three performance contexts were significantly different. For the rest of this paper I shall look at each in turn, focusing on ways in which such similarities and differences may have affected the audience's reception of the divine defense.

Homer

Homeric epic found its full meaning in performance.[16] Rhapsodes wandered the Greek world in search of receptive audiences, performing in various venues, especially at festivals.[17] In Athens, they could be heard "nearly every day" (Xenophon *Symposium* 3.6), but they competed most conspicuously every four years at the great festival of the Panathenaea. Many scholars think this took place in the theater of Dionysus, which could seat some 15,000 spectators.[18] Other possibilities include Pericles's Odeion or the Pnyx, both of which could hold a crowd of several thousand.[19] On such occasions the rhapsode stood on a platform (*bēma*), alone in front of his audience, dressed, in the words of Plato's Socrates, "as beautifully as possible," and "decorated with many-colored clothing and golden wreaths" (*Ion* 530b, 535d). The winner won both acclaim and valuable prizes (presumably including the aforementioned wreaths).

Success was achieved by arousing the audience's emotional engagement with the story and characters (cf. Plato *Ion* 535e). The rhapsode's performance style was, accordingly, vivid and emotional, as he imitated each character in turn, using appropriate intonation and gestures, much like a theatrical actor.[20] But the only "character" visible to the audience was the rhapsode himself.[21] His signature prop was a staff (*rhabdos*), which helped to enhance his use of gesture but also marked him with the authority of the single narrator. His audience would therefore "see" the Homeric characters only to a limited degree, as conveyed by his body language. They would, however, hear them, or at least their words, ventriloquated by the performer, as he adapted his voice to each character in turn.

It is in Priam's voice that we hear the divine defense used on Helen's behalf.[22] He is addressing Helen herself, in a private conversation,[23] as they look down from the walls of Troy at the duel between Paris and Menelaus. The warriors below treat Helen as an object of struggle, to be awarded as a prize to the winner without regard for her own agency or desires. But Priam addresses Helen kindly, reassuring her (3.164–65),

οὔ τί μοι αἰτίη ἐσσί, θεοί νύ μοι αἴτιοί εἰσιν
οἵ μοι ἐφώρμησαν πόλεμον πολύδακρυν Ἀχαιῶν·

In my view you are not responsible but the gods are responsible,
who stirred up lamentable war with the Achaians.[24]

In this instance, then, the divine defense is voiced by an old man speaking privately to an exceptionally beautiful woman with whom he enjoys an affectionate personal relationship. Helen is not on trial, and no one within the framework of the story is invited to judge her or punish her for her actions. Priam is, moreover, her protector, both as her father-in-law and as the king and patriarch of the royal family. He may therefore be expected to have his own agenda. That this is in fact the case is suggested by his threefold use, in just two lines, of the word *moi*, meaning roughly "in my view," or "as far as I am concerned," suggesting that Priam may have his own reasons for excusing her.[25]

These reasons go beyond Helen's extraordinary beauty and even their personal relationship. As king of Troy, Priam also has an interest in excusing Helen in order to justify continuing the war for ten long years. As long as the Greeks and Trojans are willing to keep fighting over Helen they cannot afford to admit that she is guilty, since this would impair her value by making her damaged goods. This problem is especially acute for the Trojans, whose retention of Helen is on its face inexplicable. But this particular excuse also serves a further purpose for Priam. Everyone else agrees on the guilt of his son Paris, whose seduction of Helen was directly instigated by Aphrodite.[26] Priam's vague reference to "the gods" displaces divine causation away from this specific goddess and toward the larger divine plan, making it easier to excuse not just Helen but Paris, together with himself and the Trojans collectively.

As we saw earlier, such excuses violate on their face the principle that humans are responsible for actions inspired by the gods. But similar claims elsewhere in Homer show that the divine defense may be used, in certain circumstances, as a way of saving face.[27] The most famous such case is Agamemnon's declaration that he is not guilty (*aitios*) for insulting Achilles, since Zeus and other divine forces clouded his judgment (19.86–90). But this kind of face-saving gesture only works when responsibility is not refused but acknowledged by the guilty party. As E. R. Dodds argued long ago, Agamemnon goes on to offer restitution in a way that implies that he does indeed take responsibility for his error.[28] He is able to save face precisely *because* he offers Achilles copious compensation. Paradoxically, the more willing one is to accept responsibility, the more one is entitled to save face in this fashion.

Priam's use of the divine defense serves, like Agamemnon's, less as a cogent logical argument or effective legal ploy than as a way of saving face. But the tension between self-blame and exculpation makes it easier to use the divine defense, as he does, as a face-saver on behalf of another person—albeit one in whom he has a vested interest—rather than oneself.[29] Yet its effectiveness still depends crucially on the reaction of the person in question, who is, in this case, the speaker's internal audience. In response to Priam's exculpating words, Helen does not agree with him, or accept the proffered excuse, but instead says she wishes she had died before she followed Paris and left her family (3.173–75), calling herself "dog-faced" (3.180)—a standard insult for a shameless woman.[30] Such language is typical of the Homeric Helen, whose repeated and forceful self-blame is unique in epic.[31] Unlike the men of the *Iliad*, who never blame her, she takes full responsibility for her own actions. It is this that allows Priam to save face for her by attributing responsibility to the gods.[32] Since she blames herself so stringently, the male characters are freed from the necessity of doing so.

Helen's self-blame is the most distinctive feature of her Iliadic voice. As such it underwrites her portrayal as a "good" woman who deeply regrets her single, terrible misdeed. She does not flaunt her extraordinary beauty, but appears in public as a decorous wife, modestly veiled and attended by handmaidens (3.141–44). Nor is her beauty flaunted by the poet, who conveys it only via the reaction of the Trojan elders, which is famously lacking in specifics (3.156–58). She misses her original husband and despises Paris, whom she castigates as far inferior (3.139–40, 173–76, 428–36; 6.350–53), thereby endorsing from her own lips the linchpin of Greek gender ideology, that women's desires are excessive, unstable, and unhealthy and lead only to trouble. Such self-deprecation is a form of self-disempowerment characteristic of the Greek male portrayal of "good" women.[33] Helen's self-blame thus enhances her value as a woman, ironically, by casting doubt on that value. At the same time, however, it allows her to reclaim the agency denied to her by men and use it to her own advantage. This is demonstrated by the success of her self-deprecating voice in gaining and sustaining the affections of the most powerful men in Troy, namely Priam and Hector.[34]

Helen's expressions of inner turmoil help to produce an engaging character with a nuanced ethical subjectivity and a complex relationship to agency, responsibility, and the gods. That relationship takes narrative form in her famous encounter with Aphrodite, which fleshes out Priam's vague reference to "the gods." While Helen is still on the walls the goddess appears to her, in disguise, and tries to lure her to bed with Paris (3.390–94). When Helen resists, out of shame, Aphrodite becomes angry and threatens to destroy her (3.410–17). Even though Helen then acquiesces, her self-flagellating struggle against the divinely embodied force of erotic desire renders her deeply sympathetic.[35] Yet it does not invalidate double determination.[36] Certainly it does not do so in Helen's own eyes. Her personal remorse does not prevent her from attributing her predicament to the gods in general and Aphrodite in particular (6.349, 3.399–405; cf. 6.357). But in doing so, she is not excusing but blaming herself.[37] It is this that allows Priam's use of the divine defense to function effectively as a face-saving maneuver.

The rhapsode's putatively male external audience can likewise accept Priam's paternalistic excuse in part because Helen herself does *not* accept it. Certainly, Homer's Helen has disarmed the vast majority of the poem's modern readers, almost all of whom have found her intensely appealing. This appeal would be communicated powerfully through the performance of a skilled rhapsode. Helen's encounters with Priam and (especially) Aphrodite offer rich potential for emotional engagement; if performed successfully, they should elicit the audience's sympathy, and consequently its applause. Since that audience never sees Helen's physical beauty (except in imagination), or observes her interacting with other characters, such success will depend crucially on the rhapsode's skill in ventriloquating her powerful voice.[38] The remorse that is so central to that voice allows both performer and audience to have their cake and eat it too, accepting Priam's benevolent, paternalistic use of the divine defense as a way to save Helen's lovely face without in the last resort excusing her scandalous behavior.

Gorgias

Gorgias of Leontini was one of the most famous and successful of the Sophists who frequented Athens in the latter part of the fifth century BCE. Like others, he offered a rhetorical education to ambitious and wealthy young men, and his *Encomium of Helen* was probably a way of advertising his pedagogical wares—an elegant *epideixis* designed to showcase the rhetorical skill and bravura performance style that brought him to such prominence.

Despite its title, Gorgias's *Helen* devolves quickly into a defense speech, framed as a rebuttal of Helen's poetic detractors (2). The Sophist argues that she should not be held responsible for eloping if she "did what she did" under the influence of the gods, Chance and Necessity (*Helen* 6 DK):

> πέφυκε γὰρ οὐ τὸ κρεῖσσον ὑπὸ τοῦ ἥσσονος κωλύεσθαι, ἀλλὰ τὸ ἧσσον ὑπὸ τοῦ κρείσσονος ἄρχεσθαι καὶ ἄγεσθαι, καὶ τὸ μὲν κρεῖσσον ἡγεῖσθαι, τὸ δὲ ἧσσον ἕπεσθαι. θεὸς δ' ἀνθρώπου κρεῖσσον καὶ βίαι καὶ σοφίαι καὶ τοῖς ἄλλοις. εἰ οὖν τῆι Τύχηι καὶ τῶι θεῶι τὴν αἰτίαν ἀναθετέον, [ἢ] τὴν Ἑλένην τῆς δυσκλείας ἀπολυτέον.
>
> It is natural not for the stronger to be hindered by the weaker, but for the weaker to be ruled and led by the stronger, and the stronger to lead, but the weaker to follow. But a god is stronger than a human in force and wisdom and other respects. So if responsibility (*aitia*) is to be attributed to Chance and the god, Helen should be released from ill-repute.

Alternatively, he argues, she should be excused because she was "abducted by force (*bia*)," "persuaded by speech (*logos*)," or "captured by *erōs*" (6).[39] The four hypotheses are initially presented as alternatives, but the divine defense turns out to overlap with the other three: the gods' power is equivalent to force, *logos* is divine in its power, and *erōs* can be construed as a god. Treating all four as equivalent, Gorgias develops his argument in a way that challenges the foundations of the moral order by threatening to eliminate human responsibility as such, and with it all moral judgment, praise, and blame.[40] In other words, he defies traditional views about human responsibility grounded in the principle of double determination.

The external performance context for Gorgias's use of the divine defense will have been similiar in many respects to the rhapsodes' presentations of Homer. Indeed, fifth-century Sophists were arguably the Homeric rhapsode's heirs.[41] They not only made frequent use of epic material,[42] but, like rhapsodes, wandered the Greek world giving public displays, before large audiences, in the hope of reaping both glory and profit. They too competed at festivals, where they appropriated the prestige of poetic traditions, dressing up grandly and sometimes wearing "the purple robes of the rhapsode."[43]

The internal context of utterance for Gorgias's use of the divine defense is, however, very different. The imaginary scene is no longer an intimate conversation between a man and a woman on the walls of Troy, but a public gathering where a man is speaking on behalf of an absent woman to an assembly of other men. No other character is ventriloquated and no conversation takes place. Helen, in particular, never speaks, nor is there anything to suggest her imaginary presence.[44] We neither see or nor hear anyone reacting to her appearance, her presence, or her voice, as Priam and others do in the *Iliad*.[45] Gorgias is very conscious of his relationship to his poetic forbears (cf. *Helen* 2). His attitude toward Helen is comparable to that of the Homeric warriors (who treat her as a passive object), and his language suggests that he shares Priam's agenda.[46] But he has taken over Priam's role as Helen's protector without addressing her or conjuring her presence.

Of the three authors under discussion, Gorgias is the only one who is performing his own words and doing so in his own voice. In so doing, however, he is performing the dramatic role of Helen's advocate, in a way that evokes aspects of an Athenian trial.[47] Thanks to the huge size of Athenian juries,[48] trial speeches were delivered not in enclosed venues, but in large public spaces.[49] Since Athenian women were not permitted to speak in public on their own behalf, Gorgias replicates local practice by depriving Helen of a voice.[50] And unlike the rhapsode's audience, eavesdropping from outside the dramatic frame, the Sophist's audience is drawn into the courtroom drama to become a "jury"—an acknowledged player in the imaginary scene. This role would come quite naturally to Athenian male citizens, a great many of whom would have served in this capacity.

In other respects, however, Gorgias's imaginary trial diverges sharply from Athenian practice. The speaker is a Sicilian (who could not speak at a real Athenian trial), defending a mythical figure, in a highly mannered style of a kind that would be frowned upon in court.[51] His speech is explicitly "written" (*Helen* 21), in the polished manner of a sophistic *epideixis*, not the humbler, more personal style of a real-world defense. And of course the "verdict" will have no practical consequences. Gorgias makes no attempt to update or humanize the legendary Helen by presenting her as a concrete person whose life may be affected by the outcome of the judgment. Nor does he appeal to our emotions on her behalf, relying, rather, on an exceedingly abstract series of logical arguments. Power and agency are attributed primarily to impersonal forces (*logos*, *opsis*, *erōs*), and even the gods are presented less as personal agents (like Homer's Aphrodite) than as abstract powers like Chance and Necessity.

Gorgias claims that his goal is to arouse pity for Helen (7), but this detached stance distances us from her point of view, and thus from sympathizing with her. He further undermines our sympathy by stripping her elopement of its narrative context, explicitly dispensing, as far as possible, with the familiar details of her story (5). As a result, Priam's face-saving gesture is denuded of its conversational context. Most importantly, Gorgias silences the remorseful voice that creates Helen's appealing Homeric personality. (Indeed, the self-blame that characterizes that voice is implicitly declared erroneous (2).) This leaves her without her implicit claim to agency, and Priam's face-saving gesture without its legitimating framework.

This point comes into focus when we observe how Gorgias has reconfigured the forces at play in Homer's Aphrodite scene. There we saw Helen subjected to three of his four causes—*erōs*, divine power, and persuasive language (first from Aphrodite, then from Paris)—all of which are used to induce her to reenact the choice she made at the original elopement.[52] But Gorgias eschews the Homeric narrative that shows Helen as an agent struggling to act within a complex set of forces, thereby sacrificing the kind of sympathy that a real defense lawyer would try to elicit for his client. By stripping her action of its context in personal relationships, antecedents, and consequences, he trivializes the deeply serious issues regarding agency and responsibility that are embodied in the Homeric Helen.

Gorgias's "defense" thus leaves his client worse off than when he found her. She is neither heard, as in Homer, nor seriously defended, as she would be by her *kurios* in an Athenian trial. But that does not make the speech a failure on its own terms. Despite his self-appointed dramatic role as Helen's advocate, Gorgias's aim is not, in the end, to provide her with a plausible defense. His real "client" is not Helen but the personified art of rhetoric, and with it the Sophist himself.[53] Gorgias was not a self-effacing man. (Among other things, he was honored for a speech at the Pythian Games in Delphi with a golden statue, which he appears to have dedicated himself.)[54] In performance he stands literally at center stage—visible and audible, unlike the disempowered Helen. The event is all about *him*, the power of *his* discourse, and what *he* is doing to manipulate and delight his audience. In silencing her, he is ensuring that the only voice we hear is his; in denying her agency he is asserting his own at her expense.

The relationship between performer and audience is governed, then, not by the serious concerns of the law court, but by the Sophist's desire to entertain and impress potential clients. The fictional legal context serves its purpose, by allowing him to take the case of such a notorious "defendant." Ultimately, however, the courtroom drama is subordinated to a different rhetorical agenda. As an *epideixis*, not a real courtroom defense, the speech leaves the speaker free to privilege enjoyment (*terpsis*) over conviction (*pistis*) (5). Flattering his target audience from the outset, Gorgias claims to be addressing "those who know": people familiar with traditional stories, who will enjoy something novel (5).[55] Such an audience should be alerted by the speech's polished, playful style not to take its arguments too seriously. In this performative framework, the audience will not view the divine defense as a legitimate way of excusing Helen, but if the Sophist is successful they will nevertheless applaud it as evidence of his ingenuity. This allows them to appreciate his cleverness and be amused, not scandalized, by his argument's outrageous implications.

In his speech's final words, Gorgias informs us explicitly that it is a *paignion*—a joke, plaything, or amusement (21). As such it takes its place along with other sophistic *jeux d'ésprit* purporting to argue for obviously unacceptable conclusions. In Plato's *Euthydemus*, for example, a Sophist uses absurd logic to "prove" that his interlocutor's father is his dog, and therefore that he beats his own father (298de).[56] The speaker's goal is not to convince anyone of such absurdities.[57] (No one expects you to actually believe that your father is a dog.) The goal is, rather, to make a novel and ingenious case for an improbable point of view. Critics of the Sophists—notably Plato—were appalled by such frivolity, fearing that it encouraged a superficial and intellectually irresponsible attitude towards matters of the most vital importance.[58] But Gorgias's speech is not aimed at such scolds and killjoys. His target audience is, rather, the sophisticated connoisseur of such intellectual games.

As a result, Gorgias's performance of the divine defense produces a very different effect from the Homeric rhapsode's ventriloquation of Priam. Granted, both performers use Helen for the purposes of self-promotion, making themselves the center of attention. But the rhapsode succeeds as a performer by ventriloquating Homer's characters effectively, and thus conveying their emotional and ethical substance. In Helen's case, this means giving emotional life to her compelling Homeric voice, thereby engaging our sympathy and (not coincidentally) authorizing Priam's use of the divine defense. The Sophist, by contrast, empowers himself not with Helen, but at her expense. Appropriating the power of the female voice, instead of performing it,[59] he makes sure the only voice we hear is his. For, unlike the rhapsode, his interests are not served by a sympathetic rendition of her situation. He himself is the sole beneficiary of the emotions he arouses in his audience. He therefore uses his place at center stage not to bring Helen to life but to erase her as an agent, and thus as an ethical subject, by rendering her a silenced object and undermining her defense with frivolous arguments. His extraction of the divine defense from its epic context plays an integral role in this erasure.

Euripides

My third text, Euripides's *Trojan Women*, gives Helen an unparalleled opportunity to defend herself at length for her elopement.[60] She does so by means of a bravura speech in which she blames not herself but everybody else with any role at all in her story, regardless of their knowledge or intentions. Among others, she blames Hecuba, for bearing Paris (919–20); Paris, for choosing Aphrodite at the Judgment (924–31) and then marrying Helen "by force" (*bia* 962); and Menelaus, for being stupid enough to leave town when Paris was visiting (943–44). Above all, however, she blames Aphrodite, who offered her to Paris as a gift

(929–30). Since Paris brought with him a mighty goddess (940–42), she argues, she was not in her right mind (*phronousa*) when she betrayed her husband (946–47).[61] In consequence, she tells him (*Tro.* 948–50):

τὴν θεὸν κόλαζε καὶ Διὸς κρείσσων γενοῦ,
ὃς τῶν μὲν ἄλλων δαιμόνων ἔχει κράτος,
κείνης δὲ δοῦλός ἐστι· συγγνώμη δ' ἐμοί.

Punish the goddess and become stronger than Zeus,
who has power over the other divinities
yet is [Aphrodite's] slave; but *I* should be excused!

Helen does not deny her own agency—she never claims to have been literally kidnapped—but, like Gorgias, equates divine influence on her mental state with violence (*bia* 962), of a kind that she alleges even Zeus could not resist.[62] In consequence, she declares that she should be exonerated as a passive victim of external circumstances.[63]

The argument is structurally similar to those we saw in Homer and Gorgias, but the circumstances of performance are now very different. The performer is once again an individual conspicuously clad male, who hopes, like the rhapsode, to move his audience by ventriloquating the persona of a mythic character.[64] But this time his costume is not merely a sign of status or narrative authority. Rather, it helps to construct a fictional persona distinct from that of the performer. The mask, in particular, clearly signals this new identity, indicating social status, age, or gender by such basic features as skin and hair color.[65] The actor's voice remained vitally important,[66] but now the audience could identify characters by sight as well as sound. As a result, the theatrical audience sees not a narrator but the legendary Helen herself, physically embodied upon the stage, speaking and moving within a material fictional context.[67] This presentation of the performers as visibly distinct fictional personae is the key difference between dramatic performance and narrative modes such as epic and oratory.[68]

Another key difference is the presence of multiple performers embodying several characters (whether simultaneously or in sequence). No matter how histrionically a rhapsode performed each part, he could only present one character at a time; on the dramatic stage, by contrast, the audience is exposed to a variety of voices and persons, no longer mediated by a controlling narrator. Since each of these characters has his or her own dramatic agenda, this results in a dispersal of narrative authority. As soon as we see two or more characters in the same scene, it raises immediate questions about the relationships among them, including who, if anyone, deserves our sympathy or credence. As the scene proceeds, we see them addressing each other face to face, and note the reactions of the addressee and any bystanders (such as the chorus). A narrator can, of course, describe such reactions, but on the stage we can observe them while a speech is in progress, which will influence our own responses in their turn.

This theatrical mode enables Euripides not only to place Helen's behavior in a larger narrative context (as Homer does), but to place a multifaceted rendition of her story before our eyes, as well as in our ears. It allows, in particular, for a much fuller rendition of a trial scene that the courtroom of Gorgias's imagination.[69] Far from being erased from her own trial, Helen is now visibly present, restored to the center of the issues that she literally and figuratively represents. Menelaus is visible too, as the injured party, the implicit prosecutor (cf. 916–17, 938–39), and the judge to whom Helen addresses her speech (914–18 and *passim*). The chorus of enslaved Trojan women serve as witnesses. Most significantly, a further prosecutor steps forward in the person of Hecuba; even as Helen defends herself, we know that we shall soon be hearing from her archenemy (cf. 906–10).[70] As for the audience, like the rhapsode's they are not participants but eavesdroppers. But their civic identity, along with the agonistic format, makes them more than mere voyeurs. It constitutes them as a kind of democratic "jury," inviting them to bring to bear their experience assessing public rhetorical performances, whether in court, at the Assembly, or at festivals.[71]

That experience would include assessment—and appreciation—of display-speeches like Gorgias's *Helen*, with which Helen's self-defense in *Trojan Women* has a clear affinity.[72] But the performative context invites the tragic audience to judge Helen's speech as more than a mere *paignion*. We saw earlier that Gorgias gets away with such frivolity in part by isolating his ingenious arguments from the kind of practical context that would force their moral consequences on our attention. But tragedy, as a genre, uses legendary material to explore serious issues confronting contemporary Athens. It is concerned, in particular, with the complexities of human choice, autonomy, and responsibility. In this context, as at a real Athenian trial, clever rhetoric was liable to arouse suspicion.[73] A Sophist like Gorgias might win applause by entertaining an audience with such a tissue of sophistries.[74] But now Helen herself is the speaker standing at center stage, ostentatiously dressed (1022–028), competing with other speakers for the approval of an audience. She herself appears in the role of a Sophist, offering arguments of a kind that the Athenian audience is primed to enjoy, but not to believe.

Judged from this perspective, Helen's denial of double determination in *Trojan Women* constitutes a shameless refusal of personal responsibility.[75] As we saw earlier, the divine defense is most easily employed as a face-saver when used on behalf of someone else. By placing it in Helen's own, utterly unapologetic, mouth, Euripides transforms it into a self-condemnation. In the *Iliad* Helen is convinced of her guilt and therefore seems less guilty; in *Trojan Women* she proclaims her innocence, and therefore seems less innocent. In the epic, she is the only person to explicitly blame herself; in the drama she is the only person who does *not* do so. In the *Iliad* she calls herself "hateful" (3.404); but now she is hated by all the Trojan women. Reminiscences of the Homeric Helen therefore work to this Helen's disadvantage. The verb *hespomēn* (946), which echoes her Homeric self (*Il.* 3.174), underscores her contrasting failure to take responsibility. Her blame of Paris in the *Iliad* reinforced her sense of personal shame (3.427–36, 6.349–53), but here it has the opposite effect. By blaming Aphrodite in *Trojan Women* she evokes their scene in *Iliad* Book 3, but the allusion backfires, since this Helen makes no claim to have struggled against Aphrodite's power.[76]

As a performance, Helen's argument is self-defeating for an additional reason. In the *Iliad* she asserts her own agency through the eloquence of her voice, but does so in a way that allows both internal and external audiences to respond with sympathy. Gorgias's defense strategy, in contrast, depends on Helen's absence, and her silence, which enable him to present her as a completely powerless object. In *Trojan Women*, however, the divine defense is part of an emphatic performance of agency on her part. In Gorgianic style, she defends herself by disempowering herself, drawing upon stereotypes of female weakness and passivity to the point where she denies that her own agency has any implication at all for responsibility. But this objectifying strategy backfires, because Helen is talking about herself. By *voicing* her own lack of agency she is using the power of language to assert her own powerlessness. She is no longer, as in Gorgias's speech, a passive object or vehicle of such rhetoric, but its author and agent.

Still worse, this role is now occupied by a "woman" speaking on her own behalf. In so doing she is appropriating the role and status of a male citizen with all the prerogatives that this implies.[77] In Athens, male citizens had to defend themselves in a court of law, but such behavior was prohibited to women. When Helen acts as her own advocate, then, she is adopting a distinctively masculine mode of public discourse, and in so doing acting as her own *kurios*. For both Priam and Gorgias, Helen's gender helps the divine defense by making it easier to present her a mere object; but here it undermines the implications of feminine passivity on which her argument is built. Her forceful self-presentation in a masculine role renders her claim to weakness—as a woman who cannot be left unattended by her husband—less than persuasive.

Helen's brash, scolding attitude toward her husband is also a marked departure from properly "feminine" comportment.[78] It makes for a striking contrast with the self-abasing, apologetic tone that serves her more "feminine" counterpart so well in Homer The latter, as we saw, is a model of decorum and modesty. Such a "good" woman would perform on the stage, as in life, with downcast eyes and modest demeanor.[79] But Euripides's Helen flaunts her beauty shamelessly, to the point of declaring that Aphrodite herself was "stunned" (*ekpagloumenē*) by it (929).[80] Like Xenophon's Kakia—the personification of bad womanhood—she parades herself in public, dolled-up to draw the eyes of men, looking her husband in the eye and drawing repeated attention to her face and body (cf. Xenophon *Memorabilia* 2.1.22).[81] This glamorous appearance and seductive demeanor are the visual counterpart of the "feminine" power of manipulative language, which she employs so differently from Homer's Helen.

Like Homer, then, and unlike Gorgias, Euripides locates Helen within her story and gives her a powerful voice, to which he adds a compelling theatrical presence. But instead of deploying these circumstances to elicit sympathy, he uses them to damn her. This negative judgment is endorsed by the larger dramatic context. No other character, divine or human, regards the gods' agency in the destruction of Troy as a reason to excuse their human instruments. The play begins with the appearance of two actual divinities—Athena and Poseidon—who have no hesitation in blaming humans, including Helen, for their actions.[82] The other women attribute their suffering to the gods (613, 766–73, 775–76), but without excusing Helen, whom they passionately loathe. Cassandra explicitly emphasizes Helen's personal agency in the elopement (373). These hostile women—not the affectionate and paternalistic Priam—are the lens through which the playwright focuses our response to Helen.

Euripides also uses these women to rebut the divine defense dramatically, by showing it to be untenable within the concrete circumstances presented to us on stage. The fate of the other women demonstrates vividly what it is really like to be "forced" into "marriage." Cassandra, in particular—the canonical legendary victim of forcible rape—was dragged away by Ajax by force (*bia*) (70), and is to be raped by Agamemnon, who will "marry" her by force (*biaios*) (44; cf. 617). Helen's argument that she too "married by force" (*bia*) to Paris (962) rings hollow in comparison. For if Helen is to be excused because of Aphrodite, then Agamemnon should be too, since he is equally a victim of *erōs* (255, 413–14). Hecuba highlights the speciousness of Helen's argument in her response, when she responds to the claim that Paris took Helen by force by asking who, if *bia* was in question, heard her cry out as she was taken from Sparta (998–1001).[83]

The drama also implicitly challenges Helen's claims to helpless passivity by presenting us with a world where women are responsible for their actions, capable of controlling their desires and of virtuous, rational agency.[84] Andromache, as usual, is a paragon of wifely virtue (645–56). She and the other women can and do take responsibility for what little action is allowed to them, even if that is only to speak or stay silent.[85] As enslaved women, all of them fully understand the meaning of constrained choice. Again, this makes a mockery of Helen's argument that she was "forced" by Aphrodite—an alleged constraint that she does not claim to have resisted in any way.

Euripides also uses the other Trojan women to focus our gaze in a more literal sense. There is an acute visual contrast between Helen's glamorous appearance and the degradation of the other women. Hecuba, in particular, is a visible image of suffering, debased by age and appearance, a queen reduced to the cropped hair and wretched clothing of slavery.[86] She is on stage throughout the whole play (something highly unusual in Greek drama), which helps to focalize everything through her. Her presence also amplifies the identification of the audience with the enslaved women of the chorus, who likewise remain present throughout, as degraded, suffering figures who have paid the price for Helen's adultery. As such they provide a constant background for our evaluation of her self-defense.

All this prepares us, before Helen even appears, to see through her sophistries, including her self-serving use of the divine defense. Its speciousness will be reaffirmed by Hecuba, in her rebuttal, which provides a withering critique of Helen's self-serving account of divine involvement.[87] Hecuba denies that the beauty contest took place at all,[88] or that Aphrodite "accompanied" Paris; rather, seeing the exceedingly beautiful Paris made Helen's "mind" (*nous*) into Aphrodite and drove her out of her wits (*phrenes*) (983–92).[89] Despite this way of framing the issue, she does not really disagree with Helen about what happened.[90] Her focus is not on challenging Helen's facts, but on explaining them in a way that reinstates personal responsibility. Aphrodite did in some sense "accompany" Paris. She might even truthfully be said, as Hecuba sarcastically puts it, to have transported Helen without leaving her divine home (985–86). But to say that this drove Helen "out of her mind" with erotic craziness is, as always, not an excuse but a condemnation.[91] The judge, Menelaus, agrees with Hecuba on this central issue: Helen left of her own volition and used Aphrodite in her speech as a way of boasting about her beauty (1036). Helen's death sentence therefore stands (1039–041). The audience knows that this sentence will never be carried out; but this is despite, not because of, the arguments she puts forward in her speech.[92]

Euripides could easily have given Helen a more persuasive defense (for example, by taking a leaf from Homer's book). Unlike Gorgias, however, he does not pose as her attorney.[93] He is free, if he chooses, to endow her with an alienating, sophistic voice for his own dramatic purposes. His reasons for doing so become clearer when we consider the tension between Helen's verbal arguments and the visual impact of her beauty. To create this tension, Euripides takes advantage of the particular resources of theater, as distinct from epic. In Homer, where the beautiful Helen is visible only to the eyes of the imagination, her seductive persona is constituted primarily through the charm of her voice. In tragedy, by contrast, the concreteness of theatrical performance allows Euripides to present the visual power of her extraordinary beauty on its own terms.[94] By complementing that beauty with a speech that makes her seem more guilty, not less, Euripides makes it very clear that when Menelaus ends up sparing her, it will be against his better judgment. The more offensive and implausible Helen's arguments, the worse Menelaus looks and the more effective the demonstration of her nonverbal erotic power.

Euripides's use of the divine defense in Helen's mouth is, then, just as specious as it is when used by Gorgias. But in this performance context, that speciousness produces a very different effect. Gorgias purports to be defending Helen, but the frivolity of his arguments turns attention away from her and toward the author and performer at her expense. For the playwright, on the other hand, that very frivolity serves a serious ethical function, by contributing to the dramatic characterization of Helen as shameless, shockingly irresponsible, and ultimately guilty. This deployment of sophistic arguments serves, within its larger context, to rebuke the rhetorical trivialization of serious questions about human choice, agency, and responsibility, which caused such concern to the Sophists' critics.[95]

At the same time, Euripides's script gives the actor who performs Helen's role a fine opportunity for histrionic self-display.[96] Both he and the dramatist can take advantage of the Athenian taste for sophistic rhetoric to win the favor of the theatrical audience. Unlike Gorgias, who feels the need to reassure us that he was just kidding, the actor who takes the part of Helen in *Trojan Women* is free to play the role of sophist-Helen to the hilt. If successful, such a performance would presumably elicit the mixed reaction, of enjoyment and moral disapproval, that was provoked by the intellectual games of Sophists like Gorgias.[97] But that dual response can now be bifurcated between actor and character. The audience can admire the bravura of the actor playing Helen-as-Sophist, while disapproving of such specious arguments in the mouth of Helen as a character. Euripides (and his actor) can amuse the audience with Helen's ingenious but shocking denials of responsibility, while allowing them to share in the condemnation conveyed by the drama as a whole. Both elements of the Athenian audience—the amused, frivolous sophisticate and the judgmental critic—should be satisfied. Like the Homeric rhapsode, but in a very different way, Euripides enables us to have our cake and eat it too.

I have tried to show how various aspects of the performance context affect the audience's reaction to an argument that, on its face, has the same logical content in all three cases. In none of them is the divine defense presented seriously as a compelling reason for finding Helen not guilty in judicial terms. Nevertheless, the contexts of utterance, both internal and external, shape our responses to the argument in ways that significantly affect our judgment of Helen and her responsibility. In Homer, she is clearly guilty, but her own remorse makes Priam's face-saving gesture possible, contributing to the epic's portrait of an ethically complex and sympathetic character. In Gorgias, she is defended effectively only insofar as she is erased as an agent, leaving her not guilty only because she and her behavior are both trivialized in service to the Sophist's rhetorical game. As a result, we blame her no less but also no more than we did at the start. In Euripides's *Trojan Women*, Helen presents the divine defense as if it were cogent, but by doing so in her own voice ends up condemning herself, a judgment reinforced on every level of the drama. Despite the logical similarity, then, in these three uses of the same argument, their full meaning becomes clear only when we view them in their full context, as acts of communication informed by their conditions of performance.

Notes

1. I am most grateful to the University of Chicago Classics Department for their warm welcome and helpful response to the Walsh lecture on which this article is based. Thanks also to John Kirby and William Wians, both of whom have discussed it with me at various stages.

2. On the myth of Helen in ancient Greek texts see Blondell 2013 (from which this paper was developed).

3. The classic treatments are Dodds 1951, ch. 1; Lesky 1961. See also Dover 1974, 144–60; Fenik 1974, 217–27; Redfield 1975, 97–98; Halliwell 1990, 59; Neuberg 1991; Williams 1993, ch. 5; Teffeteller 2003, 26; Holmes 2010, ch. 1.

4. Aphrodite's power extends to Zeus himself (cf. below), but not even he is normally *excused* for his amours on this account; insofar as he escapes blame, it is because he is a supremely powerful male, a beneficiary of the sexual double standard that prevails on Olympus as well as on earth.

5. Antiphon's *Tetralogies* offer an early examination of such issues. On "double determination" in ordinary life see Dover 1974, 136–38, 149–50.

6. Cf. Plato *Ion*, Xenophon *Symposium* 3.5–6, Lycurgus *Leocrates* 102, Plato *Laws* 658bcd, and see Ford 1999.

7. It could also have circulated in written form, but oral performance seems more appropriate; this was still the primary mode of delivery for most texts (especially oratory), and *Helen*'s style is highly aural (cf. Consigny 2001, 162).

8. It is written in Attic Greek (cf. MacDowell 1982, 18; Duncan 1938, 409); it alludes to distinctively Athenian genres (tragedy, oratory); and it focuses on a theme (the power of persuasion) that was of special interest in democratic Athens.

9. Cf. Aristophanes *Birds* 1694–1705. His style had a striking impact on the Athenians when he first visited the city (see e.g., Sansone 2012, 123–25). He subsequently gave displays there in private houses (cf. Plato *Hippias Major* 282b, *Gorgias* 447b), and public venues such as theaters (see Kerferd 1981,

28–29). His students are said to have included the Athenians Pericles, Isocrates, Thucydides, and Agathon (cf. Duncan 1938, 411–12).

10. Xenophon's Niceratus listens to rhapsodes "nearly every day" (Xenophon *Symp.* 3.6), and Plato presents Sophists expatiating in private houses (see previous note and cf. the setting of *Protagoras*).

11. On competitive display at Athens, and festivals as a site for such display, see Goldhill 1999, 3–9, 20–23.

12. Cf. Boegehold 1999, 15–16; Hall 2006, 297, 371–72; Kremmydas et al. 2013, 7–9; Bers 2013, 36–40. On the vocal equivalence of rhapsodes, actors, and orators cf. Aristotle *Rhet.* 3.1.4, 7–9 with Sansone 2012, 12–13; González 2013, 308–11; see also Easterling 1999. For other interconnections among them see Blondell 2002, 96–99.

13. Gorgias was known for his poetic style, which was heavily influenced by tragedy (see Sansone 2012, 126–45).

14. On the authority of the rhapsode, designated by his staff (*rhabdos*), see González 2013, 205–06, 305–08, 336–38. Fifth-century actors were Athenian citizens performing with and for their peers; in the late 5th century actors became celebrities, and in the 4th developed into itinerant figures, like rhapsodes, with international stature (Csapo & Slater 1995, 223–24; Easterling 2002; cf. 1999, 165–66). The Sophists' role in Athens was more adversarial, but nonetheless they exercised considerable influence (cf. Goldhill 1986, 226–29).

15. The notional audience is the audience to whom the works seem to be addressed by the implied author. The actual audience may also have included others, such as women, foreigners, or slaves. But the composition of the tragic audience, in particular, remains controversial (see Goldhill 1997 and cf. Hall 2006, 29, 378–79).

16. See Martin 1989, 5–7; Nagy 1996.

17. On rhapsodes see Ford 1988; Herington 1985, 10–15 and Appendix II; Boyd 1997; González 2013; Bundrick 2018; Tsagalis 2018.

18. The theater was large enough to notionally represent the whole city or even "all Greece" (Goldhill 1997, 57–58).

19. For these three possible venues see Boyd 1997, 111–13. The Odeion held "a huge crowd of spectators" (Shear 2016, 225), numbering in the thousands, and the Pnyx at least 6,000.

20. The word *hupokritēs* was used for both rhapsodes and actors (see González 2013, 296–305). The rhapsode's performance would presumably reflect the various performance styles attributed to speakers within the epic, on which see Martin 1989, ch. 3.

21. The epic "I" is "perhaps the most dramatic of all the characters in heroic song" (Nagy 1996, 80).

22. For a full discussion of Helen in the *Iliad*, with further argument and documentation, see Blondell 2010; cf. also Blondell 2013, ch. 3.

23. Priam tells Helen, "come here and sit by me" (3.162). Later Antenor, an elder, addresses her (3.203), but this is a new development.

24. This and all subsequent translations are my own.

25. On *moi* in Homeric excuses cf. Teffeteller 2003, 18. For the importance of context in reading such excuses see Cairns 2001, 14–20; Teffeteller 2003, 21–23.

26. Aphrodite "gave" him lust (24.28), and he was "overcome" by *erōs* (3.442–46).

27. On "face' in Homer see Scodel 2008 (esp. ch. 5 on apology and face-saving).

28. Dodds 1951, ch. 1. For a nuanced development of this idea see Teffeteller 2003.

29. Both Deianeira and Phaedra's nurse use the divine defense on behalf of someone they care about (Sophocles *Trachiniae* 441–48, Euripides *Hippolytus* 451–58). Menelaus uses it for Helen at Euripides *Andromache* 680, but this time it fails, in part because of Menelaus's own sophistic evasion of responsibility (*Andr.* 683–86).

30. See Franco 2014.

31. See Graver 1995 and cf. *Iliad* 6.344, 6.356, *Odyssey* 4.145.

32. Cf. Scodel 2008, 111.

33. See, e.g., Xenophon *Oeconomicus* 7.14, 39; Euripides *Orestes* 605–06, *Iphigenia at Aulis* 1393–394, *Andromache* 269–73; Sophocles *Antigone* 61–62; and cf. Blondell 2013, 24.

34. For the way Helen's discourse serves to win Priam's sympathy see Roisman 2006, 11–15. She is equally successful with Hector (cf. *Iliad* 24.767–75). On the Helenic, "feminine" power of manipulative language see esp. Bergren 1983.

35. Cf. the sympathy elicited by women who struggle against *erōs* in tragedy, notably Deianeira in *Trachiniae* and Phaedra in *Hippolytus* (on whom see Donzelli 1985, 397–400).

36. Pace, e.g. Homeyer 1977, 5–6; Friedrich 1978, 61; Atchity 1978, 41, 52; Holmberg 1995, 25. See further Mark Edwards 1987, 318; Reckford 1964, 14–19; Farron 1979, 17–20; Schein 1984, 23; Taplin 1992, 98–101.

37. Cf., e.g., Worman 2001, 25; 2002, 50.

38. It is unclear how a rhapsode would "feminize" his physical voice to indicate female speech (cf. below, n. 44). But I am concerned here primarily with Helen's "voice" in a less literal sense.

39. The last phrase is a supplement but structurally necessary and generally accepted by editors.

40. See further Blondell 2013, ch. 8.

41. Cf. Plato *Protagoras* 316cd and see González 2013, ch. 9.

42. See Blondell 2002, 298.

43. Kerferd 1981, 29.

44. Male litigants, like rhapsodes, ventriloquated women's voices "when it suited them to do so" (Hall 2006, 383), but Gorgias does not employ this tactic.

45. As in Homer, the power of her beauty is indicated through its impact on men, in this case, her suitors (4); but we do not hear from those men how they are affected, i.e., we do not hear the point of view of a viewer of Helen.

46. The word *aitios*, in particular, pervades the speech.

47. Cf. Consigny 2001, 189–91, 197. Cf. Gorgias's appropriation of the Athenian genre of the *epitaphios*, which, as a non-citizen, he could not have delivered officially (de Romilly 1992, 231).

48. Juries ranged from 200 to 6,000 (MacDowell 1978, 35–40).

49. The Odeion, for example, though built as a music hall, was also used as a courtroom (Boegehold 1995, 24).

50. A woman involved in a case had to be represented by her *kurios*; she may have been present (scholars disagree on the point), but if so she could not speak. See Just 1989, 33–39 and cf. 112.

51. Cf. Boegehold 1999, 78–79; Schloemann 2002, 134, 137–41; Hall 2006, 370–74; Bers 2009, 2013; Mike Edwards 2013. Rhetorical cleverness and sophistry were viewed as undemocratic and un-Athenian (Hesk 1999, 208–18). It is true that the same Athenian audiences who distrusted expertise in speechmaking enjoyed clever arguments and polished style, even in serious contexts (see Schloemann 2002, 141–46; cf. Ober and Strauss 1990, 250–55; Hall 2006, 369). But an Athenian defendant would not use arguments like Gorgias's in court (see Poulakos 1983, 3–4; Gagarin 2001, 281; cf. also Adkins 1960, 127; Dover 1974, 149).

52. The fourth (force) is threatened, but not in the form of violent abduction: the goddess threatens Helen with death if she does *not* go and sleep with Paris.

53. The phrase *logon grapsai* (21), in particular, is self-referential, equating Gorgias's power with that of the writer mentioned earlier (cf. Steiner 2001, 287–88).

54. For the evidence see Dodds 1959, 9. On Gorgias's brash persona, generally, see Consigny 2001, 191–94.

55. Speaking to "those who know" is "traditionally, a wink from poets and a sign of irony" (Porter 1993, 279).

56. Cf. Agathon's playful Gorgianic argument that Eros is "most self-controlled" (Plato *Symposium* 196b; cf. 197e, 198c). The sophistically trained Pheidippides argues that it is just for a son to punish his father (Aristophanes *Clouds* 1405). Plato's Lysias argues that a love-object should yield to the non-lover rather than the lover (*Phaedrus* 227c). Athenian audiences clearly loved this kind of thing (cf. Plato *Euthyd.* 303b; *Phdr.* 228a, 236b).

57. See esp. Gagarin 2001; cf. also Porter 1993, 267–70, 284–86.

58. On Plato see Irwin 1997. Cf. also Cleon at Thuc. 3.38.2–7.

59. For Gorgias's appropriation of the Helenic, "feminine" power of language see esp. Bergren 1983, 82–86.

60. For a full discussion of Helen's role in *Trojan Women* see Blondell 2013, ch. 9.

61. Most scholars take 946 to imply that she was out of her senses, a traditional symptom of erotic passion (see esp. Biehl 1989, ad loc.; Donzelli 1985, 394–95). Lee 1976, ad loc. translates "sane as I was," but that makes less sense in the context.

62. Besides invoking Aphrodite, she refers to *erōs* as a *nosos* sent by the gods (1042–043), evoking Gorgias *Helen* 19. Cf. also 953.

63. *Sungnomē* is often translated as "forgiveness." Insofar as forgiveness requires an acknowledgment of responsibility, however, Helen wants to be excused, not forgiven (on the difference see Griswold 2007, 49–52, 3–7). For parallels to Helen's usage see Lloyd 1984, 307.

64. Plato uses the same word (*kosmeō*) for the "decking out" of actors and rhapsodes (Boyd 1997, 116). On dramatic acting see Csapo and Slater 1995, 221–74; Csapo 2002; Green 2002, 105–11; Valakas 2002. Like rhapsodic performance, it appealed powerfully to the emotions (cf. Lada-Richards 2002, 412–15).

65. On costume see Wyles 2011; Green 2002, 93–97. On masks see esp. Halliwell 1993; Marshall 1999; Green 2002, 97–104; Hall 2006, ch. 4.

66. See Hall 2006, ch. 10. We do not know exactly how the male actor rendered feminine speech. In Aristophanes's *Thesmophoriazusae*, Euripides says Agathon can pass as a woman in part because he is *gunaikophōnos* (192), but it is unclear what exactly this means (see further Lada-Richards 2002, 401–05) On male performance of the female voice cf. also Hall 2002, 24; 2006, 297–98 (she is discussing lyrics, not iambics, but similar caveats apply). On actors' verbal mimicry generally see Csapo 2002, 135–40.

67. The sets for Greek drama were probably minimal, but material scenery is not necessary to transform the theatrical place into an otherwhere.

68. See Sansone 2012, part I and cf. Herington 1985, 118–19; Slater 1990, 385; Hall 2006, 21, 111–15.

69. On the close affinities between tragedy and Athenian trial see Hall 2006, ch. 12; Halliwell 1997; Ober and Strauss 1990.

70. In a real lawsuit the defendant would speak second, but the dramatic *agōn* is not strictly bound by courtroom procedure (cf. Sansone 2012, 203).

71. At an Athenian tragedy, "to be in an audience is above all to play the part of democratic citizen" (Goldhill 1997, 54; cf. also Sansone 2012, 111; Ober & Strauss 1990, 237–38, 270). On the verbal performativity of Euripides's characters and the expectation that the audience will judge them by contemporary standards see Scodel 1999/2000.

72. We do not know whether Gorgias influenced Euripides directly (or vice versa). Gorgias's *Helen* is usually dated to sometime in the last quarter of

the fifth century BCE, but we do not know if it preceded *Trojan Women* (first produced in 415). On the relationship between them see MacDowell 1982, 12; Croally 1994, 222–27; Lloyd 1992, 99–112; Giuliani 1998, 41–42.

73. On suspicion of rhetoric in tragedy see esp. Pelling 2005.

74. In a list of reprehensible sophistries, Plutarch warns against admiring Helen's blame of Hecuba as witty and ingenious, and disapproves of a woman blaming her husband when she falls for another man (*de audiendis poetis* 28a). The Zeus argument evokes the sophistic Wrong Argument at Aristophanes *Clouds* 1079–081. Note also the word κρεῖσσον, which has sophistic overtones (cf. Gorgias *Helen* 6).

75. Those who have tried to defend this Helen have not gotten very far. The most that can be said is that she does, indeed, successfully draw attention to the large number of causal factors involved in starting the war, but this does not mitigate her own behavior. See further Goff 2009, 661–62, 66, 69; Barlow 1986, 206–07; Amerasinghe 1973; Lloyd 1984, 306–08. Worman 1997 argues that Helen's speech places her "outside ethics" (182–83); for her "there is no question of moral choice" (196); but that in itself is an ethical position (and note that Helen herself makes the issue about justice: 904, 961–62).

76. Contrast the claim that she did struggle to escape from Troy, where she was held against her will after Paris's death (951–60; cf. 1008–009).

77. Note that, unlike the other women, she has no "feminine" lyrics in this play, but only the "masculine" discourse of iambics (Hall 2006, 308–15).

78. Contrast Andromache's "quiet tongue" toward her husband (654–55; cf. Euripides *Andromache* 213–14).

79. Cf. Green 2002, 106–07, 109, 115–21.

80. See further Blondell 2013, 195–97. On *ekpagloumenē* cf. Worman 1997, 192.

81. Cf. Hall 2006, 378–79 (on Apollodorus's deictic use of the beautiful Neaera).

82. Poseidon remarks that she is "justly" held captive (34–35).

83. For the shift in the meaning of *bia* see Biehl 1989, on 998; Donzelli 1985, 396. Hecuba is not perversely misunderstanding Helen here (as some have thought), but literalizing Helen's implication that erotic passion is as exculpating as physical violence.

84. Helen's claim that she is a slave "at home" at Troy (963–64) is similarly undermined by the contrast with Andromache, who accepted her domestic role as a wife who stays in the house (650; cf. 653), and will now be a slave in the house of her husband's killers (660). (The significance of the verbal echo is noted by Biehl 1989, 357–58.)

85. On women's agency in *Troades* see Scodel 1998; Mossman 2005, 362–63.

86. On Hecuba (in her eponymous play) as an "exemplary sufferer" who forces identification with the powerless see Michelini 1987, 133, 179–80.

Helen and the Divine Defense 221

87. For various views on who "wins" the *agōn* see Davidson 2001, 74–76; Goff 2009, 70–71; Croally 1994, 136–59. Hecuba's speech is as rhetorical as Helen's (see Michelini 1987, 142–57; Croally 1994, 153; for a comparison of their styles see Mossman 2005, 362). But her degraded appearance and victim-status help to protect her from the negative associations of a woman appropriating masculine discourse. On rhetoric as a tool of the powerless in Euripides, see Scodel 1999/2000.

88. Scholars disagree about whether Hecuba denies Helen's particular version, or that the judgment took place at all. See Lloyd 1984, 308–12, who defends the latter but argues that it does not really matter.

89. Hecuba's view of the world is idiosyncratic in certain respects, but standard in its attitude toward human responsibility in face of divine power. For parallels to her religious views see Biehl 1989 on 884ff.; Susanetti 2007, 156–57.

90. The point is not really whether or not the beauty-contest (literally) took place, or Aphrodite (literally) accompanied Paris. Here I sympathize with Vellacott 1975, 145, who asserts that Helen's judgment story is not "literal or factual." Note, too, that Hecuba believes the Dioscuri were turned into stars (1000–001), i.e., she does not reject all mythological phenomena.

91. Cf. Holmes 2010, 228–29.

92. Menelaus notoriously dropped his sword at the sight of Helen's beauty. In the *Odyssey* they are both still alive and well at Sparta.

93. *Pace* Dale 1954, xxv.

94. The fact that she is played by a male actor in a mask would not detract from this effect. As "painted sculptures worn by men" (Hall 2006, 115), masks evoked the association of (feminine) beauty with art, especially sculpture (see Hall 2006, ch. 4 esp. 122–23).

95. Hecuba comes close to calling Helen's defense a *paignion* when she says that the idea of the goddess accompanying her son is laughable (983).

96. Cf. Gorgias *Palamedes*, where the title character speaks in his own voice, allowing the orator to perform the roles of character and Sophist simultaneously.

97. The trilogy that included this play won second prize. The actor who played Helen would not be eligible for the "best actor" prize, since that could only go to the protagonist (who presumably played Hecuba, since she is on stage throughout), but as Csapo notes, the prize was awarded to the troupe as a whole (Csapo 2002, 136). Note too that parts for all three actors might be shaped to a specific actor's strengths (see Slater 1990, 388–89; Hall 2006, 49–51).

8

The Hero and the Saint

Sophocles's Antigone and Plato's Socrates

ROSLYN WEISS

It is easy to become persuaded that Antigone is a paragon of piety, that her dangerous and courageous defiance of mere earthly authority is piously motivated.[1] She summons the gods and their laws to validate her outsized deed. In performing the sacred rite that costs her her life, it is the divinities of the Underworld whom she seeks to please and appease (*Antig.* 74–75; 450–60).[2] Sacrificing the earthly rewards of marriage and children, of domestic happiness and fulfillment, she submits to the godly demand to care for the dead.

When set alongside Socrates's piety, however, Antigone's devoutness dims. For Socrates's piety is a life of humble service, not a single grand gesture. His piety is reverential, but Antigone reveres no one. His piety is loving, but is there anyone Antigone loves? And his piety is self-effacing, but Antigone is enthralled by her own greatness, by her supreme strength and determination, by her female virility.[3] She is a woman who is no mere woman. In the enactment of an ancient sacred rite she makes herself a god.

It is Plato's Socrates who is a saint. Sophocles's Antigone is only a hero.[4]

Antigone: Early, Middle, Late

The larger-than-life Antigone who dominates the play's first two-thirds shrinks to rather paltry human proportions in her final speech (*Antig.* 806–943). Her character thus evolves: it has a beginning, middle, and end. The stalwart Antigone sags in the play's middle but regains her composure before long; she stumbles but not irretrievably. Projecting at first an image of self-sufficiency, of needing nothing and no one, she is later seen to have expected—and needed—the gods' support and rescue.[5] When she confronts at last the inevitability of her imminent execution, when she recognizes that there will be for her no divine savior, it is then that her suppressed yearnings, her masked vulnerabilities, her fragile hopes, are revealed—and she falters. She laments the wretched condition in which she finds herself. Moreover, she becomes conciliatory—at least to the extent that her sense of self and her pride will permit.

THE EARLY ANTIGONE: THE DEFIANT PERIOD (1–581)

The opening of the play finds Antigone and her sister, Ismene, huddled together in a clandestine predawn meeting.[6] Antigone, determined to bury Polyneices's body but unable to do so alone,[7] solicits the help of her sister. The solicitation appears half-hearted: Antigone needs her sister's help (the work is painful and laborious–41), but wishes she didn't (*Antig.* 69–70; cf. 538–39, 542–43, 546–47). She treats her sister cruelly: she speaks twice of hating Ismene (86, 93) and once of having no love (*ou stergō*) for her (543). She ridiculously accuses Ismene of being in Creon's corner (549), just at the point, no less, when Ismene has asked to share Antigone's fate, to die with her rather than live without her.

Why does Antigone hate Ismene but not Polyneices, who killed his own brother, her own brother? Ismene is weak, a woman who knows her place and won't overstep her bounds. Polyneices, by contrast, is prepared to attack his own brother in order to take back the power that was wrongfully denied him. Antigone has no sympathy for the timid. The moment Ismene betrays weakness, Antigone writes her off: "I would not encourage you—no, nor, even if you were willing later would I welcome you as my partner in this action" (*Antig.* 70). It is not true that she loves her own, as is so commonly thought.[8] Indeed, despite her famed pronouncement at 523 that it is not in her nature to join in hatred but in love, she hates Ismene (*Antig.* 86, 93). Ismene is her sister, is her own (note her initial address to Ismene: "O [of] common [blood] sister of my own self [*autadelphon*], Ismene"), yet Antigone despises her. What Antigone admires, and what she associates for the most part with her relatives by blood, is boldness, bravery. Ismene in her squeamish ordinariness is no sister of hers; she is an embarrassment to the family (". . . you will soon show whether your nature is patrician [*eugenēs*] or you are the cowardly [*kakē*] descendant of valiant ones"; *Antig.* 37–38). Even Ismene's belated bravery and willingness to die alongside her sister does not measure up. Maybe Antigone discounts Ismene's newfound fortitude insofar as it stems from love and from the unbearableness to her of the thought of living without Antigone. Perhaps this more "feminine" brand of courage strikes Antigone as smacking of neediness rather than conviction. Or possibly Antigone is put off by the tentativeness with which Ismene seeks permission to lay claim to her sister's deed: "if she agrees" (*Antig.* 536). It is clear that Ismene does not share Antigone's reasons for risking death: she does not care about glory or about doing what others will see as *kalon*. All she sees, and all that matters to her, is that Antigone is facing hardship (*kakois* 5; *Antig.* 40). Yet Antigone shows no appreciation, extends no warmth, to her devoted sister, her sister who has now found the strength to stand with her: "Do not try to share my death, and do not claim as your own something you never put a hand to," she harshly says (*Antig.* 546–47). Antigone loves not her family but those members of her family who meet her standard of nobility. It is exclusively with them that she wishes to align herself.[9]

Scholars have somehow seen in Antigone a loving, even motherly figure (motherly, perhaps, because of the guard's comparison of her to the mother bird distressed at the sight of her empty nest; *Antig.* 424–25). Jebb (1891, xxvi), for example, speaks of her "intense tenderness, purity, and depth of domestic affection; manifested in love of sister for brother, a love which death has not weakened, but only consecrated" (xxvii). He sees in Antigone "a true woman, most tender-hearted" (xxxiv). "Nowhere else," he says, "has the poetry of the ancient world embodied so lofty or so beautiful an ideal of woman's love and devotion" (xxxiv). He even interprets the heartless accusation she hurls at Ismene, "ask Creon; your care is for him" (549), as Antigone's attempt to get Creon to spare Ismene's life (1891, xxix).[10] Or consider Knox (1964, 116), who says of Antigone that her "deepest motive" was love."[11] Or Segal (1981, 179), who speaks of her as "devoted to love and family." Yet the love Antigone professes for Polyneices is only *fealty* to one's own; there is no warmth in her love. It is not a love of the heart.[12] In addition, her declaration of love for her brother (73) can only be hurtful to Ismene, to whom she pledges not only her own hatred but that of Polyneices as well (93–94). It is utterly heartbreaking to hear Ismene say to Antigone: "You are foolish, but *to those you love* you are truly loving" (99). (Consider also Antigone's assertion: "Why, I know I am giving pleasure to those I must please most" [89]: not, of course, to Ismene whom she has just promised to hate [86–87], but only to her other, dead kin.)[13] Antigone's treatment of Ismene is sufficient in itself to refute any characterization of her as loving, or even as loving toward her own.[14]

The two characters who are "truly loving" are Ismene and Haemon. Ismene therefore understands the depth of Haemon's love and Antigone's irreplaceability in his affections: "Dearest Haemon," Ismene cries out, "how your father dishonors you!" (572). Even though all the manuscripts have Ismene speaking the words, scholars such as Jebb, who insist on seeing Antigone as loving, attribute the line to her. Indeed, for Jebb (1891, xxx), even if the line is spoken by Ismene it is only because Sophocles wishes to portray Antigone as "raised above every selfish thought." It is not, however, because Antigone is unselfish that she is not the speaker of this line. It is, rather, because she has no concern for Haemon. Unless 572 is assigned to her, she speaks not a single word to or about him.[15] In this conversation between Ismene and Creon, Ismene has just said: "But will you kill her who is to be your son's bride?" (568). It is in response to Creon's ugly, "Yes, for there are other furrows that can be plowed" (569), that she insists: "But not fitted to him as she was" (570). It is then Ismene, too, who, in reaction to Creon's outburst, "I hate evil wives for my son" (571), calls out in sympathy to Haemon as if he were present.

Antigone lives to embody her vision of nobility (this is what Ismene characterizes as her love or passion [*erāis*] for the "impossible" [*amēchanōn*]–90; cf. 92). Because she wishes to be thought great both by herself and by others, because she is bent on playing the hero, she is determined that her deed not go unnoticed. When Ismene proposes that they keep the burial secret "beforehand" (*promēnusēis*) (84–85), Antigone warns her that unless she shouts it from the rooftops, Antigone will hate her far more (86–87). When Antigone isn't caught the first time, she goes back a second. Although Antigone's return to the scene for a repeat performance has generated a cottage industry of solutions,[16] the reason for the second burial is simple: for a deed to be heroic—and for its agent to be a hero—it must be witnessed. Unlike genuine moral goodness, which can go undetected yet remain undiminished, heroic magnificence requires an audience. ("Yet how could I win greater glory than by placing my own brother in his grave?"–502–03). The first burial took place before dawn. Antigone had good reason to expect to be caught even in darkness since there were guards in place. Yet she was not seen. The second time, therefore, she takes no chances: she sets out when "the bright circle of the sun took its place in the sky"; and she cries out loudly (kanakōkuei [423], exōimōxen [427]) when she sees the body unburied. Nor is she shocked when she is captured (433); why indeed would she be surprised when it was her intention that her deed be witnessed? She wants to be caught not because she yearns to die;[17] not because she is bent on spiting Creon[18]; not because she did not quite fulfill her duty the first time;[19] and not because she is simply stubborn.[20] The reason she returns is that she cannot make a name for herself unless her deed is seen. (It is no doubt for the same reason—namely, to secure her future renown—that Antigone later refuses Ismene's offer to die with her: she is determined that no one share her glory. She needed Ismene to share the labor of the burial—not the notoriety it would bring. Now that the deed is done she has no further use for her.)

Antigone consequently makes no attempt to deny her deed—not to the guard (435) and not to Creon (443). Even when Creon tries to offer her a way out—he suggests that she may not have heard the decree (447)[21]—she refuses his offer. Instead, in her belligerent way, she contrasts Creon's decree, which in her eyes lacks the authority to bind, with the "laws" (nomoi) that Zeus, along with the Justice that dwells below among the netherworld gods, established long ago and that remain in force forever. Moreover, she scorns Creon's pronouncement as impotent: since everyone dies, Creon cannot by his words effect anything that would not have occurred anyway (465). She brazenly embraces death before her time, calling it beautiful (kalon–72, kalōs–97) and a gain (kerdos–462): for anyone who lives as she does among many troubles, she says, death is a gain (kerdos–464). She declares death to be in no way painful for her (466, 468). And she even encourages Creon not to delay (499). She reaches the height of impudence when she none too subtly implies that Creon is a fool: "And if you think my actions foolish, that amounts to a charge of folly by a fool" (469–70). She is dismissive of the claims of the city and of Creon's legitimate responsibility to make laws that put the city first.

In the course of Creon and Antigone's exchange, however, Creon says something to Antigone whose full impact she feels only later. He suggests that Eteocles may not take kindly to what she has done for Polyneices: the grace she bestowed upon Polyneices, Creon says, is impious toward Eteocles, and Eteocles will be none too happy to have the impious brother, who sought to destroy the very city that he sought to protect, honored equally with him; the good and the bad do not have equal claim to honor (512–20).[22] In response to Creon, Antigone poses the possibility[23] that Polyneices's action might be blameless below (katō–521)—that is, in the eyes of her dead kin.[24] But Creon is adamant: "An enemy is never a friend, even when he is dead" (522). Antigone can boldly declare now that she, by nature, does not share the mutual hatred of the brothers but joins them only in love (523), yet Creon has given her reason to suspect that not only Eteocles but all her dead family members may be ill-disposed toward Polyneices.

The Middle Antigone: The Conciliatory Interlude (806–943)

Once Antigone can no longer believe that the gods will save her,[25] she descends into what would seem to be uncharacteristic self-pity.[26] The commentators, not surprisingly, excuse this "momentary" lapse; after all, they say, she is facing death.[27] Yet Antigone's lapse is hardly momentary. She goes on for more than 150 lines lamenting her miserable fate, calling herself unhappy and wretched (850, 866, 877, 880, 919, 922), bemoaning never having been married (813–16, 867, 875–76, 891, 917–18), feeling abandoned and unmourned by friends (847, 876, 881–82, 919) and neglected by gods (921–24), and laying blame for her wretched condition on her parents ("from what parents I was born, miserable one! To them I go, to live with them, accursed, unmarried"—866–68) and on Polyneices and his marriage ("Ah, brother who made a disastrous marriage, in your death you have destroyed my life" [869–71];[28] cf. 902–03: "and, now Polyneices, for buying your body I get this reward"). What this change in Antigone's behavior reveals, of course, is not a new Antigone but the real Antigone: she is not quite one with the image she projected earlier. She does not welcome death, certainly not death before her time (895–96), as she had so proudly proclaimed at first (461–62). No longer does she speak of it as a gain (462, 464). Instead, she says of her premature descent to the underworld that it "will be by far the worst of all" (*kakista dē makrōi*) (895). She does not wish to dwell with her "beloved" family in Hades. She wants to live, to have a husband and children. And yet she is cold. It is not Haemon she longs for but a husband.[29] Neither of the two people who truly love her, and in whose eyes she is irreplaceable, matters to her.[30] She is unmoved by Haemon's and Ismene's love, and does not seem to care that she will be leaving them alone in the world, bereft of her.

Antigone dramatizes her situation beyond its reality. She is not unwept and alone though she chooses to describe herself that way (847, 876). In fact, she is present when Ismene enters with "sister-loving tears streaming down her flushed face, wetting her fair cheeks" (527–30). Even the chorus does not restrain its tears (802–03).[31] Nor is she alone; Ismene loves her so deeply that she is willing after the fact to share her sister's blame and dire fate. Ismene is worthy of Antigone's love after all; indeed, she is more than worthy. And, of course, Haemon so loves her that rather than witness her death (762), he elects in the end to die with her.

When Antigone finally turns to the dead members of her family to cast her lot with them, she "nurtures the hope" (*en elpisin trephō*–897) that they will receive her warmly. But she clearly has her doubts.[32] Although she reminds them that she has performed for them the requisite burial rites,[33] she nevertheless is no longer certain that her father, mother, and brother Eteocles[34] will approve of her burial of Polyneices. Whereas at first she was so caught up in the exhilaration of executing the forbidden deed that she could not for a moment doubt her own righteousness, Creon has by now posed the terrifying possibility that Eteocles may resent her honoring the traitorous murderer Polyneices, and that, moreover, her parents may not look favorably upon her deed.[35] And so she turns, not unreasonably, to address Polyneices: surely he, for whom she sacrificed so much, will be appreciative of her efforts on his behalf.

In what follows, however, Polyneices is only her apparent or ostensible target. It is Creon, present and attentive, to whom her remarks are directed. She has, after all, no reason to be *justifying* her action to Polyneices, no reason to be citing the "law" that requires burying his body in particular. The only person who needs to be convinced that what she has done was something she had to do, something she might be forgiven for doing, is Creon. And although Antigone does not lower herself to address Creon directly, to solicit his empathy directly, she mounts her defense in his presence.

In a passage that has caused scholars no end of consternation (904–20 or 905–13),[36] Antigone cites a "law" to support her singular care for her brother. The law to which she refers would have a woman give priority to her brother—above her husband and children—once their parents had died, on the grounds that such a brother, unlike a husband and children, is irreplaceable.[37] Unless one is willing to take the radical step of excising the passage as spurious, one can only see it as pivotal: if it is genuine then it does not confuse, obscure, or distort Antigone's character but rather illuminates it. For the truth is, as we have seen, that Antigone's demeanor had begun to change at 806, well before this passage, as soon as she realized she was really going to die.[38] The offending passage is not jarring within the context of the Antigone encountered from 806 on; it is only disturbing when read against the backdrop of the Antigone who inhabits the first two-thirds of the play.

The "law" cited is ruthlessly callous;[39] it replaces depth of feeling with crude calculation.[40] Moreover, as Antigone applies it to her current situation it is deeply flawed: once her brother has died, there is no longer an irreplaceable family member left to save.[41] Ismene, of course, is still alive, and so would Antigone be, if she hadn't tended to Polyneices's corpse. Moreover, Antigone would have married and had children. Is she not the one who destroys by her action the last vestiges of the Theban legacy? Instead of remaining alive to preserve and perpetuate her family, she chooses to die for the sake of burying an "irreplaceable" brother. It is striking that Antigone does not speak of having special feelings for this brother; she does not say that he can't be replaced in her affections. He is irreplaceable simply because dead parents can produce no more offspring. Presumably, then, if her parents were still alive, she would have let Polyneices's body rot and be preyed upon by animals and birds. Such an argument is unlikely to endear Antigone to Polyneices. And she has already completed her address to her parents and other male sibling. These words, it would seem, can be spoken only for Creon's benefit.[42]

In her last-ditch effort to be spared, then, Antigone presents an argument designed to appeal to what Charles Segal calls "Creon's masculine rationality" (1981, 200) or his "legalism" (160).[43] It has been frequently noted how eerily similar this reasoning is to that employed by Intaphernes's wife when, as Herodotus relates in his *Histories*, the Persian king Darius, who had condemned her traitorous husband along with the rest of his family to death, offered to spare but one of her relatives and she chose her brother.[44] Her reasoning was as follows: "There would be another husband for me, if the deity wishes, and other children if I lose these, but with my father and mother no longer living, there would never be another brother" (3.119). Now, of course, Intaphernes's wife's brother was not yet dead, so for her to appeal to her brother's unique irreplaceability is not quite as bizarre as Antigone's appealing to Polyneices's. What is important for our purposes is that Darius, who reasonably expected Intaphernes's wife to choose her husband or child, a relative to whom she would naturally have felt closer than to a brother,[45] is duly impressed with the justification she offers. Sophocles, then, in assigning the very same reasoning to Antigone, is enabling her to make the sort of case to Creon that Creon just might respect and be pleased and even swayed by. Rather than make an emotional pitch—Creon, after all, already thinks Antigone is mad (*anoun*–562)—Antigone presents an argument that sounds eminently rational—indeed it is hyper-rational—even if upon close inspection it makes little sense.[46] She makes it clear that she would have permitted no personal feeling—no natural devotion to husband or love of child—to thwart her obedience to Creon's edict. She thus obliquely assures Creon that it is not love that determines her actions in her brother's case. One might say she speaks Creon's language: as Creon had earlier said that wives are replaceable (569), Antigone now implies that husbands and children are.

For Antigone to say in effect that were it not for this law, a law that bids her to accord "special honor" (*ekprotimēsas'*–13) to her brother,[47] she would not have defied the king's ordinance—that she would not indeed have disobeyed the decree had it concerned even a husband or child—is for her to submit to Creon's authority as she never had before. It is to regard his decree or proclamation (*kērugma*–8; 27; 32; 34), which she formerly dismissed as the non-binding product of Creon's flexed autocratic muscles, as a legitimate one to be trumped not by any general divine *nomos* but only by the newly cited law (*nomou*–908). She further validates Creon's edict by assigning its provenance to the citizens, the *politai* (as Ismene had done as early as 79, and in contrast to 506, where Antigone says of Creon: "But tyranny is fortunate in many ways"), and by deeming its violation on her part an act of violence (*biāi*–907). Rather than call Creon a fool as she did earlier (470), she invites Creon in this way—she indeed mentions Creon by name (914)—to align himself with the wise men (*tois phronousin*–904) who recognize that, *because of this law*, she was right to accord her brother "special" honor (913).[48]

Antigone readily acknowledges that from Creon's perspective she seemed to do wrong and to be reckless (914–15). Nothing new here, to be sure: she had similarly said earlier, "my attitude displeases you" (501).

But, whereas in the earlier exchange she also said—indeed said first—"There is nothing to please me in your words, and may there never be" (499–500), here she is silent about finding Creon's stance offensive. If only Creon could now view her act in a different light, regard it, that is, as mandated by this peculiar law, perhaps he would no longer count it as transgressive (*hamartanein*–914), and as an instance of "terrible daring" (*deina tolmān*–915). If Creon thought badly of Antigone before, surely that is because he was as yet unaware of the sound reason behind her disobedience. Might not the law to which Antigone now appeals represent a new consideration for Creon to take into account, one he has not yet heard, one that might provide sufficient grounds for him to forgive Antigone?

Still ostensibly addressing Polyneices, yet speaking no doubt for Creon's benefit, Antigone depicts herself being led by Creon's hands, "without marriage, without bridal, having no share in wedlock or in the rearing of children," encouraging him to feel her loss, a loss that is no less his: the children she won't have are his grandchildren. Not surprisingly, Antigone does not carry on as Intaphernes's wife did, seeking to arouse the king's pity. Antigone would never demean herself in that way. Yet, she does indirectly, and at no cost to her dignity, hint at the loss Creon, too, stands to sustain.

And in what is arguably a further concession to Creon, Antigone admits that the gods have apparently forsaken her, that despite her piety she has been convicted (perhaps by the gods themselves?) of impiety. Creon has made it clear that he regards her burial of Polyneices as "impious" (*dussebē*) (514); he is appalled at the chorus's suggestion that the gods may in some way have instigated Polyneices's burial (278–79): the gods, he says, do not honor evil men (288). And more: Antigone acknowledges that the gods—no longer limited to the Underworld gods—may not approve of her deed.[49] That the gods may well not support her is something Creon had said earlier: "And there she can pray to Hades, the only one among the gods whom she respects, and perhaps be spared from death; or else she will learn, at that late stage, that it is wasted effort to show regard for things in Hades" (777–80). Moreover, Antigone is prepared to submit to her penalty: if the gods indeed disapprove, she says, she accepts her suffering as deserved, "for I have transgressed." If, however, "they" are the transgressors—note that Antigone leaves Creon unnamed and thus only implicitly blamed—she wishes on them no more evil than what she has unjustly (*ekdikōs*) endured at their hand. If indeed they and not she have done wrong, she has been the victim of their injustice. Nevertheless, for her part, she would have them suffer no more than justice requires—no more than what they have visited upon her.[50]

No longer does Antigone "choose death" (as she did at 515), no longer does she boast of the boon (*kerdos*–462, 464) that death will be to her, certainly as compared with her present troubles (*kakois*). On the contrary, she now calls herself a "poor creature" (*dusmoros*–919), an "unhappy one" (*dustēnon*–921), on account of her impending premature death. Moreover, it is clear that she is now stalling for time (note Creon's remark at 883–84), and bemoans the fact that "there is delay no longer" (939); in her first exchange with Creon, as we recall, she urges him not to dally: "Why do you delay (*melleis*)?" she asks (499).

In this protracted speech, Antigone provides an opportunity for Creon to rethink his punishment. She is far less insolent, far less defiant, than she was when the play began. She would bow, she says, to Creon's edict in all cases but the current one—the current one being an exception only because there is a "law" that makes it so.[51] The law she cites is, moreover, one that has some chance of impressing Creon, as it did Darius, with its seeming emotion-free levelheadedness. She can appreciate how she must appear in Creon's eyes, and she asks, without asking, that he reconsider his assessment. She recognizes her own fallibility, even the possibility that the gods see her as impious. Finally, she refrains from raining down upon Creon a whole host of curses.[52] Regarding his punishment, she wishes, justly, that he suffer no more than what she has suffered, unjustly, at his hands.

Creon does not detect the change in Antigone. The differences are admittedly subtle. After all, she doesn't speak directly to Creon. She doesn't beg for his forgiveness. She doesn't beseech the gods to spare her. She never lowers herself. It is up to Creon, therefore, to be sensitive to shifts in Antigone's demeanor, to notice her greater restraint, to respond to her new argument, to credit her admission that she might be wrong, to appreciate her wish that he, even if wrong, not be punished more than she. Creon, however, lacks the requisite subtlety; moreover, he is not one to think for himself. Once the chorus pronounces that "The same blasts of the same winds of the spirit still possess her" (929–30),[53] Creon proceeds to berate those who are to accompany Antigone to her cave for their slowness. It is then that Antigone realizes that her attempts at conciliation have fallen on deaf ears: "Ah me (*oimoi*)," she laments, "that which was spoken has reached close to death' (933–34).

Once it becomes clear to Antigone that she will die, once she realizes that Creon has not been swayed, that he will give her no reason to hope that her death sentence will not be carried out forthwith (935–36), she parades her suffering before her city and the gods of her ancestors. "Look, rulers of Thebes," she says, "upon the last of the royal house,[54] what things I am suffering from what men, for having shown reverence for reverence" (940–43).

THE LATE ANTIGONE: RESIGNATION AND RETURN (1220–022)

Antigone speaks no more. The next time she appears, Creon's men have discovered her at the bottom of her tomb hanging by the neck in a noose of woven linen. She has taken her own life. To the bitter end, then, Antigone maintains her dignity. She has gone as far as she could in seeking reprieve; she has not fallen to her knees before Creon to beg for her life. And she will not now allow him to kill her. She will not die a slow and passive death. She is courageous; she is not afraid. She does what she always does: she take matters into her own hands. She is, as the chorus noted, *autonomos* (821), a law unto herself.[55] She goes to her death because, as Knox puts it (1964, 42), "she lives on her own terms."

Antigone and the Gods

Despite Antigone's protestations of piety, there are several reasons to regard her piety with suspicion. First, one wonders if Antigone has the proper humility to be genuinely pious. Might she not be taking the opportunity of her brother's death to aggrandize herself, using her obedience to the gods' law to add gravitas to what is essentially a self-promoting deed? Indeed she says to Creon: "Yet how could I have gained greater glory than by placing my own brother in his grave? (502–04). Moreover, the sacred duty that Antigone takes to be hers alone (or hers and Ismene's, at least at first) may well not be confined to her. Although she certainly has an obligation to bury the body, inasmuch as she is a close relative of the deceased, so, too, does Creon, and for the same reason. Moreover, it appears that from the point of view of the gods, what is most important is not who buries the body but simply that the body not be left unburied. Creon suspects first that a man covered the body with dust

(248), and then that some rebellious men bribed other men to do so (289–94): it does not dawn on him that it must have been a relative of Polyneices who did so. And as Teiresias makes quite clear (1070–1071), what the gods find noxious is the unburied corpse: ". . . you have kept here something belonging to the gods below, a corpse deprived, unburied, unholy." He consequently orders Creon to see to it that the body is buried. It seems, then, that so long as the corpse is buried, the city can avoid pollution and be spared the gods' wrath. Whereas Creon takes it as his personal responsibility to free Antigone ("I who imprisoned her shall myself be present to release her" [1112]), he does not regard it as his task to bury Polyneices: he sends his servants to do so (1108–1110). Thus Antigone, by casting the duty to care for the corpse as one that only she can fulfill, does not so much serve the gods as rivet attention on herself and on her deed.[56] Although she calls her deed "a holy crime" (74), the fact that she eventually says she would not have done the same for husband or children indicates that what the gods require is not what is most important to her. She is well aware that the gods ("Hades") require these rites for all deceased (519).

Antigone seems to recognize no distance of any consequence between herself and the gods. Not only does she narrow the gap between herself and the gods by way of the comparison she sets up between herself and Niobe (823–33) (the chorus chastises her for likening herself to a goddess, even though they are also at the same time somehow impressed that such a comparison might be reasonably made in Antigone's case [834–38]), but in looking to the gods to be her ally, her fellow combatant (*xummachōn*–923), she brings them down to her level or herself up to theirs. As Knox (1964, 43) so aptly puts it: "The heroes refuse to accept the limitations imposed on human beings by their mortality, resist the strong imperatives of time and circumstances—all things change but they will not—and this is a conception of divinity."

Second, Antigone does not think well of the gods. She lays all the evils her family has suffered at Zeus's door (2). She sees the gods as demanding and unforgiving (74–76). (Ismene, interestingly, does not see them so [65–66]. Ismene expects the gods to understand her predicament and sympathize with her on its account.) How odd for a paragon of piety to believe that the gods do wrong and, in particular, that they have wronged her. Moreover, Antigone never speaks approvingly of the gods' laws as just. She thinks only that Justice demands that she obey them.

Third, Antigone on occasion appears to calculate her advantage. Her stated reason for pleasing the gods is that "there will be a longer span of time for me to please those below than there will be to please those here; for there I shall lie forever" (74–76).[57] Is this the reckoning of a pious woman?[58] Indeed, why would a pious woman believe the gods owe her something in exchange for her reverence? Does true reverence, real devotion, demand something in return? Antigone surely seems to think she shouldn't have to suffer "for having shown reverence for reverence."

One wonders, finally, if an utterly selfish person can be pious. Antigone shows no concern for others—for live others. She isn't concerned with Ismene's soul or Ismene's end, beyond a single perfunctory admonishment her: "Have no fears for me! Make your own course go straight!" (83). On the contrary, when Ismene wants to share Antigone's fate, Antigone discourages her from doing so, recommending instead that she "Save yourself!"—Ismene has made her choice and Antigone bars her from sharing in her death (553, 555, 559). If Antigone believes that the gods demand that she and Ismene bury Polyneices, why does she not concern herself with the dire consequences that await Ismene at the hands of the gods should she fail to act? And why does she not worry that Ismene may be committing an act of injustice and impiety? Why does she not argue with her, work to persuade her to do what is right? She wants neither to share the glory nor to protect her sister. After Antigone says she's better off pleasing the gods because of the longer time—forever—that she will be spending below (74–76), she then says to Ismene: "As for you, if that's what you prefer, dishonor what the gods honor!" (76–77).

Antigone shows herself in the end to care little for the gods. They serve as her ticket to grandeur: she appropriates to herself a divine duty that is not hers alone; she does not ultimately feel bound to honor the impartial law she herself takes to be the gods' law and hence neglects to serve them consistently; and she lacks the humility to regard the gods as her superiors. Antigone regards the gods as the source of evil and injustice; indeed, she complains about the inappropriate treatment she receives at their hands. She seeks to please the nether gods for the crassest of reasons—that she will dwell among *them* forever. She shows no concern for others, and, in particular, takes no trouble to encourage others to be pious and just.

Antigone's Heroism

Antigone is at beginning and end heroic—though, as we have seen, she falters somewhat in the middle. She has what Jebb calls (1891, xxvii) "an enthusiasm, at once steadfast and passionate, for the right, as she sees it—for the performance of her duty." And Knox detects in Antigone a "self-centered, inflexible temper" (1964, 70), an "uncompromising determination . . [a] high sense of [one's] own worth and a consequent quickness to take offense . . . [as well as a readiness to die rather than surrender" (1982, 51), features that are characteristic of the Sophoclean hero. Heroism, it seems, comes with prideful doggedness; it is the pursuit of an end at any cost, and particularly at the very highest cost: life itself. Heroes cannot be deflected from their determination; no argument can penetrate their cloak of righteousness—that is, of the righteousness of their cause as they perceive it. When Antigone indulges in self-pity, lays blame on others, feels betrayed by men and gods, and seeks, however subtly, to reverse her fate, her heroism wavers. She reverts to type, however, by ending her own life, by taking her destiny into her own hands. Nevertheless, that she commits suicide indicates that life for her is not worth living unless she is visible, unless she is admired or even feared as one who is exceptional, as one who dares to exhibit terrifying boldness (*deina tolman*—915).

Even as heroes single-mindedly pursue a course they believe to be honorable and glorious, they typically describe themselves as doing their duty. But heroes take themselves to have more stringent, more taxing, obligations than other, ordinary, people have—duties, moreover, that no one else would impose on them. As Antigone sees it, to bury a brother at the cost of one's life is more than what is required of the general run of people; Ismene would have proved herself extraordinary, noble, by seeing Polyneices's burial as her obligation. From Antigone's perspective, Ismene, by refusing to undertake this frightful deed and by trusting that the gods will forgive her, demonstrates her commonness; she fails in this way to honor her noble and patrician heritage. Antigone's disgust derives not from Ismene's failure to satisfy some pedestrian standard—the standard that applies to the coward no less than to the brave of heart—but from her taking *that* as her standard. To be noble is to regard oneself as obligated to do what is "impossible"; to require of oneself only what is possible—and expected—is to be just ordinary.

Thus, the moment Teiresias makes it clear to Creon that it is his strict duty to bury Polyneices's body, there ceases to be anything heroic about his doing so; he engages in only the quotidian business of morality.[59] In heroism there is heightened drama; ordinary goodness is humdrum by comparison. Heroism lives on the edge.

To say that the hero takes as his or her duty more than what others do should not be construed to imply that any cause a hero takes on is of necessity a worthy one. Heroes take themselves to be bound by a cause of their own choosing, and are then prepared to do whatever it takes to succeed—or die trying. They set their own standards and place themselves beyond the reach of ordinary moral judgment or reproach. They pursue their ends no matter the cost to themselves or to others.

Except in Antigone's unheroic middle stage, she is unable to recognize and will not concede the merit of any view but her own. She accords no value to Creon's care for the city and its gods; she dismisses any claim the city might have on her; and she is disdainful of the opinion others have of her. She shows no allegiance to or care for her city or its people or its gods. She is right; everyone else is wrong; there is no grey.

Because heroes perceive themselves as bound by rules that apply to no one else, to be heroic is often to fail at even the most basic decency. Heroism can make one harsh and unforgiving. It can make one intolerant and unloving. Heroism can make one think oneself superior, extraordinary; it can make one regard others, by contrast, as inferior and common. When Creon asks Antigone if she is not ashamed (*epaidē*) to have beliefs that are at odds with everyone else's (510), she insists that "there is no shame (*aischron*) in showing regard for your own stock" (511). Rather than doubt herself for holding views that are not shared, her nonconformity is for her a source of pride. She does not, at least in her heroic moments, stop to ask herself if she might be wrong. To doubt oneself is inexcusable weakness.

The Saintly Socrates

Whether or not the portrait of Socrates that follows constitutes (as it is intended to) an accurate representation of the Socrates of Plato's dialogues, indeed even if Plato's Socrates is not all the things I say he is, it is this Socrates from whom I have learned much of what I understand about piety, and it is his insights and practice that have helped me to raise doubts about and challenge Antigone's presumed piety. Although Plato's Socrates may be unable or unwilling to produce a perfect definition of piety, nevertheless, profound piety is manifest in his personal conduct, and both the things he says and the questions he asks reveal a sure grasp of at least what piety is *not*.[60]

To cast Plato's Socrates as a saint[61] seems a grotesque distortion of a character who is complex and enigmatic, vexed no less than vexing.[62] Arguably, however, the odd nuances of Socrates's persona are themselves manifestations of his piety, of his devotion to the god. To be sure, Socrates is no dogmatic moralist, no prophet who simply relays to the people what the god tells him regarding what they should believe and how they should behave. But his god is also no ordinary god. What Socrates's god demands is care for truth and virtue and the practice of philosophy (*Ap.* 29c–30c). To obey *such* a god is "to obey nothing else of what is mine than that argument which appears best to me upon reasoning" (*Crito* 46b). Socrates can be a philosopher and a saint at the same time, for what his god demands is that people philosophize, that they think for themselves.

Not only are Socrates's exemplary character—which he would call the state of his soul[63]—and his noble ends a testament to his piety, but so too are his means. Were it not for his devotion to the god (*dia tēn tou theou latreian*–*Ap.* 23c), could anything induce him to engage in practices that keep him mired in poverty, sap his leisure time, win him few friends and many enemies, and eventually get him killed? What else could account for his persistent recourse to cheap and offensive tactics even at the cost of becoming hated (*Ap.* 22e–23a; 28a)? His irony, his mock humility, his setting traps in the form of sophistic "gotcha" arguments for even his best-intentioned interlocutors, his shaming, frequently in public, of those whose views he opposes, and his almost always steering his dialogic exchanges to unsettling *aporia*—all these idiosyncratic and irritating features of his regular routine contribute to his divine mission to pursue, with others, truth, morality, and philosophy.[64]

As Socrates conceives piety, it seems to include the following two components. On the one hand, it requires that one be just or refuse to commit injustice. This is for him piety's non-negotiable necessary condition, its sine qua non. It is also its essentially negative aspect. It is because piety has this negative aspect that Socrates believes that those judges who would pervert justice by doling out favors to defendants whose emotional pleas they find gratifying cannot be pious, no matter how orthodox their views of the gods or how punctilious their ritual practice. On the other hand, however, piety surpasses justice in requiring service to the god in the form of helping others: this is its positive aspect. In the *Euthyphro*, where Socrates explicitly distinguishes piety from justice, Socrates encourages his interlocutor to think of piety in terms of the service human beings might render to the gods, the work with which they might promote the gods' noble agenda—on earth. To be the gods' servant is to acknowledge both their superiority and one's own inferiority: only those who are humble before the gods can be their faithful emissaries.

On both counts, Socrates makes the grade. As both Socrates himself and others attest, Socrates is just—certainly in the sense that he assiduously avoids injustice. Socrates declares that "my whole care is to commit no unjust or impious deed" (*Ap.* 32d); he is "convinced indeed that I do not do injustice to anyone" (37b); if he is brought before a court, he says, "some base man will be my prosecutor—for no worthwhile person would prosecute a human being who does no injustice" (*Gorg.* 521d). And in the *Phaedo*, Phaedo pronounces at the dialogue's close that Socrates was "of all those we have known, the best and also the wisest and most just (*dikaiotatou*)." But Socrates does more for others than refrain from harming them. He tends to their souls and fights for *their* justice. It is this activity that he almost invariably refers to as his serving the gods.[65]

Socrates as Hero

Socrates strikingly resembles Antigone in her heroic phases. First, like Antigone, Socrates sees himself as a person of distinction. And this is so not only in the *Apology*, where Socrates presents himself as the god's envoy, sent to save Athens's soul (*Ap.* 30e), but also in the *Gorgias*, where he identifies himself as the only (or nearly the only) true politician (see 521d: "I think that with a few Athenians—so as not to say myself alone—I put my hand to the true political art and I alone of the men today practice politics"), and in the *Theaetetus* (149a–151d), where he reserves to himself the special gift of midwifery, the skill, in his case, of aiding "pregnant" men in the birthing of their ideas. In addition, Socrates frequently sets himself apart from the many, whom he tends to regard with disdain (Crito 44d; Prot. 351c). Second, Socrates, like Antigone, respects himself and will not compromise his dignity—though whereas Antigone's self-regard has its source in her noble birth, Socrates's derives from the justice that informs everything he does and from his dogged pursuit of philosophy. "For I am old," Socrates says, "and have this name; and whether it is true or false, it is reputed at least that Socrates is distinguished from the many human beings in some way" (Ap. 34e–35a). Neither Antigone nor Socrates begs that their life be spared: Antigone has too much pride; Socrates sees any attempt to get judges to substitute sympathy for honest and considered judgment as a perversion of justice (Ap. 35b–c; 38d–e).

Third, neither Antigone nor Socrates values life itself above all else. When asked if he is not ashamed (*aischunē*) to have followed the sort of pursuit from which he now runs the risk of dying (Ap. 28b), Socrates, like Antigone, insists he is not. Antigone is willing to die if that is the only way she can bury her brother; Socrates is prepared to die if to live means to disobey the god or to act in an unworthy, unphilosophical, way. Like Antigone, Socrates is fearless when facing death. Antigone tells Creon that those who seek to kill her have no real power; after all, everyone dies (460–61); Socrates says much the same: "if you had waited a short time, this would have come about for you of its own accord" (Ap. 38c); moreover, Socrates puts his would-be executioners in their place: though he can be killed, he says, he cannot be harmed by those who are his inferiors (Ap. 30c–d). Fourth, neither seeks to delay death: Antigone professes at first to welcome death and in the end commits suicide; Socrates has no interest in lingering for the sake of prolonging his enjoyment of the pleasures of food and sex (Phaedo 116e–117a); indeed, the prison guard remarks that no one has ever given him so little trouble (Phaedo 116c–d). Fifth, both exhibit extraordinary courage, though it is not easy in Antigone's case to keep her courage from shading into recklessness.[66]

Sixth, both are reputed to be impious and must defend their piety. Antigone says: "I have acted piously but have been thought impious" (923–24). And Socrates, of course, was indicted on the charge of "not believing in the gods of the city but in other new divinities (*daimonia*)" (Ap. 24b–c). Seventh, Socrates, like Antigone, can be defiant, even insolent. That is certainly how he was at his trial, particularly after the verdict was in. As Knox puts it (1964, 58):

When Socrates, whose life of patient intellectual probing for moral definitions seems as far removed from the careers of the heroes as north is from south, seeks in his defense in court for comparisons with his own case, it is Achilles and Ajax whom he cites. Strange authorities for a philosopher—and yet, not so strange. For in his refusal to abandon what he considers his mission, imposed by the god, he shows the familiar heroic stubbornness, and in his ironic but outrageous proposal that his punishment should be that entertainment at the public expense offered to Olympic victors he shows the defiant arrogance which is the mark of the heroic temper. In his deliberate choice of death rather than surrender he enters the ranks of the heroes himself.

The clearest point of contact between Antigone and Socrates is their respective refusals to obey a ruler's decree despite the very real possibility that their refusal would result in their death. Antigone defies Creon's decree that Polyneices is to remain unburied; in Socrates's case, there are three instances of disobedience, all of which he refers to in the *Apology*: (1) the mass trial of the generals of Argenusae (*Ap.* 32b), and (2) the Leon of Salamis affair (*Ap.* 32c–d)—Socrates cites both incidents as occasions on which he chose justice over personal safety—but also, and most important, (3) his hypothetical refusal to obey Anytus rather than the god, should Anytus make it a condition of his pardon that he cease philosophizing (*Ap.* 29c–d).

Surprisingly, however, it has frequently been the Socrates of the *Crito*, the Socrates who *submits* to the city's sentence, who has been compared—and, of necessity, contrasted—with Antigone. Jebb (1891, 12–13), for example, contrasts the case of Antigone whose positive religious duty to bury her brother conflicts with Creon's law, with that of Socrates, who has no comparable obligation to break out of prison. According to Jebb, Socrates is therefore entitled to weigh (1) how much good he would accomplish by escaping, against (2) the bad example he would then set, and to conclude that (2) is greater. Jebb thinks Plato, unlike Sophocles, fails to address the question of the limit of the state's authority over the individual conscience.

It is because Jebb neglects the *Apology* that he does not see that Plato in fact does raise the pressing question that is central to Sophocles's *Antigone*. It is evident that for Socrates the state's authority ends at the moment it requires the commission of acts of injustice or impiety. Socrates therefore defies Athens by doing what is right rather than complying with what its rulers have ordered; and he declares his intention to resist any new order that would bar him from pursuing his divinely mandated philosophical inquiries.

It should be clear, moreover, from even a cursory reading of the *Crito* that Socrates does not weigh the good he would accomplish if he escapes against the bad example he would set by doing so, but raises instead the single question: is escape unjust?[67] If escape is just, he would have little reason to be concerned about setting a bad example; indeed, it is only by doing injustice that he sets a bad example and causes harm.[68] From Socrates's perspective, one harms others by teaching them that injustice is the superior choice. Whatever Socrates's reasons for not escaping are, we can be sure they concern justice.[69]

Where Socrates Differs

Although, as we have just seen, Socrates has much in common with Antigone, their differences far outstrip their similarities. Most critically, Socrates, unlike Antigone, is devoted not to one particular person but to people generally. He is in no danger, therefore, of succumbing to the harsh indifference to others that infects the heroic Antigone. When he imagines himself being asked by the Athenians if he isn't ashamed to be engaged in a pursuit for which he might incur the death penalty (*Ap.* 28b) he responds out of his concern for them: "Are *you* not ashamed?" (*Ap* 29d)—and determinedly persists in his unwelcome badgering. Antigone, however, does nothing to try to persuade the reluctant Ismene to do what she ought and is instead simply glad to be rid of her unspectacular sister.

Antigone's scorn for Ismene and indifference to Haemon has no counterpart in Socrates's attitude toward his friends and companions who want to save him or who dread his impending death.[70] Socrates appreciates his friends' concern for him, however misplaced. He addresses his friends philosophically, remonstrating with them gently and encouraging in them a more rational and reflective approach to death. When they mistakenly assume that something bad is happening to him, he reproaches them only for their lack of insight. Unlike Antigone who absurdly lashes out at Ismene for supporting Creon, and who, in her moments of weakness, thoughtlessly complains that she is unwept and friendless, Socrates acknowledges the genuineness of his friends' concern. "Crito," Socrates says, "your eagerness (*prothumia*) is worth much if some correctness be with it. If not, the greater it is, the harder it is to deal with" (*Crito* 46b). Socrates never gives up on anyone, not even on Thrasymachus: "we've just become friends; though we weren't enemies even before" (*Rep.* 6.498c–d).

Socrates, then, does not select a single brother as the object of his concern. Instead, he approaches *each* of his fellow Athenians, as he says, as a father or older brother would (*Ap.* 31b). He will talk to anyone, though to the Athenians, his fellow-citizens, first and foremost (*Ap.* 30a).[71] To speak to people as a father or brother is, as Saxonhouse says, to engage them in their particularity. It is an approach characterized by personal care. If "political life for him reflects the relationships of the family in which differences are acknowledged rather than suppressed," he may be said to "transform[s] the city into his family" (Saxonhouse 1992, 104). Socrates may of course anger people when he seeks to divest them of some nonsensical view, but, as he says, he does so out of goodwill (*eunoiāi*) and certainly not out of malice (*dusnoiāi*) (*Theaet.* 151c–d). For it is possible, he notes, for an unjust man, when he is made to give and take an account "in private"—that is, when he is questioned by Socrates, the quintessential "busybody in private" (*Ap.* 31c), who "always does your business, going to each of you privately" (*Ap.* 31b)—to come to see that what he says "fails to satisfy even himself" (*Theaet.* 177b). To recognize the inadequacy of one's beliefs is, from Socrates's perspective, a good thing; that Socrates brings people to that recognition makes him their benefactor.[72]

Socrates cares not only for his friends and family and for people generally; he cares, too, for the city. He fights for his city, remaining at the post where he is stationed by his commanding general—so long, at least, as to do so seems right to him,[73] that is, when it involves no injustice (*Ap.* 28d). He obeys the city's laws so long as they are not unjust (see *Ap.* 18e–19a, where Socrates agrees to make his defense speech despite the objectionably short time allotted for it because "the law must be obeyed.") He understands himself to be a gadfly sent by the god *to the city of Athens* to awaken her from her slumber (*Ap.* 30e–31a). And when he rebukes his city, he is doing precisely what he thinks one ought as a matter of course to do for those for whom one cares—oneself, one's parents, comrades, children, or fatherland who have committed injustice: rather than enable them to avoid a deserved punishment and so to persist in evildoing, one ought to see to it that they are punished so that they may return to virtue (*Gorg.* 430b). When Socrates says to the Athenians, "I will obey the gods rather than you," there is no belligerence in his words. In fact, his words follow an express affirmation of his affection for his countrymen: "I, men of Athens, salute you and love you" (*Ap.* 29d). Socrates considers himself Athens's greatest benefactor: he does more for the Athenians than the Olympic victors do; they only "make you seem to be happy" whereas he "makes you be so" (*Ap.* 36d–e). If Socrates refuses to "be quiet" it is because he believes his reticence would hurt the city. Antigone, by contrast, as we have seen, does not care at all about her city of Thebes. She answers to a higher authority not for the sake of the city but with callous disregard for its interests. Antigone does not try to persuade Creon that his decree is not good for the fatherland; it takes Teiresias to make that point.[7] The city's welfare is not Antigone's concern.

If it is true that Socrates cares for his city, is everyone's father, and seeks the moral improvement of everyone he meets, we may wonder what to make of his apparent neglect of his family's "affairs" (*praxai*) (*Ap.* 23b; 31b) and his belittling as pedestrian the concerns regarding "spending of money and reputation and nurture of children" (*Crito* 48c) in which Crito grounds his case for Socrates's escape.

It seems likely that the neglect of which Socrates speaks is financial. At 23b he associates his inattentiveness to his family with the "ten-thousandfold poverty" to which his devotion to the god has led. Indeed, if it were his children's nurture and education of which Socrates was careless while he was alive, Crito's appeal on their behalf would have been both senseless and ineffective: Socrates's dying would in that case not make his children's situation any worse, nor would it matter to Socrates if it did. Although Socrates does assuredly assert that not only matters of money and reputation, but also nurture of children, are "considerations of the many who act mindlessly," he does so in response to Crito's suggestion at *Crito* 45c–d that his neglect of his children isn't even just: in abandoning them, Crito charges, Socrates is abdicating his responsibility and leaving them as orphans to chance. What Socrates wants Crito to understand is that he would indeed abandon even his children if that were the only way to avoid injustice. That he would do so, however, is patently not because his children are of no consequence to him; on the contrary, almost the very last thing he says in the *Apology* (41e–42a) is that the way he will attain justice at the hands of those who voted against him is if they punish and pain his children for caring about the wrong things—that is, if they care for money or anything else above virtue (*Ap.* 41e–42a). Once Socrates determines that escape is unjust, it is only by remaining in prison that he can avoid harming his children; only thus can he protect them from the corruptive influence of a mistaken moral message.

Interestingly, although Socrates does not pardon those who sought his execution, he also wishes them no harm. They are blameworthy, to be sure, but he is neither indignant (*aganaktōn*) (*Ap.* 35e) nor angry (*chalepainō*) (*Ap.* 41d). In the speech Socrates makes in the *Apology* after his conviction, he *predicts*—but he doesn't wish—that harsher people will force them to a reckoning. He predicts, too—again, without wishing it—that Athens will do worse without him, unless and until the gods see fit to send her another benefactor in his place. His hope, of course, is that the god would send someone in his stead. Antigone's sense of justice, as we recall, requires that those who condemned her, if indeed they were in the wrong, undergo a fate no worse than hers. Until they suffer in nearly equal measure, however, there can be no justice.

Socrates's sometimes innovative moral views, the products of prolonged and concerted thinking, depart markedly from Antigone's unreflective and perhaps underdeveloped beliefs. Ismene must even say to Antigone: "Think, sister" (*phronēson, ō kasignētē*–49). Moreover, Socrates holds his views not for the moment but for a very long time: should we suddenly relinquish our long-held principles, he asks Crito, just because we now face death? (*Crito* 49a). Socrates is sought after as a source of moral wisdom because he is known for reflecting deeply and wisely about questions of justice. In the *Republic* Glaucon wants Socrates to defend justice because "I suppose I would be most likely to learn that from you"—to learn, that is, why justice should be extolled all by itself, why indeed it is better than injustice (358c–d). Meno, too, approaches Socrates to get an answer to a question about justice that had been troubling him: can justice be taught? And, of course, Chaerephon's consulting of the oracle to determine if anyone is wiser than Socrates attests to his own suspicion that the answer would be no. Because Antigone's deed is not the culmination of a life devoted to a set of moral principles, she weakens when she confronts the reality of her impending death, bemoaning the fate of "unhappy me." Socrates, however, because of his solid commitments, soldiers on; he never wavers, never falters. He remains steadfastly "at his post." Socrates doesn't change; he has no reason to. And he is serenely happy even as he awaits an undeserved execution.

Because Socrates is a thinker, his friends do not write him off as impossible to reason with—the way Haemon must have done with Antigone, choosing to speak to Creon instead. In the *Crito*, Crito is not afraid to go to the prison to talk to Socrates and even to attempt to influence his decision. In the *Phaedo* several of Socrates's other friends engage him in conversation even as he awaits execution; not only do they try to understand him but they also challenge his views. Of course, some of his friends, and Crito in particular, don't understand him. But Socrates never gives any of his friends the impression that there is no point in talking, that he is wedded to his decision and will never reconsider. Socrates scrutinizes the choices he makes: are they right? He listens for the *daimonion*, to his deeply engrained sense of right and wrong, to weigh in—or not.[75] He is thoughtful—not impetuous or impulsive.

Perhaps in part for that reason, Socrates does not take his own life. Instead, he considers in the *Phaedo*, at 61c–63c, whether or not to do so is right, concluding that suicide is improper (*ou themiton*). Genuine philosophers, Socrates says (*Phaedo* 61c–62c), despite yearning for the transcendent reality they suppose awaits them after death, nevertheless don't kill themselves because they are the gods' possessions (*ktēmata*), or, as Cebes puts it, they perform a service (*therapeias*) for the gods who are their masters (*despotas*). Philosophers therefore may not, and do not wish to, cut their service short. Antigone, however, as we know, commits suicide: insofar as she serves not the gods but herself, she has no role to continue playing in the world once her brother is buried. Rather than be executed by the state, then, she seizes the moment to end her own life her own way.

Antigone likely has no humility—not before men and not before gods. As we have seen, she goes so far as to compare herself to the goddess Niobe. She expects the gods to be her ally. Socrates, by contrast, is humble—if not before men then at least before gods. He never compares himself to the gods. And he insists upon the chasm that yawns between human knowledge and divine with respect to the most important things, *ta megista* (*Ap.* 22d; see, too, *Rep.* 3.392b; *Laws* 3.688c; 10.907a): the just, the noble, and the good. Socrates calls less attention to himself than he might. In the Leon of Salamis affair, for example, he simply goes home without making a show of his defiance. His elenctic activity is by its nature public, but there is no deliberate intent on his part to seize the spotlight. Despite his commanding presence in each of the dialogues in which he is featured, his interest lies not in showcasing himself but in confronting his interlocutors. Unlike Antigone, who is not inclined to share her glory, Socrates wants others to live the way he does, examining each other and speaking daily about virtue. He may be unique, but still his wish is for everyone to live the examined life, the only life that is "worth living for a human being." Antigone's suicide is so much more dramatic than Socrates's calm and serene drinking of the hemlock is.

Although Antigone becomes less sure of herself as the play progresses, she has little doubt at first that upon her death she will be welcomed by the gods below; indeed, she determines her course of action in part by taking into account the longer amount of time she is likely to spend in their presence. Socrates, by contrast, avoids the hubris of thinking he knows what happens after death. He may hope for and expect the gods' continuing care, but he faces death in the dark. Are there Forms? Will he see them? Socrates does not even claim to know whether it is better for him to live or die. This, he says, is known to the god alone (*Ap.* 42a).

Socrates and the Gods

Socrates presents himself (or Plato has him present himself) as a believer in a supernatural being (or beings). In this section I will take Socrates at his word, yet I will raise doubts in the the paper's final section about so literal a reading of him, and will suggest that Socrates is a paragon of piety whether he believes in a supernatural being who is god—or not. For whether or not one believes literally in beings who are gods, one's view of the gods—what one thinks they *are* like or what one thinks they *would* be like—colors one's piety. Those who believe in gods who must be pleased and appeased, who are the source of evil as well as good, and whose response to human beings is determined by how well their desires are fulfilled by them will have the kind of piety that is marked and marred by complaint, disappointment, despair, and anger. Those who believe in gods who are just and generous, who are above caprice and whim, and whose only wish is that people be virtuous and seek truth, will never blame the gods, will never be enraged, will never feel neglected and resentful, and will wish only to serve them. Antigone belongs, as we have seen, to the first of these two types of believer, and Socrates to the second.

Socrates spends his life remaining at the post to which he is stationed by the god, the post of practicing philosophy and pursuing virtue. He never has complaints against the gods. For him, gods who aren't just, just aren't gods. The gods are good generally and, in particular, are good to good men. In the *Apology* Socrates is convinced that "there is nothing bad for a good man, whether living or dead, nor yet are the gods without care for his troubles" (41c–d). In the *Theaetetus*, too, Socrates says of the god that "in him there is no wrong whatsoever"; indeed, "the god is most just" (176c); furthermore, "no god can wish evil to men" (151c–d). Socrates therefore believes that it must be the case that his dying now is good. It is inconceivable that he would expect, as Antigone does, to be saved at the last minute from death because of his reverence—as remuneration for his reverence. Socrates trusts that all will be well. Regardless, however, of how things turn out, it is not possible that the gods are in any way at fault.

Most important, Socrates does not make deals with the gods. Doing something for them in return for something from them is not piety. It is the practice of barter; it is a business transaction. It is for just such a conception of holiness that Socrates reprimands Euthyphro in the *Euthyphro*.[76] Socrates's piety is one-way. He serves the gods, pursues justice, and even dies, without a hint of anguish. Since he thinks the gods owe him nothing, he never feels abandoned, betrayed, or shortchanged.

Piety without God

To be a saint or regularly to perform acts that can reasonably be called saintly or pious, is it necessary that one believe literally in gods? Socrates would no doubt readily admit that he does not in the end know if there is a single god, many gods, or, for that matter, any gods, or what their nature is. By the same token, he would have to confess that he does not know that there are no gods. Just as he declares it the height of audacity "reproachable ignorance," to assume that death is bad (*Ap.* 29a–b), so he would surely acknowledge that he knows nothing of the existence or nature of the gods. All he can do is what any of us can do: imagine a god or gods worthy of the name and serve him or them. One can live one's life *as if* there is a god of justice and truth, performing only those deeds that are consistent with the existence of such a god. It is this sort of life that Socrates would consider holy or pious.

To live a saintly life in this sense would require that one (1) do no injustice, (2) dedicate oneself to a just cause in a way that goes above and beyond the call of duty, (3) be willing to risk something of great value for the sake of the cause, (4) do so not for oneself alone or mainly, and (5) approach the task with a measure of humility. To be pious is to be more than a hero. For heroes often embrace a cause that is not just (Antigone's "holy crime" [*hosia panourgēsas'*–74], for example); they typically see to it that their act does not go unwitnessed or unknown; and they exhibit an unwavering self-satisfied assurance that is not open to change by reasoned argument.[77]

For Socrates, a god (if there is one) can only be consummately just (*dikaiotatos*). Therefore, as Socrates says in the *Theaetetus*, the just man, "the one of us who has become as just as possible (*hoti dikaiotatos*)," is "most like the god"; "there is nothing more like him [the god] than the one of us who has become the most just possible" (*Theaet*. 176c). This is the simple truth: "Let us articulate the truth this way" (*to de alēthes hōde legōmen* [176c]).[78] If to be godlike is only to be just, and to be most godlike is no more than to be most just, it would seem that the godlikeness of the just man depends not at all on there actually being a god.

The *Apology*, for all its god talk, casts each of its "religious" point in secular terms. For example, when Socrates seeks to explain why he cannot simply go into exile and "keep quiet," that is, relinquish his practice of philosophy, he offers two reasons: first, that keeping quiet or ceasing to philosophize "is to disobey the god" (*Ap*. 37e6), and, second, that ". . . this even happens to be the greatest good for a human being—to make speeches every day about virtue and the other things about which you hear me conversing and examining both myself and others" (*Ap*. 38a2–5). Moreover, each of his references to his *daimonion*, his presumably "divine" sign, is similarly secularized. At *Ap*. 31c7–d6, Socrates says that his *daimonion* turned him away from participation in politics. Yet there is considerable evidence in the *Apology* that Socrates, independent of, and even prior to, any warning by the *daimonion*, decides that politics is not for him. At *Ap*. 23b7–9, he says: "And because of this occupation [namely, his service to the god], I have had no leisure, either to do any of the things of the city worth speaking of or any of the things of my family." And, later in the dialogue, after the guilty verdict has been announced, Socrates, making no reference to the *daimonion*, presents his own reasons for avoiding politics and expresses his lack of interest in—even his disdain for—political affairs:

> What am I worthy to suffer or to pay because I did not keep quiet during my life and did not care for the things that the many do—moneymaking and household management, and generalships and popular oratory, and the other offices, and conspiracies and factions that come into the city—since I held that I myself was really too decent to survive if I went into these things? I did not go into matters where, if I did go, I was going to be of no benefit either to you or to myself. (emphasis added; *Ap.* 36b5–c3)

Socrates, then, has reasons of his own that keep him from entering politics, namely, his lack of leisure owing to his mission, his disinclination to involve himself in the sorts of occupations and intrigues that appeal to the many, his sense that because of his decency he would not live long if he were to be politically active, and his belief that he would benefit no one.

The other sources Socrates cites for the divine origin of his mission are "oracles, dreams, and every other way a divine allotment ever ordered a human being to practice anything at all" (*Ap.* 33c). Note, however, that he continues: "These things, men of Athens, are both true and easy to test (*euelenkta*)." It is not in fact easy to test whether a god has communicated with a human being by way of a dream; and it is no simple matter to trust the veracity of an oracle. Indeed, the primary meaning of *euelenkta* is not "easy to test" but "easy to refute."

Whether or not Socrates believes in gods, there are for him certain things, namely, truth and justice that gods who are really gods would care about. His service to the god consists therefore in practicing philosophy and promoting individual virtue, the main noble thing gods worthy of the name would produce on earth with the help of human assistants (*Euthyph.* 14a.) The gods need helpers in this venture no less—and perhaps more—than human craftsmen do in theirs. Socrates is the gods' helper. Socrates can speak of being the possession of the gods or the servant of the gods because he has bound himself to work for the justice and truth that the gods would wish to promote if there were gods.

As noted in the previous section, Socratic piety is especially worthy in that it seeks nothing from the god. Socrates doesn't pray—not for his own needs; not even for those of others.[79] He has nothing but appreciation for the gods; he neither makes demands nor has expectations of them. He has no desire to bend the gods' will to his own for any reason. Not only does he not bargain with the gods as Euthyphro does; he does not ask them for anything. Even the Hebrew prophets and patriarchs petition God for justice and mercy. They indeed at times ask for things for themselves. Since Socrates does not ask for anything, does not pray for anything, his piety does not require a being to hear his pleas and grant his wishes. Socrates's piety can endure even without gods.

Socratic piety surpasses strict justice. What justice ostensibly requires of people is that they refrain from harming others (see *Ap.* 37b-c, 41d-e; *Crito* 49a-e; *Rep.* 1.335a-e). But to serve God is to do more than not harm people; one would have to help people. For if there is a god, what would he need? What could we human beings give him? These are questions that occupy the last part of Plato's *Euthyphro*. But is it Euthyphro the piety expert, the man who is privy to amazing stories about the gods, who can teach us how to serve them? Is it he who can say what kind of service (*hupēretikē*) to the gods holiness is? Is it he who can specify the work that men assist the gods in accomplishing on earth? Euthyphro is unable to name that work because it has no place in his narrowly self-centered conception of piety: the only work that is of concern to him is that of pleasing the gods in hopes of securing their favor. It is Socrates who can readily identify the work that is holiness, for this work is none other than the divine service that occupies him daily: the admonishment, examination, and exhortation of his fellow men to care for truth, justice, and the condition of their souls. As he says, "For I believe, men of Athens, as none of my accusers does" (*Ap.* 35d).

Notes

1. See, for example, Ahrensdorf (2009, 104): "The key to understanding Antigone's uncanny, heroic daring is her piety."

2. Antigone's devotion to the underworld gods and Creon's to the gods of the city have been duly noted by scholars. Segal (1981, 172), for example, speaks of the clash between Creon's Olympian and Antigone's chthonic allegiances. See, too, Knox 1964, 76-77, 102.

3. Creon is acutely aware of Antigone's manliness. "Indeed, I am no man, but she is a man, if she is to enjoy such power as this with impunity" (484-85). Although he was at this point in the play planning to put to death both Antigone and Ismene (488-89), it is only Antigone who he fears will be

the man. But cf. Segal (1964, 51) who alludes to Antigone's "full acceptance of her womanly nature." Also Knox (1964, 78-79), who thinks devotion to family is a womanly trait.

4. I use the terms "saint" and "hero" to capture two types. Both, to be sure, have connotations and associations that are foreign to Antigone and Socrates. Perhaps it is best to think of these terms as I use them as moderately stipulative, straying, but not by much, from ordinary usage. As I use "hero," it is intended to evoke the Greek heroes who are larger than life, bold, and single-mindedly committed to a cause at all costs; my "saint" is someone who exhibits supererogatory care for others in service of something transcendent.

5. Benardete 1975, 154.

6. Not all scholars regard the meeting as taking place in the predawn semi-darkness, as Benardete (1974, 148) and Bradshaw (1962, 201-03) do—rightly, in my view. Jebb (1891, xi), for example, puts the meeting at daybreak, as does McCall (1972, 108-09).

7. See Knox 1964, 64.

8. It is fairly common for scholars to contrast the family-oriented Antigone with the city-oriented Creon. Segal (1981, 189), for example, speaks of Creon's "undervaluation of blood ties" and Antigone's overvaluation of them. See, too, Knox 1964, 102; Winnington-Ingram 1980, 120.

9. It seems unfair for Sophocles's readers to accord less value to Ismene's love for her sister than they routinely accord to what they take to be Antigone's love for her brother.

10. It is arguably actually the loving Ismene who tries to save Antigone. She implies that Antigone acted as she did because in her misery she was not in her right mind (563-64). See Ahrensdorf 2009, 106n28.

11. Knox, interestingly, seems to change his view. Speaking earlier of how Antigone responds to intolerable pressure, he says that she "falls back on purely personal considerations, unrelated to family, city gods . . . [she is] laid open for us to see, and there is nothing there but the stubborn, individual, private will" (1964, 103).

12. See Nussbaum (1986, 64): ". . . there is no sense of closeness, no personal memory, no particularity animating her speech." Cf. Hegel who thinks Antigone's love for Polyneices is "without the slightest implication of anything blameworthy or egotistical" and that she is "the noblest of figures that ever appeared on earth" (1962, 147, 360; also 268-70). Or Norwood (1960, 140), who speaks of Antigone's "unswerving affection" for her brother. And Jebb (1891, xxx, xxxv): "Sophocles has preferred to portray Antigone as raised above every selfish thought, even the dearest—'earthly happiness'"; her "sole reward was to be in the action itself."

13. Here "those I must please most" are Antigone's dead family members: she most recently mentioned "my dearest brother" (81), and mentions him

again immediately following "you will justly incur the hatred of the dead man" (94). Ismene confirms at 99 that family is intended. At 75, those below whom Antigone intends to please are the gods. At 521 and 527, those "below" are once again Antigone's dead relatives.

14. If Antigone loves and acts lovingly toward one sibling but hates and acts hatefully toward another that ought to suffice to disqualify her as someone whose essence is love, someone whose "deepest motive" is love. The truth is, however, that she loves neither sibling.

15. It should come as no great surprise, therefore, that Antigone later declares that what she has done for Polyneices she would not have done for husband or child. It is already abundantly clear that she wouldn't risk her life for love of a particular husband. What Haemon does for her she would never do for him.

16. The views range from that the matter of the two burials is inconsequential (see Kamerbeek 1978, on ll. 429–31), to that the gods performed the first burial or in some way participated in it (Adams 1931, 110–11; Sheppard 1947, 51; Segal 1981, 160; see, too, Knox 1964, 69), to that Ismene did it—why else, after all, would she say she did (536)? (Rouse 1911, 40–42), to that there are "dramatic" purposes served by Antigone's return, see Cowser 1989, 38–40. Coleman (1972, 10–12) argues that, according to the guard, she admits to both (at 435), and so must have done both. (It is not impossible, of course, for Antigone to "admit" to something she did not in fact do. But why would she "call down curses on those who had done the deed" [427–28] unless she knew them to be undoing her work?) For a review of the literature, see McCall 1972.

17. The chorus does say, however, that Antigone is "in love with death" (220). For the view that Antigone wishes to achieve immortality through her act, see Ahrensdorf 2009, 108.

18. Cowser 1939, 38–40.

19. Knox 1964, 64.

20. Norwood 1920, 140; Meikeljohn 1932, 4–5; Flickinger 1933, 136. Norwood argues that Sophocles has Antigone return "simply to remind us" that, as she well knows, she cannot succeed and will not succeed in burying Polyneices: the king's guards will remove the dust she scatters each time. She thus "throws away her life"—as well as the lives of Haemon and Eurydice—for no good reason; she displays a tragic "blindness," an "inability to see the crude facts of a hateful situation." Were this Sophocles's intention, however, why would she be caught the second time?

21. Knox 1964, 65.

22. Creon had already spoken of his own relation to Polyneices as one of enemy to enemy (187–90), insofar as Polyneices showed himself to be an enemy of the city. See Saxonhouse (1992, 72), who says of Creon that "he

can only know Polyneices as an enemy and not as a friend." See, too, Segal 1964, 52; Winnington-Ingram 1980, 123, 129–33, 148; Benardete 1974, 173; Nussbaum 1986, 57.

23. Antigone says: "Who knows if these things are blameless (*euagē*) down below?" By phrasing the question positively rather than negatively (as: "Who knows if these things aren't blameless down below"), Antigone betrays her own uncertainty. Note that Jebb translates Antigone's question as if it were in the negative: "Who knows but this seems blameless in the world below?" (1891, 101); and in the corresponding note: "She means: 'who can tell if Eteocles, in the world below, will not think it consonant with piety that Polyneices should be honoured?'" (102) (emphasis added).

24. Creon understands by those who are "below," *katō*, as the human dead: "Then go below and love those friends, if they are to be loved" (524–25).

25. As Knox explains (1982, 49), "the ancient Greek expected if not direct intervention at least some manifestation of favor or support from his gods when he believed his cause was just—a flight of eagles, the bird of Zeus, or lightning and thunder."

26. See Winnington-Ingram (1980, 137): "Was Creon right about the effect of the approach of death even upon the bold?" At 580–81 Creon had said that even the bold flee when they see Hades nearing their lives. For Winnington-Ingram (140) the reason Antigone now fears death is that she fears its manner: she will be neither with the living nor with the dead.

27. See, for example, Jebb (1891, xxxiv): ". . . then, indeed, there is a brief cry of anguish from that brave and loving spirit."

28. Polyneices married Adrastus's daughter Argeian. It was Adrastus whose support enabled Polyneices to mount his attack on Thebes and on Eteocles.

29. Knox is not right to think (1964, 107) that what is revealed in Antigone's last long speech is that she cares not about "the family as an institution" but about her individual dead family members whom she loves. For she laments not even once the loss of the man to whom she is betrothed; what she regrets is having to forgo marriage (813–16, 867, 875–76, 891, 917–18)—and hence family as an institution.

30. It is perhaps worth noting that Antigone does not ask Haemon for help with the burial nor does he make any attempt to persuade her to soften her stance and win his father's pardon. It is arguable that Antigone does not want to ask a man for help and thus appear weak (note that Creon is sure a man must have done the deed–249 290), and that Haemon knows better than to try to reason with Antigone, nor even to offer to intercede for her with his father. (See Knox [1964, 25]: "There is no dealing with such incorrigible natures.") He approaches Creon directly instead. (In Euripides's version of the story, Haemon does indeed assist Antigone in the burial; Antigone doesn't die but marries Haemon.)

31. The chorus of this play consists of fifteen Theban elders. All members of the chorus are male.

32. Jebb (1891, xxxi) is surely not right to say: "She feels sure of love in the world of the dead." Similarly, Knox (1964, 113): "She is rightly confident of the gratitude of those beloved dead she goes to join."

33. Perhaps Antigone rehearses for her parents and brother what she did for them in the hope that they will therefore not now hold against her that she did the same for Polyneices. (I owe this insight to my colleague Mark Bickhard.)

34. For the view that the brother Antigone addresses is Eteocles, see Benardete (1975, 151) and Ahrensdorf (2009, 129). Since Antigone turns to Polyneices immediately after addressing her parents and brother, it stands to reason that it was Eteocles who was the first brother addressed. That she is addressing Eteocles also makes sense of her uncertainty that upon her death she will be welcomed by her brother. For the view that the brother is not Eteocles see Winnington-Ingram (1980, 144n79). He argues that it is not Eteocles because Antigone had not addressed Eteocles before. The fact is, however, that Antigone hadn't addressed Oedipus or Jocasta before, either, so it is not at all unlikely that when Antigone turns to the dead members of her family, she turns to her parents and her brother Eteocles.

35. Ahrensdorf (2009, 129) rightly suspects that it is Creon's objection at 512–22 that causes Antigone to lose confidence in the unqualified rightness of her decision. Benardete (1975, 150) attributes Antigone's insecurity to the likelihood that the burial rites that she performed for her family members will not be performed on her corpse. It would seem, however, that if anyone would spurn her because of the impurity of her dead body it would be the gods rather than her family.

36. Many scholars either treat the vexing text as an excisable interpolation (Jebb 1891, 164) or wish they could (Goethe 1998, 178). The passage appears, however, in all the manuscripts and is quoted in Aristotle, *Rhet.* 1417a32–33. Since Jebb believes that Sophocles wishes the reader to regard Antigone as being wholly in the right, yet the passage in question does not show Antigone in the most flattering light, it is not surprising that he would think it inauthentic. It is not easy to imagine who would later insert such a passage—or why.

37. As we have seen, Creon had sinisterly told Ismene that Haemon can do without Antigone since "there are other furrows that can be plowed" (569).

38. Creon's demeanor and behavior also change—even before Teiresias reprimands him: he spares Ismene and delays Antigone's death, sequestering her in a cave rather than ordering her immediate stoning. It appears that something Haemon said may have caused Creon to rethink his plan: no one before had spoken to him plainly, as Haemon does, in terms of justice (728, 743). Haemon's appeal to justice may have recalled for Creon Antigone's having just refused to

permit Ismene to share the blame for the forbidden deed on the grounds that "justice will not allow you this, since you refused and I was not your associate" (538–39). Creon, unlike Antigone, has allegiance to something outside himself to which he remains faithful throughout: the city. It is surely for that reason that he goes first to bury Polyneices and then to free Antigone.

Ismene and Haemon also change, though they remain true to their ideals. Ismene finds her courage—too little, too late. She loves Antigone; she discovers she would rather die than live without her. All she says and does is motivated by that love. Haemon is trickier, though he too finds courage too little, too late. He remains steadfast in his love for Antigone; one wonders what would have happened had he killed Creon earlier rather than later. In the end, Antigone's motivation may be the least noble.

39. Segal (1981, 201) mischaracterizes Antigone's citing of the "law" as an emotional outburst: "The reasoning is emotionally, if not logically, consistent." Of the argument Segal says: "It is not reasonable, refuses to be reasonable." On the contrary, however, the argument strains to be reasonable, to appeal to some law that serves as justification—something that Creon might understand.

40. See Goethe 1998, 178: Antigone's speech "appears . . . to savour too much of dialectical calculation."

41. Benardete 1975, 151. See, too, Knox 1964, 107; also 1982, 46. Knox argues that the illogicality escapes Antigone because for her "the distinction between living and dead has ceased to exist."

42. Knox (1964, 105–06) thinks Antigone is addressing neither Creon nor the chorus, nor anyone present on stage but "the dead of her family, whom she is shortly to join." Yet she has turned from her family to Polyneices, and addresses only him specifically. None of what she says, however, would recommend itself to anyone but Creon.

43. Knox notes (1964, 67) that in this speech Antigone employs spoken iambics, "the medium of reflection, discussion, analysis." Knox assumes that Antigone is trying to clarify for herself the motivation behind her deed, but is it likely that the law she cites would be needed to justify her deed to herself? Surely she has seized on a justification that stands a chance of impressing Creon.

44. For an intriguing take on the role of the Herodotus story in the Antigone see Honig (2010). Honig understands Antigone to be showing Creon that "he is no Darius" (15): Darius feels pity but Creon is cold. "She charges him with inadequacy and injustice right to his face" (16). On her interpretation, the dirge "parodies Pericles, mimics Creon, and cites . . . Herodotus" (10).

45. There is little reason to assume that the "Greeks" simply saw husbands, wives, and children as replaceable. It is clear that neither Ismene nor Haemon thinks Haemon could do just as well with any wife. And it is clear that Darius expects Intaphernes's wife to choose to save her husband or child,

precisely because he understands the strong bond that exists between spouses and between parents and their irreplaceable children. We dare not generalize from Creon's ugly remark.

46. See Honig (2020, 11), who calls Antigone's argument "a parody of reason giving."

47. By paying special tribute to her brother, Antigone in effect relinquishes her earlier insistence that all the dead are equal (519, 521).

48. "The wise" are no doubt those who agree with Antigone as against Ismene (557).

49. Jebb (1891, xxxi–xxxii) finds "infinitely touching" "this supreme trouble which clouds her soul at last," but he assumes she surmises that "there has perhaps been something wrong in her way of doing the duty," not that she was mistaken about the duty "which was so clear and so binding."

50. In all the secondary literature I have read on Antigone I have encountered no one fully sensitive to the nuance in Antigone's expression, "no greater evils" (*mē pleiō kaka*–927). Even the meticulous Benardete has, first, "she now hopes that Creon will suffer *no less* than she has suffered" (150), and later, "in hoping that Creon suffer *as many* evils as she unjustly has" (154–55) (emphasis added in both). Knox (1964, 31) has: "the same injustice he has used against her." Granted that in many contexts the expression "not more" can mean "the same," nevertheless "not more" would be a most peculiar way of wishing on someone suffering that is "at least as much as but certainly not less than" what one has endured oneself. Jebb suggests that because Antigone can imagine no suffering worse than her own, she wishes on those who treated her unjustly no more suffering than she was subjected to. But, that is not what she says; it is only the sort of thing a commentator would read into what she says. Of course she thinks she has endured terrible suffering. But is that a reason for her to wish on her tormenters nothing worse? If she can imagine no worse suffering than her own, she would make a point of wishing on them the same—if that is what she intended. Moreover, she has just said that she accepts her punishment if she is judged to be in the wrong; to wish on those who wrongly caused her to suffer no worse evils than hers is, in this context, to regard her travails not as excessive but as what is merited. It appears that scholars attribute to Antigone a harshness that she pointedly avoids in this conciliatory speech.

51. One wonders if Antigone would really not have done the same for a husband or child if she could by doing so have won for herself the same sort of glory. Now that she is in conciliatory mode, however, she declares that she would defy the citizens only for a brother.

52. Raining down curses is something Antigone knows how to do; when she discovers that the dust she had sprinkled on Polyneices's corpse had been removed, she calls forth evil curses on those who did the deed (427–28).

53. The chorus, of which Winnington-Ingram is generally contemptuous (1980, 128) ("Choruses are not always right, and the chorus of Antigone is more likely to be wrong than many"), suddenly rises in his estimation as recognizing "her tone better perhaps than some modern interpreters. . . . She is still the same Antigone who faced the threats of Creon; her spirit is still unbroken; indignant rather than perplexed, in her ultimate and total isolation she confronts the gods with boldness and justifies her action in the teeth of fate" (146).

54. Antigone has here written Ismene off completely—and not only here but at 895 as well, where she calls herself "the last" (*loisthia*) of those of her own who are dead and among the shades, and says of her fate that it will be the worst (*kakista*) of all. How poignant is the difference between these words of Antigone and Ismene's earlier ones: "And now consider how much the worse (*kakist'*) will be the fate of us two (*nō*), who are left alone."

55. The chorus also attributes to Antigone *autognōtos orga*, "self-willed (or self-knowing, or self-conceived) passion" (875).

56. Sophocles leaves ambiguous how Antigone's deed is received, so that it is not clear if even the people think she has done right, though they probably have been persuaded that she did right by the gods. Haemon reports to Creon that the people are behind Antigone, that they think she deserves "to be honored with a golden prize" (699). It is not at all certain, however, that what Haemon reports is so. Antigone at first seems to think she has the people's support and tells Creon so (504–05). Yet she later believes herself to be mocked (838) and without support (876–78). Moreover, if the chorus is any indication of general sentiment, then the people do not approve of Antigone's headstrong rebelliousness.

57. Ahrensdorf (2009, 104) thinks Antigone is pious because she believes "she will not truly die but will rather enjoy the divine reward of eternal wellbeing . . . [she] places her hopes in supernatural beings who enable . . . mortals to win the divine reward of immortality in another, nether world, after death." In this way, he thinks, she confirms Ismene's contention that "human beings are incapable of rising above their concern for themselves" (108). There is no evidence in the text, however, to support the idea that Antigone calculates her advantage in quite this way, although she does say that she would prefer to anger Creon than to irritate the gods below because she will be spending far more time below (74–75). Ahrensdorf also thinks that Antigone's faith "buckles and collapses at the end," once she no longer has hope that the gods will save her (105). Yet if she wants to die in order to secure for herself a blissful afterlife, why would she want to be saved?

58. This is reminiscent of John Austin, who recognizes that one might have to disobey a sovereign whose law conflicts with divine law because of the greater severity of divine punishment.

59. For an analysis of heroism that is in some ways similar to this, see Urmson 1958.

60. It is my belief that formulaic definitions of the virtues or a specification of their necessary and sufficient conditions are not what Socrates is after; for that reason, among others, he regularly undermines the formulas he and his interlocutors reach. The search for formulas or definitions is only a first step: it is a way to begin thinking about things that will always exceed their formulaic bounds. The best formulas can identify features of the virtues but cannot say what they are.

61. Erasmus in his *Colloquium Convivium religiosum* (LB I, 683D–E) famously wrote: "Saint Socrates, pray for us": *sancte Socrates, ora pro nobis*, though these words were apparently written only in the margin of the original manuscript. See Thompson's 1957 edition, in which the colloquy appears as "The Godly Feast," and the plea is found on p. 158. As I argue, however, one distinctive feature of Socrates's piety is that he never prayed for things—for himself or for others.

62. See David Mikics's smart and sassy review of *Paul Johnson's Socrates: A Man for Our Times*. Johnson wrongly "gives us a pious Socrates rather than a Socrates who interrogates piety." As I understand Plato's Socrates, he sees the interrogation of piety, particularly when conducted with a pompous "piety expert" such as Euthyphro, as itself a pious act.

63. Alcibiades in the *Symposium* compares Socrates to a statue of Silenus that contains within it statues of the gods (215b); the figures Socrates contains within, Alcibiades says, are "golden" (*chrusa*), completely beautiful (*pankala*), and extremely amazing (*thaumasta*)" (217a).

64. Witness his effect on Alcibiades as recounted in the *Symposium*. Socrates is able to shame him; he is the only one who can do so (216b). Socrates can make him feel that his life as he lives it is not worth living (216a).

65. A view that had great currency in Socrates's day was that justice is a matter of helping friends and harming enemies. This is implicitly Crito's view in the *Crito* (it is the view that both motivates him to plan Socrates's jailbreak and causes him to be troubled by Socrates's acquiescence in his plight), and explicitly Polemarchus's view in *Rep.* 1. In responding to both of these interlocutors Socrates makes a point of characterizing justice as a matter of not harming anyone. Yet he conspicuously avoids including in his characterization of justice any reference to helping others, whether friend or foe. Justice is at its core impartial: it does not differentiate friend from foe. Piety, however, that is, Socrates's service to his fellow men, permits him to favor those closest to him ("but more so for my fellow-citizens, inasmuch as you are closer to me in kin"–*Ap.* 30a), though, as he says in the very same passage, he will converse with "whomever I happen to meet—younger or older, foreigner or fellow-citizen." Even in *Rep.* 7, where philosophers, whose clear preference is not to rule, are persuaded to rule by considerations of justice, justice is framed as repaying a

debt to those who nurtured them (see 520a–e). The implication of this way of framing the obligation is that justice requires that one play fair, that one return good for good. The consideration of "helping others" forms no part of the argument from justice.

66. Socrates tries to keep the two distinct both in the *Protagoras* at 349e–350c, and in the *Laches* at 196d–197c.

67. See *Crito* 48b–c; also 48d; cf. *Ap.* 28b.

68. It may appear that Socrates capitulates to the arguments of the Crito's personified Laws but, on my reading of the dialogue, Socrates has both reached his decision and offered his reasons for it before he introduces the Laws. The Laws merely bully; they are reminiscent of Creon in his worst moments. When pressed by his son, Creon, like the Laws, inflates the dangers of a single instance of "insubordination": "This it is that ruins cities, this it is that destroys houses, this it is that shatters and puts to flight the warriors on its own side! But what saves the lives of most of those that go straight is obedience! In this way we have to protect discipline . . ." (673–677). The Laws similarly charge Socrates and Crito with nothing less than "attempting to destroy us" (*Crito* 50d; 52c–d). For a discussion of the role of the Laws in the *Crito*, see Weiss 1998, chapters 5, 6, and 7.

69. I argue in Weiss 1998, chapter 4, that Socrates sets forth his reasons for refusing to escape before he introduces the Laws, and that it is only because, and when, Crito fails to grasp Socrates's reasons that Socrates offers an alternative in the form of the Laws' rhetorically charged speech. In brief, Socrates's reasons for refusing to escape are (in my view) that escape would require him to break his just agreement to "abide by my penalty" (*Ap.* 39b) and also to engage in the unsavory practices of deception and bribery.

70. In Plato's account in the *Phaedo*, Socrates is kind to his distraught wife, Xanthippe, and sees to it that his good friend Crito look after her (60a)

71. It is in the context of his trial that Socrates professes to favor Athenians. The trial is conducted, of course, by Athenians in Athens.

72. It is arguable that it is not best for all people to question their beliefs and to doubt them. But for Socrates "the unexamined life is not worth living for a human being" (*Ap.* 38a). One's life, he thinks, is not a fully human one if one has not reflected upon it.

73. I read this passage as Woozley (1979, 49) does

74. There is every reason to believe that Creon would have buried Polyneices had he come to see that the presence of an unburied body in its midst is dangerous for Thebes. No sooner does Teiresias tell him that the body must be buried than he goes ahead and sees to its burial.

75. For a full discussion of the *daimonion*, see Weiss 1998, 17–23.

76. Arguably, the same criticism is implicit as well in the following question posed by Socrates to Nicias in the *Laches*: "And do you regard that man

as lacking in temperance or justice and holiness to whom alone belongs the ability to deal circumspectly with both gods and men with respect to both the fearful and its opposite, and to provide himself with good things through his knowledge of how to associate with them correctly?" (*La.* 199d–e).

77. It is not sufficient that one's cause be thought just by oneself; it must actually be so. Heroes are self-righteous and so of necessity regard their cause as just. Justice, however, is something to which they have generally given little thought and is not what they consistently look to, to guide their choices. People cannot qualify as pious if their cause parades as just while being in fact merely vengeful or cruel, reflecting no more than their own narrow passion. Achilles in the *Apology* is a case in point (*Ap.* 28b–d). Whereas he is unmistakably heroic, someone who stands his ground at the cost of his life, his cause is not a just one nor is justice his first consideration. He illustrates the first part of Socrates's point, namely, "that a man who is of even a little benefit" should not "take into account the danger of living or dying" (*Ap.* 28b)—as Socrates says to the jury: "Surely you do not suppose that he gave any thought to death and danger?" (*Ap.* 38d)—but not the second: "and rather consider this alone whenever he acts: whether his actions are just or unjust" (*Ap.* 28b).

78. It is striking that in this part of the *Theaetetus* where the question of relativism is still alive and prominent, Socrates does not hesitate to announce this plain "truth."

79. How ironic, then, is Nephalius's entreaty of Socrates in Erasmus's colloquy (see n61) that he "pray for us," when it is a mark of his piety that he does not pray for things—for himself or for others.

9

Myth and Argument in Glaucon's account of Gyges's Ring and Adeimantus's Use of Poetry

MARINA McCoy

In this paper, I examine Glaucon's narrative about Gyges's ancestor and the ring and how it contribute to the argument of *Republic*, Book Two. Glaucon's adaptation of the story from Herodotus introduces new features that are both philosophically and psychologically significant to the argument. His use of narrative form invites philosophical reflection on one's own motivations for acting justly or unjustly, by asking us to identify or dis-identify with one who possesses the ring. Such mimetic identification puts poetic and narrative form to philosophical use, in contrast to the criticisms of mimesis that Socrates levels against poetry.[1] Building on his brother's approach, Adeimantus also uses poetry as an argumentative resource. Rather than reading Socrates's critique of poetry as the full Platonic view, Adeimantus uses Hesiod, Homer, and other authors in order to argumentatively strengthen the challenge to which Socrates must respond.[2]

Glaucon himself holds the opinion that the just life is better, but restores the position that the unjust life is happier with the hope that Socrates can show why that view is wrong. To begin, he suggests that doing injustice is good while suffering it is bad, but that the bad in suffering it exceeds the good in doing it—a kind of a social contract theory, whereby citizens agree not to do unjust acts so that they also do not suffer from them (358e–359a).[3] Justice is the mean between doing injustice without consequences and suffering it. He adds that even those who do justice do it unwillingly from an inability to do justice (359b). To illustrate the claim that even those who act justly would act unjustly if they were given the opportunity (359b), Glaucon retells the story of Gyges from Herodotus (358d–360b). In shifting to a narrative account, Glaucon is not simply making an appeal to poetic authority. The use of the mode of narrative invites Glaucon's audience to situate himself in the story and to examine whether his motives would align with those of the shepherd, should he find himself in a similar situation. It thus encourages the audience to explore whether the view that justice is undertaken merely for the good effects such as reputation, is psychologically adequate.

Glaucon adapts elements of the story for his own purposes, not simply retelling the version found in Herodotus, but changing its central message so that the question of what the shepherd chooses once he has the ring heightens the psychological dimensions of his choice. Whereas in Herodotus's version, the shortcomings of the king are emphasized, here, the shepherd's response to finding himself in the midst of power without consequences is the story's center. In Herodotus, Gyges is not a shepherd, but rather the bodyguard to the king, Candaules. Herodotus describes Candaules as a man overly in love with his wife, in excess of passion even for his lawful partner, who persuades Gyges to look at his wife naked because Gyges does not believe him as enthusiastically as King Candaules would like. Gyges is his most trusted bodyguard. Gyges initially does not want to do what he believes to be wicked, but he eventually capitulates to Candaules's wishes. It is the king who contrives a situation where Gyges can hide and see the queen naked, unknown to her. The queen discoverers that she has been seen and Gyges flees. She later tells Gyges that either he must kill the king and take over the throne, or die immediately. While Gyges elects to marry the queen, he does so reluctantly, since his choice is either his own death or the king's. His choice is between his own life and the king's life, and so when the queen places a dagger into his hand, he slays the king. In Herodotus's story, the king's foolishness and queen's power drive the action. While Gyges does choose to spy and to kill, those choices are framed within a context of a king and queen who try to "force his hand." Herodotus's story is a story about sexual shame and passion. In his version, a servant capitulates to the forces around him: it's the social forces—the king and the queen—that push him to act unjustly, and only when he succumbs to them and does not listen to his internal sense of morality does he become unjust. In Glaucon's version, it is exactly the opposite: the just man becomes unjust when he can escape notice, when *no* social pressure touches him. The queen has no part in Glaucon's version of the plan and she is overcome by Gyges, rather than being the instigator.

Several elements of Glaucon's narrative are novel and not found in Herodotus: a ring is discovered deep in a chasm of the earth and is removed from a corpse inside a bull. This language of descent into the chasm is another instance of the language of ascent and descent that occurs throughout the dialogue. The discovery of the corpse inside the brass horse suggests a man who is eventually tortured and killed despite, or even on account of, its possession—especially if one notes the parallel to the torture device of Phalaris who roasted his human victims within a brass bull.[4] Here we find a quiet foreshadowing of the Myth of Er, in which exceptionally evil souls descend into the earth and do not re-ascend. Glaucon also changes the main character to a shepherd rather than a bodyguard—perhaps taking up the prior paradigm from Thrasymachus of the shepherd who cares for his sheep for his own good (343b). Glaucon's story's main character is not Gyges but his ancestor from generations before, thus pushing the story back into a more foundational mythical past.[5]

The presence of details such as lightning and the bronze horse with windows and the earthquake convey also a sense of mythic power and the possibility of violence in nature. The myth asks, if we could have something that could remove a person from the realm of human society, would we still want to be just? What happens to man when one takes away convention and descends deeply into his own depths, out of the light of day? Yet, in Glaucon's description, there is something strange about even *speaking* about what human beings are like without shame or without social forces to influence their growth of their persons, since no such people exist. They are mythical, and so we need, then, a myth to be able to speak of the pre-conventional, natural man.

In Herodotus's version, an otherwise good man is led into unjust choices by others who seem to have power over him and yet ascends to the throne. In Glaucon's retelling of the story, Glaucon lacks all shame and self-restraint once he possesses the ring. Moreover, the temptation to which Herodotus's shepherd submits is due to the King's overvaluation of sight as opposed to hearing. Herodotus writes that the king tells his servant: "I see you do not credit what I tell you of my lady's loveliness; but since men's ears are less credulous than their eyes, contrive some means whereby you may see her naked." That is, on Herodotus's account, Candaules finds *logos* to be powerless in conveying the truth of his wife's beauty; instead, a visual experience is needed to directly convey the reality that Candaules wishes to share. Yet, such an experience is also morally dangerous: had Gyges simply trusted in the king's words and refused firsthand knowledge by sight in favor of secondhand knowledge, he would have been saved from other unjust actions. Thus there is an implicit critique of sight as an adequate model for all moral knowledge, despite the eventual centrality of vision as a model for "seeing" the forms.

In the *Republic* as a whole, we find dialectical movement between sight and hearing as a means to understanding the nature of justice. On the one hand, Socrates and his friends use a variety of narratives and argumentative strategies in order to discover and to test ideas about justice. Here, listening is central to discovering the nature of justice, and verbal accounts are intended to draw the borders and to give definition (*horos*) to justice. On the other hand, in the middle books, Socrates offers primacy to sight in his description of the form of the good as the cause of intellectual insight, and in the forms themselves as modeled on a visual metaphor of "shape" or something that can be seen or imaged. This movement between sight as a metaphor for knowledge—especially for the "coming to see" something about justice by an individual inquirer—and *logos*, which in the characters' verbal communication requires hearing, is a continual dialectical movement of the *Republic*.[6] The *Republic*'s critiques of poetry will go on to suggest that the dangers of knowledge as "seeing for oneself" presented by Herodotus, are not exclusive to visual approaches to knowing. Hearing the traditional stories of heroes and gods is also powerful; the question of moral corruption is not exclusive to either sight or to hearing.

However, the form in which Glaucon tells this story also allows for a critical response to the narrative. Listening to a narrative in which a character must make a key choice between just and unjust acts invites those who listen to identify or to dis-identify with the character. Glaucon's concluding remarks at the end of his mythological account especially encourage such a self-identification.[7] He asserts that the just man and unjust person would act identically if in possession of the ring, having sexual relations with whom he wishes, freeing or slaying those in bonds, and in general, universally stating of all persons, "Indeed, all men suppose injustice is far more to their private profit than justice" (380c).[8] Glaucon, in other words, moves from a universal claim about why men act justly (to protect themselves from injustice), to a narrative that provides the possibility of identification with such those who act unjustly, and back to a universal claim about the nature of human beings.

This movement from universal to particular to universal in his argument may be mirrored in an audience response to the argument that moves from listening to Glaucon's story, to assessing the motivations of one's own particular just or unjust actions, with the opportunity then to agree or to disagree with the adequacy of Glaucon's universal claims about human beings. The listener who critically engages with the story can more easily make judgments about the adequacy of the general account when faced with a narrative representation that invites finding similarity and difference between oneself and this iconic character of the shepherd. That is, the person who listens to Glaucon (e.g., Socrates or his friends in Cephalus's house, and also those who read a Platonic text) is invited to undertake a mimetic identification or dis-identification with the character in order to assess the argument.[9] Both a member of Glaucon's audience and of the Platonic audience may say to herself, "I would never use the ring in such a way!" and so actively dis-identify (or perhaps identify with the shepherd). At the moment of identification or dis-identification, the person who does so might begin to have better access as to *why* she would choose as she thinks that she would. For example, a listener might say that he would feel ashamed to commit adultery and make an examination of shame and its motivational and ethical significance. Or a listener might assert that murder is always wrong and then offer rational principles as to why taking the life of another is worse than suffering death. The use of narrative presents an opportunity for examining any felt psychological isomorphism or lack of one between the image of the shepherd with a ring, and that of the soul of the person listening to the story. In other words, Glaucon's use of narrative here encourages a philosophical movement toward self-knowledge.[10] As human beings, we can only recognize who others are by their actions: a courageous man is known to be courageous through the courageous acts that he does. We also come to know ourselves through comparing ourselves to the actions of others, for example, asking whether I would respond in the same way as another did, if placed in identical circumstances.

If one wishes better to understand how such identification or dis-identification might work, one need look no further than Socrates's own later account of how mimesis affects those who perform in dramatic works. Tragedy and comedy both proceed through the use of mimesis (394c). In the ideal city in speech, the city's guardians should only imitate those who possess the virtues that are necessary to be capable guardians, such as characters who display moderation, courage, and piety (395c). One reason is that one cannot be good at imitating everything. More importantly for our purposes here, such imitations make impressions on the soul that leave lasting effects. Socrates says, "Haven't you observed that imitations, if they are practiced from youth onwards, become established as habits (ἔθη) and nature in body (σῶμα) and sounds and in thought (διάνοιαν)?" (395d). In mimetic imitation, one may become other than who one already is through imitation of another's actions and the resulting habits that may arise. For example, in ordinary life, if I want to learn how to cook a complex dish, I might begin by watching a chef undertake the same activities that I wish to learn, and note which skills I already have (mixing pastry dough), and which skills I still lack (making a meringue). Through practicing the skills that I lack, I can become a better pastry chef. In observing others from whom we actively wish to learn, we naturally compare our current state to that of others, and form comparisons between their actions and our own. Such comparisons result in greater self-knowledge. Deliberately imitating the skill that I lack over time can produce a capability to undertake actions that I previously did not know how to do, through force of habit. However, imitations of others can also produce negative traits: imitating a man who wails too easily over his misfortune might lead me also to become such a kind of a person (395e). Imitations harm the soul because they lead the imitator to act "as though he were someone else" (393c). Over time, imitations produce habits, changing one's character.

The guardians should only use narration when describing others whom they do not wish to be like, such as blacksmiths or those who practice other crafts, women, or slavish or mad men (395e–397b). Socrates says remarkably little about how and why narration saves speakers from the problems inherent in pure mimesis, but we can reasonably infer that narration does not demand of the speaker or listener that he choose to be "someone else."[11] Narration does not produce the same immediate habits and impressions on the body and soul as does mimesis. However, narration still allows both the speaker and the listener access to the character being portrayed, but with greater distance, on account of the mediated narrative. Glaucon's narrative of the shepherd invites the listener to consider whether he is *already* like the shepherd, or would be like him were he to possess a similar power of invisibility and its accompanying lack of consequences.

If we consider Socrates's comments about the power of imitation for producing habits in the person who undertakes the imitation and the greater advantages of narrative, then we might glean an understanding of how listening to Glaucon's story might work. Glaucon narrates the story of Gyges's ancestor for us and provides a kind of distance from the story—one that would be lacking in simply imitating the shepherd's words and actions—by framing it within the context of exploring the question of justice. Narrative itself provides a kind of critical distance by which the power of mimesis becomes mediated. In effect, rather than passively becoming habituated to act like the shepherd through repeated imitations of his story, a reader is encouraged to consider the very question of whether she would or would not be like the shepherd. Glaucon's narrative framework offers a freedom and openness to compare oneself to the shepherd that mimesis alone does not. Narration is not a completely mimesis-free form of speech, but rather is a more mediated way of undertaking mimetic comparisons. With narration, one does not already assume the voice of the character being imitated. Rather, one is invited to imagine, to observe, and to assess the character. Glaucon's account, although narrated, is nonetheless imaginatively vivid and encourages some self-identification with the shepherd. But his framing that story within the context of what others—"they"—say about the value of injustice also asks any audience also to situate this image within a larger framework of judgment and criticism.

We see a similar phenomenon is at work with the presentation of characters in the Platonic dialogue. While Socrates describes Thrasymachus as akin to a wild beast (336b), he approves of Glaucon as courageous and as worthy of honorific poems (357a; 368a). Elsewhere, Glaucon is presented as highly erotic (368a; 402e; 450a; 468a), and as many commentators have argued, this eros is not limited to sexual desire but extends also to a yearning for better argument.[12] Socrates himself is another example of a just man who had a reputation for injustice, as one brought to court for the corruption of youth and yet in the *Apology*, devoted to justice regardless of consequence.[13] Yet Socrates also narrates the entire account to us, providing a kind of distance also from the characters that are being imitated.[14] Thus, for the Platonic audience, there is a double set of images at play: the unjust shepherd and beastlike Thrasymachus, on the one hand, and the tortured just man and the just Socrates (who will later in his life be punished unjustly) on the other hand. This "layering" of narrative further invites an audience member to find himself or herself in the dialogue.[15]

Here we can see an interesting element of a Platonic approach to eikastics within the text's argumentation. A true likeness or image—*eikasia*—is both like and unlike that of which it is an image, i.e., the *paradeigma*. *Phantasia* in the *Sophist* is defined as that "appears but does not resemble" (*Soph.* 236b).[16] In Book Nine, Socrates will emphasize the dissimilarity of images from that which they imitate, and thus their relative unreality in comparison to the forms. But to the extent that a likeness *is* a likeness, it also bears some similarity to that which it is like; it is, to some extent or another, truthful. This combination of likeness and difference is important for Plato's purposes, insofar as we who listen to or read a dialogue are invited to examine the extent to which the shepherd is like and unlike ourselves, and so to have better information to evaluate the degree of likeness and unlikeness of this *eikasia* of the human being in the image of the shepherd. As Tanner writes of Plato more generally, "the imagination plays a philosophical role: it is analytical because it enables the seeing of differences within identity, and thus enables philosophical inquiry."[17]

The difficulty, of course, is that unlike a painting that can be compared to the *paradeigma* of which it is an image, the very nature of justice is in dispute. There is no indisputable mode of access to the paradigmatic "just soul." In fact, in the ring of Gyges story, the just soul is really only a self-interested and unjust soul who has not yet found his freedom, i.e., the unjust soul is the paradigmatic "original." Given that immediate access to the paradigmatic soul is unavailable, Glaucon instead offers a narrative account that allows comparison between an image of an unjust soul (the shepherd with the ring) and oneself. Self-knowledge is a means by which the Platonic audience may enter into the possibility of making the distinction between *eikasia* and *phantasia* with respect to the specific image of the shepherd that Glaucon has presented. In other words, a person who denies her own similarity to the shepherd may find reasons that the story is inadequate as model for human character, through delving more deeply into her own soul and disposition.

Glaucon next offers a *synkrisis* (comparison) of the just and unjust man as a means of making the best judgment about them: "As to the judgment (κρίσιν) itself about the life of these two of whom we are speaking, we'll be able to make it correctly (κρῖναι ὀρθῶς) if we set the most just man and the most unjust man in opposition; if we do not, we won't be able to do so" (360e). On each side of the comparison is the "perfection" (τέλεον) of each man: that is, the man who is unjust but appears to be perfectly just, and gets all the rewards of justice, and the man who is perfectly just but seems to be perfectly unjust, and is whipped, racked, bound, and has his eyes burned out before finally being crucified (362a). Glaucon challenges Socrates to judge which of the two is happier. Moreover, Glaucon cleverly reincorporates each of the previous visions of justice from the earlier discussion of Book One: by asserting that the unjust man benefits in contracts and partnerships; is better able to help his friends and to harm his enemies; and is better able to make sacrifices to the gods (362b–c). That is, he suggests that the perfectly unjust person accomplishes many of the actions of the just person as presented by Cephalus and Polemarchus, too. He thus caps off his epideictic speech by asserting a kind of verbal triumph over all the previous speeches given about justice insofar as it can also account for many of these earlier points.

Before Socrates can answer, Adeimantus joins in and asserts that Glaucon's argument has not been adequately stated (362d). He takes up an agonistic position not only against the Socratic claim that the just person is happier, but also competitively against his brother's skill in speechmaking. Adeimantus argues that poets also do not sufficiently defend justice and that their ideas can be reconstrued as the view that justice is praised only for external goods such as reputation, offices, wealth, and divine rewards (363a–367e).[18] Just as Glaucon retrieved from Herodotus a useful *muthos* for making his points, Adeimantus treats the poets of the past as a resource for his own argumentative "case" against justice. They are literally "witnesses" (μάρτυρας; 364c), that is, evidentiary material for Adeimantus as he makes his own case.[19] A defendant or prosecutor in a courtroom is not usually interested in making a point about the witnesses whom he brings to the stand, so much as using those witnesses in order to build up an argument about some other matter. Similarly, Adeimantus here is not attempting to show that the poetic tradition has *itself* taken the view that injustice is preferable to justice. Rather, he utilizes poetic resources in order to build a kind of forensic argument of his own, alongside the defense of injustice that has been offered by Glaucon, but with the hope that Socrates will later be able to tear it down with a counterargument.

With respect to the larger movement of the evening's discussion, Adeimantus also begins the trajectory of criticizing the poets for whether they are adequate educators, a question which Socrates will soon take up and expand even further. Adeimantus uses multiple poets—Hesiod, Homer, Musaeus, Simonides, and Pindar—without making any kind of argument for the consistency of thought of any one of these poets on the point. His purpose is not to offer the best possible critical commentary of any one of these poets, or of the poetic tradition as a whole, but only to show why the view that "injustice is better" might be concluded even from the mainstream poetry of the day. If the poetic tradition wants to defend the goodness of justice—and clearly the passages he cites from Hesiod and Homer suggest that they do want to make such a defense—their teaching is inadequate, given the kinds of justifications unjust people can find even in the same poets for only *seeming* to be just. Near the end of his discourse, Adeimantus says, "no one has ever, in poetry or in prose, adequately developed the argument that the one [injustice] is the greatest of evils a soul can have in it, and justice the greatest good" (366e). Adeimantus's biggest criticism of the poets is that they do not offer sufficient philosophical justification for the claims that they make on behalf of justice. Such an argument is what he hopes Socrates will be able to give, however.

This is not to say that poetry is not a source of philosophical learning, for the inclusion of the poets as part of Adeimantus's argument is intrinsic to how Adeimantus deepens the philosophical questions about justice. This inclusion of poetry into the discussion of justice also extends to Plato as author, such that the total banishment of poetry from the ideal city in speech is not true of Plato's own philosophical process in this imperfect city. While Socrates will go on to criticize certain forms of poetry, its inclusion here in the voice of Adeimantus is an act of Platonic reincorporation of the poetic tradition, not a total rejection of it as inappropriate for argument.[20] However, Adeimantus's claim that no poet has adequately defended justice seems to be a moment when we can see that Plato's text is at least attempting to take up the project of defending the goodness of the just life in a more thorough way than any of his poetic predecessors. The poets do not actively corrupt but to the extent that they do teach that justice and piety are goods, they are unable to answer the kinds of questions that Glaucon and Adeimantus have, as those who basically believe in justice as a good but want to know why. The poets are also insufficient teachers, insofar as their poetry does not shape the souls of those who listen but still have doubts about the goodness of justice. At best, they can only move others who already share in the conviction that justice is good, and cannot defend against criticisms that the mere appearance of justice is enough. In other words, the poetic tradition is not sufficient philosophically, psychologically, or pedagogically.[21]

Adeimantus's use of poetic sources adds to Glaucon's argument that justice is praised for its rewards by not only listing concrete instances of those rewards (which might be done even without naming any poets), but also by attributing the origin and causation of those rewards to divine sources. Adeimantus cites Hesiod who says that the gods give to the just bees, acorns, and "fleecy sheep heavy laden with wool," while Homer attributes productive land and plentiful crops, fish, and herds to lands ruled by a just king (363a–c). Musaeus says that the just receive the divine reward of neverending drunkenness at an eternal symposium, while others punish the unjust in Hades (363c–d). Hesiod and Homer offer examples of rewards given not to just individuals, but rather to whole lands ruled by just kings.[22] The reference to Musaeus's poem brings in a larger cosmic dimension of eternal reward or punishment after death, although Adeimantus does not particularly extol the notion of "eternal drunkenness" as the noblest of all rewards for a just life, either! Still, only the poets can serve as witnesses of the consequences of justice from this larger, divine and cosmic perspective, for the inspired poet's perspective exceeds that of any ordinary person, who does not have access to divine motivations and causes.

Adeimantus next moves to instances of poetry and prose that praise injustice as more profitable and as shameful only by "opinion and law" (364a). Again, Adeimantus gives most of his attention in this analysis to the gods, who sometimes are said to give misfortune to many good men and good things to bad men (364b). Priests and prophets persuade the rich that certain recitations and sacrifices can remedy the injustices that they have committed, or that rites can benefit the dead who may be in need of them (364b–365a). Adeimantus does not himself concur with these claims, but rather concludes that those who listen to these poets might reasonably conclude that the advantage of justice lies in appearing just, while still being unjust (365b). Although getting away with injustice is difficult, "nothing great is easy" and perhaps the poets are incorrect even in believing that there are gods or that they care about human matters (365d–e). Or, if the gods do accept sacrificial and votive offerings as payment for wrongdoing, this ought to lead one to be unjust and then to offer appropriate sacrifice later for the best possible overall outcome (365e).

Adeimantus introduces at least two important novel elements here: the place of the divine in human happiness—especially whether the gods really reward justice or not—and the place of poetry in education. He identifies a fundamental tension between the Greek understanding of the gods as presented in poetry and the claim that justice is inherently good and rewarding. In this way he contextualizes their conversation about the human being's justice or injustice in terms of Greek theology. Moreover, while Glaucon keeps the domain of justice confined to the individual just soul, Adeimantus expands justice to include the interrelationships with others in our own society, and the relation between the human and the divine. Adeimantus also asks Socrates not only to prove that justice is best for a human being, but also to show how justice affects the person himself, when the "wages" of justice are removed. That is, he wants to know what justice and injustice are and what "power" (*dunamis*) each has in the soul. Adeimantus believes that Socrates is best suited to answer this question, since he has "spent your whole life considering nothing other than this" (367e).

These reformulations of the Thrasymachean vision by Glaucon and Adeimantus considerably focus the questions that Socrates must answer. The two brothers utilize the resources of myth and poetry in order to give Socrates multiple tasks. First, Glaucon wants Socrates to give better evidence that justice really is the kind of good that he said it was, that is, both a good for its own sake and good for the consequences. Glaucon removes these good consequences from the just man altogether when he unlinks justice from its effects in his two idealized "statues" of the just and unjust man and invites listeners to consider whether they might act in the same way as the shepherd. Second, Adeimantus suggests that the poetic tradition about religious sacrifice provides a psychological motivation for those who listen to poetry to *choose* the unjust life, since religious practices can become a practical means to acquire being unjust while still gaining all the benefits of justice both in this life and afterwards. He thus challenges Socrates to describe how justice can be psychologically motivating, in light of Greek poetry and religion. Third, Adeimantus wants to know not only what *kind* of good justice is, but *what* it is in itself, and what power (*dunamis*) it has in the soul. Socrates is thus challenged to give an account of what justice is; its effect on the soul; its goodness; its manner of acquisition; and the role of the divine in attention to human justice. It will take the entirety of the dialogue to fully address all of these questions.

Socrates expresses both wonder and delight at the Glaucon's and Adeimantus's challenges. He briefly praises them, himself citing a poetic line in their praise for distinguishing themselves in battle at Megara: "Sons of Ariston, divine offspring of a famous man" (368a). His delight lies not only in their capacity to offer a substantial argument on behalf of justice, but also because they are not persuaded that injustice is better than justice even after offering such speeches (368a–b). Here, Socrates notes a certain gap between persuasive argument and belief. It is possible to believe that justice is better than injustice and still to offer a strong argument on behalf of the opposite of this idea. In Aristophanes's *Clouds*, this manner of approaching *logos* is presented as dangerous: to make the weaker argument the stronger destroys tradition and corrupts souls. Here, Plato presents characters who are engaged in strengthening what they believe to be the "weaker" argument, but their commitments to justice and goodness do not waver. Socrates names this as something "divine" that has happened to them, suggesting that the cause of belief in justice and injustice is not restricted to persuasive argumentation alone but has some other source.[23] Indeed, Socrates says of himself that he would distrust (ἀπιστέω) them on the basis of their argument alone except that he knows them not to be persuaded (οὐ πεπεῖσθαι) that justice is better than injustice, on the basis of their character (τρόπος) (368b). Glaucon and Adeimantus take up the challenge to justice not from the standpoint of being unjust men looking for justification for their actions, but as good men seeking to understand better why what they believe to be good, really *is* good. Myth and poetry are central to their accomplishment of this pursuit, not only for these two brothers, but also for the reader of the dialogue itself.

Notes

1. This paper was initially presented in shorter form at the Ancient Philosophy Society annual meeting in 2016. I am grateful to my commentator,

Anne Marie Schultz, and APS audience members for helpful feedback. Thanks also to Drew Alexander for research assistance with this paper.

2. Jacob Howland also argues extensively for the view that *muthos* is indispensable to the *Republic* and its *logos*. See Howland 2005.

3. For a fuller argument that Glaucon's initial argument here is contractarian, see Santas 2010, 37–41. Santas takes this contractarian view to be Glaucon's own, but it seems clear to me that Glaucon offers it as part of building up a Thrasymachean case with the hope that Socrates will be able to demolish it by giving a counterargument.

4. Diodorus Siculus, *Bibliotheca historica*, IX, 18–19. Phalaris ruled Acragus from 570–554 BCE. Tradition says that Phalaris himself was killed within the same bull when he was dethroned. See also Pindar, *Pythian I*, 103–04.

5. Thanks to Jacob Howland for pointing this out to me.

6. The critiques of poetry will go onto suggest that the dangers of knowledge as "seeing for oneself" presented by Herodotus, are not exclusive to visual approaches to knowing. Hearing the traditional stories of heroes and gods is also powerful; the question of moral corruption is not exclusive to either sight or to hearing but a possibility for all forms of representative thinking.

7. Here, I am arguing that the example of the shepherd and the ring is not merely a thought experiment, although it does accomplish some of the aims of a thought experiment. For example, Miščević helpfully points out some features of the story as akin to a political thought experiment while noting difficulties with thought experiments that ground themselves in counterfactual conditions (such as utopian scenarios); see Miščević 2012, 153–65. Instead, Glaucon uses a narrative form of *muthos* in order to allow his audience to explore their own similarities and differences from the shepherd, as a means of self-knowledge and knowledge about justice. Plato is not only after our moral intuitions, but furthermore is also displaying the power of *muthos* and especially its mimetic powers.

8. All translations of the *Republic* are from Bloom 1991.

9. As Sonja Tanner argues, Horace later explicitly links poetry's emotional effects on its audience to mimesis, and Plato's Ion connects the partial mimetic identification of the actor to the character whom he imitates as fundamental to his ability to act well (*Ion* 535c); see Tanner 2010, 77. Here I depart from Howland, who takes the stance that Glaucon uses the story of the ring in order to *show* that any person would use the ring for the sake of deception. I argue instead that Glaucon offers it, like the image of the man tortured on the rack, as a poetic counterargument to his own belief that justice is best. He offers the image as part of the argument that "they say" that doing injustice is naturally good, and not as his own view—a view that he hopes his audience (Socrates and perhaps others) will challenge.

10. Schultz argues that Socrates's narration and his frequent inclusion of his feelings about the situation at hand, such as responses of fear, models a form of self-mastery in which Socrates shows the listener how to be responsive to emo-

tions in which one neither ignores emotions nor is ruled by them, but rather is responsive to them. See, for example, her helpful reflections on Socrates's *aporia* in Book Two, and his capacity to regulate his desire for answers to questions about justice in Schultz 2013, 179.

11. For the purposes of this paper, I focus solely on Glaucon's use of narrative and its contrast to mimesis. However, it should be noted that in another way, the reader of the dialogue does take on a kind of mimesis of *all* of the dialogue's characters, in the very act of reading. Thus, a longer account of how narration and imitation function in the *Republic* will have to also incorporate how the Platonic reader's acts of imitation differ from the passive imitators described here in Book Three of the *Republic*. Such an argument is beyond the scope of this paper.

12. See, for example, Rosen 2005, 12; Howland 1993, 78–83; Roochnik 2003, 55–57; and Schultz 2013, 160.

13. Here I am thinking of his refusal to harm the thirty generals and Leon of Salamis.

14. Again, see Schultz 2013 and her chapters on narration in the *Republic*.

15. As Howland writes, "Like Socrates, we attempt to move by means of imagination and inference from the visible exterior of Plato's *dramatis personae* to their invisible interior"; Howland 2005, 217.

16. Tanner examines this contrast between *eikasia* and *phantasia* as indicative of a deep Platonic engagement with imagination in Plato's *Sophist*. Tanner persuasively argues that translation of *paradeigma* as "original" mistakenly communicate an ontological or temporal priority that may not always be present and so I use "paradigm" as a translation where possible. I am indebted to her work on the *Sophist* and general reflections on the imagination in Plato for my own work on the *Republic* here. However, I want to add a further psychological dimension to the use of images in argument. Images encourage both analysis of philosophical ideas and self-knowledge or concern for one's own soul as part of the basis of assessing claims about justice and injustice. See Tanner 2010 92–103 for more on eikastics and phantastics in the *Sophist*.

17. Tanner 2010, 103.

18. See Lake 2011, 126.

19. Ausland 2003 also notes the use of epideictic, forensic, as well as deliberative elements in Adeimantus's speech.

20. Similarly, Plato's *Protagoras* has Socrates protest the value of the interpretation of poetry in contrast to speaking on behalf of one's own ideas, but Socrates also offers an interpretation of Simonides that is more reflective of Socratic concerns than of anything the original poem might have meant. See McCoy 1999.

21. In contrast, Rosen 2005, 67–68 argues that the poets are for Adeimantus a "powerful contribution to the corruption of the many" and even pandering to the many.

22. The Hesiodic reference is to *Works and Days*, 232–34 and clearly concerns the benefits accorded to an entire land, not only an individual, when the ruler makes just judgments.

23. Howland 2005, 216 notes the brothers' openness to the question of the good life as what Socrates names as "divine."

10

Myth Inside the Walls
Er and the Argument of the *Republic*[1]

PIERRE DESTRÉE

As several recent works have suggested, the myth of Er has a rather strangely ambiguous status.[2] It is arguably the sort of poetic device that may prove "not only pleasurable but also useful for political regimes and private human lives," as Plato famously proposes at the end of his critique of poetry (*Rep.* 607d). And it is at the same time a philosophical rewriting of a Homeric piece of poetry, namely the famous Nekuia from *Odyssey* 11, which offers a rather different, in fact critical, version of what we find in Homer. In a way, this comes as no surprise. If Plato wants to be seriously and effectively considered as offering a new moral-cum-political guidance, it is much more to be expected that he would choose to criticize Homer, who has been considered to be the Greeks' moral guide (see esp. 598d-e, 600c, 606e). And yet, as he fully recognizes at the beginning and end of his critique of poetry in Book 10 (595b-c, 607e-608a), even Socrates cannot help but feel deep love and respect for Homer—after all. It may seem that the reason why Plato comes back to poetry in Book 10 is precisely because he wants to ensure that Glaucon and his readers do not fall back into their childish love of poetry and Homer; so far from being a sort of afterthought, Plato's second critique of poetry would actually aim at banishing Homer for good. But, in fact, it is worth emphasizing that Glaucon is not prohibited from going to the theater and enjoying it; instead, he is offered protection against the potential damages such poetry might inflict on his soul (or rather, the government of his soul) whenever he listens to it, that protection consisting in repeating to himself the arguments Socrates has just defended (608a). And along the same lines, one may doubt that Plato's injunction to stick to the lyric poetry that praises the virtuous gods and men, which alone is to be admitted into a well-governed city, might actually work. It might perhaps do so in Kallipolis, but certainly not in real cities and with real people who do indeed take immense pleasure in going to the theater or listening to rhapsodes reciting Homer's work. Remember Glaucon's famous response when Socrates proposes feeding the people of the first city olives and cheese, figs, chickpeas, and beans, and also myrtles and acorns: "But that's a city of pigs" (372d4), meaning that this food is only fit for pigs (that were fed such things), that is for humans without any decent, properly human culture. In other words, a city without pleasurable poetry, like Homer's, would be exactly like that first city: a city where you could survive, but not live a properly human life. So here is the challenge, I propose, that Plato had to face in wrapping up the *Republic*: since Homer was the moral-cum-political guide who needed to be replaced, Plato had to get back to Homer to make his case all the while offering something poetical if he was to respond to Glaucon's outcry. In brief, the myth of Er is designed for poetry lovers like Glaucon and Plato's readership, but poetry lovers who have followed the argument of the *Republic* so far where the critique of poetry has played a very important role.

In this paper, I want to focus on the two main issues that have been under particular scrutiny in the last two or three decades of scholarship, from that perspective. First, I'll be dealing with the problem of the status of this myth in the framework of the whole work by focusing on the addressee of the myth. And second, I will explore the possible meaning of some crucial parts of the myth (or what I take to be its crucial parts) through a comparison with the message that seems to be conveyed in Homer's myth of the Nekuia.

A New Platonic Hero

Before going into these two related issues, let me emphasize how this paradoxical claim—that the myth of Er is a critical, yet poetical, rewriting of poetry—can be seen at work in the famous sentence that begins the myth:

> Well, it is not an Alcinous-story I am going to tell you, but that of a brave man called Er, the son of Armenios, by race a Pamphylian.

> Ἀλλ' οὐ μέντοι σοι, ἦν δ' ἐγώ, Ἀλκίνου γε ἀπόλογον ἐρῶ, ἀλλ' ἀλκίμου μὲν ἀνδρός, Ἡρὸς τοῦ Ἀρμενίου, τὸ γένος Παμφύλου·

Plato could not be clearer: he is going to offer a rewriting of the tales Odysseus offers the king Alcinous, and more precisely of the Nekuia that takes place in Book 11 of the *Odyssey*. And, as we will see, this will be a very different account of Hades from what Odysseus has reported. But still, it is meant to be a poetical rewriting of a sort, as the tone and style of this introductory sentence shows—saturated by alliterations, repetitions and puns. The word *alkimos*, a hapax in Plato, typically refers to Homeric heroes. Plato is very emphatic: Er is a "particularly courageous man" (ἀλκίμου μὲν ἀνδρός).[3] If ἄλκιμος is not used specifically for Odysseus, numerous passages in the *Odyssey* underline his exceptional strength and courage (see notably 22.226–32 where μένος, ἀλκή, and ἄλκιμος are used for Odysseus); and πολύτλας, "much enduring," is his epithet (*Il.* 8.97; *Od.* 7.1, 16. 90). Thus, with this unexpected, and emphatic, usage of the term *alkimos*, and the wordplay with the name of the recipient of Odysseus's tale, Alcinous, Plato wanted to alert his readers to the fact that Er is going to tell a story as if he were a sort of new Odysseus, with a revised version of the Nekuia. And perhaps, more precisely, readers are meant to understand that the soldier introduced by Socrates must be, as S. Halliwell proposed, "standing for a deeper courage than the traditional paradigm of endurance, Odysseus."[4] This might also explain the origin and meaning of his very name: interpreters have tried all sorts of possible etymologies and puns, but perhaps the solution to the origin of that rather awkward name which best suits the context, I suggest, is simply to hear a pun on the genitive form Ἡρός—and note that, in fact, the name of Er is only used here by Plato, so only in the genitive form: Ἡρός can be very easily understood as a pun on the word ἥρως (which may be heard as either a nominative, or a contracted form of the genitive), which is another current word, like ἀνήρ, for naming the great soldiers, indeed the heroes, of the *Iliad*.[5] In other words, Er/Ἡρός/ἥρως is presented as the truly "heroic" figure, or the new Platonic "hero," who is going to deliver an important message from Hades that is meant to replace the report we got from Odysseus. (Indeed, when criticizing the Homeric vision of Hades at the beginning of *Rep.* 3, Plato began by citing three verses from the Nekuia—the famous ones where Achilles boldly admits that he would prefer farming the land for another man, however poor, than being king of the dead).[6]

Also, the strange patronymic and ethnic name of Ἐρ/Ἡρός, τοῦ Ἀρμενίου, τὸ γένος Παμφύλου cannot have been chosen by random. τοῦ Ἀρμενίου literally means "son of Armenios" which is an existing male name but the name itself means the Armenian. Even if the Armenian people (as Herodotus already reports: 1.194; 5.52) lived in a much more northerly region than Pamphylia, these two names refer to Persia (at least at the time of Plato, Pamphylia and Armenia were part of the Achaemenid Empire), and lend a sort of mysterious flavor to the origin of Er, perhaps simply a way for Plato to underline that his tale will not correspond to what traditional Greek ears might have been expecting to hear. But it is also very likely that the noun Πάμφυλος, 'Pamphylian,' should be understood in its etymological meaning, that is, the whole human race.[7] Thus, Er, or Ἡρός, is a sort of new hero, coming from a foreign country, who is a representative of human being as such, and, we may suppose, speaks for all humanity.

Er and the Temptation to Tyranny

Before getting to what Er has to tell us, let us turn to the first question I have announced: how does the myth of Er relate to the rest of the *Republic*? And more generally why end this work with a myth? Perhaps the last sentence, indeed the conclusion Socrates draws from the myth he has just reported, may give us a clue:

> And so, Glaucon, the myth was saved and not lost, and it would save us, too, if we were persuaded by it (ἂν πειθώμεθα αὐτῷ), since we would safely cross the river Lethe, with our souls undefiled; and if we are persuaded by me, we will believe that the soul is immortal and able to endure every evil and also every good (δυνατὴν πάντα μὲν κακὰ ἀνέχεσθαι), and always hold to the upward path, practicing justice with wisdom every way we can, so that we will be friends to ourselves and

to the gods, both while we remain here on Earth and when we receive the rewards of justice, and go around like victors in the games collecting prizes, and so both in this life and on the thousand year journey we have described, we will fare well (εὖ πράττωμεν).

It is a detail which curiously has not attracted scholarly attention that I want to focus on: the addition that Socrates makes here on his own behalf that, "if we are persuaded by me, and accept that the soul is immortal and able to endure every evil and also every good, [. . .] we will fare well." It is this last phrase that interests me here, "able to endure every evil and also every good," or as another translator has it, perhaps more rightly, "capable of coping with all evils and all goods" (Griffith). If we read this in the context of the myth of Er, I suppose the goods and evils Plato refers to are the ways, fortunate or unfortunate, we will choose our next life when our turn comes. But perhaps, in a wider context, Socrates may want to remind Glaucon of the beginning of Book 9 where the description of the tyrant's life began. This is probably one of the most striking passages in Plato, not only for its modern, Freudian resonances, but more immediately for the admission that Plato gives us there: "What we want to pay attention to is this: there are appetites of a terrible, savage, and lawless kind in everyone—even in those of us who seem to be entirely moderate. This surely becomes clear in sleep" (572b). In other words, anyone can become a tyrant if he fails to keep his epithumetic appetites, and his thumetic desires too, in check. Tyranny, that is the tyranny of our own desires, as Plato says (τύραννος ὁ Ἔρως, 573b6-7), is a constant threat to human life. And it should come as no surprise then that tyranny is also what is most vividly underlined in the myth of Er.

There are two places where tyranny comes to the fore. First, when Er mentions the life of a certain Ardiaeus who "was a tyrant in a certain city of Pamphylia" (615c: οὗτος τῆς Παμφυλίας ἔν τινι πόλει τύραννος ἐγεγόνει), echoing the ethnic name of Er, and alluding, at least if one accepts the etymological wordplay of Pamphulia, to the fact that tyranny is indeed a desire every human being shares, even if secretly. And second, in the famous, central scene of our myth, when the souls in Hades have to choose their new life, tyranny comes first again, and strikingly enough, the person who opts for tyranny (and who is fated to eat his own children) is the only one who will remain nameless while the other *psuchai* who choose their lives are expressly named: Orpheus, Thamyras, Ajax,

Agamemnon, Atalanta, Epeos, Thersites, and, finally, Odysseus. Most certainly, ancient readers would have immediately thought of Thyestes who (unknowingly) ate his own children, but might also be reminded of that former passage of Book 9 where the same graphic feature was on display, when Plato says about our dreams that "there is no food one refuses to eat" (571d2–3: βρώματός τε ἀπέχεσθαι μηδενός), alluding to the figure of Thyestes too. In brief, the unnamed figure of Thyestes may really be nothing more than the personification of the desire for tyranny that we all share, even if unconsciously.

So what I would like to stress is the very fact that this is the message Socrates wants to repeat once again in the last sentence of the dialogue he has so far had with Glaucon: every single soul, or human being, is capable of the best and of the worst, and it is because of that permanent temptation of evil, of which tyranny is paradigmatic, that we need the myth to be saved. And the myth will save us, that is, Glaucon to whom the myth is told, but also Socrates's audience and Plato's wider readership, provided we repeat it for ourselves; we must repeat it again and again, so as to make sure we'll arrive in Hades with an unpolluted, just, soul. In a way, the myth of Er, with its insistence on tyranny, is a sort of last call before we are left in the next day, or the real world, after this long, all-night discussion.

So the myth of Er is in no way an unnecessary appendage to the whole work, as some, notably Julia Annas, have claimed[8]: it may not add anything substantially new to the arguments that have been developed earlier, but it warns us of the urgency that something must be done if we want to avoid tyranny, that is, being tyrannized by our own irrational desires. And the fact that Plato has chosen to make this final call through a myth, and not, say, through a cold, rational, argumentative address, comes as no surprise since he is not dealing with fully rational persons but indeed with people who love poetry and cannot renounce the irrational pleasures it provides them. To be sure, one should avoid making a clear-cut dichotomy between *logos* and *muthos*, as if philosophical arguments were addressed only to the *logistikon* while *muthos* would be addressed to the irrational parts of the soul alone. Indeed, even tragedy can persuade our reason: what Plato in fact fears most is that through repeated exposure to poetry, one's *logistikon* may end up being persuaded that, as the tragic worldview would have it, happiness is indeed impossible, and therefore virtues are worthless. But the purveyor of that worldview is not argument per se, but, roughly speaking, emotions, or rather the hearer's emotional involvement in poetry. So from this perspective, it may be the case that by ending with a myth, which is mainly presented as a spectacle the new hero Er is reporting, Plato wanted to reach the sort of deep persuasion and forceful motivation that only both reasoning and emotional involvement can provide.

As several interpreters have rightly stressed, Glaucon is repeatedly described, notably by his own brother Adeimantus, as a man with very strong epithumetic and thumetic desires; so he is certainly a man who must be very much tempted by tyranny.[9] A crucial step, therefore, is adding some sort of protreptic last call addressed to his irrational part too; and since poetry, as Plato repeatedly emphasized in his second critique of poetry in Book 10, is aiming at that irrational part, it is all the more natural for Plato to use such a poetic device. So, from this perspective, the myth of Er is the addition to the argumentation of Book 9 that is needed if one wants to have Glaucon heading back to Athens, fully convinced by what he has heard during that night, and strongly motivated to eventually keep the paradigm of Kallipolis seriously in mind, through which he would be able "set up the government of his own soul" (these are the last words of Book 9, 592b).

Cephalus in Hades

The myth of Er is also intimately related to the other parts of the *Republic*, especially its beginning. Remember, Socrates is invited to Cephalus's house by his son Polemarchus. Cephalus is an old, rich, and reputable man who shows great esteem toward Socrates: he even kindly takes him to task for not coming more often; for now that he is old and no longer feels the desires one usually does when young, roughly the strong appetitive desires for food, drink, and sex, he craves the pleasures of conversation, which will indeed lead to this long conversation we are going to attend between his guest Socrates, his son, and the rest of his guests. Socrates, too, seems eager to engage in conversation:

> SOCRATES: In fact, I enjoy engaging in discussion with the very old (χαίρω γε διαλεγόμενος τοῖς σφόδρα πρεσβύταις). I think we should learn from them—since they are like people who have traveled a road that we too will probably have to follow—what the road is like, whether rough and difficult or smooth and easy. And I would be particularly glad to find out from you what you think about it, since you have reached the

point in life the poets call 'old age's threshold' (ἐπὶ γήραος οὐδῷ). Is it a difficult time of life? Or what have *you* to report about it (πῶς σὺ αὐτὸ ἐξαγγέλλεις)? (328d–e)

The tone of this passage must sound familiar to readers of the so-called Socratic dialogues, where we see Socrates feigning ignorance and willing to get some *sophia* from an interlocutor he will soon be refuting. But perhaps, in contrast to those earlier dialogues, as soon as Socrates begins the questioning that will lead to his interlocutor's refutation, Cephalus, despite his apparent willingness to converse, leaves the room, goes to his sacrifice, and will never be heard from in the rest of the work. But if he disappears, what he introduces will be echoed in the myth of Er.

The most evident echo is of course the theme of death: Cephalus is an old man and now fears death and Hades—where he is going to be judged sooner rather than later. At the outset, when Socrates says he would be pleased to hear what Cephalus has to say since he likes listening to old people, this should most probably be understood as irony: for surely Socrates is hardly likely to be taught some traditional *sophia*, he who is always at pains to refute common ideas and prejudices. But this insistence on old age is a way of emphasizing the urgency of the question of justice: since we may well be asked to account for our lives in Hades, it is urgent that we know what justice amounts to. In the myth of Er, this will take on dramatic importance in the famous scene where the souls have to choose their next life. Also, Cephalus is a man who likes poetry and seems to reflect on important issues in life from poetry: poetry provides him with a certain knowledge—something that the second critique of poetry will duly refute. He even talks like a poet in saying to Socrates: you don't really come that often, where the verb *thamizein* is in fact a typically Homeric one.[10] Thus, getting back to Homer and offering a revised version of the Nekuia seems to be the expected answer to what Cephalus's conversation was all about.

Also, there is a rather curious word Socrates uses here: ἐξαγγέλλειν. Socrates wants Cephalus to report what he has experienced so far, being now at old age's threshold. So it cannot be by mere chance that Er too is repeatedly called an ἄγγελος (614d2; 619b2; and cf. 619e2). Commentators have sometimes suggested that this term may evoke a religious context, but it more likely evokes a theatrical context where messengers were often used in key passages to announce something important which will initiate a turning point in the play. To be sure, the way that message should be received is rather different from one case to another:

while Cephalus's message has been duly refuted by Socrates in front of Polemarchus, who is Cephalus's son and heir to his message, the myth of Er, as Socrates will urge Glaucon, is to be saved—in order to save us. In brief, the myth of Er is meant to replace the message we received from old Cephalus—and of course the usage of poetry in the myth of Er, which is a replacement for Homer's Nekuia, is also part of that. If it is a replacement for Cephalus's message, one must also suppose that the message is meant to be addressed to the same sort of people we find in Cephalus' house, i.e., the inhabitants of "our beautiful cities" where people love poetry.

In Book 3 Plato insists that the depiction of Hades is not to be presented to the future guardians of Kallipolis: they must be prevented from hearing such dreadful myths, which would create unnecessary fears and not help in shaping the virtue of courage (386a–387b). But here we are, let me underscore this again—in the real world, in the house of Cephalus where people have been brought under the sway of poetry—it is to them that the myth is addressed. Jonathan Lear has proposed reading the myth or Er as a cure for those who have been brought up that way, that is, as a cure for their fears.[11] I want to propose another picture along the same lines: Plato wants to use our fears of the afterlife's judgment as a sort of emotional tool toward our better understanding of, and our total commitment to, the main idea conveyed by Er's message: that only practicing philosophy will help you be happy.

In contradistinction to the way the myth of retribution in Hades is used in the *Gorgias*, here that traditional picture is used as a sort of preliminary step toward something more important. Indeed, the description of the terrible fate unjust people suffer in Hades, with the example of Ardiaeus, only occupies the very beginning of Er's report. As the reader will soon discover, the main scene is obviously the famous one in which people are choosing their next life. In brief, Plato seems to use the power of the fear these men have, notably because of their love of poetry depicting Hades that way, in order to make them react emotionally to the spectacle of the souls choosing the life that awaits them.

Tragedy and Responsibility

Before trying to assess what sort of emotional reaction Glaucon, and Socrates's audience, is supposed to get involved in, we should first turn to the second issue I announced, that is the meaning and aim of the myth, or rather of its central scene. As I have said, one central feature of this myth is its critical rewriting of poetry. And indeed, there is one crucial point at stake in this rewriting, which is best seen in the famous announcement made by the prophet of Lachesis that begins the central scene of the choices of life:

> The word of Lachesis, maiden daughter of Necessity: Ephemeral souls (Ψυχαὶ ἐφήμεροι—the beginning of another death-bringing cycle for mortal kind! Your daimon will not be assigned to you by lot: you will choose it! (οὐχ ὑμᾶς δαίμων λήξεται, ἀλλ' ὑμεῖς δαίμονα αἱρήσεσθε) The one who has the first lot will be the first to choose a life to which he will be bound by necessity. Virtue has no master: as he honors or dishonors it, so shall each of you have more or less of it. The chooser's responsibility—the god is not responsible (αἰτία ἑλομένου· θεὸς ἀναίτιος). (617d–e)

Leaving aside the problem of what Plato actually means by agency and responsibility here,[12] I would like to point to the most striking phrase of this sentence, literally translated: 'It is not you that the *daimōn* will choose, but you will choose the *daimōn*.' This sounds like a firm and strong rejection of a more traditional view. But what view exactly?

I suggest that the worldview Plato wants to oppose here, and which he has opposed all along in the *Republic*, is the tragic worldview that typically takes human happiness to be subject to external fate. Perhaps one of the most brilliant and celebrated texts expressing such a view comes from Pindar's eighth *Pythian* which exposes the core of the tragic worldview we find from Homer to the great tragedians:

> But the delight of mortals grows in a short time, and then it falls to the ground, shaken by an adverse thought. Creatures of a day (*epameroi*). What is someone? What is no one? Man is the dream of a shadow. But when the brilliance given by Zeus comes, a shining light is on man, and a gentle lifetime. (*Pyth.* 8.92–98)

Here is the typical way of using the Homeric word, *ephēmeros* (or *epameros* in Pindar's Dorian Greek): human beings are just mortal beings who not only do not last long, but also get their happiness, or only some portion of sweet time, from the gods' willingness. As 'Creatures of a day,' human beings are essentially frail and their happiness essentially depends on the gods. As Pindar has said, just a few lines earlier:

> For if anyone has noble achievements without long toil, to many he seems to be a skillful man among the foolish, arming his life with the resources of right counsel. But these things do not depend on men. It is a god (*daimōn*) who grants them; raising up one man and throwing down another. (73–76)

One cannot but be struck by close similarities between our two texts. According to Pindar, even the "noble achievements," that is virtues or virtuous actions in Plato's vocabulary, are not up to us, human beings; it is a *daimōn*, be that the general name for fate or a god, who grants all this, that is, allows us to live a happy, or morally good, life or not. It is difficult not to see Lachesis's word as a sort of anti-Pindaric, or more generally anti-tragic rallying cry: no, says Plato, contrary to what you are used to hearing in your previous life from the tragic poets of the Greek city you lived in, you 'Ephemeral souls' are in charge of choosing your *daimōn* and virtue is up to you, not up to an external and imposed *daimōn*. Thus, 'the responsibility is of the chooser; god is not responsible' is Plato's reply to Pindar, and more generally, traditional poetry.

This tragic, near to fatalist picture is also what we already find in the Nekuia. The whole episode takes place because of Circe, who told Odysseus to go down into Hades (or in fact to evoke the dead through some sort of magical ritual) find old Tiresias who is blind, but still has his intellect (*nous*) intact, in order to know his future. When the *psuchē* of Tiresias finally comes up to claim his part of the sacrificial blood, he tells Odysseus the truth (96: νημερτέα εἴπω; 137: τὰ δέ τοι νημερτές εἴρω) about his future, that he will indeed end up safely in Ithaca and there spend a happy life. To which Odysseus replies in full acceptance: "Tiresias, this is all the destiny the gods themselves have spun" (139: Τειρεσίη, τὰ μὲν ἄρ που ἐπέκλωσαν θεοὶ αὐτοί). In brief, we have here the worldview Odysseus fully accepts, of one's destiny as almost completely decided in advance by the gods, or the Moira, and from which not even a Homeric hero could dream of trying to escape. This is the worldview Plato vigorously opposes through the mouth of Lachesis who here works as a sort of ironic goddess of destiny who, instead of allotting each person her fate, gives each of them the burden of responsibility for her choice.

Now if Plato proposes a very different worldview from the one we find in that passage of the Nekuia, he nonetheless shows no hesitation in drawing on how Homer presents his story. In the *Odyssey*, the message Odysseus gets from Tiresias is that he will return home safely and live a happy life back home, and in order to do so he should beware of Poseidon's nasty attempts to prevent his returning home safely. In the myth of Er, the message is for Glaucon (and the rest of the audience), obviously not for Er himself, but in a situation is very similar to Odysseus's: the problem Glaucon faces is also, in a way, finding good counsel in order to eventually reach happiness in avoiding bad choices. And indeed, as several interpreters have stressed,[13] the paradoxical phrase, *ephēmerai psuchai* (it is paradoxical because souls are supposed to be immortal) must refer to living people, not dead (the poetic word *ephēmeros* referring to human beings as they are alive for a short period of time). Thus, the word of Lachesis is not so much addressed to dead people in Hades as to living people who face hard choices here and now, like Glaucon and the rest of us. But what sort of choices?

It is very tempting to see in this choice of life what an Aristotelian reader would call a way of life, such as the political or the philosophical life. But I don't think that can be right. As Socrates himself tells Glaucon just before narrating this scene, philosophy, or philosophical life, in fact constitutes the very condition necessary for choosing well when forced to choose one's next life (668c–d).[14] So, if you follow the logic of this argument, that must mean that the life to be chosen is really nothing but the metaphor (or in fact the metonymy) for any and every choice when acting in such-and-such a way—the tyrannical life being the metonymy for each and every possible tyrannical act. And indeed, as we have seen, the message Socrates wants Glaucon to get from all of this is that only philosophy can help him cope with all the irrational desires urging him on to make fatal choices. Thus, since philosophy is the very condition for us choosing a new life well, that is, the right decisions in our acting, the hortatory message bears on this rather than on our choosing well, or acting itself.[15]

This hortatory message is evidently not only a purely intellectual one: for a person like Glaucon, as we said, understanding that philosophy is the only condition for acting rightly, and therefore being happy, is not sufficient. That understanding must be accompanied, or perhaps enhanced, by some emotional involvement on his part. But what sort of involvement?

As I have said, it is remarkable that Plato has Er repeatedly use words that tend to describe what he is reporting as a spectacle: "it was a sight worth seeing how the various souls chose their lives, since seeing it caused pity ridicule, and surprise" (Ταύτην γὰρ δὴ ἔφη τὴν θέαν ἀξίαν εἶναι ἰδεῖν, ὡς ἕκασται αἱ ψυχαὶ ᾑροῦντο τοὺς βίους· ἐλεινήν τε γὰρ ἰδεῖν εἶναι καὶ γελοίαν καὶ θαυμασίαν, 619e6–620a2; trans. Reeve). At first sight, this scene seems to be typically tragic, especially with the case of Thyestes who realizes what the consequences of his choice will be only too late. But in Plato's eyes, the core of the scene, and where its aim resides, is this: once he has seen all the terrible acts he will be determined to do, that are actually the consequences of his acts, that man (who in fact was lucky enough to be the first chooser) accuses the gods and destiny of being *aitios*, i.e., of having caused, or of being responsible for all that, while he himself, and no one else, chose those acts. This is not pitiable anymore (as Aristotle will explicitly state, we don't pity those who merit their fate),[16] but barely ridiculous: that soul makes a fool of himself in denying being *aitios* for the consequences of his choice. And note that the way he is described, as "beating his breast and bemoaning his choice" (619c2–3), typically corresponds to lamenting as it usually takes place in mourning and in tragedies. Except that here, this is all ridiculous. In brief, Plato rewrites a typically tragic ending of a play as if it were a comedy.

The second part of the scene is in the same spirit, which corresponds to the one Odysseus describes when he meets the heroes of the *Iliad*, after Tiresias has withdrawn to Hades again. In Homer, it is striking that all these heroes—Agamemnon, Ajax, and Achilles—not only are definitely unhappy about their fate down there, but also complain about their past life on earth, all weeping and lamenting quite heavily. (Homer emphasizes this by repeating words related to pity and tears; see, e.g., 11.301, 388, 391, 466.) This is, in sum, a tragic vision that must have produced strong emotions of pity in the audience at Alcinous's court—typically, a scene that anticipates a tragic show (and indeed, Plato took Homer to be "the guide of tragedy," 598d8). In the myth of Er, we also meet those heroes who are all unhappy about their previous lives; and it is because of such a disappointment of what they have lived previously that they choose the life of an animal: Ajax, the life of a lion, Agamemnon, the life of an eagle, Thersites, that of an ape. And this is, as Plato just said, a scene that is "ridiculous and surprising": instead of wanting to live the extraordinary life of the great heroes they have been, they prefer being reborn as mindless animals. And for those who did not choose the life of an animal, their fate is ridiculous as well: while Atalanta decides for the life of a male athlete, Epeos, the hero who built the horse of Troy, chose the life of an industrious woman—two rather awkward choices in the eyes of this male, aristocratic audience in Cephalus's house, which can be imagined laughing with derision and contempt at those characters who make such ridiculous choices. In a way then, it is not exaggerated to say that Plato has rewritten a comedic version of the Nekuia.

At the same time, this scene is also meant to be seen by Glaucon as a sort of mirror of his own life. Indeed, when Socrates explains that the man who choose the life of a tyrant "was one of those who had come down from heaven, having lived his previous life in an orderly constitution, sharing in virtue through habit but without philosophy" (619c6–8), one may suppose that Glaucon and Plato's audience, all decent citizens, could hardly not help thinking of themselves. And so if confronted with the same sort of choice, even they might make such bad, tyrannical choices. Thus, laughing at such ridiculous people choosing so badly should help them realize how they may be in urgent need of philosophy if they want to be happy. And the same goes for the second part of the scene. Admittedly, this scene of the *Iliad* heroes choosing the life of an animal can hardly be meant to mirror of their own lives. But as is clear from Book 3 where Achilles is meant to work as a role model for young people (as he indeed was, in a way, in Athens), these characters are the heroes of the poetical education they have received. (To be sure, Thersites is not a role model to be emulated; but being a sort of ancestor of comedic poetry, people such as Glaucon who may "very much enjoy" such poetry, must have somehow admired him).[17] Thus, laughing at their choice in Hades, instead of admiring them as they used to, should be a vigorous way of making them see why they should not hesitate in opting for philosophy.

Conclusion

As a way of concluding my reading I would like to add a few remarks on the description of the last one to choose his next life, Odysseus himself being here one of the dead in Hades instead of the Homeric messenger:

Now it chanced that Odysseus's soul drew the last lot of all, and came to make its choice. Remembering its former sufferings, it rejected love of honor (φιλοτιμία), and went around for a long time looking for the life of a private individual who took no part in politics (βίον ἀνδρὸς ἰδιώτου ἀπράγμονος), and with difficulty it found one lying off somewhere neglected by the others. When it saw it, it said that it would have done the same even if it had drawn the first-place lot, and chose it gladly (ἀσμένην ἑλέσθαι). (620c–d)

There seem to be several reasons why one may be tempted, as indeed many interpreters have been, to see this last case with a very favorable eye. As M. McPherran writes, "Odysseus the Cunning, it seems, has been transformed into a virtuous and philosophically reflective individual by means of the purification that suffering and punishment provide."[18] Indeed, Odysseus has now understood, so it seems, that honor is not the good he should pursue in order to be happy, at least if those honors might turn out to be a source of trouble as Socrates warned at the end of Book 9 (592a). And note also Plato's emphasis on Odysseus's being allotted the last place in the queue, which is meant to remind his reader of the priest's words of encouragement: "Even for the one who comes last, if he chooses wisely and lives earnestly, there is a satisfactory life available, not a bad one available. Let not the first to choose be careless nor the last discouraged" (619b3–6). Odysseus is indeed a courageous hero who can even cope with his share of hard luck. So it is hard to escape the conclusion that, indeed, we have an Odysseus finally realizing that going after honors is not worth it, and who firmly decides to become a more reasonable, or philosophical hero.

But one may wonder if this picture is to be taken completely seriously. Despite his final realization, Odysseus can hardly be Glaucon's new role model as it were. First of all, it seems that his decision is rather a sort of ersatz choice: it is because his trip was so tough that he decided to retreat from any sort of public business; his retreat appears to be what is left when one tires of honors. Strikingly enough, we find here a last echo of the figure of Cephalus when Odysseus's *psuchē* is said to be "glad (ἀσμένη)" to have found and chosen her new life: this is also the adjective Plato used when he had Cephalus report his friend Sophocles's answering the question of whether he was still able to have sex: "I am very glad (ἀσμενέστατα) to have escaped from all that, like a slave who has escaped from a deranged and savage master" (329c3–4). Thus, while Cephalus has become temperate by defect since he is now too old to have sex, Odysseus has become "philosophically reflective" (as McPherran says) because he is simply exhausted from looking for honor—not a very promising picture of Odysseus. And finally, let's remember that this whole scene of the choices, indeed "how each of those souls choose their lives," is described by Plato as "ridiculous," and I don't see why Odysseus should be any exception. All of these supposedly great heroes, Agamemnon, Ajax, and Odysseus, make their choices in "automatic reaction" (as McPherran rightly says)[19] to what they have lived previously, which is certainly not how Plato wants us to turn to philosophy. So perhaps mentioning Odysseus as an inhabitant of Hades, from where Er reports that his message is, after all, nothing more than the final reminder that Homer is definitely a poor guide for people if they want to be happy. And that, Plato had to tell them in a sort of poetic, Homeric way.

Notes

1. This chapter is the descendant of a keynote I gave at the conference "Myth, Ritual and Initiation in Plato's *Republic*" organized by Hallvard Fossheim at the University of Båergen, Norway, in June 2016; I also read a first version of it at a conference on "Mythes et philosophie ancienne' organized at the Sorbonne, Paris, by Fabienne Baghdassarian and Jean-Baptiste Gourinat, in June 2014. I am grateful to them and their respective audiences, for their questions that have forced me to reconsider, or qualify, some of my contentions.

2. See esp. Morgan 2000, 204–10; Halliwell 2007.

3. Here μέν is equivalent to μήν.

4. Halliwell 1988, *ad loc*. Actually, Proclus already had a similar interpretation, if for other reasons (2.111.23–112.16; see esp. 112, 13–4: ταύτην [Plato's own Nekuia] δὲ ὄντως ἀνδρικοῦ φησιν ἀνδρὸς εἶναι. David Reeve has suggested that a more sophisticated pun might be involved between the two words: "*Alkinou* might be taken as a compound of *alkê* + *nous* and *alkimou* as a compound of *alkê* + *Mousa*. Socrates would then be saying something like: it isn't a tale that shows strength of understanding that I'm going to tell but one that shows the strength of the Muse of storytelling" (Reeve 2004, 319n25). However interesting, this suggestion seems rather overstretched as nothing alludes to the word Μοῦσα in the context.

5. I have argued for that suggestion in Destrée (forthcoming).

6. βουλοίμην κ' ἐπάρουρος ἐὼν θητευέμεν ἄλλῳ / ἀνδρὶ παρ' ἀκλήρῳ, ᾧ μὴ βίοτος πολὺς εἴη / ἢ πᾶσιν νεκύεσσι καταφθιμένοισιν ἀνάσσειν (Od. 11.489-91, cited at 386c).

7. For such a pun, see Platt 1911, 14. Some interpreters have doubted this, but we do find a similar pun on the name *Kreōphulos* earlier, at *Rep.* 600b6-8 (of the race of meat). On the other hand, the adjective πάμφυλος can have such an etymological meaning, 'of mingled tribes or races,' which one finds in one passage of the *Politicus* (291a7).

8. Annas 1982. For a detailed critique of Annas's view, see Johnson 1999.

9. On the figure of Glaucon, see in particular Gallagher 2004, 295-302; and O'Connor 2007, 64-68; see also Blondell 2002, 203-14, for a different perspective.

10. It has also been argued that Cephalus may remind Plato's readers of the figure of Nestor, the oldest of the Achaeans: note that Cephalus's wealth comes from his fabricating shields, while Nestor is said to have a golden shield (e.g., *Il.* 8.192-93). Nestor is the great counsellor of the Iliad's warriors—perhaps a sort of irony on Plato's part as Cephalus is in his eyes a rather poor counsellor as regards justice.

11. Lear 2006.

12. For which I take the liberty to refer to Destrée 2014.

13. See esp. Halliwell 2007, 461-62, who also notes that Er uses alternatively the feminine term *psuchē* and masculine grammatical forms. See also Ferrari 2009 and Gonzales 2012; both emphasize that the myth is all about the living and their choice of life, not about any sort of future life in the literal sense of the term.

14. Also, and consequently, no philosophical life is on display (Ferrari 2009, 129, also notices this but curiously adds that "the philosophical life is certainly meant to be one of the available choices").

15. On the hortatory, or protreptic, aspect of the myth of Er, see in particular Gonzalez 2012, and Segal 1978, 331; on that aspect in the *Republic* more generally, see Gallagher 2004, and Yunis 2007.

16. See *Poetics* 13, 1453a1-4; *Rhetoric* 2.8, 1385b13-14.

17. It is noteworthy that in the only passage on laughter in the critique of poetry in Book 10, Socrates is addressing directly to Glaucon: "If there are jokes you would be ashamed to tell yourself but that you very much enjoy when you hear them in a comedy, or even in private, and that you don't hate as something bad, aren't you doing the same as with the things you pity? For the element in you that wanted to tell the jokes, but which you held back by means of reason, because you were afraid of being reputed a buffoon, you now release, and by making it strong in that way, you are often led unawares into becoming a comedian in your own life" (606c)—in which Glaucon fully acquiesces (606c).

18. McPherran 2010, 141. For a positive assessment of the figure of Odysseus in the myth of Er, and in the *Republic* more generally, see Bouvier 2001; but see Reeve 2013, 45–47, for a more qualified view.

19. McPherran 2010, 136.

11

Priam's Despair and Courage
An Aristotelian Reading of Fear, Hope, and Suffering in Homer's *Iliad*

MARJOLEIN OELE

Among the groundworks of Western civilization, Homer's *Iliad* occupies an extraordinary space. While offering insights in a long bygone mythical world dominated by illustrious gods and powerful warriors centered around honor (τιμή), the epic also acutely affects us with its phenomenal description of the most profound and intimate affections (πάθη) that seem to drive humans of any place and era. Indeed, ranging from wrath to grief, fear, love, and pity, the *Iliad* is, in its reflections upon our human—all too human—affections, all but far removed from the themes of many of our most popular current novels or movies, although its brilliant style and intellectual imagination make it stand out far above many of those current sources. Yet, what makes Homer's analysis so effective is not only its mastery in describing the range and depth of human emotions, but more specifically its consideration to view affections as underpinning both virtue and vice, especially where suffering is at its pinnacle.[1] This very possibility to envision our affections as underlying vice or virtue is what fascinates us and captures our moral imagination. For instance, how can anger turn into an all-consuming, deadly wrath, and how and why can pity be wrongly denied but also be made productive and felt even for one's staunchest enemy?

One of the central characters in the *Iliad* who demonstrates that even, or precisely, amidst incredible suffering, affections can be shaped into virtue, is King Priam.[2] Although Homer mentions Priam in multiple instances in the *Iliad*, it is not until Books 22 and 24 that we can clearly witness Priam's ability to transform his affections into unparalleled paradigms of beauty and nobility among intense suffering. In Book 22, Priam's growing despair is visible in his expressions of hope and fear as he pleads with his son Hector to withdraw from facing Achilles by himself. In Book 24, Priam courageously travels to the camp of Achilles, his enemy opponent, and asks for his son's body. In those two books in particular, Priam's expression of the affections of hope and fear offer fruitful ways to consider possible reactions to despair, offering insight into how the fear and hope evoked by desperate situations can find fruitful symbiosis in the expression of courage.

Aristotle's ideas on affectivity (πάθος) can further clarify the relationship between affections and virtue. In particular, Aristotle discusses how (oftentimes painful) affections can serve as the very underpinnings of virtuous behavior, and that affections can be the very *embodiment* of our dispositions.[3] In other words, Aristotle shows that how we are *affected* is the other side of how we *act* and an intrinsic part of who we *are*. In this view, affections are not just incidental happenings, but an inherent component of a (potentially) virtuous life. While tragic circumstances have to be acknowledged and cannot be undone (*NE* I.9, 1100a4–9), even extremely painful affections, those related to our own suffering or that of others, can be "worked up" to beautiful demonstrations of virtue.

Even more applicable to the specifics of Priam's ordeals in Books 22 and 24, Aristotle offers in the *Nicomachean Ethics* and in the *Rhetoric* an enriching account of the seemingly paradoxical relationship between fear (φόβος) and hope (ἔλπις) evoked by despair. His remarks indicate that we need to distinguish between *empty*, blind hope and *productive* hope. While hope may blind us to suffering and dispel fear of suffering, hope can have a "positive" role in dispelling resignation, invoking fear and allowing for fruitful deliberation and courageous handling of the situation. It is my thesis that Priam's plea with his son Hector in Book 22 shows some of Aristotle's insights on the powerful interaction between despair, fear, and hope; however, it is not until Book 24 that we can truly see the full realization of their fruitful interaction. When seemingly all hope is lost and despair seems to be all that can be left, Priam embraces human finitude—specifically his own and his son's finitude—and invests hope in what *transcends* this finitude: the meaning of human life as embodied by human burial rites. It is this noble hope that underlies his fear and transforms it into the courage he manifests in visiting Achilles in the enemy camp.

This analysis will begin with a brief description of Priam's situation in Book 22, which functions as the springboard for providing an account of fear, hope, and suffering from Aristotle's perspective, and further complemented by insights from Hesiod and Aeschylus on the nature of hope. Subsequently, Aristotle's understanding will be applied to Priam's situation in Books 22 and 24, with Book 24 offering the most suitable context for grasping how, ideally, even amidst extreme suffering, affections such as fear and hope may give rise to the virtue of courage.

Aristotle, Hesiod, and Aeschylus on Fear, Hope, and Suffering

As we find him in Book 22, Priam is the once-powerful and prosperous king whose city has been under siege for numerous years. He has lost most of his children and is on the verge of losing his most beloved son Hector, to the cruel rage of Achilles. Priam is the first to see illustrious and swift-footed Achilles approach his son Hector (22.25), who stands alone and unprotected outside the city walls. Homer describes Priam's initial reaction in the following way:

> The old man groaned aloud and with both hands high
>   uplifted
> Beat his head, and groaned again, and spoke supplicating
> His beloved son. . . . (*Il.* 22.32–35)[4]

Priam's groaning and beating express the great distress that Priam must feel in the face of anticipating the demise of his own son Hector. The anguish he senses can be further explained by Aristotle's definition of fear in the *Rhetoric*, which states:

> Let fear be understood as a certain pain and agitation (λύπη τις ἢ ταραχή) from the imagining of an impending evil of a destructive or painful sort. (*Rhet.* II.5, 1382a23–30)[5]

Fear, perhaps the most universal emotion according to Aristotle,[6] involves the anticipation of that which will destroy or harm us greatly,[7] and only arises when that danger is imminent and not far away: otherwise we do not give particular thought to that which is fearful. Certainly, this definition applies to Priam since the destruction that he anticipates is great, and the danger is indeed very near with Achilles's appearance. Crucially applicable to the case of Priam, Aristotle includes in his discussion of fear that people must have left some sense of "hope (τινὰ ἐλπίδα) of being saved from the thing causing their agony" (Rhet. II.5, 1383a8) to be capable of feeling fear. People who have lost hope, those "who regard themselves as having already suffered every kind of terrifying affliction (τὰ δεινὰ), when all feeling toward the future has grown cold" (Rhet. II.5, 1383a4–6), are incapable of feeling fear.

Thus, according to Aristotle, fear and hope form by necessity a pair. Fear is felt for great harms, but can only be felt when somehow we are also trusting in delivery from that harm. We really need to feel safe somehow to be able to feel fear and anticipate and imagine loss. Thus, paradoxically, we can only feel the worst fear if we can also imagine being saved from it. But how exactly would this work? Is hope on an equal par with fear—as its complementary feeling? Is hope perhaps the underlying condition that makes fear possible? If we consider the structure of Aristotle's text, then the latter seems to be the case: Aristotle's discussion of hope is part of his account of the "dispositions" (ἕξεις) that make us feel a particular affection (cf. Rhet. II.1, 1378a25–26) and, in particular, the dispositions that make us feel fear (Rhet. II.5, 1382b28–1383a13). This would mean that hope is the pre-condition for fear. If we imagine fear as a whole, then hope is perhaps part of the "double bottom" that makes up the structure of this emotion: it is the "secret compartment" of feeling and anticipating security that allows us to truly feel fear for great suffering. As Gravlee puts it: "hope underlies fear, in a certain sense, for without any hope, resignation replaces the anxiety of fear."[8]

Moreover, not only does Aristotle make it clear that hope provides the underpinning for feeling true fear, but hope and fear also function as complements toward mutual productivity. In this vein, Aristotle writes that for fear to be felt:

> Some hope (τινὰ ἐλπίδα) of being saved (σωτερία) from the thing causing their agony has to be left; a sign of this is that fear makes people deliberate (βουλευτικοὺς), and yet

no one deliberates about things that are hopeless." (*Rhet.* II.5, 1383a7–8)[9]

This thought conveys that hope might not only be an underlying condition for fear, but also functions as an affection that works in tandem with fear—allowing fear to become productive in seeking deliberation. Accordingly, hope is both a precondition of fear and a paradoxically antonymic, yet essentially collaborative, co-affection of fear as hope and fear together estimate and seek to find ways out of possible future suffering.[10]

Notably, hope functions here in a very different role than the affection that seems closely related to it: confidence (θάρρος). While Aristotle argues that hope *enables* fear to emerge, confidence does not fulfill such a foundational role. Instead, confidence seems to function on the same level as the affection of fear, as Aristotle repeatedly stresses the fact that fear operates on a spectrum with confidence (e.g., *NE* III.6, 1115a7). Along these lines we could argue that hope can inspire both affections of fear and confidence as they emerge on the same affective level. And, in fact, evidence for this can be found in *Rhetoric* II.12, where Aristotle argues that hope may "create confidence" (1389a26–28), which parallels claims that hope might underlie fear (*Rhet.* II.5, 1383a8).[11]

Returning to the issue of the relationship between hope and fear, the above passages show Aristotle's commitment to a positive interpretation of hope, emphasizing how hope underlies fear and leads to the necessary deliberations. Since deliberation for Aristotle is pivotal to virtuous action and passion in providing a guide for our desire (*NE* III.3, 1113a9–14), this means that hope does not only ground fear as such, but possibly also its particular expression as courage (ἀνδρεία), with courage defined as the mean between fear (φόβος) and confidence (θάρρος) (*NE* III.6, 1115a7).

However, this positive appreciation of hope—underlying fear, stimulating deliberation, and possibly underlying courage—is not always present in Aristotle's texts. In fact, in some instances Aristotle contrasts people of courage with sheer optimists (οἱ εὐέλπιδες). In this vein, *NE* III.6 argues that the optimism and fearlessness exhibited by sailors at sea should not be confused with courage, as it is solely based on experience (*NE* III.6, 1115a33–1115b7). Similarly, *NE* III.8 opposes courage to optimism, but for a slightly different reason:

> Nor are optimists (οἱ εὐέλπιδες) courageous, for they gain their confidence in danger from having won many victories

over many people. They resemble courageous men in that both are confident (θαρραλέοι): the confidence of courageous men, however, is inspired by the motives discussed above, while the confidence of optimists is based upon their belief that they are the strongest and will suffer (παθεῖν) no harm. (NE III.8, 1117a10–14)

Experiences gained on the battlefield lead soldiers to express a certain confidence that resembles courage. However, their confidence should not be confused with courage, since, due to the absence of enduring fear, there is not any question of the invocation of courage. And perhaps, as Gravlee remarks, the confidence established here is based less on experience and more on belief and "induction from good fortune," which might distinguish this form of optimism from the preceding one.[12]

These passages on optimism indicate that hopefulness, fear, and courage are not linked *per se*: in fact, sheer hopefulness based on experience or belief does not invoke fear, and thereby stands in shrill contrast to courage, as does hopefulness based on "ignorance of danger" (NE III.8, 1117a23). This more tempered and unproductive view of hope, disconnected from fear and courage, echoes, to some degree, the mixed views of hope found in the earlier Greek literary tradition. For instance, Hesiod's influential account of hope in his *Works and Days* distinguishes empty hope from wholesome hope:

> A man out of work, a man with empty hopes (κενεὴν ἐπί ἐλπίδα μίμνων)
> And no livelihood, has a mind that runs to mischief (κακά).
> It's no good (οὐκ ἀγαθη) kind of hope [that] comes to a man who's broke
> Sitting in the blacksmith's with no sure living. (Hesiod, *Works and Days* 498–501)[13]

Although hope may be good and wholesome, hope can be ungrounded and may lead to deception and harm, providing empty confidence where it is unwarranted. Hesiod warns against the vacuous dreams that may hold us back from truly preparing for and achieving things necessary. This warning against the emptiness of hope runs parallel with Aristotle's idea that hope may very well be based on empty belief or ignorance, and should thus be sharply distinguished from the hope that makes fear productive and that seeks to call up courage and provide true insight into practical situations.

Furthermore, Hesiod's recounting of the myth of Pandora in his *Works and Days* includes a puzzling account of hope, offering us seemingly contradictory, and certainly mixed, views on both the positive and negative aspects of hope. Since hope is contained in Pandora's box or jar together with evils such as illnesses and pains (*WD* 91–100), it seems at first sight that hope is unambiguously defined as an evil as well.[14] However, an alternative interpretation of hope can be distilled from this passage once it is realized that hope stands out from all the miseries distributed to humans since it remains, as the only one, in the jar while the rest escape from it (*WD* 96–99). Allowing hope to remain in the jar signals a more positive view, since it may mean that hope is not an evil as such, but something that often *accompanies* human suffering and evil. Also, taking into consideration that the Greek term for hope (ἐλπις) might simply mean anticipation, keeping hope or anticipation in the jar might be interpreted as positive, since it prevents humans from not only suffering evils, but also anticipating them constantly.[15]

Another provocative, mixed view of hope is offered in Aeschylus's *Prometheus Bound*. The story recounts how Prometheus has given human beings not only the gifts of fire and transformative crafts, but also something else: hope. In response to the Chorus-leader, Prometheus reveals the following: "I stopped men from foreseeing their fated end (προδέρκεσθαι μόρον) . . . I placed in man blind hopes (τυφλὰς ἐλπιδας)" (*Prom.* 248–50). Prometheus's special gift consists of depriving humans of the capacity of foreseeing their own destruction and finitude and giving them hope. The hope given by Prometheus is blind in that it gives humans the illusion of being able to defeat death. Simultaneously, there is a positive aspect to the blindness of this hope: hope is the capacity to creatively think and imagine freely, outside of one's own material and bodily limitations.[16] In this vein, hope to a certain degree aligns with the transformative and creative skills that are also part of Prometheus's gifts to humanity.

If, after this detour to Hesiod and Aeschylus, we now return to Aristotle's account of hope, we find overlap in many different directions. Just as Hesiod and Aeschylus warn against the emptiness and blindness of hope that may hold us back in truly preparing constructively for the future and our finitude, Aristotle warns against a hope that is divorced from fear and based solely on experience, empty beliefs, or expectations of good fortune. Being divorced from authentic fear, such hope cannot inform courage and does not allow for proper deliberation and acquiring true insight into situations. Moreover, Hesiod's account of Pandora's jar offers us a complicated view of hope, which possibly includes the idea that hope is evil, but also the view that hope is not evil as such but accompanies and offers solace to suffering. It may be argued that Aristotle's account elaborates on aspects of Hesiod's myth, insofar as Aristotle appears to show the productivity of hope in allowing us to contemplate solutions out of possible suffering. Like Hesiod's myth of Pandora, for Aristotle hope and suffering go together, but instead of being a part of suffering, hope for Aristotle is the condition of the possibility of fearing suffering *and* the very way *out* of suffering. It is also at this point that Aristotle's narrative of fear intersects with Aeschylus's view, as both Aristotle and Aeschylus stress hope's ability to think and imagine outside of our limited, finite existence to imagine another, better existence.

Understanding Priam's Fear and Hope: The Petition of Hector in Book 22

After this overview of the complex intersection of fear, hope, and suffering in Aristotle, which finds conceptual underpinnings in Hesiod and Aeschylus, we are better equipped to understand Priam's desperate, yet hopeful, predicament in Book 22 of the *Iliad*. Whereas both his actions—groaning, beating his head, and pleading with his son—and his words manifest great desperation and fear, Priam also expresses immense hope. The first instance of such hope is found in the early part of his speech to Hector, when Priam mentions that he still has hope that two of his sons (Lykaon and Polydoros) are alive (22.46–51). However, as readers we already know that Achilles has brutishly killed the defenseless Lykaon (21.34–135), allowing us to pity Priam in that one of his sources of hope is already undermined.

The second and more complex instance of hope in Book 22 consists in Priam seeking to convince Hector that he needs to withdraw and not fight Achilles alone. In particular, his way of convincing Hector is to ask him to withdraw inside the city walls so as to protect the Trojans inside, save his own life, and consider and lighten the fate of his father, Priam:

> Come then inside the wall, my child, so that you can rescue
> the Trojans and the women of Troy, neither win the high glory
> for Peleus' son, and yourself be robbed of your very life.
>   Oh, take
> pity on me, the unfortunate still alive, still sentient (φρονέοντ')
> but ill-starred, whom the father, Kronos' son, on the threshold
>   of old age
> will blast with hard fate (δύσμορον) . . . (*Il.* 22.56–61)

In his speech, Priam utters hope for Hector's return and his protection of his fellow citizens. Yet, despite the appeal for hope, fear of suffering seems most of all prevalent, as Priam's speech becomes gradually more disturbing and even macabre. First of all, he reminds Hector of Priam's harsh fate—describing himself as someone who is only living in the mere sense of "possessing one's senses" (φρονέοντ'), but who is hardly alive in any other way, being broken "at the threshold of old age" with such a horrible destiny. Having specified the fate that has befallen himself and his close family members, Priam continues to describe his own fate in the following details:

> And myself last of all, my dogs in front of my doorway,
> will rip me raw, after some man with stroke of the sharp bronze
> spear, or with spearcast, has torn the life out of my body;
> those dogs I raised in my halls to be at my table, to guard my
> gates, who will lap my blood in the savagery of their anger
> and then lie down in my courts. For a young man all is decorous
> when he is cut down in battle and torn with the sharp
>   bronze, and lies there
> dead, and though dead still all that shows about him is
>   beautiful (καλά);
> but when an old man is dead and down, and the dogs mutilate
> the grey head and the grey beard and the parts that are secret,
> this, for all sad mortality, is the sight most pitiful. (*Il.* 22.67–76)

Priam seeks to make Hector fully aware of all the suffering that he as king and father has already gone through and might still have to undergo. In his speech, the great fear and concern that Priam has for his son are translated mostly in reminders concerning his own suffering. In wording his fear (and hope) in this way, we see Priam dwelling on his fate. He contrasts his dishonorable death with the beautiful (καλόν) sight of a young man dying an honorable death on the battlefield. Furthermore, to continue the theme of his imagined dishonor, he allows his chilling imagination to truly soar: imagining his naked body, his private parts included (and thereby his progeny), to finally be mauled by what used to be his close animal companions, his very own dogs. Accordingly, Priam's speech spoken out of fear and hope ends in an "apocalyptic vision"[17] of violence and abandonment, with—at least at first sight—no honor, trust, or beauty in sight.

The very fact that first Priam's, and later Hecuba's, address to Hector (22.79–89) culminate in references to dogs deserves more attention as it sheds light on the exact nature of Priam's and Hecuba's fear, hope, and desperation.[18] While in ancient Greece pet dogs could very well be objects of affection and some dogs were even eulogized and given burial places amongst humans,[19] the image that Priam paints here shows the darker side of the relationship between humans and dogs. Instead of being the embodiment of humans' loyal and trustworthy companions, the pet dogs Priam envisages here turn the tables of power and assert their supremacy over human beings.[20] While he imagines to be killed not by animal but by human hand, the sheer fact that his own guardian dogs would "rip him raw," "lap his blood," and mutilate "grey head, beard and secret parts" is most pitiful to him because it expresses not just deep personal betrayal but the threat of losing our very *humanity*. For, what is at stake in this takeover of animals is ultimate disrespect for one of the most sacred social human rites: the respect and burial of the human body.[21] Thus, ultimately, the destructiveness of Priam's vision is not so much oriented around his own death as it is focused on the loss of meaning of human social life, with its biggest threat a return to a bestial kind of state initiated by a takeover by its former animal companions.[22]

Likewise, Hecuba's consecutive speech to Hector ends with a visualization of how, after his death outside the city walls, dogs will attack and eat his body. Her speech is prefaced by the dramatic, desperate gesture of her baring and holding one of her breasts. She asks him to obey and pity the mother who nursed him as a baby and who offered solace in a world so overwhelming to a newborn child:

> Hector, my child, look upon these and obey, and take pity
> (αἴδεο καί μ' ἐλέησον)

On me, if ever I gave you the breast to quiet your sorrow.
Remember all these things, dear child, and from inside the wall
Beat off this grim man. Do not go out as champion against him,
O hard one; for if he kills you I can no longer
Mourn you on the death-bed, sweet branch, o child of my
  bearing,
Nor can your generous wife mourn you, but a big way from us
Beside the ships of the Argives the running dogs will feed
  on you. (*Il.* 22.82–89)

The persuasive arc of Hecuba's speech consists in confronting Hector with the very beginning of his life, protected and nursed by the woman with whom he once shared a body, and his imminent death on the battlefield, *outside* of the circle of homely protection, where not even his body can be properly respected and cared for by his wife and mother. Instead, his body would be simply dehumanized and being made into food for another species, the dog. In addition, the final image of the dogs eating his flesh makes an especially shrill contrast with the nourishing and comforting suckling of the newborn at the breast of his mother. Where in the final instance a human body is decomposed into simple matter to be consumed by another species, in the initial image a human body finds its growth, development, nourishment, and comfort through establishing its connection with its original, human, maternal home.

Comparing the two speeches, we can note how Hecuba's address is keenly to be distinguished from Priam's due to its dramatic gestures and its feminine, motherly orientation emphasizing the home. Additionally, Hecuba's focus throughout her speech is Hector himself and his development, growth, and destruction; contrarily, the theme of Priam's speech is mostly his own suffering: he recounts the losses he himself has suffered so far and underlines that his only hope for survival will be extinguished with the death of Hector, culminating in an image of his own violent death. Yet, a remarkable resemblance between Priam's and Hecuba's speeches can be found in the respective endings of their addresses. Both ultimately conclude with images of dogs desecrating human bodies, namely those of Priam and Hector. While Hecuba laments the fact that she would not be able to take proper care of Hector's dead body if he dies outside the city walls, and Priam envisions his own body being taken apart by dogs without being buried, their visions coalesce in stressing the violent overtake by dogs over humans and the withholding of proper human burial rites. Thus, their darkest fears unite in the object of their primal fear: the devolution to a more primitive, bestial state and the collapse of social rites and humanity.

Having explored the speeches by Priam and Hecuba in greater detail, the question can be raised whether Priam's affections offer proof of Aristotle's ideas that hope underlies fear and that hope can make fear productive and allow for deliberation and courage. For sure, Priam's actions and speech clearly indicate that hope and fear intersect and form a symbiosis. The suffering and dishonor he fears—being torn up by his own dogs—is enabled through the hope he expresses for the survival of his son, himself, his family, and his people. Moreover, the extreme fear he expresses for his own death seems to be made possible by a hope that beauty and nobility (τo καλὸν) will be sustained as long as humans are offered proper burial. In addition, we can clearly witness here that, as Aristotle writes, fear and hope can be made productive and lead to deliberation. For, Priam's plea with Hector, similar to Hecuba's, is, if not itself aiming for deliberation with Hector, then certainly the *result* of his personal reflections and deliberations on the practical situation and how to escape suffering. While Priam's petition with Hector ultimately falls flat in that it does not convince Hector to act otherwise and withdraw within the city walls (22.78), the petition itself allows all involved—including the reader—to gain further insight into the situation and to mark the irreversible nature of Troy's tragedy.

Yet, it is the question of whether the interaction between Priam's affections of fear and hope realizes itself ultimately in the virtue of *courage*. While the desperation in Priam's plea is all too human and understandable, especially given the fact that Priam likely anticipates Hector's steadfast resolve in facing Achilles all alone on the battlefield (22.77–78), the speech seems very Troy-centered and self-focused. This becomes especially apparent in contrast with Hecuba's speech that culminates in concern for the well-being and burial of their son Hector, whereas Priam's speech seems to highlight mostly his own fear and fate. In fact, the description of his predicament and his imaginary ghastly ending appears to emphasize too much absorption with his own mortality and, arguably, pushes fear in the direction of cowardice. Simultaneously, however, considerations of beauty (τo καλὸν) and proper burial also indicate that Priam's fear is not solely self-centered, but driven by concerns of respect for humanity's purpose—concerns that are associated with a virtuous character.

Ultimately, then, Book 22 offers us unsatisfactory and limited evidence of the fruitful connection between hope, fear, and courage. This is in contrast with Priam's predicament as described in Book 24, to which we turn next. To truly do justice to the question of courage in respect to Priam's affections, that reflection will be paired with an analysis of Aristotle's discussion of courage in Book III of his *Nicomachean Ethics*.

Aristotle on Courage and Priam's Courageous Mission to Achilles in Book 24

Book 24 of the *Iliad* depicts Priam in all his misery after his worst fear has become true: his dearest son Hector has been killed by Achilles.[23] Homer describes Priam's initial reaction in the following way:

> . . . the old man
> sat veiled, beaten into his mantle. Dung lay thick
> on the head and neck of the aged man, for he had been rolling
> in it, he had gathered and smeared in on with his hands.
> (*Il.* 24.161–65)

With Hector dead, Priam is overcome with grief and he has surrendered himself to the very excrements our physical lives expel. The dung that Priam has scraped up and that covers him speaks to his willingness to humble himself in the face of this overburdening loss, demarcating an abrupt departure from all common social behavior and a return to the earthly.

While his extreme suffering cannot be undone and is the kind of suffering of which Aristotle argues that it deprives even the most prosperous man, such as Priam, of happiness (*NE* I.9, 1100a4–9), respect for his son Hector urges Priam to gather all his strength.[24] Under divine guidance by Hermes, "man's dearest companion," Priam penetrates into the enemy camp to petition Achilles for his son's body. During this mission, fear is never far away, as in his initial encounter with Hermes, Priam is described as "badly frightened" at the sight of this stranger, with his hairs "standing up all over his gnarled body" (24.358–59). Even more poignantly, during his encounter with Achilles, fear directly erupts when Achilles gets angry after Priam has urged him to not delay in giving him the body back (24.552–55). Achilles asks not to be further pushed and stirred, as he wants to do things on his terms. In response, Priam is said to be "frightened and did as he told him" (24.571).

Yet, the fear that Priam feels only rarely emerges in a "merely" fearful form, but for most of his expedition to the camp of Achilles, Priam also manifests significant hope. Even while consulting his wife Hecuba about this mission, he seems set on it and speaks of "his heart and strength as terribly urgent" (μένος καὶ θυμὸς ἀνώγει; 24.198), indicating an enormous drive and strong trust in the divine support of his mission. His hope to succeed in this mission and his fear that things may go awry struggle with each other and seem to manifest themselves in a rare and noble shape: courage.

To understand his courage more deeply, Aristotle's ideas on the relationship between undergoing fear and manifesting courage can be of aid. Aristotle defines courage as the mean regarding the painful feeling of fear and the feeling of confidence (cf. *NE* II.7, 1107a35). The virtue of courage expresses itself par excellence in anticipating and undergoing death (*NE* III.6, 1115a26). Aristotle states that:

> Death and wounds will be painful for a courageous person and he will suffer them unwillingly (ἄκοντι), but he will endure (ὑπομενεῖ) them because it is noble (καλόν) to do so or base to do otherwise. (*NE* III.9, 1117b8–9)[25]

The importance of *enduring* fearful, and thus painful, events, is repeated time and again in *NE* III.6–7. For instance, Aristotle notes that no one but the courageous person "endures (ὑπομενετικώτερος) what is terrifying more steadfastly" (*NE* III.6, 1115a26) and that the attitude the courageous person has to a fearful event is to "endure (ὑπομενεῖ) it in the right way and as *logos* (speech, account) directs for the sake of what is noble (τοῦ καλοῦ)" (*NE* III.7, 1115b12–13). Moreover, Aristotle states that the courageous person "endures (ὑπομενεῖ) and fears as courage demands" (1115b18), and that "the courageous person endures (ὑπομενεῖ) and acts (πράττει) for the sake of what is noble" (1115b23).[26]

Aristotle's repetitive use of the verb ὑπομένω with regard to the relationship that the courageous person has toward fearful events is very instructive for our understanding of King Priam's attitude during his mission to Achilles. As a composite of ὑπο and μένω, the Greek verb ὑπομένω literally expresses the notion of "to remain," or "stand," "while being subjected."[27] Endurance thus entails an interesting "passive activity"—that of *actively* holding out or withstanding, while being *passively* under the pressure of hardship or stress.[28]

If we now return to the case of King Priam visiting the camp of Achilles, we can clearly see how Priam's courage is not without enduring severe pain. In fact, since he submits himself to the most unthinkable mission ever—going into the enemy camp by himself and facing possible discovery and death—his fear must be unthinkably intense. Nonetheless, as his response shows to his wife Hecuba, who tries to dissuade him from his mission on the basis that it is based on pure madness, he is willing to withstand this pain and fear because of deep respect and commitment to his son, hoping to hold his son in his arms one last time:

> I am going, and this word shall not be in vain. If it is my destiny
> to die there by the ships of the bronze-armored Achaians,
> then I wish that. Achilles can slay me at once, with my own son
> caught in my arms, once I have my fill of mourning above him. (24.224-25)

Thus, Priam illustrates very prominently Aristotle's concept of courage as actively withstanding, while being passively under the pressure of stress: the hope he has for being reunited with his son allows him to truly fear suffering. Still, while suffering and feeling fear he simultaneously actively shapes and counteracts his fear through his hope for being reunited with his son and trusting the aim and beauty of his actions: paying final respect to his son by holding him, if not burying his body. The epithet given to Priam—he with the "iron heart" (24.205, 521)—echoes this beautiful endurance: while not without feelings, his heart has also been shaped and toughened through hope against hardship.[29]

Aristotle writes that "courageous action ought to be motivated by the fact that it is noble (κάλον)" (*NE* III.8, 1116b2-3). The hope that Priam expresses here, to be reunited with his son and to offer him proper burial, certainly qualifies as such a noble motivation and allows for Priam's courage to come to the forefront. Moreover, the fear that Priam experiences here is intense, but is different from the kind of fear expressed in Book 22. Fear concerning his own mortality is still there, but does not preoccupy him. According to Aristotle, the courageous person still considers death a great evil that is to be feared (cf. *NE* III.6, 1115a27), but the vision of his own death leaves him "undisturbed" (ἀτάραχος) which is what happens to the courageous person in situations that evoke fear (*NE* III.9, 1117a31). Similarly, Priam shows himself fearful, but also embracive of his son's and his own mortality. What transforms Priam's fear and what preoccupies him instead is the hope to leave intact the *meaning* of human life. Upholding the uniqueness and sanctity of human life through offering proper burial to his son has thereby taken precedence over securing his own personal destiny. Locating his hope beyond the ramifications of his own life and death, Priam demonstrates in a Promethean vein that hope can align with transformation and creativity.

The courage that is Priam's manifests itself also in his speech to Achilles. In Priam's speech, he proves himself to be utterly vulnerable, aiming to invoke pity, but simultaneously strong and generous in his ability to acknowledge the very humanity in Achilles. Priam asks Achilles to remember his own father, Peleus, who is currently defenseless and deprived of his dearest son, and to recognize the fate of Priam, who, unlike Peleus,[30] has lost all hope of being reconciled in life with his noble children:

> Achilles like the gods, remember your father, one who
> Is of years like mine, and on the door-sill of sorrowful old age
> And they who dwell nearby encompass him and afflict him,
> Nor is there any to defend him against the wrath, the
>   destruction . . . (24.486–89)
> Honor then the gods, Achilles, and take pity upon me
> Remembering your father, yet I am still more pitiful;
> I have gone through (ἔτλην) what no other mortal on
>   earth has gone through;
> I put my lips to the hands of the man who has killed my
>   children. (24.503–06)

Priam's words allow Achilles to view Priam no longer as his enemy, but as the man and father who has suffered much. With his noblest son dead, the hope to bury him has given his fear an unimaginable courageous shape: traveling to Achilles and kissing the hands of the man who has killed his children. While possibly otherwise interpreted as a symbol of weakness, Priam's gesture expresses both great strength and humility as it breaks through preconceived patterns of hostility, war making, and pride. What takes the place of these patterns is the simplest yet most profound recognition there can be: the recognition of Priam and Achilles as human beings with their own unique, yet universal family connections as, respectively, a father and a son.[31]

Much is alluded to here: the death that is Hector's may soon be Achilles's fate; the abandoned father that is Priam may soon be Peleus's ordeal; the hope that Priam has to bury his son, may be foregone to Peleus. Et cetera. Wherever we look, we see references of each life and fate as connected to the other. What all these references effect is emphasize the universally human dimension of Priam's and Achilles's life and, consequently, understanding for each other.[32]

Conclusion

Homer's description of King Priam in Books 22 and 24 of the *Iliad* offers a fruitful way to understand Aristotle's idea that, even amidst incredible suffering, affections can be shaped into remarkable examples of virtue. More precisely, Priam's expression of the affections of hope and fear in those books provide further insight into Aristotle's ideas that hope is essential as the precondition for fear, and that hope, when aimed for what is beautiful and noble, can transform fear into courage. The symbiosis of fear and hope makes itself felt in Book 22, but the true transformative power of fear and hope emerging as courage only makes itself truly visible in Book 24. While Priam is still afraid for his life, the hope to leave intact the *meaning* of human life takes precedence over the fear for securing his own destiny. The transcendence achieved by embracing one's mortality and prioritizing proper human relationships allows for mutual understanding between Priam and Achilles as they come to recognize and relate to each other's suffering.[33]

Notes

1. My view here is opposite to that of Nick Smith, who denies that for Homer ἀρετή made any specific contact with moral concepts "but measured, instead, forms of excellence in non-moral domains" (Smith 2001, 7).

2. Achilles's affections as described by Homer also offer fruitful ways to think about the connection between affections, virtue, and vice. Especially the transformation that Achilles undergoes from rage and absorption in himself to

pity and understanding for another is what we could call, with Zanker, "the poem's central gift" (Zanker 1994, 73).

3. For a more elaborate analysis of the relationship between affections and dispositions, see Oele 2012.

4. All translations from the *Iliad* will be from Lattimore 1951.

5. All translations from Aristotle's *Rhetoric* will be from Sachs 2009.

6. The most commonly held view on fear is that it is the most universal feeling "across human cultures but pertaining to higher animals as well," as Konstan clearly articulates (Konstan 2006, 129). By contrast, Konstan tries to show that fear is a "socially constituted response" and not an instinctive aversion, since fear involves evaluation: generals and orators may use it and make it subject to reasoned analysis (Konstan 2006, 142). While Konstan's argument is sophisticated and nicely builds off Aristotle's *Rhetoric*, it perhaps overemphasizes the social aspects of fear at the expense of its biological components. Especially since the *Rhetoric* is aimed at discussing the social level of the πάθη, a more biological account of fear could find its underpinnings elsewhere in Aristotle's works, such as in *De Anima*.

7. As Sorabji points out, Aristotle's definition of fear oscillates "between reference to the appearance of past or future evil and belief in such evil" (Sorabji 1996, 319).

8. Gravlee 2000, 468.

9. Heidegger cites this particular passage to argue that people who become anxious approach others to deliberate and to obtain advice. He concludes that fear is the kind of disposition (*Befindlichkeit*) that brings us to speak, especially when we are not simply fearful, but when we experience dread and a sense of uncanniness (Heidegger 2002, 261). Heidegger's point that dread (*Angst*) might lead to social deliberation is interesting, and has led many of his commentators to discern here a "social" dimension to Heidegger's thoughts of the attunements. With regard to Aristotle's account of deliberation, we could doubt whether it always *necessarily* has a social aspect, especially since Aristotle does not explicitly mention the need for others to be present for such a process, and could thus very well consist of a conversation with oneself. Still, Heidegger's point regarding the social nature of *Angst* and deliberation might be valid insofar as even a mostly "solitary" deliberation springing from a fundamental attunement cannot be disconnected from a character's embeddedness in the world and the corresponding functions that represent one's role in society.

10. Gravlee argues that it is primarily hope, and not fear, that leads to deliberation. He grounds this argument on the basis of *De Anima* III.10, 433a23–30, which he interprets as stating that it is mostly positive desires (such as hope), and not aversions (such as fear), that, according to Aristotle, seem to drive our actions (Gravlee 2000, 471). While Gravlee's take on this passage is thoughtful, the ground for his argument is, nonetheless, rather "thin," since

Aristotle's argument in that particular passage in DA III.10 concerns very generally desire's direction for the good or the apparent good. Due to its very general description, the passage does not necessarily imply that "positive" desires prevail over aversions, because avoiding negative things could still be a desirable good to be achieved. In fact, since Aristotle explicitly writes that it is *fear* (and not hope) "that makes people deliberate," I think good ground remains to argue that fear—inspired by and collaborating with hope—seeks for deliberation.

11. Admittedly, the underpinning of hope for confidence asks for more exploration. However, because of the already challenging and complex nature of explaining the connection between hope and fear, this paper has to forego such considerations at this time.

12. Gravlee 2000, 464. Gravlee continues to distinguish a third form of hopefulness in Aristotle (separate from its basis on experience or good fortune) namely one that is based on being ignorant of the danger at hand (ibid.).

13. Translation Lombardo 1993.

14. The idea that hope might be understood here as an evil has led some commentators to speak of a possible "lapse of logic" in Hesiod's text, since they underline that hope, in offering consolation, could never be counted among evils. Cf. Lamberton 1993, 52.

15. Verdenius offers a summary of various interpretations of why hope is kept in the jar. Ultimately, influenced by Proclus's interpretation, he argues that the Greek term *elpis* might best be neutrally translated as "expectation" (from the root: to suppose) and not necessarily as "hope." This has repercussions for how we understand the fact that hope is left in the jar: keeping "expectation" in the jar is a good thing, because we are, at least, not continuously anticipating evil in addition to suffering it (Verdenius 1985, 69–70).

16. Cf. Conacher, who states that "Prometheus' gifts to man are allowed to soar beyond the merely technological: freed from the acute awareness of his limitations, man's reach will exceed his immediate grasp: the key to all true advances in 'civilization'" (Conacher 1980, 42).

17. Lonsdale 1979, 152.

18. As Jones keenly points out, the theme of "maltreatment of the dead—being left out in the open for scavengers, rather than being properly buried" finds special emphasis in Homer. It can be found already early in the *Iliad* (1.5), is referenced by Odysseus contrasting his fate with Socus's (11.455) and finds it climax in Achilles aiming to mutilate Hector's body, which is prevented by the gods (Jones 2003, 49 and 178).

19. Lonsdale 1979, 151. Opposite the nuanced and rich historical perspective of Lonsdale, Nussbaum sketches a generally far more narrow and negative view of how dogs were perceived by the ancient Greeks, mentioning how the dog, in contrast to the lion and eagle, "ranks very low on the scale of animal nobility" (Nussbaum 2001, 414).

20. Lonsdale speaks in this regard of the dog essentially becoming "man's successor" (Lonsdale 1979, 152).

21. While Nussbaum's perspective on the general meaning of dogs for the ancient Greeks is too narrow (as mentioned in a preceding note), her claim about how the dog may evoke contempt and fear as "it devours the flesh of human corpses, indifferent to the most sacred law of human society" is certainly applicable and true to Priam's vision (Nussbaum 2001, 414).

22. The shamelessness and lack of respect for social rites associated in some instances with dogs was actually one of the main reasons that Cynics such as Diogenes of Sinope came to praise dogs and other animals. These animals represented for Diogenes a fine role model for humans to emulate as they embody freedom of action, honesty, and self-sufficiency vs. the artificial, insincere, and dependent lifestyle that humans have in society. It would not have been an insult but rather praise to Diogenes knowing that his philosophy came to be associated with the Greek term for dog, κυνος. Cf. Diogenes Laertius, 1961, Vol. II: 6.

23. Selected paragraphs of this section on Homer's *Iliad* Book 24 rely textually on my article "Suffering, Pity and Friendship: An Aristotelian Reading of Book 24 of Homer's Iliad" (Oele 2010, 51–65).

24. For a more elaborate account of Aristotle's conceptualization of the vulnerability of existence in the face of tragic events and the resilience embodied by Priam, see my article "Suffering, Pity and Friendship: An Aristotelian Reading of Book 24 of Homer's *Iliad*" (Oele 2010, 53–56).

25. All translations from the *Nicomachean Ethics* are from Ostwald 1962.

26. Other instances of Aristotle's use of ὑπομένω can be found at NE II.2, 1104a20; III.1, 1110a21, 22, 26; III.6, 1115b18, 23, 33; III.7, 1116a12, 15; III.8, 1117a17; III.9, 1117a35.

27. As Liddell and Scott explain, in composites, ὑπο can "express subjection or subordination."

28. Plato's *Laches* speaks very similarly about courage as endurance: see especially *Laches* 192a–94c.

29. Interestingly, after their battle, Hector pleads with Achilles to have his body be given to the Trojans for burial. When Achilles denies his request, he describes Achilles as having an "iron heart" (22.357). Notably, the meaning of the expression "iron heart" is very different in this passage, as in the case of Achilles "iron heart" seems to indicate insensitivity and stubbornness, while in Priam's case sensibility, endurance, and courage are invoked. Interestingly, the French and Latin etymology underlying the English term "endurance" also speaks of "to make hard" or "to harden" as explanations for the root of this noun ("endure, v. OED Online. September 2012. Oxford University Press. http://0-www.oed.com.ignacio.usfca.edu/view/Entry/62035 (accessed November 10, 2012).

30. According to Priam, Peleus may still have hope. See *Iliad* 24.491.

31. In her analysis of force in the *Iliad* Simone Weil argues contrarily that Achilles does not really values Priam as a human being, as he forgets the presence of the suffering creature that is Priam and does not see Priam as "a suppliant, but as an inert object" (Weil 1991, 4). I argue here the opposite: that eventually there is on many levels, and certainly on a very fundamental level, a mutual understanding between Priam and Achilles. While Weil's argument is persuasive in understanding the factor of reification in force, I think she overlooks the depth of the interaction between Priam and Achilles.

32. Christopher Smith has persuasively underscored that Priam seeks to be welcomed as a friend (φίλος; 24.309): Smith 2002, 392. For a further elaboration of this move from pity to friendship, see Oele 2010, 61–63.

33. I am thankful to the anonymous reviewers of this volume for their comments on this article, and owe special gratitude to William Wians for his insightful and constructive comments on an earlier draft of this paper. A special note of gratitude is due to my research assistants Daniel O'Connell and Lex Wochner for their fruitful suggestions and editorial assistance with this article. I also benefited from the feedback of the participants of the 2014 Annual Meeting of the Ancient Philosophy Society at the University of South Florida, and the commentary provided by Milton Wilcox.

12

Poets as Philosophers and Philosophers as Poets

Parmenides, Plato, Lucretius, and Wordsworth

A. A. LONG

This study owes its theme to Eric James. High Master of Manchester Grammar School (1945–1962), who taught me a class on "divinity" in 1953. James was an agnostic but a fervent Platonist. His exposition of the Sun, Line, and Cave has been one of the strongest influences on my academic life. What made James's teaching especially memorable was his simultaneously introducing the class to Wordsworth. James interpreted Plato with the help of Wordsworth's "Intimations of Immortality." From both authors he derived support for his own philosophy of education, which included a strong commitment to *a priori* ideas. In my turn, I acquired a lifelong conviction that philosophy and poetry may coexist at the highest level in a few exceptionally rich texts.

To many in this era of post-modern disparagement of literary aesthetics and humanism such a conviction will be thought naïve or worse. So be it! What I offer here is no formal defense of an unfashionable thesis but a selection of empirical observations. I attach them not only to Plato and Wordsworth but also to Parmenides and Lucretius. Why do I choose the latter pair? In truth they are two of my favorites, but if that is insufficient reason, the poetry of Parmenides and the philosophy of Lucretius deserve special emphasis because they have sometimes been subject to question. I also propose that reflection on these four authors underscores the difficulty of precisely differentiating either activity, the one from the other.

It goes without saying that one of these four figures, Plato, is so gigantic and so central that he would be anyone's first choice as an author for stimulating thought on the relation of philosophy to poetry. Would I not have done better, then, to devote these remarks exclusively to Plato? That may well be so. But I hope that my choice of these four authors proves to be more than an evasive eccentricity. By discussing them conjointly, I aim to provoke thought about general aspects of the connections and relationships between poetry and philosophy, which is a major theme of this book.

Setting aside the differences between the freedom of prose rhythm and the strictness of metrical form for ancient verse, I propose that each one of my chosen authors, in his own distinctive way, combines philosophy and poetry. My point in saying this is neither the truism that Parmenides composed philosophy in verse form, nor the fact that Plato's philosophic prose can be highly imaginative in tone and content, but the substantive claim that their medium and their message are inherently reflective *and* poetic, and so engage both reason and feeling. So too, I will argue, in the case of Lucretius and Wordsworth. I also propose that my collective focus on Plato, Parmenides, Lucretius, and Wordsworth can underscore the difficulty of precisely differentiating poetry from philosophy.[1] That issue in turn raises the question of whether there are poetic and philosophic universals, or whether these literary practices are irreducibly particular and various in time and culture. I will give a brief response to this question at the end of my paper. Now I turn to some introductory remarks about my chosen four, taking them in chronological order.

An Impassioned Expression of Science?

Parmenides of Elea, thanks to his pioneering metaphysics and novel method of deductive argument, was Plato's most influential and illustrious predecessor as a writer of philosophy in the early years of the fifth century BCE. Yet, unlike Plato's limpid Attic prose and dialogue style,

Parmenides composed in the dactylic hexameter form practiced by the hallowed epic poets Homer and Hesiod. Why did Parmenides choose this verse medium? Is he a poet in any sense other than in rhythm and diction? What does his poetry contribute, if anything, to his thought and his manner of engaging listeners or readers?

Plato is notorious for holding that poetry is the enemy of philosophy, and that the mimetic influence of Homer and the tragedians is extremely dangerous to people's characters and intellects.[2] Yet, in the view of numerous interpreters Plato, notwithstanding his prose dialogues sometimes writes in a manner that is supremely poetic. To quote the English poet and critic Samuel Coleridge: "Plato's writings furnish undeniable proofs that poetry of the highest kind may exist without metre and even without the contradistinguishing objects of a poem."[3] Actually in spite of the absence of any original verse from his dialogues, except for a possible line or two, Plato was credited in antiquity with writing several epigrams, and some of these, including a beautiful poem mourning the death of Dion of Syracuse, may well be genuine.[4] Creative writers (we may think of Jose Sarramago's novel *The Cave*) frequently draw inspiration from Plato even when the context of their indebtedness is quite remote, as when John Milton draws on the concluding myth of the *Republic* in describing Satan's journeys in Book 3 of *Paradise Lost*.[5]

Plato writes positively about poetry in the *Laws* where the Athenian Stranger calls the discussions about the Cretan city "the most beautiful and finest tragedy."[6] Plato's Socrates drops dialectic and adopts a poetic style in his second speech in the *Phaedrus* (249d–253c), a passage he prefigures by declaring that he is breaking into verse (241e). Shortly after that, Socrates attributes the "madness" of true love to divine inspiration, and likewise the "madness" that enables poets to glorify past achievements and teach them to future generations.[7] A comparably lyrical passage is the "ladder of love," told to Socrates by the wise woman Diotima in *Symposium* (210a–212b), who praises the poetic offspring of Homer and Hesiod (ibid. 209d). The remarkable discourse Plato assigns to Socrates in the erotic and psychological contexts of the *Phaedrus* anticipates Wordsworth's romantic evocations of nature and subjective responses to visual beauty. From Aristotle onward Plato's most sensitive readers have found it impossible to place him in a single literary category.[8] Yet no one, reading the current periodicals for ancient philosophy, will find any treatment of Plato the poet. This omission says a lot about Plato's present location within academic discourse rather than the general culture where he was fully at home in the nineteenth century.[9]

Lucretius, with his theme of instructing the Roman statesman Memmius in Epicurean physics, is often called a didactic poet, but didactic is a false modern category. Lucretius's literary genre is hexameter epic, and Epicurus's salvational discoveries are a heroic theme throughout the *De rerum natura*, making Epicurus virtually a *deus*, as Lucretius calls him (5.8). Because we have lost so much of Epicurus's writings, modern historians of philosophy turn to Lucretius as a doctrinal source of paramount importance for Epicureanism. Yet Cicero, who knew and admired the work of Lucretius, never mentions him in any of his many books of philosophy, even though he includes in them detailed accounts of Epicurean philosophy.

For his Roman audience, Lucretius was not a philosopher but an inspired poet through and through.[10] On the other hand, many modern readers find him only intermittently and contingently poetic, as if his imagery and other stylistic qualities were merely the "honey," as he called it (4.22), to sweeten his faithful and austere reproduction of Epicurean physics and make it more palatable to his less scientific readers. As with Parmenides, so in the case of Lucretius there is a strong tendency to think that he alternates between poetry and philosophy but does not satisfyingly integrate them.

Wordsworth, my fourth author to consider, wrote poetry in many styles, but he is most renowned for the poems in which he conveys his own feelings about nature and humanity. He was also strongly affected by Plato's notions of ideal Forms, recollection of forgotten knowledge, and the soul's immortality. Unlike my other three authors, Wordsworth wrote at length about his conception of poetry and philosophy and also about his own aims as a poet.[11] A few quotations will show the relevance of his observations to my chapter's theme, especially his conviction that poetry and philosophy, so far from being at variance, are intimately related:

> Poetry is the breath and finer spirit of all knowledge; it is
>   the impassioned
> expression which is in the countenance of all Science.[12]

In a different context Wordsworth set out his notion of an authentic philosopher:

> The true province of the philosopher is not to grope about in the external world, and when he has perceived or detected an object [with] such or such a quality or power, to set himself to the task of persuading the world that such is a sublime or beautiful object, but to look into his own mind and determine the law by which he is affected . . . To talk of an object as being sublime or beautiful in itself, without reference to some subject by whom that sublimity or beauty is perceived, is absurd.[13]

Wordsworth defines poetry as "the spontaneous overflow of powerful feelings" arising from "emotion recollected in tranquility."[14] His criteria for poetry are psychological rather than formal or literary, as when he explains his use of everyday language:

> There neither is, nor can be, any essential difference between the language of prose and metrical composition. What is a poet? . . . He is a man speaking to men but one endowed with more lively sensibility, more enthusiasm and tenderness, who has a greater knowledge of human nature, and a more comprehensive soul, than are supposed to be common among mankind.[15]

Wordsworth's focus on the poet's internal world and the necessary connection he draws between what is "beautiful in itself" and the perceiving subject recall the two Platonic dialogues I have mentioned before—the *Symposium*, where Diotima reveals to Socrates "the higher erotic mysteries," culminating in the vision of Beauty Itself, and the philosophical lover of the *Phaedrus*, who by observing the visual beauty of his beloved recollects the ideal Form of Beauty. Although Wordsworth's context (early nineteenth century) was utterly remote from Plato's Athens, the Romantic poets of his time saw no difficulty in imagining themselves to be Plato's companions.

Shelley, Wordsworth's younger contemporary, spoke in absolutist terms about poetry, as if there were a Platonic form of authentic versification.[16] I have the impression that German critics of this period such as Friedrich Schlegel had a similar view. Not so Wordsworth himself. He was acutely aware of composing a quite different kind of poetry from that which had been fashionable in the eighteenth century, and of having to defend himself from critics who found his style and subject matter unrefined. Rather than bowing to convention, Wordsworth took himself as a poet to be doing something fresh, philosophical, or universal in its general message, but intensely personal in its expression and appeal to the emotions.

Was it the same, *mutatis mutandis*, in the case of Parmenides, Plato, and Lucretius? I will try to establish this thesis. Underlying my argument will be the assumption that there is nothing that intrinsically connects philosophy and poetry, but nothing either, that intrinsically separates them. In the rare cases where the two creative practices are fully combined, that is a very deliberate choice by the writer. If the outcome is successful, we get a product that seeks to combine the objective truths and appeals to reason, that we associate with philosophy, and the subjective tone and emotive power of poetry that is more than mere versification. After this brief introduction of my four poet philosophers I now turn to each of them in more detail, starting with a few comments on early Greek conceptions of poetry.

The Visionary Philosopher

The English words for poet, poem, and poetry are taken directly from the Greek *poietes, poiema, and poiesis*. These are not the earliest Greek terms for poet, poem, and poetry. For Homer the epic poet is a singer (*aoidos*), but by the fifth century the poet—*poietes*—is the quintessential "maker." As Plato says at *Symposium* 205bc: "All the productions of every craft are *makings* (*poieseis*) . . . but we have marked off one part, the part the Muses give us, with melody and rhythm alone as poetry." For the Greeks of this period, and thereafter, the poet, or the poet's muse, is the quintessential maker or creator. We can see the etymological significance of this linguistic usage by a contrast with Latin, where the corresponding agent noun for the verb *facio* is the humble word *factor*, which, to the best of my knowledge, is never associated with poetry.

I cannot prove that Parmenides, my earliest philosopher poet, was already familiar with the Greek use of *poiesis* for poetry specifically. But we can confidently assume that his poem was designed to strike his hearers as a supremely creative production, inspired by the unnamed goddess who instructs "the man who knows" in the respective "ways" of Truth and Opinion. It is often assumed that Parmenides wrote in verse because prose at this date (about 500 BCE) was not yet an established form of composition, but I find this proposal unconvincing. Heraclitus and other early "scientific" writers composed in prose. Parmenides's choice of verse was clearly deliberate and not continued by his Eleatic successor Zeno. Diogenes Laertius (9.22) couples Parmenides as a philosophical poet with Hesiod, Xenophanes, and Empedocles, but the association obscures big differences between these four authors. Hesiod, whether or not we call him a philosopher, was an epic poet at a time when epic poetry was the only literary genre. Xenophanes was a professional rhapsode, who recited his poems at symposia. Empedocles's hexameter poetry alludes to Parmenides, but, unlike Parmenides, Empedocles also wrote poems on non-philosophical themes; and his choice of verse for his great poem on nature may well have been influenced by his strong sympathies with Orphism and Orphism's use of hexameter poetry. We need to explain Parmenides's choice of verse through his particular intention and message.

I propose to examine his work as a philosopher poet by reference to four criteria—speculative creativity, cultural authority, emotional intensity, and memorable phraseology. Once I have done that, I shall proceed to apply these criteria to my other three philosopher poets.

Parmenides begins his poem with a 32-line prologue that pictures him travelling rapidly on a horse-drawn chariot, guided by divine maidens, daughters of the sun, to the house of Night. This journey fulfils his heart's desire. It will bring him eventually through the mighty gates of Day and Night, which are guarded, high in the sky, by "inexorable Justice." To secure his passage, the sun maidens must first soothe Justice, personified as a divine figure, and persuade her to open the great doors secured by double bolts. Once Parmenides has passed through, he continues his journey until the goddess meets him, and addresses him as follows:

> Greetings, young man, escorted by immortal charioteers who have brought you with their horses to my dwelling. No evil fate has summoned you to make this journey—far from the path of human beings—but Right and Justice. You are to learn all things, both the stable mind of well-rounded Truth, and the opinions of mortals that contain no true assurance.

This double agenda, the Way of Truth and the Way of Opinion, announces the poem's philosophical theme. Before recounting the antithetical ways the goddess instructs Parmenides to "bring her words back" to his human starting place, where people are characterized in uncompromisingly negative terms: they "know nothing," because they are utterly confused about the stark difference between "what is" and "what is not." Indeed, so great is their confusion that they "wander, two-headed, helpless, bemused, deaf and blind, identifying being and not-being, and yet also distinguishing them from one another." Parmenides, in contrast, characterizes himself, the privileged acolyte of the goddess, as "the knowing man."

In short, the poem he has composed describes a spiritual journey from the domain of human error to enlightenment, truth, and knowledge. This spiritual journey is divinely sanctioned and supported by Justice, who, as a controlling divinity, ensures that reality is utterly stable—subject to neither becoming nor perishing nor any change or motion whatsoever. Parmenides is to receive not only this absolute truth about nature, but also an account of the deceptive appearances of the phenomenal world. Then he is to convey the news back to his fellow mortals.

The narrative of Parmenides's miraculous journey to the goddess is a remarkable piece of writing. It draws on Homeric and Hesiodic mythology and vocabulary to create something entirely new in Greek literature—the speculative experience of a philosophical hero, whose spiritual journey mimics the physical travels that taught Odysseus on his visits to the cities of mortal men. Other early Greek philosophers were acutely aware of the need to distance their findings from traditional myth and poetic authority. Rather than denouncing the lies of Homer and Hesiod directly, as Heraclitus did, Parmenides marginalizes his poetic predecessors in a richly symbolic parody of traditional epic style and diction.[17]

Parmenides the poet has been completely overshadowed by Parmenides the philosopher, but that is because many readers have poetic expectations of imagery and color that he does not, to their satisfaction, fulfill. I disagree. It would be difficult to imagine a more intense and imaginatively phrased prologue to his work, as I hope my summary conveyed. In the limits of time I can do no better than quote Werner Jaeger's comments on Parmenides's salvational notion of rationality:

> Parmenides was a natural poet, because he was carried away by his conviction that he must preach his discovery, the discovery which he believed to be in part at least a revelation of the truth . . . he feels that he is only the instrument and servant of a power far higher and more worthy than him-

self . . . Parmenides considers thought and the truth which it apprehends to be something very like religion. It was the consciousness of his high mission which left him . . . to draw the first real picture of a philosopher.[18]

Traditionally the Greek poets had seen themselves as merely the vocal instruments of divine inspiration, who might, for all they knew, deliver falsehoods as well as truths, and be unable to distinguish the one from the other. Parmenides's goddess, by contrast, puts him in the privileged position of not only knowing the difference but also understanding why one account is true and the other account deceptive. We can interpret Parmenides's philosophy without reference to its poetic form and tone. Most readers do that, but the price for doing only that is high. What we chiefly lose is a feeling for his work's extraordinary intensity and density, which is as much emotional as it is cognitive. Heraclitus had told his audience to listen not to him but to his *logos*—which we may take to mean the objective rationale of nature. Parmenides, much more boldly registers his own subjective identity by imagining that he himself—a mere mortal—is the privileged addressee of a goddess whom he has visited on a transcendental journey to learn the truth about reality. Thus, each one of us, as we read and work through his poem, is invited to take our own place on the chariot journey to meet the goddess and have the privilege of hearing her disquisition about reality.

Greek poets at this date wrote to be heard by a group and not for private reading. Even prose writers typically delivered their work in this way, as Plato imagines Zeno doing at the beginning of his dialogue *Parmenides*. Poetry was a performance. Are we, then, to imagine Parmenides delivering his poem in a sympotic gathering? Hard though that is to believe, it may well have been the case; and if so, this occasion will have contributed to impressions of the author's authority, solemnity, and intensity. Plato characterizes Parmenides as speaking in both verse and prose (*Sophist* 237a).

To follow chronology, I should now proceed to Plato himself, but, because Wordsworth's philosophy is Platonism, I want to conclude my paper with these two writers; so I turn next to the question of how Lucretius integrates poetry and philosophy in his Epicurean epic.

As I already said, modern readers tend to find Lucretius alternating between dry argument (versified prose in effect) and powerful images such as Epicurus's heroic conquest of the monster superstition (*De rerum natura* 1.62–79), his shattering the *moenia mundi*, so as to disclose atoms moving through the void (3.14–17), and analogies of the atoms' behavior like motes of dust fighting, as virtual armies, in a sunbeam's illumination (2.112–24). As I also said, Lucretius's own figuration of his verse as honeying the scientific medicine may seem to lend credence to such disjointed assessment of his work. I don't question that such alternations occur and recur throughout the immense poem; by the same token I don't claim that Parmenides continues the personifications of his prologue throughout all the rest of his work. What I do want to resist, in the case of both philosopher poets, is that their poetic identity is present or evident only in purple passages, as it were, and in abeyance elsewhere. Lucretius, of course, is an immensely more complex writer than Parmenides. For that reason, his poetic qualities are far more various, and they are amenable to analysis by reference to local features of rhythm, sound, and imagery. But, as with Parmenides, I want to focus our attention on Lucretius's work as a whole. I will ask what, apart from versification, makes the entire *De rerum natura* (and not just its most memorable passages) a great poem in addition to its detailed exposition of Epicurean physical theory.

Actually, I think even this question is not entirely well formed; for my response to it, in essence, is that what confers greatness on the poem in its entirety *as a poem* is precisely Epicurean philosophy, as presented and interpreted by Lucretius. Form and content are integrated in all manner of ways, whether at the very outset where Lucretius invokes *Aeneadum genetrix* (as if he were writing Rome's national epic), or where we are promised to learn how Epicurus, superstition's triumphing hero, has made his journey into outer space (3.14–17) and brought back the scientific gospel to liberate us from fear of death and superstition (recall Parmenides's spiritual journey), or where we learn how Epicurus has outdone the labors of Hercules (5.23–54) by conquering the much more grievous internal enemies constituted by such vices as envy, sloth, and pride.

Still, is such integration of form and content sufficient to make Lucretius's poetic voice, brilliant though that often is, indispensable to the poem's subject matter and total effect? What Lucretius has added to Epicurus is powerful rhetoric, variety, readability, and color. But he has hardly contributed important semantic content that you could not have found in the voluminous works of Epicurus himself. Is there something else that the poetry essentially contributes?

I think there is, but how does one articulate that additional feature? Words that come to mind include vision and intensity, but for now I repeat Wordsworth's saying that the philosopher's task is "to look into his own mind and determine the law by which he is affected." Philosopher's or poet's task? For Wordsworth, as we have already seen, you cannot truly have the one without the other, and I think his dictum is peculiarly apt for understanding Lucretius. The *De rerum natura* is the record of Lucretius's inspection of his own mind, as mediated by the philosophy of Epicurus, and of determining how *he* the poet has been affected. What he has been affected to create was far more than an Epicurean text book or treatise, even though Lucretius has extraordinary command of that material and displays great intelligence in his representation of its most recondite details.

Let us pause over the word "affected"; for I take it to be crucial to Wordsworth's critical stance, given his preoccupation with emotion and enthusiasm. Lucretius has not simply versified Epicurus. He has used poetry to convey two things in particular—first to show how he has been affected by his internalization of Epicurean philosophy, and second, how he can affect us his readers, rather than just his official addressee Memmius. He affects us, works on us, by his peremptory use of the second-person singular imperative (*nunc age*) and by other ways of marking the urgency of his message, taking us into his confidence, with such words as *vidimus, nonne vides*, and treating us as grown-ups who will accept his science in place of childish fictions. We do not need Lucretius in order to assess the cogency of Epicurean doctrine and argument. We can get the logic and evidence he presents elsewhere. What we cannot get elsewhere is the personal affect. It could also be called "vision," and vision in turn recalls Jaeger's observation about Parmenides's *religious* mentality. Lucretius was hostile to all traditional forms of religion, but the awe in which he voices his feelings about the divine Epicurus is Roman *pietas* in full.

At this point, I need to raise a question that I have concealed so far. Must the poet as philosopher or the philosopher as poet be a visionary, whose words transport us out of our everyday selves in order to sense a non-mundane reality? If that is so, does it help to explain why poets and philosophers have completely parted company in the modern world? A few concluding words about Plato and Wordsworth may help us respond to these questions.

Ask anyone who knows Plato where, in his prolific works, he is at his most poetic and they will almost certainly respond: in certain contexts of the *Phaedo*, *Symposium*, *Republic*, and *Phaedrus*. Scholars have traditionally and rightly dated these dialogues to Plato's middle period—later than the early so-called Socratic dialogues and prior to the most analytically sophisticated works *Theaetetus*, *Sophist*, *Statesman*, and *Philebus*. Plato's Socrates is no enemy of poetry in general—not in the least—but it is in the middle period dialogues, where the philosophy appears to have gone well beyond anything historically Socratic, that we find the ideas that became the hallmark of Platonism—the soul's immortality, recollection of truths we learned before birth, the identity of Reality, Truth, Goodness, and Beauty, and the philosopher's desire to transcend embodied life and experience the immaterial, changeless, and perfect Forms.[19]

Does Plato attempt to prove these doctrines? In the case of immortality and recollection, certainly. But he is notoriously reticent in justifying the Forms—his most famous doctrine—by explicit arguments. Moreover, the ways he talks about the Forms are too varied and imprecise to settle their exact nature to the satisfaction of modern interpreters, leaving unresolved such questions as: Are the Forms universals or ideal particulars? How do they cause or explain everyday objects? Is our knowledge of them propositional or intuitive? Plato talks of everyday objects "imitating" Forms, and "participating" in or "striving after" Forms. How does imitation relate to participation or striving? Plato leaves it to us to figure out as best we may.

Aristotle decisively rejected Plato's transcendent Forms. Even Plato himself raised cogent logical objections to the doctrine in his dialogue *Parmenides*, but, to the best of our knowledge, he never abandoned it altogether. Could he not prove it to his own satisfaction? Did he never settle all its details? My response to these questions brings us back to Plato the poet. His theory of Forms is a doctrine of metaphysics and epistemology, but it is much more than just that. It is also a doctrine about value, especially beauty, the objects of desire, and an intuition that human life here and now is only a transient phase in the soul's millennial journeys.

How could anyone prove these things? Clearly not by discursive reasoning. Hence, I take it, the great poetic passages—Diotima's ladder of love in the *Symposium*, the allegory of the Cave in the *Republic*, and the soul's celestial journey, loss and recovery of wings in the *Phaedrus*. These passages are poetic because they appeal to our imagination, and they appeal to our imagination because they invite us to transcend our present existence by picturing our encounter with a better and more desirable reality.

If this is right, Plato's poetry, at least in these passages, is not a mere embellishment of what could be said in prosaic philosophical language. The poetry is the indispensable means of expression. Plato will not have thought that the soul literally grows and loses wings, but how could he better express the idea that human beings are capable of both identifying with their bodily desires and identifying, alternatively, with their longing for spiritual truth and beauty? The image of the soul's wings is unforgettably potent. It enables Plato's philosophical thoughts about transcendence to lodge in the mind as an ever-living presence, as all true poetry does.

These few remarks on Plato can convey only a hint of his extraordinary integration of philosophy and poetry. Fortunately, I can now turn again to Wordsworth, to illustrate how a poetic genius with a philosophical mind was able to capture the Platonism I have briefly characterized and do so in splendid verse. Wordsworth romanticizes Plato by his focus on the innocence and ideals of youth as contrasted with the drab conventionality of maturity, and with nostalgic talk of Nature; but I need not go on about that. Wordsworth's Platonic themes are too obvious to need detailed discussion—immortality, recollection of truths we learned before birth, the Cave or prison allegory, extra-mundane reality and beauty, and the vision of Sun or light as the source of all goodness. All of these heady ideas are packed into the fifth stanza of Wordsworth's Ode: *Intimations of Immortality from Recollections of Early Childhood*.[20]

> Our birth is but a sleep and a forgetting:
> The Soul that rises with us, our life's Star,
> Hath had elsewhere its setting,
> And cometh from afar:
> Not in entire forgetfulness,
> And not in utter nakedness,
> But trailing clouds of glory do we come
> From God, who is our home:
> Heaven lies about us in our infancy!
> Shades of the prison-house begin to close
> Upon the growing Boy,
> But he beholds the light and whence it flows,
> He sees it in his joy;

> The youth, who daily farther from the east
> Must travel, still is Nature's Priest,
> And by the vision splendid
> Is on his way attended;
> At length the Man perceives it die away,
> And fade into the light of common day.

The philosopher poet or the poet philosopher is a rare bird. When such birds appear, we need to ask, in each case, why they take on this hybrid identity rather than compose in a single way. Do Parmenides, Plato, Lucretius, and Wordsworth share anything that can throw light on this question? I think they do. Each of them is a visionary with a message that they take to be supremely important to us. They seek to communicate that message in ways that will impress us imaginatively and emotionally as well as rationally. We can abstract from their poetic images and discuss their stripped-down philosophical content—Parmenides's Way of Truth (forgetting its being a journey), Plato's immortal soul (forgetting its wings), Epicurus's atoms moving in the void (forgetting the motes dancing in the sunbeam), and Wordsworth's intimations of immortality (forgetting the nostalgic evocation of childhood). But I hardly need to argue that such abstraction would rob the original context of all its personality.

Conclusion

For better or worse, today's philosophy and poetry proceed on separate tracks and largely address quite different audiences. The principal goal of modern philosophy, at least in the Anglo-American tradition, is to get as clear as possible about the concepts we use in order to negotiate language and experience of the everyday world. Nothing could be further from that agenda than Platonism's transcendental ambition. As to modern poetry, Wordsworth's visionary style has been largely superseded by miniature poems that treat experience in a fractured, impressionistic way. There are, then, no poetic or philosophical universals, nor is there a determinate formula for combining or connecting poetry and philosophy. Just occasionally, though, a philosopher has also been a poet, and a poet has been a philosopher—Parmenides, Plato, Lucretius, and

Wordsworth. No doubt there are others in other languages, but these four must suffice for now.[21]

Notes

1. I am not suggesting that it is generally difficult to distinguish philosophy from poetry, but the other way round, and only in the case of certain types of poetry. Most philosophy, because it is discursive and eschews linguistic artifice for its own sake, is evidently not poetry. On the difficulty of distinguishing philosophy from literature in general, see Cascardi 1987, x.

2. Standard discussions include Murdoch 1977, Ferrari 1989, and Asmis 1992. All too often Plato's alleged hostility to poetry is treated as a blanket condemnation of all poetic forms and abstracted from the political contexts of the *Republic* where the critic of the poets is Socrates and not Plato in propria persona. Contrast Fr. Schlegel, *Athenaeum Fragments* 450, who says: "Plato is more against poets than he is against poetry; he thought of philosophy as the most daring dithyramb and the monodic music," translated in Bernstein 2003, 260.

3. Coleridge (1817) 1960, ch. 14; cf. Shelley (1821) 1975. Such judgments were standard in Britain throughout the nineteenth and early twentieth centuries, and can be extravagant: for instance Pater 1883, 127: "He [Plato] breaks as it were visible colour into the very texture of his work; his vocabulary, the very stuff he manipulates, has its delightful aesthetic qualities; almost every word, one might say, its figurative value;" and Adam 1911, 9: "We realize that the high quality of the language is not due to a clever manipulation of imagery or a felicitous choice of words, but rather to an intensely vital and even exuberant creative impulse taking everything in its stride, and expressing itself with an ease that comes naturally only to one who is a poet at heart." I take these quotations from Hartland-Swann 1951. For the twentieth century, see Nussbaum 1986, 227.

4. See Bowra 1938.

5. See Bennett 1939.

6. Plato, *Laws* 817b2-3, in contrast with the actual genre of tragedy; see Padilla Longoria 2010 and Nightingale 1995, 88.

7. See Hackforth 1952, 61: "Plato himself is a compound of rationalist and poet . . . in the *Phaedrus* the poet definitely gets the upper hand [and] is exceptionally conscious of the value of the imaginative, as against the rational, power of the human soul."

8. See Diogenes Laertius 3.37.

9. The only such study known to me is Hartland-Swann 1951. I find his work chiefly valuable for the literary assessments of Plato that he quotes from

others and for his observation that "Plato still had one foot in the semi-myth world of the Presocratics" (139).

10. Note especially the assessment of Statius, *docti furor arduus Lucreti, Silvae 2.7.76*, where *furor* "certainly refers to poetic inspiration," Smith 1975, xx.

11. See Abrams 1953, 103–14, and Eldridge 2001.

12. *Preface to the Lyrical Ballads*, in Hutchinson, 938. Cf. Fr. Schlegel, *Athenäums Fragment*, 255: "Je mehr die Poesie Wissenschaft wird, je mehr wird sie auch Kunst. Soll die Poesie Kunst werden, soll der Künstler von seinen Mitteln und seinen Zwecken, ihren Hindernissen und ihren Gegenständen gründliche Einsicht und Wissenschaft haben, so muss der Dichter über seine Kunst philosophieren."

13. "The sublime and the beautiful," in W. J. B. Owen and J. W. Smyser, eds., *The Prose Works of William Wordsworth*, vol. 2 (Oxford, 1974), 357.

14. *Preface to the Lyrical Ballads*, 935.

15. *Preface to the Lyrical Ballads*, 937.

16. For instance: "A poem is the very image of life expressed in its eternal truth . . . A story of particular facts is as a mirror which obscures and distorts that which should be beautiful: poetry is a mirror which makes beautiful that which is distorted," cited in Shawcross 1909, 155, 128, and poetry "strips the veil of familiarity from the world and lays bare the naked and sleeping beauty, which is the spirit of its forms," cited in Abrams 1953, 127.

17. See Mourelatos 2008, ch. 1. "epic form."

18. Jaeger 1947, vol. 1, 177.

19. Socrates in Plato's *Apology* declares that he found the poets at Athens "inspired" but incapable of understanding their "fine sayings" (23c). He also looks forward to the possibility of encountering Orpheus, Musaeus, Hesiod, and Homer after death (ibid. 41a).

20. If, as has been argued, Wordsworth had no direct acquaintance with any work by Plato at the time he composed this poem (1802–1804), his Platonic intuitions were quite remarkable: see Price 1994.

21. I originally wrote this study as the keynote address for an international conference on philosophy and poetry held at the University of Munich in March 2010. That version of my paper was published as Long 2011. It is reprinted here in lightly revised form with the editor's and publisher's permission.

Bibliography

Abrams, M. H. 1953. *The Mirror and the Lamp*. Oxford: Oxford University Press
Adam, J. 1911. *The Vitality of Platonism*. Cambridge: Cambridge University Press
Adams, S. M. 1955. "The Burial of Polyneices." *Classical Review* 45:110–11.
Adkins, A. W. H. 1960. *Merit and Responsibility*. Oxford: Oxford University Press
Adkins, A. W. H. 1982. "Values, Goals, and Emotions in the *Iliad*." *Classical Philology* 77:292–326.
Ahrensdorf, P. 2009. *Greek Tragedy and Political Philosophy: Rationalism and Religion in Sophocles' Theban Plays*. Cambridge: Cambridge University Press.
Algra, K. 1999. "The Beginnings of Cosmology." 45–65 in Long 1999.
Allan, W. 2006. "Divine Justice and Cosmic Order in Early Greek Epic." *Journal of Hellenic Studies* 126:16–25.
Amerasinghe, C. 1973. "The Helen Episode in the *Troiades*." *Ramus* 2:99–106.
Anderson, G. 2005. "Before *Turannoi* Were Tyrants: Rethinking a Chapter in Early Greek History." *Classical Antiquity* 24:173–222.
Annas, J. 1982. "Plato's Myths of Judgment." *Phronesis* 27:119–43.
Asmis, E. 1992. "Plato on Poetic Creativity." 338–64 in R. Kraut (ed.), *The Cambridge Companion to Plato*. Cambridge: Cambridge University Press.
Atchity, K. 1978. *Homer's Iliad: The Shield of Memory*. Carbondale: University of Southern Illinois Press.
Ausland, H. 2003. "Socrates' Argumentative Burden in the *Republic*." 123–51 in A. Michelini (ed.), *Plato as Author: The Rhetoric of Philosophy*. Leiden: Brill.
Austin, J. 1832. *The Province of Jurisprudence and the Uses of the Study of Jurisprudence*. London: J. Murray.
Ayer, A. J. 1936. *Language, Truth and Logic*. London: Gollancz.
Barnes, J. 1979. *The Presocratic Philosophers*. London: Routledge.
Benardete, S. 1974. "A Reading of Sophocles' Antigone I." *Interpretation* 4:148–96.
Benardete, S. 1975. "A Reading of Sophocles' Antigone II." *Interpretation* 5:1–55.
Benardete, S. 1975. "A Reading of Sophocles' Antigone III.' *Interpretation* 5:148–84.

Benardete, S. 1981. "Physics and Tragedy: On Plato's *Cratylus*." *Ancient Philosophy* 1:127–40.
Benardete, S. 2000. *The Argument of the Action: Essays on Greek Poetry and Philosophy*. Chicago: University of Chicago Press.
Benardete, S. (trans.) 2001. *Plato's Symposium*. Chicago: University of Chicago Press.
Benardete, S. 2002. *Encounters and Reflections: Conversations with Seth Benardete*. Chicago: University of Chicago Press.
Benardete, S., and M. Davis (trans.) 2002. *Aristotle: On Poetics*. South Bend, IN: St. Augustine's Press.
Bennett, J. W. 1939. "Milton's Use of the Vision of Er." *Modern Philology* 36.4:351–58.
Bergren, A. 1983. "Language and the Female in Early Greek Thought." *Arethusa* 16:69–95.
Bernabé, A. (ed.) 2005. *Orphicorum et orphicis similium testimonia et fragmenta. Poetae epici Graeci. Testimonia et fragmenta* pars II, fasciculus 2. Munich and Leipzig: K. G. Saur.
Bernstein, A. E. 1993. *The Formation of Hell*. Ithaca, NY: Cornell University Press.
Bernstein, J. M. (ed.) 2003. *Classic and Romantic German Aesthetics*. Cambridge: Cambridge University Press.
Bers, V. 2009. *Genos Dikanikon: Amateur and Professional Speech in the Courtrooms of Classical Athens*. Washington, DC: Center for Hellenic Studies.
Bers, V. 2013. "Performing the Speech in Athenian Courts and Assembly: Adjusting the Act to Fit the Bema?" 27–40 in Kremmydas et al. 2013.
Bickerman, E. J. 1968. *Chronology of the Ancient World*. Ithaca, NY: Cornell University Press.
Biehl, W. 1989. *Euripides Troades*. Heidelberg: C. Winter.
Blondell, R. 2002. *The Play of Character in Plato's Dialogues*. Cambridge: Cambridge University Press.
Blondell, R. 2010. "'Bitch That I Am': Self-Blame and Self-Assertion in the *Iliad*." *Transactions of the American Philological Association* 140:1–32.
Blondell, R. 2013. *Helen of Troy: Beauty, Myth, Devastation*. Oxford: Oxford University Press.
Bloom, A. 1991. *The Republic of Plato*, translated with notes, interpretive essay, and a new introduction. 2nd ed. New York: Basic Books.
Boegehold, A. L. 1995. *The Lawcourts at Athens: Sites, Buildings, Equipment, Procedure, and Testimonia*. Princeton, NJ: Princeton University Press.
Boegehold, A. L. 1999. *When a Gesture Was Expected*. Princeton, NJ: Princeton University Press.
Bouvier, D. 2001. "Ulysse et le personnage du lecteur." 19–53 in M. Fattal (ed.), *La philosophie de Platon* vol. 1. Paris: Harmattan.

Bowra, C. M. 1938. "Plato's Epigram on Dion's death." *American Journal of Philology* 59:394–404.
Boyd, T. 1997. "Where Ion Stood, What Ion Sang." *Harvard Studies in Classical Philology* 96:109–21.
Bradshaw, A. T. 1962. "The Watchman Scenes in the *Antigone*." *Classical Quarterly* 12:200–11.
Bremmer, J. M. 2022. *The Rise and Fall of the Afterlife*. New York: Routledge.
Brill, S. 2009. "Violence and Vulnerability in Aeschylus's *Suppliants*." 161–80 in Wians 2009b.
Brisson, L. 1994/1999. *Plato the Myth Maker*. Trans. G. Naddaf. Chicago: University of Chicago Press.
Brisson, L. 1995. "'Le corps 'dionysiaque.'" *L'anthropogonie décrite dans le Commentaire sur le Phédon de Platon (1, par. 3–6) attribué à Olympiodore est-elle orphique?*" Reprinted in *Orphée et l'Orphisme dans l'Antiquité gréco-romaine*. Aldershot: Variorum reprint.
Brisson, L. 2002. *Sexual Ambivalence*. Berkeley and Los Angeles: University of California Press.
Broadie, S. 1999. "Rational Theology." 204–24 in Long 1999.
Bryan, J. 2012. *Likeness and Likelihood in the Presocratics and Plato*. Cambridge: Cambridge University Press.
Buitron-Oliver, D. (ed.) 1992. *The Greek Miracle: Classical Sculpture from the Dawn of Democracy*. Washington: National Gallery of Art.
Bundrick, S. D. 2018. "Reading Rhapsodes on Athenian Vases." In Ready and Tsagalis 2018.
Burkert, W. 1972. *Lore and Wisdom in Ancient Pythagoreanism*. Trans. E. L. Minar. Cambridge, MA: Harvard University Press.
Burkert, W. 1979. *Structure and History in Greek Mythology and Ritual*. Berkeley and Los Angeles: University of California Press.
Burkert, W. 1984. *Die Orientalisierende Epoche in der griechischen Religion und Literatur*. Heidelberg: Carl Winter Universitätsverlag.
Burkert, W. 1985. *Greek Religion*. Trans. J. Raffan. Cambridge, MA: Harvard University Press.
Burkert, W. 1987. *Ancient Mystery Cults*. Cambridge, MA: Harvard University Press.
Burkert, W. 1998. *Kulte des Altertums: Biologische Grundlagen der Religion*. Munich: C. H. Beck Verlag.
Burkert, W. 2000. "Mythen um Oedipus: Familienkatastrophe und Orakelsinn.'" *Freiburg Universitätsblätter* 48(1):7–20.
Burkert, W. 2000 *Creation of the Sacred: Tracks of Biology in Early Religions*. Cambridge, MA: Harvard University Press.
Burnet, J. 1920. *Greek Philosophy: Thales to Plato*. 2nd ed. London: Macmillan.
Burnet, J. 1930. *Early Greek Philosophy*. 4th ed. London: Macmillan.

Buxton, R. 1994. *Imaginary Greece: The Contexts of Mythology*. Cambridge: Cambridge University Press.
Buxton, R. (ed.) 1999. *From Myth to Reason?* Oxford: Oxford University Press.
Cairns, D. L. (ed.) 2001. *Oxford Readings in Homer's Iliad*. Oxford: Oxford University Press.
Cascardi, A. J. (ed.) 1987. *Literature and the Question of Philosophy*. Baltimore, MD: The Johns Hopkins University Press.
Cherubin, R. 2009. "*Alêtheia* from Poetry into Philosophy: Homer to Parmenides." 51–72 in Wians 2009b.
Claus, D. B. 1981. *Toward the Soul: An Inquiry into the Meaning of Psuchē Before Plato*. New Haven, CT: Yale University Press.
Clay, D. 1992. "The World of Hesiod." *Ramus* 21:131–55.
Coleman, R. 1972. "The Role of the Chorus in Sophocles' *Antigone*." *Proceedings of the Cambridge Philological Society* 198 (n.s.), 18:4–30.
Coleridge, S. 1960. *Biographia Literaria*, ed. G. Watson. London and New York: Dent/Dutton.
Collobert, C. 2009. "Philosophical Readings of Homer: Ancient and Contemporary Insights." 133–157 in Wians 2009b.
Collobert, C., P. Destrée, and F. J. Gonzalez (eds.) 2012. *Plato and Myth: Studies on the Use and Status of Platonic Myths*. Leiden: Brill.
Conacher, D. J. 1980. *Aeschylus Prometheus Bound: A Literary Commentary*. Toronto: University of Toronto Press.
Consigny, S. P. 2001. *Gorgias: Sophist and Artist*. Columbia: University of South Carolina Press.
Copernicus, N. 1543/1939. *On the Revolutions of the Heavenly Spheres*. Trans. C. G. Wallace. Chicago: Encyclopedia Britannica Great Books.
Cornford, F. M. 1912. *From Religion to Philosophy: A Study in the Origins of Western Speculation*. London: E. Arnold.
Cornford, F. M. 1952. *Principium Sapientiae: The Origins of Greek Philosophical Thought*. Cambridge: Cambridge University Press.
Couprie, D. 2011. *Heaven and Earth in Ancient Greek Cosmology*. New York: Springer.
Couprie, D., and R. Kočandrle. 2013. "Anaximander's Boundless Nature." *Peitho, Examina Antiqua* 4:63–91.
Cowser, J. 1939. "The Shaping of the *Antigone*." *Proceedings of the Classical Association* 36:38–40.
Croally, N. T. 1994. *Euripidean Polemic: The Trojan Women and the Function of Tragedy*. Cambridge: Cambridge University Press.
Csapo, E. 2002. "Kallippides on the Floor-Sweepings: The Limits of Realism in Classical Acting and Performance Styles." 127–47 in Easterling and Hall 2002.
Csapo, E., and W. J. Slater. 1995. *The Context of Ancient Drama*. Ann Arbor: University of Michigan Press.

Dale, A. M. (ed.) 1954. *Euripides: Alcestis*. Oxford: Oxford University Press.
Davis, M. 1988. *Ancient Tragedy and the Origins of Modern Science*. Carbondale, IL: Southern Illinois University Press.
Davis, M. 1999. *The Poetry of Philosophy: On Aristotle's Poetics*. South Bend, IN: St. Augustine's Press.
Davis, M. 2009. The Fake that Launched a Thousand Ships: The Question of Identity in Euripides' *Helen*." 255–271 in Wians 2009b.
Deneen, P. 2000. *The Odyssey of Political Theory*. Lanham, MD: Rowman & Littlefield.
Densmore, S. 2009. *Riders on the Storm. My Life with Jim Morrison and the Doors*. New York: Random House.
Destrée, P. (forthcoming). "Who is Plato's Soldier Er? A note on Ἡρὸς τοῦ Ἀρμενίου, τὸ γένος Παμφύλου (*Rep*. 614b3–4)."
Destrée, P. 2014. "How can our Fate be Up to Us? Plato and the myth of Er." 25–38 in P. Destrée, R. Salles and M. Zingano (eds.), *What is Up to Us? Causality and Responsibility in Ancient Philosophy*. Sankt Augustin: Academia Verlag.
Detienne, M. 1967/1996. *The Masters of Truth in Archaic Greece*. Trans. J. Lloyd. Paris: F. Maspero; New York: Zone Books.
Detienne, M., and J.-P. Vernant. 1991. *Cunning Intelligence in Greek Culture and Society*. Trans. Janet Lloyd. Chicago: University of Chicago Press.
Dicks, D. R. 1966. "Solstices, Equinoxes, and the Presocratics." *Journal of Hellenic Studies* 86:26–40.
Dicks, D. R. 1970. *Early Greek Astronomy to Aristotle*. Ithaca, NY: Cornell University Press.
Diels, H., and W. Kranz. 1952. *Die Fragmente der Vorsokratiker*. 6th ed. Berlin: Wiedmann.
Dodds, E. R. 1951. *The Greeks and the Irrational*. Berkeley and Los Angeles: University of California Press.
Dodds, E. R. 1959. *Plato: Gorgias*. Oxford: Oxford University Press.
Dodds, E. R. 1966. "On Misunderstanding the *Oedipus Rex*." *Greece and Rome* 13:37–49.
Donlan, W. 1999. *The Aristocratic Ideal and Selected Papers*. Wauconda, IL: Bolchazy-Carducci Publishers.
Donzelli, G. B. 1985. "La colpa di Elena: Gorgia ed Euripide a confronto." *Siculorum Gymnasium* 38:389–409.
Dover, K. J. 1974. *Greek Popular Morality in the Time of Plato and Aristotle*. Berkeley and Los Angeles: University of California Press.
Duncan, T. S. 1938. "Gorgias' Theories of Art." *Classical Journal* 33:402–15.
Dynes, R. W., and S. Donaldson, (eds.). 1992. *Homosexuality in the Ancient World*. New York: Garland Publishing.
Easterling, P. E. 1999. "Actors and Voices: Reading between the Lines in Aeschines and Demosthenes." 154–66 in Goldhill and Osborne 1999.
Easterling, P. E. 2002. "Actor as Icon." 327–41 in Easterling and Hall 2002.

Easterling, P. E., and E. Hall (eds.) 2002. *Greek and Roman Actors: Aspects of an Ancient Profession*. Cambridge: Cambridge University Press.
Edmunds, L. 1996. *Theatrical Space and Historical Place in Sophocles' Oedipus at Colonus*. Lanham, MD: Rowman and Littlefield.
Edwards, M. W. 1987. *Homer, Poet of the Iliad*. Baltimore, MD: Johns Hopkins University Press.
Edwards, Mike. 2013. "*Hypokrites* in Action: Delivery in Greek Rhetoric." 15–25 in Kremmydas et al. 2013.
El-Shahawy, A. 2005. *Das Ägyptische Museum von Kairo. Ein Streifzug durch das Alte Ägypten*. Cairo: Farid Atiya Press.
Eldridge, R. 2001. *The Persistence of Romanticism*. Cambridge: Cambridge University Press.
Evelyn-White, H. G. (trans.) 1914. *Hesiod, Theogony*. Trans. H. G. Cambridge, MA: Harvard University Press.
Farron, S. 1979. "The Portrayal of Women in the *Iliad*." *Acta Classica* 22:15–31.
Fenik, B. 1974. *Studies in the Odyssey*. Hermes Supp. 30. Wiesbaden: Steiner.
Ferrari, G. R. F. 1989. "Plato and Poetry." 92–148 in G. A. Kennedy (ed.), *The Cambridge History of Literary Criticism*. Cambridge: Cambridge University Press.
Ferrari, G. R. F. (ed.) 2007. *The Cambridge Companion to Plato's Republic*. Cambridge: Cambridge University Press.
Ferrari, G. R. F. 2009. "Glaucon's Reward, Philosophy's Debt: The Myth of Er." 116–33 in Partenie, C. (ed.), *Plato's Myths*. Cambridge: Cambridge University Press.
Finley, M. I. 1978. *The World of Odysseus*. Rev. ed. New York: Viking Press.
Flickinger, M. K. 1933. "Who First Buried Polynices?" *Philological Quarterly* 12:130–36.
Ford, A. 1988. "The Classical Definition of *Rhapsoidia*." *Classical Philology* 83:300–07.
Ford, A. 1999. "Reading Homer from the Rostrum: Poems and Laws in Aeschines' *Against Timarchus*." 231–56 in Goldhill and Osborne 1999.
Franco, C. 2014. *Shameless: The Canine and the Feminine in Ancient Greece*. Berkeley and Los Angeles: University of California Press.
Fränkel, H. 1962/1973. *Early Greek Poetry and Philosophy*. Trans. M. Hadas and J. Willis. New York: Harcourt Brace Jovanovich.
Fränkel, H. 1974. "Xenophanes' Empiricism and his Critique of Knowledge (B34)." 118–31 in A. D. P. Mourelatos (ed.), *The Presocratics*. Garden City, NY: Anchor Books.
Friedrich, P. 1978. *The Meanings of Aphrodite*. Chicago: University of Chicago Press.
Gagarin, M. 1987. "Morality in Homer." *Classical Philology* 82:290–91.
Gagarin, M. 2001. "Did the Sophists Aim to Persuade?" *Rhetorica* 19:275–91.

Gallagher, R. L. 2004. "Protreptic Aims of Plato's *Republic*." *Ancient Philosophy* 24:293–319.
Gibbs, S. 1976. *Greek and Roman Sundials*. New Haven, CT: Yale University Press.
Gide, A. 1961. *Two Legends: Oedipus and Theseus*. Trans. J. Russell. New York: Vintage Books Publishing.
Glessmer, E., and M. Albani. 1999. "An Astronomical Measuring Instrument from Qumran." 407–442 in D. W. Parry and E. Ulrich (eds.), *The Provo International Conference on the Dead Sea Scrolls*. Leiden: Brill.
Goethe, J. W. 1998 *Conversations of Goethe with Johann Peter Eckermann*. Trans. J Oxenford. Ed. J. K. Moorhead. Cambridge, MA: Da Capo Press.
Goldhill, S. 1986. *Reading Greek Tragedy*. Cambridge: Cambridge University Press.
Goldhill, S. 1997. "The Audience of Athenian Tragedy." 54–68 in P. E. Easterling (ed), *The Cambridge Companion to Greek Tragedy*. Cambridge: Cambridge University Press.
Goldhill, S. 1999. "Programme Notes." 1–29 in Goldhill and Osborne 1999.
Goldhill, S., and R. Osborne (eds.) 1999. *Performance Culture and Athenian Democracy*. Cambridge: Cambridge University Press.
Gonzalez, F. 2012. "Combating Oblivion: The Myth of Er as Both Philosophy's Challenge and Inspiration." 259–78 in Collobert, Destrée, and Gonzalez 2012
González, J. M. 2013. *The Epic Rhapsode and His Craft*. Washington, DC: Center for Hellenic Studies.
Gould, J. 1973. "Hiketeia." *Journal of Hellenic Studies* 93:74–103. Reprinted in J. Gould, *Myth, Ritual, Memory, and Exchange* (Oxford: Oxford University Press, 2001), 22–77.
Gould, J. 1985. "On Making Sense of Greek Religion." 1–33 in P. E. Easterling and J. V. Muir (eds.), *Greek Religion and Society*. Cambridge: Cambridge University Press.
Graver, M. 1995. "Dog-Helen and Homeric Insult." *Classical Antiquity* 14:41–61.
Gravlee, G. S. 2000. "Aristotle on Hope." *Journal of the History of Philosophy* 38 (4):461–77.
Green, R. 2002. "Towards a Reconstruction of Performance Style." 93–126 in Easterling and Hall 2002.
Gregory, J. (ed.) 2005. *A Companion to Greek Tragedy*. Malden, MA: Blackwell.
Griffin, J. 1980. *Homer On Life and Death*. Oxford: Oxford University Press.
Griswold, C. 2007. *Forgiveness: A Philosophical Exploration*. Cambridge: Cambridge University Press.
Grube, G. M. A. (trans.) 1992. *Plato, The Republic*. Indianapolis, IN: Hackett.
Guthrie, W. K. C. 1962. *A History of Greek Philosophy*. vol. 1. Cambridge: Cambridge University Press.
Gutjahr, O. 2010. *Ödipus, Tyrann von Sophokles*. Würzburg: Königshausen & Newmann Verlag.

Hackforth, R. 1952. *Plato's Phaedrus*. Cambridge: Cambridge University Press.
Hadot, P. 2002. *What is Ancient Philosophy?* Trans. M. Chase. Cambridge, MA: Harvard University Press.
Hahn, R. 2001. *Anaximander and the Architects: The Contributions of Egyptian and Greek Architectural Technologies to the Origins of Greek Philosophy*. Albany: State University of New York Press.
Hahn, R. 2010. *Archaeology and the Origins of Philosophy*. Albany: State University of New York Press.
Hahn, R., D. Couprie, and G. Naddaf (eds.) 2003. *Anaximander in Context: New Studies in the Origins of Greek Philosophy*. Albany: State University of New York Press.
Hall, E. 2002. "The Singing Actors of Antiquity." 3–38 in Easterling and Hall 2002.
Hall, E. 2006. *The Theatrical Cast of Athens: Interactions between Ancient Greek Drama and Society*. Oxford: Oxford University Press.
Halliwell, S. 1988. *Plato Republic 10: With an Introduction, Translation and Commentary*. Warminster: Aris and Phillips.
Halliwell, S. 1990. "Traditional Greek Conceptions of Character." 32–59 in C. Pelling (ed.), *Characterization and Individuality in Greek Literature*. Oxford: Oxford University Press.
Halliwell, S. 1993. "The Function and Aesthetics of the Greek Tragic Mask." 195–211 in N. Slater and B. Zimmermann (eds.), *Intertextualität in der griechisch-römischen Komödie*. Stuttgart: M&P.
Halliwell, S. 1996. "Plato's Repudiation of the Tragic." 332–49 in M. S. Silk (ed.), *Tragedy and the Tragic*. Oxford: Oxford University Press.
Halliwell, S. 1997. "Between Public and Private: Tragedy and Athenian Experience of Rhetoric." 121–41 in C. Pelling (ed.), *Greek Tragedy and the Historian*. Oxford: The Clarendon Press.
Halliwell, S. 2000. "The Subjection of Muthos to Logos: Plato's Citation of the Poets." *The Classical Quarterly* 50:94–112.
Halliwell, S. 2002. *The Aesthetics of Mimesis*. Princeton, NJ: Princeton University Press.
Halliwell, S. 2007. "The Life-and-Death Journey of the Soul: Interpreting the Myth of Er." 445–73 in Ferrari 2007.
Hammer, D. 2002. "The *Iliad* as Ethical Thinking: Politics, Pity, and the Operation of Esteem." *Arethusa* 35:203–35.
Hannah, R. 2005. *Greek and Roman Calendars: Constructions of Time in the Ancient World*. London: Duckworth.
Hare, R. M. 1952. *The Language of Morals*. Oxford: Oxford University Press.
Hare, R. M. 1963. *Freedom and Reason*. Oxford: Oxford University Press.
Hartland-Swann, J. 1951. "Plato as Poet. A Critical Interpretation." *Philosophy* 26.96:3–18 and 26.97:131–41.
Hatab, L. 1990. *Myth and Philosophy: A Contest of Truths*. Chicago: Open Court.

Hatab, L. 2008. *Nietzsche's On the Genealogy of Morality: An Introduction.* Cambridge: Cambridge University Press.
Havelock, E. A. 1963. *Preface to Plato.* Cambridge, MA: Harvard University Press.
Heath, T. L. 1921. *A History of Greek Mathematics.* Oxford: The Clarendon Press.
Hegel, G. W. F. 1962. *Hegel on Tragedy,* ed. A. and H. Paolucci. Garden City: Anchor Books.
Heidegger, M. 2000. *Introduction to Metaphysics.* Trans. G. Fried and R. Polt. New Haven, CT: Yale University Press.
Heidegger, M. 2002. *Grundbegriffe der aristotelischen Philosophie.* Frankfurt am Main: V. Klostermann.
Heidel, W. A. 1937. *The Frame of the Ancient Greek Maps. With a Discussion of the Discovery of the Sphericity of the Earth.* New York: American Geographical Society.
Heiden, B. 1997. "The Ordeals of Homeric Song." *Arethusa* 30:221–40.
Herington, J. 1985. *Poetry into Drama: Early Tragedy and the Greek Poetic Tradition.* Berkeley and Los Angeles: University of California Press.
Herman, G. 1987. *Ritualized Friendship and the Greek City.* Cambridge: Cambridge University Press.
Herrero de Jáuregui, M. 2011. "Priam's Catabasis: Traces of the Epic Journey to Hades in Iliad 24." *Transactions of the American Philological Association* 14:37–68.
Herron, M. 2017. *The Anatomy of Myth.* Oxford: Oxford University Press.
Hesk, J. 1999. "The Rhetoric of Anti-Rhetoric in Athenian Oratory." 201–30 in Goldhill and Osborne 1999.
Holmberg, I. 1995. "Euripides' *Helen*: Most Noble and Most Chaste." *American Journal of Philology* 116:19–42.
Holmes, B. 2010. *The Symptom and the Subject: The Emergence of the Physical Body in Ancient Greece.* Princeton, NJ: Princeton University Press.
Homeyer, H. 1977. *Die spartanische Helene und der trojanische Krieg: Wandlungen und Wanderungen eines Sagen-Kreises vom Altertum bis zur Gegenwart = Palingenesia* 12. Wiesbaden: Steiner.
Howland, J. 1993. *The Republic: The Odyssey of Philosophy.* Philadelphia: Paul Dry Books.
Howland, J. 2005. "Storytelling and Philosophy in Plato's *Republic*." *American Catholic Philosophical Quarterly* 79.2:213–32.
Hussey, E. 1972. *The Presocratics.* London: Duckwoth.
Hussey, E. 1990. "The Beginnings of Epistemology." 11–38 in S. Everson (ed.), *Companions to Ancient Thought 1: Epistemology.* Cambridge: Cambridge University Press.
Hussey, E. 1999. "Heraclitus." 88–112 in Long 1999.
Irwin, T. 1997. "Plato's Objections to the Sophists." 568–90 in A. Powell (ed.), *The Greek World.* London: Routledge.
Jaeger, W. 1947. *Paideia.* Oxford: Oxford University Press.

Jebb, R. C. 1891. *Sophocles: The Plays and Fragment*. Part III: *The Antigone*. Cambridge: Cambridge University Press.
Jebb, R. C. 1894. *Homer: An Introduction to the Iliad and Odyssey*. London: James Maclehose and Sons.
Johannes, H. 1937. "Saulenbasen von Heratempel des Rhoikos." *Mitteilungen des deutschen archaologischen Instituts, Athenische Abteilung* 62:13–37.
Johansen, T. K. 1999. "Myth and *Logos* in Aristotle." 279–91 in Buxton 1999.
Johnson, R. R. 1999. "Does Plato's Myth of Er Contribute to the Argument of the *Republic*?" *Philosophy and Rhetoric* 32:1–13.
Jones, P. J. 2003. *Homer's Iliad. A Commentary on Three Translations*. London: Bristol Classical Press.
Jones, P. J. 1988. *Homer's Odyssey*. Bristol: Bristol Classical Press.
Just, R. 1989. *Women in Athenian Law and Life*. London: Routledge.
Kamerbeek, J. C. 1978. *Sophocles' Antigone*. Leiden: Brill.
Kaufmann, W. (trans.) 2000. *Basic Writings of Nietzsche*. New York: Random House.
Kemball-Cook, B. (trans.). 1993. *Homer. Odyssey*. New York: Calliope Press.
Kerenyi, C. 1973. *The Religion of the Greeks and Romans*. Trans. C. Holme. Westport, CT: Greenwood Press.
Kerferd, G. B. 1981. *The Sophistic Movement*. Cambridge: Cambridge University Press.
Kern, O. 1922. *Orphicorum fragmenta*. Berlin: Weidmann.
Kienast, H. 1991. "Fundamentieren in Schwierigem Gelande: Fallenstudien aus dem Heraion von Samos." 123–27 in A. Hoffmann (ed.), *Bautechnik der Antike*, band 5. Mainz: Phillipp von Zabern.
Kirk, G. S. 1974. *The Nature of Greek Myths*. Harmondsworth: Penguin Books.
Kirk, G. S. 1985. *The Iliad: A Commentary*. Volume 1; books 1–4. Cambridge: Cambridge University Press.
Kirk, G. S., J. E. Raven, and M. Schofield. 1983. *The Presocratic Philosophers*, 2nd ed. Cambridge: Cambridge University Press.
Kirkland, S. 2014. "Tragic Time." 51–67 in Chanter, T., and S. Kirkland (eds.), *The Returns of Antigone: Interdisciplinary Essays*. Albany: State University of New York Press.
Knox, B. 1964. *The Heroic Temper: Studies in Sophoclean Tragedy*. Berkeley and Los Angeles: University of California Press.
Knox, B. 1982. "Introduction" and notes. *Sophocles: The Three Theban Plays*. Trans. R. Fagles. New York: Penguin Books.
Knox, B. 1998. *Oedipus at Thebes*. New Haven, CT: Yale University Press.
Kočandrle, R., and Couprie, D. 2017. *Anaximander on Generation and Destruction*. Berlin: Springer.
Konstan, D. 2006. *The Emotions of the Ancient Greeks: Studies in Aristotle and Classical Literature*. Toronto: University of Toronto Press.

Kosman, A. 1992. "Acting: *Drama* as the *Mimēsis* of *Praxis*." 51–72 in A. O Rorty (ed.), *Essays on Aristotle's Poetics*. Princeton, NJ: Princeton University Press.

Kremmydas, C., J. Powell, and L. Rubinstein (eds.). 2013. *Profession and Performance. Aspects of Oratory in the Greco-Roman World*. London: Institute of Classical Studies.

Lada-Richards, I. 2002. "The Subjectivity of Greek Performance." 395–418 in Easterling and Hall.

Lake, P. 2011. "Plato's Homeric Dialogue: Homeric Quotation, Paraphrase, and Allusion in the *Republic*." *ETD Collection for Fordham University*. AAI3474142. https://fordham.bepress.com/dissertations/AAI3474142.

Laks, A. 2018. *The Concept of Ancient Philosophy*. Trans. G. Most. Princeton, NJ: Princeton University Press.

Lattimore, R. (trans.) 1951. *Homer, The Iliad*. Chicago: University of Chicago Press.

Lattimore, R. (trans.) 1959. *Hesiod*. Ann Arbor: University of Michigan Press.

Lattimore, R. (trans.) 1965. *The Odyssey of Homer*. New York: Harper Collins.

Lear, J. 2006. "Allegory and Myth in Plato's *Republic*." 25–43 in G. Santas (ed), *Blackwell's Companion to Plato's Republic* Malden, MA: Blackwell.

Lee, K. H. 1976. *Euripides: Troades*. Bristol: Bristol Classical Press.

Lesher, J. H. 1992. *Xenophanes of Colophon-Fragments: Text and Translation with Notes and Commentary*. Toronto: University of Toronto Press.

Lesher, J. H. 1999. "Early Interest in Knowledge." 225–70 in Long 1999.

Lesher, J. H. 2009. "Archaic Knowledge." 13–28 in Wians 2009b.

Lesky, A. 1961. *Göttliche und menschliche Motivation im homerischen Epos*. Heidelberg: C. Winter.

Lloyd-Jones, H. 1971. *The Justice of Zeus*, 2nd ed. Berkeley and Los Angeles: University of California Press.

Lloyd-Jones, H. (trans.) 1994. *Sophocles, Volume I. Ajax. Electra. Oedipus Tyrannus*. Cambridge, MA: Harvard University Press.

Lloyd, G. E. R. 1987. *The Revolutions of Wisdom*. Berkeley and Los Angeles: University of California Press.

Lloyd, G. E. R. 1999. "Mythology: Reflections from a Chinese Perspective." 145–65 in Buxton 1999.

Lloyd, M. 1984. "The Helen Scene in Euripides' *Troades*." *Classical Quarterly* 34:303–13.

Lloyd, M. 1992. *The Agon in Euripides*. Oxford: Oxford University Press.

Lombardo, S. 1953. *Hesiod. Works and Days, Theogony*. Indianapolis, IN/Cambridge: Hackett.

Long, A. A. (ed.) 1999. *The Cambridge Companion to Early Greek Philosophy*. Cambridge: Cambridge University Press.

Long, A. A. 2011. "Poets as Philosophers and Philosophers as Poets." 293–308 in B. Huss, P. Marzillo, and T. Ricklin (eds.) 2011. *Para/Textuelle Verhandlungen. Zwischen Dichtung und Philosophe in der frühen Neuzeit*. Göttingen: De Gruyter.
Lonsdale, S. H. 1979. "Attitudes towards Animals in Ancient Greece." *Greece and Rome* 26.2:146–59.
Loraux, N. 1979. "L'autochtonie, une topique athénienne. Le mythe dans l'espace civique." *Annales (ESC)* 34:3–26. Trans. C. Levine as "Autochthony: An Athenian Topic," in *The Children of Athena*. Princeton, NJ: Princeton University Press, 1993.
Lynn-George, M. 1996. "Structures of Care in the *Iliad*." *Classical Quarterly* 46:1–26.
MacDowell, D. M. (ed.) 1982. *Gorgias: Encomium of Helen*. Bristol: Bristol Classical Press.
MacDowell, D. M. 1978. *The Law in Classical Athens*. Ithaca, NY: Cornell University Press.
Mansfeld, J. 2000. "Presocratics Myth Doxography," *Phronesis* 45:341–356.
Marchant C. E., and W. G. Bowersock (trans.). 1925. *Xenophon Scripta Minora VII*. Cambridge, MA: Harvard University Press.
Marshall, C. W. 1999. "Some Fifth-Century Masking Conventions." *Greece and Rome* 46:188–202.
Martin, R. P. 1989. *The Language of Heroes: Speech and Performance in the Iliad*. Ithaca, NY: Cornell University Press.
McCall, M. 1972. "Divine and Human Action in Sophocles: The Two Burials of the *Antigone*." 103–18 in A. Parry (ed.), *Studies in Fifth Century Thought and Literature*. New Haven, CT: Yale University Press.
McCoy, M. 1999. "Socrates on Simonides: The Use of Poetry in Socratic and Platonic Rhetoric." *Philosophy and Rhetoric* 32.4:349–67.
McPherran, M. 2010. "Virtue, Luck, and Choice at the End of the *Republic*." 132–46 in M. McPherran (ed.), *Plato's Republic. A Critical Guide*. Cambridge: Cambridge University Press.
Meikeljohn, K. W. 1932. "The Burial of Polynices." *Classical Review* 46:4–5.
Meineck P., and P. Woodruff 2000. *Sophocles: Oedipus Tyrannus*. Indianapolis, IN: Hackett.
Michelini, A. 1987. *Euripides and the Tragic Tradition*. Madison: University of Wisconsin Press.
Mikics, D. 2011. "The Unexamined Socrates." Review of P. Johnson, *Socrates: A Man for Our Times* (New York: Viking Press, 2011). *The New Republic*, online.
Miller Jr., F. D. 2009. "Homer's Challenge to Philosophical Psychology." 29–50 in Wians 2009b.
Miščević, N. 2012. "Plato's *Republic* as a Political Thought Experiment." *Croatian Journal of Philosophy* 12.2:153–65.

Morgan, K. 2000. *Myth and Philosophy from the Presocratics to Plato*. Cambridge: Cambridge University Press.
Morgan, M. H. 1914. *Vitruvius. The Ten Books on Architecture*. Cambridge, MA: Harvard University Press.
Mossman, J. 2005. "Women's Voices." 352–65 in Gregory 2005.
Most, G. 1999a. "The Poetics of Early Greek Philosophy." 332–62 in Long 1999.
Most, G. 1999b. "From *Logos* to *Muthos*." 25–47 in Buxton 1999.
Most, G. (tr.) 2006. *Hesiod: Theogony, Works and Days, Testimonia*. Cambridge, MA: Harvard University Press.
Mourelatos, A. D. P. 2014. "The Conception of *eoikos/eikos* as Epistemic Standard." *Ancient Philosophy* 34:169–91.
Mourelatos, A. P. D. 2008. *The Route of Parmenides*. 2nd ed. Las Vegas, NV: Parmenides Publishing.
Muellner, L. 1996. *The Anger of Achilles: Mēnis in Greek Epic*. Ithaca, NY: Cornell University Press.
Murray, A. T. (trans.) 1995. *Homer, The Odyssey*, 2nd ed. Cambridge, MA: Harvard University Press.
Murray, G. 1924. *The Rise of the Greek Epic*. Oxford: Oxford University Press.
Naddaf, G. "Allegory and the Origins of Philosophy." 99–131 in Wians 2009b.
Naddaff, R. 2009. "No Second Troy: Imagining Helen in Greek Antiquity." 73–97 in Wians 2009b.
Nagy, G. 1996. *Poetry as Performance: Homer and Beyond*. Cambridge: Cambridge University Press.
Nestle, W. 1940. *Vom Mythos zu Logos: Die Selbstentfaltung des griechischen Denkens von Homer bis auf dis Sophistik und Sokrates*. Stuttgart: Kröner.
Netz, R. 1999. *The Shaping of Deduction*. Cambridge: Cambridge University Press.
Neuberg, M. 1991. "Clytemnestra and the Alastor (Aeschylus, *Agamemnon* 1497ff)." *Quaderni Urbinati di Cultura Classica* 38:37–68.
Nietzsche, F. 1962. *Philosophy in the Tragic Ages of Greeks*. Trans. M. Cowan. Washington, DC: Regnery Gateway.
Nightingale, A. W. 1995. *Genres in Dialogue. Plato and the Construct of Philosophy*. Cambridge: Cambridge University Press.
Norwood, G. 1960. *Greek Tragedy*. New York: Hill and Wang.
Nussbaum, M. C. 1986. *The Fragility of Goodness: Luck and Ethics in Greek Tragedy and Philosophy*. Cambridge: Cambridge University Press.
O'Connor, D. 2007. "Rewriting the Poets in Plato's Characters." 55–89 in Ferrari 2007.
Ober, J., and B. Strauss. 1990. "Drama, Political Rhetoric, and the Discourse of Athenian Democracy." 237–70 in J. J. Winkler and F. I. Zeitlin (eds.), *Nothing to Do with Dionysos?* Princeton: Princeton University Press.
Oele, M. 2010. "Suffering, Pity and Friendship: An Aristotelian Reading of Book 24 of Homer's *Iliad*." *Electronic Antiquity* 14:51–65.

Oele, M. 2012. "Passive Dispositions: on the Relationship between Πάθος and Ἕξις in Aristotle." *Ancient Philosophy* 32:351–68.

Ogden, C. K., and I. A. Richards. 1936. *The Meaning of Meaning*. London: Routledge and Kegan Paul.

Osborne, R. 1997. "The Polis and its Culture." 9–46 in C. C. W. Taylor (ed.), *The Routledge History of Philosophy, vol. 1: From the Beginnings to Plato*. London: Routledge.

Ostwald, M. 1962 (trans.). *Aristotle, Nicomachean Ethics*. Englewood Cliffs, NJ: Prentice-Hall.

Padilla Longoria, M. T. 2011. "Platon como amante de la poesia en las *leyes y su influencia en los inicios de la edad moderna*." 179–94 in Huss, Marzillo, and Ricklin 2011.

Parker, V. 1998. "Τύραννος. The Semantics of a Political Concepts from Archilochus to Aristotle." *Hermes* 126(2):145–72.

Parry, M. 1936. "On Typical Scenes in Homer." Review of Walter Arend, *Die Typischen Scenen bei Homer* (Berlin, 1933), *Classical Philology* 31:357–60; reprinted in Adam Parry, *The Making of Homeric Verse: The Collected Papers of Milman Parry*. Oxford: Oxford University Press, 414–18.

Pater, W. 1883. *Plato and Platonism*. London: Macmillan.

Pelling, C. 2005. "Tragedy, Rhetoric, and Performance Culture." 83–102 in Gregory 2005.

Peradotto, J. 1990. *Man in the Middle Voice: Name and Narration in the Odyssey*. Princeton, NJ: Princeton University Press.

Pitt-Rivers, J. 1986. "The Stranger, The Guest and the Hostile Host." 13–30 in J. G. Peristiany (ed.), *Contributions to Mediterranean Sociology*. Paris and The Hague: Moulton.

Platt, A. 1911. "Plato, *Republic* 614b." *Classical Review* 25:13–14.

Porter, J. 1993. "The Seductions of Gorgias." *Classical Antiquity* 13:267–99.

Poulakos, J. 1983. "Gorgias' *Encomium to Helen* and the Defense of Rhetoric." *Rhetorica* 1:1–16.

Price, A. W. 1994. "Wordsworth's *Ode on the Intimations of Immortality*." 217–29 in A. Baldwin and S. Hutton (eds.), *Platonism and the English Imagination*. Cambridge: Cambridge University Press.

Prier, R. A. 1989. *Thauma Idesthai*. Gainesville, FL: Florida State University Press.

Raaflaub, K. 1997. "Homer's Society." 624–48 in I. Morris and B. Powell (eds.), *A New Companion to Homer*. Leiden: Brill.

Ready, J. L., and C. Tsagalis (eds.) 2018. *Homer in Performance: Rhapsodes, Characters, and Narrators*. Austin: University of Texas Press.

Reckford, K. J. 1964. "Helen in the *Iliad*." *Greek, Roman, and Byzantine Studies* 5:5–20.

Redfield, J. M. 1975. *Nature and Culture in the Iliad: The Tragedy of Hector*. Chicago: University of Chicago Press.

Reece, S. 1993. *The Stranger's Welcome*. Ann Arbor: The University of Michigan Press.
Reeve, C. D. C. 2009. "Luck and Virtue in Pindar, Aeschylus, and Sophocles." 215–232 in Wians 2009b.
Reeve, C. D. C. 2012. *Blindness and Re-Orientation: Problems in Plato's Republic*. Oxford: Oxford University Press.
Rehm, A., and G. Kawerau. 1914. *Das Delphinion in Milet. Milet, Ergebnisse der Ausgrabungen und Untersuchungen seit dem Jahre 1899*. Berlin: Konigsliche Museum zu Berlin.
Reinhardt, K. 1993. *Sophokles*. Frankfurt am Mein: Klostermann.
Robb, K. 1994. *Literacy and Paideia in Ancient Greece*. Oxford: Oxford University Press.
Rochberg, F. 1995. "Astronomy and Calendars in Ancient Mesopotamia." 1925–1940 in J. M. Sisson (ed.), *Civilizations of the Ancient Near East*. New York: Scribner.
Roisman, H. M. 2006. "Helen in the *Iliad*; *Causa Belli* and Victim of War: From Silent Weaver to Public Speaker." *American Journal of Philology* 127:1–36.
Romilly, J. de. 1992. *The Great Sophists in Periclean Athens*. Oxford: Oxford University Press.
Roochnik, D. 2003. *Beautiful City: The Dialectical Character of Plato's Republic*. Ithaca, NY: Cornell University Press.
Rosen, S. 2005. *Plato's Republic: A Study*. New Haven, CT: Yale University Press.
Roth, P. 1993. "The Theme of Corrupted *Xenia* in Aeschylus's *Oresteia*." *Mnemosyne* 46:1–17.
Rouse, W. H. D. 1911. "The Two Burials in *Antigone*." *Classical Review* 25:40–42
Sachs, J. (trans.). 2002. *Aristotle: Nicomachean Ethics*. Newburyport, MA: Focus Publishing.
Sallis, J. 1996. *Being and Logos: Reading the Platonic Dialogues*. Bloomington: Indiana University Press.
Sallis, J. 2012. *Logic of Imagination: The Expanse of the Elemental*. Bloomington: Indiana University Press.
Samuel, A. E. 1972. *Greek and Roman Chronology: Calendars and Years in Classical Antiquity*. Munich: C. H. Beck Verlag.
Sansone, D. 2012. *Greek Drama and the Invention of Rhetoric*. Malden, MA: Blackwell.
Santas, G. 2010. *Understanding Plato's Republic*. Hoboken, NJ: Wiley-Blackwell.
Saxonhouse, A. 1992. *Fear of Diversity: The Birth of Political Science in Ancient Greek Thought*. Chicago: University of Chicago Press.
Schein, S. L. 1984. *The Mortal Hero: An Introduction to Homer's Iliad*. Berkeley and Los Angeles: University of California Press.
Schloemann, J. 2002. "Entertainment and Democratic Distrust." 133–46 in I. Worthington and J. M. Foley (eds.), *Epea and Grammata: Oral and Written Communication in Ancient Greece*. Leiden: Brill.

Schmiel, R. 1987. "Achilles in Hades." *Classical Philology* 82:35–37.
Schultz, A. M. 2013. *Plato's Socrates as Narrator: A Philosophical Muse*. Lanham, MD: Lexington Books.
Scodel, R. 1998. "The Captive's Dilemma: Sexual Acquiescence in Euripides *Hecuba* and *Troades*." *Harvard Studies in Classical Philology* 98:137–54.
Scodel, R. 1999/2000. "Verbal Performance and Euripidean Rhetoric." *Illinois Classical Studies* 24–25:129–44.
Scodel, R. 2008. *Epic Facework: Self-Presentation and Social Interaction in Homer*. Swansea: Classical Press of Wales.
Segal, C. 1978. "'The Myth Was Saved': Reflections on Homer and the Mythology of Plato's *Republic*." *Hermes* 106/2:315–36.
Segal, C. 1981. *Tragedy and Civilization: An Interpretation of Sophocles*. Harvard, MA: Cambridge University Press.
Segal, C. 1994. *Singers, Heroes, and Gods in the Odyssey*. Ithaca, NY: Cornell University Press.
Segal, R. 2004. *Myth: A Very Short Introduction*. Oxford: Oxford University Press.
Seneca. 1983. *Oedipus*. Adapted by Ted Hughes. London: Faber and Faber.
Shawcross, T. 1909. *Shelley's Literary and Philosophical Criticism*. London: Henry Frowde.
Shear, T. L. 2016. *Trophies of Victory: Public Building in Periklean Athens*. Princeton, NJ: Princeton University Press.
Sheehan, S. 2012. *Sophocles' Oedipus the King: The Reader's Guide*. New York: Continuum.
Shelley, P. B. 1975. *A Defence of Poetry*, ed. J. E. Jordan. Indianapolis, IN: Bobbs-Merrill.
Sheppard, J. T. 1947. *The Wisdom of Sophocles*. London: Allen and Unwin.
Slater, N. W. 1990. "The Idea of the Actor." 385–95 in Winkler and Zeitlin 1990.
Smith, M. F. 1975. *Lucretius. De Rerum Natura*. Cambridge: Harvard University Press.
Smith, N. 2001. "Some Thoughts about the Origins of 'Greek Ethics'" *Journal of Ethics* 5:3–20.
Smith, P. C. 2002. "Nietzsche and Gadamer: From Strife to Understanding, Achilles/Agamemnon to Achilles/Priam." *Continental Philosophy Review* 35:379–96.
Smith, P. C. 2009. "Poetic *Peithô* as Original Speech." 199–213 in Wians 2009b.
Snell, B. 1953. *The Discovery of the Mind*. Trans. T. G. Rosenmeyer. Cambridge, MA: Harvard University Press.
Sontag, S. 2003. *Regarding the Pain of Others*. New York: Farrar, Straus and Giroux.
Sorabji, R. 1996. "Rationality." 311–34 in M. Frede and G. Striker (eds.), *Rationality in Greek Thought*. Oxford: The Clarendon Press.
Sourvinou-Inwood, C.1996. *"Reading" Greek Death*. Oxford: The Clarendon Press.

Steiner, D. T. 2001. *Images in Mind: Statues in Archaic and Classical Greek Literature and Thought*. Princeton, NJ: Princeton University Press.
Stevenson, C. L. 1937. "The Emotive Meaning of Ethical Terms." *Mind* 46:14–31.
Stevenson, C. L. 1944. *Ethics and Language*. New Haven, CT: Yale University Press.
Stevenson, C. L. 1963. *Facts and Values: Studies in Ethical Analysis*. New Haven, CT: Yale University Press.
Strassler, B. R. (ed.). 1998. *The Landmark Thucydides*. New York: Touchstone Publishing.
Strassler, B. R. (ed.). 2007. *The Landmark Herodotus: The Histories*. New York: Pantheon Books.
Tanner, S. 2010. *In Praise of Plato's Poetic Imagination*. Lanham, MD: Lexington Books.
Taplin, O. 1992. *Homeric Soundings*. Oxford: Oxford University Press.
Teffeteller, A. 2003. "Homeric Excuses." *Classical Quarterly* 53:15–31.
Thompson, C. R. (trans.) 1957. *Ten Colloquies of Erasmus*. Indianapolis, IN: Bobbs-Merrill.
Thomson, G. 1955. *The First Philosophers: Studies in Ancient Greek Society*. 2 vols. London: Lawrence & Wishart.
Tomlinson, R. A. 1976. *Greek Sanctuaries*. London: Paul Elek.
Trümpy, C. 1997. *Untersuchungen zu den altgriechischen Monatsnamen und Monatsfolgen*. Heidelberg: C. Winter.
Tsagalis, C. 2018. "Performance Contexts for Rhapsodic Recitals in the Archaic and Classical Periods." In Ready and Tsagalis 2018.
Urmson, J. O. 1958. "Saints and Heroes." 198–216 in A. I. Melden (ed.), *Essays in Moral Philosophy*. Seattle: University of Washington Press.
Urmson, J. O. 1968. *The Emotive Theory of Ethics*. Oxford: Oxford University Press.
Valakas, K. 2002. 'The Use of the Body by Actors in Tragedy and Satyr-Play." 69–92 in Easterling and Hall 2002.
Verdenius, W. J. 1985. *A Commentary on Hesiod. Works and Days* vols. 1–382. Leiden: Brill.
Vernant, J.-P. 1996. *Myth and Tragedy in Ancient Greece*. Trans. J. Lloyd. New York, NY: Zone Books.
Vernant, J.-P. 1962/1982. *The Origins of Greek Thought*. Ithaca, NY: Cornell University Press.
Vernant, J.-P. 1965/2006. *Myth and Thought among the Ancient Greeks*, 2nd ed. Trans. J. Lloyd with Jeff Fort. New York: Zone Books.
Vernant, J.-P. 1974/1990. *Myth and Society in Ancient Greece*. Trans. J. Lloyd. New York: Zone Books.
Vernant, J.-P. 1991. "*Psuchē*: Simulacrum of the Body or Image of the Divine?" 186–92 in F. Zeitlin (ed.), *Mortals and Immortals*. Princeton, NJ: Princeton University Press.

Versnel, H. S. 2011. *Coping With the Gods: Wayward Readings in Greek Theology.* Leiden: Brill.
Waterfield, R. 2018. *Creators, Conquerors, and Citizens: A History of Ancient Greece.* Oxford: Oxford University Press.
Weil, S. 1991. *The Iliad, or the Poem of Force.* Trans. M. McCarthy. Emeryville: The Lapis Press.
Weiss, R. 1998. *Socrates Dissatisfied: An Analysis of Plato's Crito.* Oxford: Oxford University Press.
West, M. L. 1966. *Hesiod, Theogony: edited with Prolegomena and Commentary.* Oxford: Oxford University Press.
West, M. L. 1971. *Early Greek Philosophy and the Orient.* Oxford: Oxford University Press.
West, M. L. 1983. *The Orphic Poems.* Oxford: The Clarendon Press.
Westerink, L. G. 1976. *Introduction to The Greek Commentaries on Plato's Phaedo, Vol. I. Olympiodorus.* Amsterdam: North-Holland Publishing Company.
Wians, W. 1996. "Odysseus the Harper." *Journal of Education* 178.3:1–16.
Wians, W. 2008. "Aristotle and the Problem of Human Knowledge." *International Journal of the Platonic Tradition* 2:41–64.
Wians, W. 2009a. "The Agamemnon and Human Knowledge." 181–98 in Wians 2009b.
Wians, W. 2009b. Wians, W. (ed.) *Logos and Muthos: Philosophical Essays in Greek Literature.* Albany: State University of New York Press.
Wians, W. 2016. Review of H. Haarmann, *Myth as source of knowledge in early Western thought. Bryn Mawr Classical Review* 2016.01.14.
Wickkiser, L. B. 2008. *Asclepius, Medicine, and the Politics of Healing in Fifth Century Greece: Between Craft and Cult.* Baltimore, MD: Johns Hopkins University Press.
Williams, B. 1993. *Shame and Necessity.* Berkeley and Los Angeles: University of California Press.
Winkler, J. J., and F. I. Zeitlin (eds.). 1990. *Nothing to Do with Dionysos?* Princeton, NJ: Princeton University Press.
Winnington-Ingram, R. P. 1980. *Sophocles: An Interpretation.* Cambridge: Cambridge University Press.
Woodruff, P. 2009. "Sophocles' Humanism." 233–54 in Wians 2009b.
Woodruff, P. 2015. "Virtues of Imperfection." *The Journal of Value Inquiry* 49/4:597–604.
Woozley, A. D. 1979. *Law and Obedience: The Arguments of Plato's Crito.* Chapel Hill: University of North Carolina Press.
Wordsworth, W. 1923. *The Poetical Works* ed. T. Hutchinson. Oxford: Oxford University Press.
Worman, N. 1997. "The Body as Argument: Helen in Four Greek Texts." *Classical Antiquity* 16:151–203.

Worman, N. 2001. "This Voice Which Is Not One: Helen's Verbal Guises in Homeric Epic." 19–37 in A Lardinois and L. McClure (eds.), *Making Silence Speak: Women's Voices in Greek Literature and Society*. Princeton NJ: Princeton University Press.

Worman, N. 2002. *The Cast of Character: Style in Greek Literature*. Austin: University of Texas Press.

Wyles, R. 2011. *Costume in Greek Tragedy*. London: Bristol Classical Press.

Yamagata, N. 1994. *Homeric Morality*. Leiden: Brill.

Yamagata, N. 2005. 'Plato, Memory, and Performance." *Oral Tradition* 20/1:111–29.

Yunis, H. 2007. "The Protreptic Rhetoric of the *Republic*." 1–26 in Ferrari 2007.

Zanker, G. 1994. *The Heart of Achilles: Characterization and Personal Ethics in the Iliad*. Ann Arbor: University of Michigan Press.

Zimmerman, E. J. 1966. *Dictionary of Classical Mythology*. New York: Harper and Row.

Zimmermann, B. 2000. "Sein und Schein im König Oidipus des Sophokles." *Freiburg Universitätsblätter* 48(1):21–33.

Zimmermann, B. 2005. *Die Griechische Tragödie*. Düsseldorf: Patmos Verlag.

About the Contributors

Ruby Blondell is a Professor of Classics and Byron W. and Alice L. Lockwood Professor in the Humanities at the University of Washington in Seattle. She has published widely on Greek literature and philosophy, and on the reception of myth in popular culture. Her books include *The Play of Character in Plato's Dialogues* (Cambridge 2002); *Women on the Edge: Four Plays by Euripides* (co-authored) (Routledge 1999); *Helping Friends and Harming Enemies. A Study in Sophocles and Greek Ethics* (Cambridge 1989); and *Helen of Troy: Beauty, Myth, Devastation* (Oxford 2013). She is currently writing a book on the portrayal of Helen in film and television.

Luc Brisson, Director of Research [Emeritus] at the National Center for Scientific Research (Paris [Villejuif], France), is known for his works on both Plato and Plotinus, including bibliographies, translations, and commentaries. He has also published numerous works on the history of philosophy and religions in Antiquity. Recent publications include Platon, *Œuvres complètes* (Flammarion, 2008), Plotin, *Traités* 51–54 and Porphyre, *Vie de Plotin* (Flammarion, 2010), and *Platon. L'écrivain qui inventa la philosophie* (Cerf, 2017).

Pierre Destrée is Associate Research Professor at the University of Louvain/FNRS (Belgium). He is the author of numerous articles in ancient Greek philosophy, mostly on Plato and Aristotle. He has edited several books, most recently *The Cambridge Companion to Aristotle's Politics* (2013), *The Blackwell Companion to Ancient Aesthetics* (2015), *Plato-Symposium—A Critical Guide* (CUP 2017). His current projects include a book-length study of Aristotle's *Poetics*, and the role of laughter and humor in ancient Greek philosophy.

Robert Hahn is Professor of Philosophy at Southern Illinois University–Carbondale and Director of the Ancient Legacies traveling seminars to Greece, Turkey, and Egypt. He is the author of *The Metaphysics of the Pythagorean Theorem: Thales, Pythagoras, Engineering, Diagrams, and the Construction of the Cosmos out of Right Triangles*; *Archaeology and the Origins of Philosophy, Anaximander in Context* [co-author]; and *Anaximander and the Architects: The Contributions of Egyptian and Greek Architectural Technologies to the Origins of Greek Philosophy*. A recent essay "Heraclitus, Milesian Monism, and the Felting of Wool" appears in *Heraklit im Kontext*. The focus of his work has been to explore how and why philosophy began in eastern Greece in the sixth century BCE.

Lawrence J. Hatab is Louis I. Jaffe Professor of Philosophy and Eminent Scholar Emeritus at Old Dominion University. He is the author of *Myth and Philosophy: A Contest of Truths* (1990), *A Nietzschean Defense of Democracy: An Experiment in Postmodern Politics* (1995), *Ethics and Finitude: Heideggerian Contributions to Moral Philosophy* (2000), *Nietzsche's Life Sentence: Coming to Terms With Eternal Recurrence* (2005), *Nietzsche's On the Genealogy of Morality* (2008), and *Proto-Phenomenology and the Nature of Language* (2017), along with several articles and essays on ancient Greek thought.

A. A. Long is Chancellor's Professor of Classics Emeritus and Irving-Stone Professor of Literature Emeritus at the University of California–Berkeley. He has published widely on Greek and Roman literature and ancient philosophy. His first book was *Language and Thought in Sophocles*, and his most recent works include *Seneca, Letters on Ethics* (with Margaret Graver) and *Greek Models of Mind and Self*.

Marina Marren is a Postdoctoral Fellow with the Department of Philosophy at the American University in Cairo. Marren's research focuses on ancient Greek philosophy and literature, especially Plato, Aristotle, and the dramatists. Her interests extend into the philosophy of art, imagination, psychology, and politics. Marren's research on temporality appears in *The Humanistic Psychologist* as well as in the volume, *On Time: Philosophical, Theological, and Literary Accounts*. Her forthcoming article on the transformative power of art will be printed in the special issue of *Pli: The Warwick Journal of Philosophy*.

Marina McCoy is Associate Professor of Philosophy at Boston College. She is the author of *Plato on the Rhetoric of Philosophers and Sophists* (Cambridge, 2007) and *Wounded Heroes: Vulnerability as a Virtue in Ancient Greek Literature and Philosophy* (Oxford, 2013). She is working on a book on images as argument in Plato's *Republic*. She has also published articles on topics in ancient rhetoric and philosophy, literary genres and devices in Plato, and self-knowledge. Prof McCoy is on the executive board of the Ancient Philosophy Society and is a former National Endowment for the Humanities fellow.

Marjolein Oele is Associate Professor of Philosophy at the University of San Francisco. Her research intertwines Aristotle's philosophy with topics and figures in Twentieth-Century and Contemporary Continental Philosophy. She is the author of *E-Co-Affectivity* and co-editor of *Ontologies of Nature: Continental Perspectives and Environmental Reorientations*. Her articles have been published in a range of journals, including *Ancient Philosophy*, *Configurations*, *Electronic Antiquity*, *Epoché*, *Graduate Faculty Philosophy Journal*, and *Radical Philosophy Review*.

Kevin Robb is Professor of Philosophy at the University of Southern California. His publications include *Literacy and Paideia in Ancient Greece* (Oxford), *Language and Thought in Early Greek Philosophy* (Open Court), and contributions to such journals as *Ancient Philosophy*, *Journal of the History of Philosophy*, *Classical Review*, *The Monist*, and *The Personalist*. His scholarly interests include early Greek philosophy and law, the alphabet and the transition from orality to literacy, and Hellenic archeology. After graduate studies at Yale, he taught at the venerable Robert Koleg in Istanbul, now the University of the Bosporus, affording access to the ruins of Troy, and the Austrian excavation at Ephesus, where he was a visiting consultant for two seasons.

Roslyn Weiss is the Clara H. Stewardson Professor of Philosophy at Lehigh University. Her fields of expertise are Ancient Greek Philosophy and Medieval Jewish Philosophy. She has published four books on Plato, *Socrates Dissatisfied: An Analysis of Plato's 'Crito'* (Oxford, 1998); *Virtue in the Cave: Moral Inquiry in Plato's 'Meno'* (Oxford, 2001); *The Socratic Paradox and Its Enemies* (Chicago, 2006); and *Philosophers in the 'Republic': Plato's Two Paradigms* (Cornell, 2012); and numerous articles on Greek and Jewish philosophy. Her current project is the first complete translation into English of a medieval philosophical work, *Light of the Lord*, by Hasdai Crescas.

William Wians, Merrimack College and Boston College, has co-edited (with Gary Gurtler, S.J.) ten volumes of the *Proceedings of the Boston Area Colloquium in Ancient Philosophy*. He has edited *Aristotle's Philosophical Development: Problems and Prospects* (Rowman and Littlefield, 1996), and *Logos and Muthos: Philosophical Essays in Greek Literature* (SUNY Press, 2009), and co-edited (with Ron Polansky) *Reading Aristotle: Argument and Exposition* (Brill, 2017). His articles include studies of method in Aristotle's *Metaphysics* and *Posterior Analytics*, and of Plato's *Meno*.

Index

Abrams, M. H., 334
Achilles, ix, 27, 31, 73, 76, 140–141, 147–150, 304, 308, 315; wrath of, 5, 12, 64–67, 149, 162, 313; and Agamemnon, 50, 145–146, 201; and Priam, 21, 39, 52, 65, 149–150, 163, 298–300, 309–313, 316, 317; in Plato's *Apology*, 242, 262; shade of, speaking to Odysseus in Hades, 139, 159, 161, 195, 282, 291–292
Adam, J., 94
Adams, S. M., 254
Adkins, A. W. H., 36, 160, 162, 218
Aeschylus, 13, 14, 49, 299; *Prometheus Bound*, 86, 303–304
Agamemnon, 65, 67, 212, 218, 284, 291, 294. *See also* Achilles and Agamemnon
Ahrensdorf, P., 252, 253, 254, 256, 259
Albani, M., 132
Algra, K., 68, 74, 76
Allan, W., 160, 161, 162
allegory and allegorical interpretation, 15
Amerasinghe, C., 220
Anaxagoras, 7, 134

Anaximander, 3, 4, 7, 11, 12, 13, 68, 95–134
Anderson, G., 163
Annas, J., 284, 295
Antigone, 14, 15, 223–262. *See also* Sophocles, *Antigone*
Archaic period, historical and cultural, 2, 6, 19, 22, 24, 27, 60, 76, 97–100, 103–104, 108–109, 114, 119, 121, 123, 132, 168, 169, 171
aretê. *See* virtue
Aristophanes, 5, 215, 218, 219, 220, 275; as character in Plato's *Symposium*, 9, 15, 80, 87–89, 93
Aristotle, 7, 55, 68, 74, 91, 107, 109, 114, 133, 183, 321, 330; and courage, 297–316; and tragedy, 187–188, 196, 290–291, 298; attitude toward myth, 4, 11, 91; *De Anima*, 314–315; *De Caelo*, 132; *Metaphysics*, 4, 9, 11, 68, 133; *Meteorologica*, 132; *Nicomachean Ethics*, 183, 298, 309–313, 316; *Poetics*, 163, 187–188, 196, 291, 295; *Rhetoric*, 216, 256, 295, 298, 299–301, 314
Asclepius, 191
Asmis, E., 333

Atchity, K., 217
Athens, city of, 99, 156, 203, 211, 215; public performance in, 198–199, 216. See also Socrates and Athens; Sophocles and Athens
Ausland, H., 277
Austin, J., 259
Ayer, A. J., 24, 49

Barnes, J., 57, 68, 74, 76
Benardete, S., 166, 167, 171, 174, 175, 176, 182, 187, 188, 189, 191, 193, 194, 196, 253, 255, 256, 257, 258
Bennett, J. W., 333
Bergren, A., 217, 219
Bernabé, A., 86
Bernstein, A. E., 164
Bernstein, J. M., 333
Bers, V., 216, 218
Bickerman, E. J., 130, 131
Biehl, W., 219, 220, 221
Blondell, R., 14, 15, 215, 216, 217, 219, 220, 295
Bloom, A., 276
body, and relation to soul, 91, 93, 139–140, 157, 268; desecration of, 234–235, 261, 305–308, 315. See also Achilles and Priam
Boegehold, A. L., 216, 218
Bouvier, D., 296
Bowra, C. M., 333
Boyd, T., 216, 219
Bradshaw, A. T., 253
Bremmer, J. M., 160
Brill, S., 14, 49, 52
Brisson, L., 12, 14, 94, 130
Broadie, S., 69, 72, 76, 77
Bryan, J., 77
Buitron-Oliver, D., 11
Bundrick, S. D., 216

Burkert, W., 11, 131, 160, 161, 167, 191, 193, 194, 195
Burnet, J., 10, 11, 122, 130, 133
Buxton, R., 12, 13

Cairns, D. L., 217
Cascardi, A. J., 333
Cherubin, R., 13, 74, 75
Classical period, 7, 19
Claus, D. B., 160
Clay, D., 132
Coleman, R., 254
Coleridge, S., 321, 333
Collobert, C., 13, 14
Conacher, D. J., 315
Consigny, S. P., 215, 218
Copernicus, N., 95, 98, 100, 130
Cornford, F. M., 4, 12, 96, 97, 122, 130, 133
cosmology and cosmogony, 4–5, 7, 8, 12, 13, 76, 88; Babylonian, 4, 96–97, 110, 120, 122, 123, 132; Egyptian, 4, 110. See also Anaximander
Couprie, D., 131
courage, 5, 12, 13, 33, 140–142, 146, 267, 268–269, 281, 287, 293; of Antigone in comparison to Socrates, 223–262; of Priam, 297–317
Cowser, J., 254
Croally, N. T., 220, 221
Csapo, E., 216, 219, 221

Dale, A. M., 221
Davis, M., 15, 187, 188, 190, 195, 196
Delphi, city of, 99, 114, 117, 128, 206
Delphic oracle. See oracles
Deneen, P., 164

Densmore, S., 192
Destrée, P., 14, 294, 295
Detienne, M., 13, 162, 164
Dicks, D. R., 133
Dodds, E. R., 163, 195, 201, 215, 217, 218
dogs, 201, 206–207, 305–308, 315, 316
Donaldson, S., 195
Donlan, W., 17, 19, 36, 47, 48, 50, 53
Donzelli, G. B., 217, 219, 220
Dover, K. J., 215, 218
Duncan, T. S., 215, 216
Dynes, R. W., 195

Easterling, P. E., 216
Edmunds, L., 191
Edwards, M. W., 75, 217
Edwards, Mike, 218
El-Shahawy, A., 193
Eldridge, R., 334
Empedocles, 13, 72, 76, 325
ethics and the ethical, 7, 12, 14, 89–91, 135–164, 202, 207, 214–215, 220, 267; and Homeric/heroic values, 6, 14, 17–53, 55–77, 138–150, 157–158, 161, 204, 210, 217, 281; emotive theory of, 14, 19, 23–27, 31, 42–44, 324
Euripides, 13, 14, 49, 219, 255; and sophistry, 9, 197, 209–210, 213–214, 219–220, 221; *Andromache*, 217, 220; *Hippolytus*, 217; *Trojan Women*, 15, 197, 207–215, 220; *Orestes*, 217
Evelyn-White, H. G., 160

Farron, S., 217
fate (*moira*) and destiny, 37, 59, 63, 160, 162, 163, 166, 303; in the Homeric/Hesiodic worldview, 84–86, 137–159, 289; in myth of Er, 287–292; in *Oedipus Tyrannos*, 178–189, 195
Fenik, B., 215
Ferrari, G. R. F., 295, 333
Finley, M. I., 18, 19, 21–23, 48, 49, 50
Flickinger, M. K., 254
Ford, A., 215, 216
Franco, C., 217
Fränkel, H., 10, 73, 130
Friedrich, P., 217

Gagarin, M., 163, 218
Gallagher, R. L., 295
Gibbs, S., 102–103, 131
Gide, A., 167, 176, 196
Glessmer, E., 132
Goethe, J. W., 256, 257
Goldhill, S., 216, 219
Gonzalez, F., 14, 295
González, J. M., 216, 217
Gorgias of Leontini, 13, 14, 197–199, 203–211, 213–215, 216, 218, 219–220, 221
Gould, J., 18, 45, 48, 50, 51, 52, 162
Graver, M., 217
Gravlee, G. S., 300, 302, 314–315
Greek miracle, 10, 11, 97, 101, 130
Green, R., 219, 220
Griffin, J., 160, 161
Griswold, C., 219
Grube, G. M. A., 160
Guthrie, W. K. C., 122, 133
Gutjahr, O., 167, 174, 182, 193–194, 195

Hackforth, R., 333
Hades/the Underworld 137, 139–140, 142, 148, 154, 157–158, 161, 163, 164, 187, 229, 232, 235, 273, 281–287, 289–292, 294

Hadot, P., 74, 75
Hahn, R., 12, 13, 130, 131, 132, 133, 134
Hall, E., 216, 218, 219, 220, 221
Halliwell, S., 163, 164, 215, 219, 281, 294, 295
Hammer, D., 163
Hannah, R., 130, 131
happiness, 56, 85, 153, 154, 157–159, 164, 173, 177, 223, 253, 274, 284, 288–290, 309
Hare, R. M., 24–25, 27, 31, 49
Hartland-Swann, J., 333
Hatab, L., 12, 14, 15, 160, 163
Havelock, E. A., 163, 164
Heath, T., 130
Hector, 21, 27, 39, 64, 67, 149, 202, 217, 298, 299–300, 304–309, 313, 315, 316
Hecuba, 207, 209, 212–213, 220, 221, 306–308, 310, 311
Hegel, G. W. F., 10, 253
Heidegger, M., 159, 162, 163, 314
Heidel, W. A., 107, 132
Heiden, B., 161
Helen, 13, 14, 15, 38, 160, 161, 197–221
Heraclitus, 3, 9, 13, 58, 69, 72, 76, 142, 325, 326, 327
Herington, J., 216, 219
Herman, G., 18–19, 48, 49
Herodotus, 14, 22, 58, 109, 120, 130, 132, 133, 176, 192, 194, 230, 257, 263–266, 271, 276, 282
Herrero de Jáuregui, M., 163
Herron, M., 10, 11, 12
Hesiod, 2, 12, 13, 24, 47, 55–63, 67–73, 74–77, 80–86, 88, 94, 96–97, 122, 123, 139, 142, 161, 164, 263, 272–273, 299, 302–304, 315, 321, 325, 326, 334; and invocation to the Muses, 6, 27, 59–63; as mythic thinker, 3, 4, 11, 14, 136–138; as authoritative teacher of Greece, 5–8, 12, 14, 58; criticized as immoral, 6, 68, 72–73, 68, 161; *Theogony*, 5, 47, 51, 59–60, 62, 75, 76, 80, 81–84, 86, 96–97, 130, 136–138, 160, 164; *Works and Days*, 6, 47, 80, 84–85, 137, 139, 278, 302–303. *See also* ethics, and Homeric/heroic values; justice in Homer and Hesiod
Hesk, J., 218
hiketeia (supplication and supplicants), 12, 14, 17–53, 64, 163, 171, 175, 191, 299, 317
Hippocrates and Hippocratic writings, 134
Holmberg, I., 217
Homer, 2, 12, 13, 17–53, 55–77, 155, 157, 158, 159, 160, 161, 164, 172, 187, 197–218, 263, 272–273, 279–282, 286–294, 297–300, 304–313, 315, 316, 321, 324, 326, 334; and invocation to the Muses, 6, 27, 59–63, 75; as expression of a tragic worldview, 14, 135, 138–150, 288–292; as mythic thinker, 3, 14; as authoritative teacher of Greece, 5–8, 12, 14, 18, 58, 155; criticized as immoral, 6, 68, 72–73, 155, 161, 321; *Iliad*, 13, 17, 21, 26, 31, 50, 51, 52, 60, 63–67, 73, 74, 75, 80, 137, 138–146, 149–150, 160, 161, 161, 163, 164, 171, 191, 193, 194, 195, 197, 201–202, 204, 210, 216, 217, 281, 291–292, 295, 297–299, 304–313, 314, 315, 316, 317; and the catalogue of ships, 12, 60–61, 64–67, 75; *Odyssey*, 12, 14, 17–20, 21–26, 28–48, 49, 50–51, 52, 60, 61–62, 73, 74, 75, 138, 139–142, 146–148, 155, 158,

160, 161, 162, 164, 171–172, 195,
217, 221, 279–282, 290, 289, 295.
See also ethics, and Homeric/heroic
values; justice in Homer and
Hesiod; Plato, criticisms of Homer;
rhapsodes
Homeric Hymns, 87
Homeyer, H., 217
Howland, J., 164, 276, 277, 278
hubris, 32, 152–153, 168, 174, 180,
185–186, 190, 191, 193, 248
human beings, origins and limits
of, 4, 5, 12, 13, 55–76, 79–94,
115, 123, 135–164, 171, 173–174,
183–184, 188, 192, 193, 235, 240,
247, 282, 299, 303
Hussey, E., 57, 60, 61, 62, 68–69, 70,
73, 74, 75, 76, 77

Ionia, 68, 109, 123, 124, 126, 128,
133
Ionian philosophers (collectively),
10, 68, 133
Irwin, T., 218

Jaeger, W., 326, 329, 334
Jebb, R. C., 36, 51, 225, 226, 237,
242, 253, 255, 256, 258
Johannes, H., 132
Johansen, T. K., 11
Johnson, P., 260
Johnson, R. R., 295
Jones, P. J., 29, 35, 49, 50, 315
Just, R., 218
justice (dikê), 63, 75, 129, 220, 227,
325–326; in Homer and Hesiod,
35, 50–51, 142–144, 161; in
Antigone, 227, 233–238, 256–257,
258; in Oedipus Tyrannus, 152,
176, 182; in Plato, 155–158, 164,
239–252, 260–261, 262, 263–277,
282–283, 286, 295

kairos (critical time), 100
Kamerbeek, J. C., 254
Kaufmann, W., 193
Kerenyi, C., 160
Kerferd, G. B., 215, 217
Kern, O., 86, 94
Kienast, H., 125, 129, 133, 134
Kirk G. S., 11, 51, 75
Kirk G. S., J. E. Raven, and M.
Schofield, 122, 131, 161
Kirkland, S., 195
knowledge, human vs. divine, 7, 13,
55–77, 135, 151, 174, 247, 262,
326; and self-knowledge, 14, 15,
151, 161, 166–167, 176–183, 184,
188–189, 267–268, 270, 276, 277;
and sight, 165, 191, 192, 266, 276
Knox, B., 167, 175, 177, 178, 179,
180, 183, 186, 191, 194, 225, 234,
235, 237, 241, 252, 253, 254, 255,
256, 257, 258
Kočandrle, R., 131
Konstan, D., 314
Kosman, A., 163
Kremmydas, C., 216

Lada-Richards, I., 219
Lake, P., 277
Laks, A., 10
Lattimore, R., 28, 29, 35, 38, 44, 45,
49, 50, 59, 74, 75, 160, 314
Lear, J., 287, 295
Lee, K. H., 219
Lester, J. H., 13, 69, 74, 76, 164
Lesky, A., 215
Lloyd-Jones, H., 74
Lloyd, G. E. R., 13
Lloyd, M., 219, 220, 221
logos, and/vs. muthos, 1–15, 58–60,
64, 67, 79–94, 95–97, 100–101,
112, 117, 122–123, 127–128,
136–138, 155–156, 166, 177, 185,

logos, and/vs. *muthos* (continued)
188, 190, 193, 196, 203–204, 205, 208, 263–278, 279–296, 297, 321, 326–327, 334. *See also* myth
Lombardo, S., 315
Long, A. A., 13, 14, 334
Lonsdale, S. H., 315, 316
Loraux, N., 93
Lynn-George, M., 162, 163

MacDowell, D. M., 215, 218, 220
Mansfeld, J., 12
Marshall, C. W., 219
Martin, R. P., 124, 216
McCall, M., 253, 254
McCoy, M., 14, 277
McPherran, M., 293, 294, 296
Meikeljohn, K., 254
Meineck, P., 160, 163, 190
Michelini, A., 220, 221
Mikics, D., 260
Milesian philosophers (collectively), 4, 122, 129
Miletus, city of, 97–99, 111–116, 121, 127–128, 130–131
Miller Jr., F. D., 14, 162
mimesis (imitation), 24, 27, 30–31, 49, 156–157, 187, 199, 276. *See also* Plato and imitation
Miščevič, N., 276
Morgan, K., 12, 77, 294
Morgan, M. H., 133
Mossman, J., 220, 221
Most, G., 10, 12, 13, 58, 74, 75, 76, 94
Mourelatos, A. P. D., 77, 334
Muellner, L., 161, 162
Murray, A. T., 160
Murray, G., 44, 51
Musaeus, 272, 273, 334
Muses, 6, 27, 28, 47, 55–67, 70, 72, 74, 75, 77, 156, 164, 294, 324

myth, definition of, 3; equated with poetry, 11; reception of, 2, 7–8, 11, 13, 17, 155, 156, 199. *See also* Plato, construction and use of myth

Naddaf, G., 15
Naddaff, R., 13
Nagy, G., 216
narrative, 8–10, 11, 31, 208, 263–264, 266–267, 269–270, 276, 277
nemesis, 26, 27, 29, 32, 41, 47, 137
Nestle, W., 10, 12, 122, 133
Netz, R., 134
Neuberg, M., 215
Nietzsche, F., 68, 76, 159, 160, 173, 193
Nightingale, A. W., 333
nomos (custom, law), 5, 63, 227, 229–234, 236, 261
Norwood, G., 253, 254
Nussbaum, M. C., 163, 253, 255, 315, 316, 333

O'Connor, D., 295
Ober, J., 218, 219
Odysseus, 5, 28, 31–32, 38, 52, 56, 61–62, 64, 74, 75, 139–140, 146–150, 161, 162, 187, 195, 326; as suppliant and *xenos*, 12, 20, 21–23, 39–46, 52; in Hades (*Odyssey* 11), 158–159, 195, 282, 315; in Plato's *Republic*, 164, 281–294, 296
Oedipus, 14, 15, 150–154, 155, 163, 165–196, 256
Oele, M., 12, 13, 314, 316, 317
Ogden, C. K., 25, 27, 49
Oinopides, 118, 134
one over many, 98, 101, 112, 125, 128
oracles, including Delphic oracle, 8, 151, 152–153, 172, 174, 178–180, 183, 192, 194, 246, 251

Orphism, 80, 86–87, 88, 92–93, 160, 325
Osborne, R., 13
Ostwald, M., 316

Padilla Longoria, M. T., 333
Pandora, myth of, 80, 84–86, 303–304
Parker, V., 168, 169
Parmenides, 13, 69, 72, 75, 76, 160, 319–322, 324–333
Parry, M., 25, 30, 50
Pater, W., 333
Pelling, C., 220
Peradotto, J., 162
performance, public, and oral culture, 3–4, 8, 9, 14, 15, 17–18, 27, 30, 32, 50, 138, 144, 155, 156, 164, 167, 197–221, 327. *See also* Athens, public performance in
Pericles, 100, 186, 199, 216
phusis (nature), concept of, 127–129, 131, 133, 138, 193, 265, 321–322, 325, 326, 327, 331–332
piety and the pious, 15, 69, 71–73, 143–144, 151–153, 162, 268, 273; of Antigone in comparison to Socrates, 223–262 *passim*
Pindar, 13, 14, 100, 131, 272, 276, 288–289
Pitt-Rivers, J., 18, 48, 50, 51
Plato, 5, 11, 14, 15, 55, 58, 72, 93, 135–136, 163, 171–172, 207, 216, 219, 223, 238–239, 260; and imitation (*mimesis*), 14, 156–157, 164, 263–270, 276, 277, 321, 330; and poetry, 11, 135–136, 154–159, 263–278, 319–334; construction and use of myth, 6, 8–9, 11, 14, 15, 91–92, 276; moral criticisms of Homer and tragedy, 72, 143, 151, 154–159, 279–282; myth of Er,
14, 156, 158–159, 265, 279–296; ring of Gyges, 14, 156, 176, 192, 194, 263–278; *Apology*, 14, 56, 238–252, 260–261, 262, 269; *Crito* 239, 241–247, 252, 260, 261; *Euthydemus*, 124, 206–207, 218; *Euthyphro*, 7, 52, 162, 240, 249, 251–252, 260; *Gorgias*, 158, 215, 240, 245, 287; *Hippias Major*, 215; *Ion*, 164, 199, 215, 276; *Laches*, 261–262, 316; *Laws*, 164, 215, 247, 321, 333; *Meno*, 177, 246; *Phaedo*, 155, 157, 164, 240–241, 247, 261, 330; *Phaedrus*, 15, 218, 321, 323, 330–331, 333; *Philebus*, 100, 131, 330; *Protagoras*, 6, 9, 15, 33, 215, 216, 217, 241, 261, 277; *Republic*, 14, 35, 72, 91, 100, 131, 135–136, 154–159, 160, 164, 192, 244, 245, 247, 252, 260–261, 263–278, 279–296, 330–331; *Sophist*, 164, 270, 277, 327, 330; *Symposium*, 80, 87–89, 195, 218, 260, 321, 323, 324, 330–331; *Theaetetus*, 160, 240, 244, 249, 250, 262; *Timaeus*, 15, 72, 77, 194. *See also* justice in Plato
Platt, A., 295
poets and poetry, 2, 3–8, 11, 47, 55–77, 135–164, 166, 177, 185, 188, 189–190, 195, 196, 216, 218, 263–278, 279–317, 319–334; and the competition for authority, 5–6 7, 12, 13, 58–59, 68, 75, 155, 163, 199, 200–201, 204, 208–209, 216, 325, 326, 327; as a vehicle for knowledge and truth, 5, 13, 58–69, 74, 155–156, 159, 163, 164, 286, 322–324; vs. prose, 4, 13, 14, 68, 76. *See also* Plato and poetry
Porter, J., 218
Poulakos, J., 218

praise and blame, 138, 145, 161, 204, 271, 273, 316
pre-Socratic philosophers (collectively), 3–4, 5, 55, 57, 68, 69, 72, 76, 77, 334
Priam, 5, 12, 21, 39, 52, 64, 65, 149–150, 163, 197, 200–203, 204, 205, 207, 211, 212, 214, 217, 297–317. *See also* Achilles and Priam
Price, A. W., 334
Prier, R. A., 164
progress, human, 1, 4, 10, 70–71, 161, 177
prose, as vehicle for rational thought, 95, 97, 101, 122–128. *See also* poetry vs. prose
Protagoras of Abdera. *See* Plato, *Protagoras*
Pyrrho, 9

Raaflaub, K., 48
Reckford, K. J., 217
Redfield, J. M., 160, 215
Reece, S., 49, 50
Reeve, C. D. C., 13, 291, 294, 296
Rehm, A., 130
Reinhardt, K., 195, 196
rhapsodes, 61–62, 68–69, 164, 198–200, 202–203, 204–205, 207, 208–209, 214, 216, 217, 218, 219, 280, 325
Robb, K., 12, 14, 49, 53, 77
Rochberg, F., 130
Roisman, H. M., 217
Romilly, J., 218
Roochnik, D., 277
Rosen, S., 277
Roth, P., 49
Rouse, W. H. D., 254

Sachs, J., 183, 314

Sallis, J., 177, 191
Samuel, A. E., 130, 131
Sansone, D., 215, 216, 219
Santas, G., 276
Saxonhouse, A., 244, 254
Schein, S. L., 217
Schloemann, J., 218
Schmiel, R., 161
Schultz, A. M., 276, 277
Scodel, R., 217, 219, 220, 221
seemliness, propriety, and what is fitting, 31, 33, 36–37, 43, 46, 50, 51, 71–73
Segal, C., 162, 225, 230, 252, 253, 254, 255, 257, 295
Segal, R., 10, 11
Seneca, 196
Shawcross, T., 334
Shear, T. L., 216
Sheehan, S., 190
Shelley, P. B., 323, 333
Sheppard, J. T., 254
Simonides, 169, 272, 277
Skepticism, 57
Slater, N. W., 216, 219, 221
Smith, M. F., 334
Smith, N., 313
Smith, P. C., 14, 317
Snell, B., 56, 61, 68, 69, 70, 73, 74, 75, 76, 122, 133
Socrates, 9, 15, 52, 56, 92–93, 124, 223, 238–252, 253, 260, 261, 262, 323, 330; and Athens, 14, 156, 240–246, 251–252, 261; as tragic hero, 155–156, 158, 240–243, 253. *See also* Plato
Sophists (collectively), and sophistry, 68, 203, 204, 205, 206–207, 213–215, 216, 217, 218, 220, 221, 239
Sophocles, 12, 13, 15, 80, 100, 131, 135–136, 138–139, 150–154, 163,

165–196, 217, 223–238, 242, 253, 254, 256, 259, 293–294; and Athens, 7–8, 14, 165–170, 185–187, 191; *Antigone (Antig.)*, 15, 163, 169, 190, 217, 223–262; *Oedipus at Colonus (OC)*, 153, 154, 160, 167, 169, 190; *Oedipus Tyrannos (OT)*, 150–154, 160, 163, 165–196
Sorabji, R., 314
soul, 155–159, 160, 164, 184, 187–188, 239, 240, 252, 265, 267, 270, 272–275, 277, 279–296, 322–323, 330–332, 333. *See also* body, and relation to soul
Sourvinou-Inwood, C., 160, 164
speech and (spoken) language, 14, 37, 42, 43, 72, 146, 196, 204–207, 218
Steiner, D. T., 218
Stevenson, C. L., 24–27, 31, 49
Strauss, B., 218, 219

Tanner, S., 270, 276, 277
Taplin, O., 217
Teffeteller, A., 215, 217
Thales, 4, 113
theology, 68–73, 77, 86, 88, 124, 274
Thompson, C. R., 260
Thomson, G., 130, 131
Thucydides, 100, 131, 186, 216, 218
Tomlinson, R. A., 133
tragedy and the tragic, 12, 13, 14, 15, 135–164, 187–189, 190, 195, 196, 198, 209, 213, 215, 216, 217, 219, 220, 268, 284–285, 287–289, 291, 298, 316, 321, 333
tragic playwrights (collectively), 2, 7–8, 9, 55, 164, 169, 209, 288–289, 321

Trümpy, C., 130, 131
Tsagalis, C., 216
tyrants and tyranny, 14, 152, 165–196, 231, 282–285, 290, 292

Urmson, J. O., 24, 49, 260

Valakas, K., 219
Verdenius, W. J., 315
Vernant, J.-P., 12, 93, 130, 133, 160, 162, 167, 178, 193, 196
Versnel, H. S., 162
virtue (*aretê*), 13, 36, 47, 76, 77, 36, 47, 138–139, 141, 144, 147, 156, 158, 189, 212, 239, 245–246, 248–251, 260, 268, 234, 288, 289–290, 292, 297–299, 313

Waterfield, R., 10
Weil, S., 317
West M. L., 76, 94, 124, 133
Westerink, L. G., 92, 93, 94
Wians, W., 10, 12, 13, 73, 74, 129, 162, 192, 215, 317
Wickkiser, L. B., 191
Williams, B., 163, 215
Winnington-Ingram, R. P., 255
Woodruff, P., 15, 160, 163, 167, 190, 191, 192
Woozley, A. D., 261
Wordsworth, W., 319–324, 327, 329, 331–334
Worman, N., 217, 220
Wyles, R., 219

xenia and the *xenos*, 12, 17–53, 195
Xenophanes, 6, 13, 49, 51, 55–58, 67–73, 76–77, 143, 325
Xenophon, 124, 133, 192, 193, 195, 199, 211, 215, 216, 217

Yamagata, N., 150, 164

Yunis, H., 295

Zanker, G., 314
Zeno, 9, 325, 327
Zeus, 5, 21, 23, 26, 37, 38–40,
  44–45, 47, 52, 59–62, 67, 73–74,
  76, 80, 81–87, 88, 89, 92–93,
  96–97, 101, 137–138, 143,
  145–146, 147, 155, 160, 162, 195,
  198, 201, 208, 215, 220, 227, 235,
  255, 288
Zimmerman, E. J., 193, 195
Zimmermann, B., 167, 183, 191,
  195

www.ingramcontent.com/pod-product-compliance
Lightning Source LLC
Chambersburg PA
CBHW021214240426
43672CB00026B/36